LITERARY
AUSTIN

For Betsy

*Who teaches literature the way
it should be taught, with great
passion, intelligence, and humor*

LITERARY AUSTIN

Don Graham, editor

TCU Press • Fort Worth, Texas

Library of Congress Cataloging-in-Publication Data

Copyright © 2007 TCU Press (compilation only)
Introduction copyright © 2007 by Don Graham

Literary Austin / edited by Don Graham.
    p. cm.
  Includes bibliographical references and index.
  ISBN 978-0-87565-342-6 (cloth : alk. paper) — ISBN 978-0-87565-347-1 (pbk. : alk. paper)
    1.   Austin (Tex.)—Literary collections. 2. American literature—Texas—Austin.
      3. American literature—21st century. I. Graham, Don, 1940-
  PS559.A9L58 2006
  810.9'76431—dc22
                              2006039771

Jacket & Book design/Margie Adkins Graphic Design

CONTENTS

INTRODUCTION: CITY OF WORDS ix

PART ONE: THE SEAT OF FUTURE EMPIRE 1

William Sidney Porter (O. Henry), Austin. A Brief
    Glance at Her History and Advantages 2

A.C. Greene, The Founding of Austin 6

Edwin Shrake, from *The Borderland* 8

Dave Oliphant, from *Austin* 11

PART TWO: CITY OF THE VIOLET CROWN: 1900S-1940S 17

John A. Lomax, from *Adventures of a Ballad Hunter* 18

Frederic Prokosch, from *Voices: A Memoir* 23

Ralph Yarborough, The Music of Running Waters 27

Margaret Cousins, from The Beatific Memories of an
    English Major 30

William A. Owens, from *Three Friends* 34

Roy Bedichek, [Letters on Sculptures] 40

Liz Carpenter, from *Getting Better All the Time* 44

Lyndon B. Johnson, from Tarnish on the Violet Crown 50

PART THREE: THIS TRUE PARADISE ON EARTH: 1950S 53

Mary Lasswell, from *I'll Take Texas* 54

John Henry Faulk, from *Fear on Trial* 59

Rolando Hinojosa-Smith, '50s Austin: A Variform Education 64

Wilson M. Hudson, from Bedichek's Rock 71

Walter P. Webb, J. Frank Dobie 73

David Richards, from *Once Upon a Time in Texas* 76

Ann Richards, from *Straight from the Heart* 80

Willie Morris, from *North Toward Home* 87

Celia Morris, from *Finding Celia's Place* 91

PART FOUR: AN OASIS FOR MIND AND BODY: 1960s 95

J. Frank Dobie, For Years We Three Sat Together 97

Bertram Rota, The Night of the Armadillos 110

Joe B. Frantz, from *The Forty Acre Follies* 116

Billy Lee Brammer, from *The Gay Place* 119

Larry McMurtry, from *In a Narrow Grave* 124

Thomas Whitbread, Argumentative Poem Against
    Certain Articles 129

Jonathan Bracker, Garten of the Gods 132

Olivia Dwight (Mary Hazzard), from *Close His Eyes* 134

Carolyn Osborn, The Vulture Descending Each Day 137

Christopher Middleton, The Armadillos 153

Harry Huntt Ransom, Frontier Museum 155

Miguel Gonzalez-Gerth, from Borges and Texas: Farewell
    To An Old Friend 156

Hazel Harrod Ransom, *Quorum Pars Parva Fui* 161

Prudence Macintosh, from *Just As We Were* 165

Julius Whittier, from The Last Bastion 172

Kinky Friedman, The Left Bank of Texas 177

Gary Lavergne, from *A Sniper in the Tower:
    The Charles Whitman Murders* 179

William J. Helmer, The Madman on the Tower 184

James R. Giles, One August Day in Texas 197

PART FIVE: AUSTIN IS THE HEART OF TEXAS: 1970s 207

Greg Curtis, Austin, May 15, 1973 208

Albert Huffstickler, The Ghosts of College City 209

Michael Mewshaw, from *Earthly Bread* 212

Pat Ellis Taylor, Spring Water Celebration 215

Zulfikar Ghose, It's Your Land, Boss 220

Jan Reid, from *The Improbable Rise of Redneck Rock* 223

Michael Adams, Crossroads at the Broken Spoke 229

Ronnie Dugger, from *Our Invaded Universities* 237

PART SIX: AUSTIN IS A HAPPY PLACE, SORT OF: 1980s 241

Andy Clausen, Conversation With a Lady I Took to the
    Airport Who Loved Austin Texas 243

Peter LaSalle, from *Strange Sunlight* 247

James Hynes, from *Publish and Perish: Three Tales of
    Tenure and Terror* 251

Max Westbrook, Bartons Creek 255

Stephen Harrigan, [A "School" of Austin Writers?] 257

Dagoberto Gilb, From a Letter to Pat Ellis Taylor 259

Kurth Sprague, from *Frighten the Horses* 262

Marian Winik, The Texas Heat Wave 265

Chuck Taylor, Texas 267

Betty Sue Flowers, Being Imagined 270

Joseph Jones, from *Life on Waller Creek* 272

Tom Zigal, Recent Developments 277

PART SEVEN: OUR SCRUFFY EDEN: 1990s-2006 297

Lars Gufstafsson, from *The Tale of a Dog* 300

Elizabeth Harris, Give 305

Thomas Cable, Trail Markers 310

Molly Ivins, How Ann Richards Got To Be
    Governor of Texas 312

Bill Minutaglio, from *First Son: George W. Bush and the Bush Family Dynasty* 322

Lynn Freed, from *Reading, Writing and Leaving Home: Life on the Page* 330

David Wevill, Home Improvement 334

Lawrence Wright, Heroes 336

Kevin Brown, Literary Playscape 338

James Magnuson, The Week James Michener Died 343

Bert Almon, Austin Odyssey 348

Robert Draper, Adios to Austin 351

Lyman Grant, Co-Op 360

Kurt Heinzelman, Way Out West at 51st and Berkman 363

Steven Moore, Salon of the West 365

John Spong, King's Ransom 373

Gary Cartwright, Statues of Limitation 378

Laura Furman, The Woods 384

Don Webb, from *Essential Saltes* 401

Scott Blackwood, Nostalgia 410

Don Graham, Ghosts and Empty Sockets 416

Karen Olsson, from *Waterloo* 425

Betsy Berry, Human Sexuality 427

William J. Scheick, Gridlock 443

Selected Bibliography of Additional Novels Set in Austin 447

Permissions 451

Acknowledgments 457

Index 459

City of Words

By all rights the city of Austin should have been named after its founder, Mirabeau Buonaparte Lamar, soldier, hero of San Jacinto, second president of the Republic, and poet. But that did not happen, and about all that remains of Lamar's memory in the city today is a north-south street bearing his name. That it is Austin's longest street is perhaps a kind of tribute, I suppose. But no statue of Lamar, for example, stands in the city (though there are ones of Stevie Ray Vaughn and Angelina Eberley, the latter a figure so obscure that you have to read the inscription at the site, in the 600 block of Congress Avenue, to learn who she was).

Lamar is not, in fact, a congenial spirit for modern Austin, whose slogan, if we can believe the evidence of innumerable bumper stickers, is "Keep Austin Weird." Old Mirabeau did not want to keep Austin weird; he wanted to extend its influence over an empire. Indeed the very founding of Austin was itself the act of an imperialist imagination. Given the settlement patterns of the Republic, it made more sense for the capital to be in southeast Texas, in Houston, where it was for a time. Austin, as yet unnamed, was on a distant and dangerous frontier where Comanches ruled and buffalo roamed.

But it was the right place if empire was the motive, and it was. According to the commissioners who recommended the site, [we] "confidently anticipate the time when a great thoroughfare shall be established from Santa Fe to our seaports, and another from Red River to Matamoros, which two routs [*sic*] must always of necessity intersect each other at this point." Old Mirabeau believed in Manifest Destiny before the term was invented. During his presidency he acted along imperialist lines. Among other ventures, he launched a war against Sam Houston's Native American friends in East Texas, the Cherokees, and he sent a filibustering expedition to New Mexico to seize Santa Fe for the financially strapped Republic of Texas. In Old Mirabeau's grand vision of geography, Texas took in Santa Fe, parts of Colorado, and stretched all the way to the Pacific Ocean. And if he had succeeded, think of it: Santa Fe wouldn't look like a Navajo theme park and Texans would have their own ski slopes. Old Mirabeau was also the first Austin writer. He wrote enough poetry to fill up a book (*Verse Memorials*, 1857). A very high percentage of his poems extolled the beauty of women, young, middling, and "on the shady side of fifty-three." Although his verse was conventional and undistinguished, he did have a talent for phrase-making. Speaking of his arch-rival, Sam Houston, Lamar once characterized Texas as "Big Drunk's Big Ranch."

To his credit, Lamar believed strongly in the importance of an educated citizenry, and in an early speech he declared: "Cultivated mind is the guardian genius of democracy, and while guided and controlled by virtue is the noblest attribute of man." To this end, Lamar proposed that every county have land set aside for the building of free public schools and that fifty leagues of land should be made available for "a university of the first class." Eventually Lamar's educational vision would be enacted into law.

In the beginning the city of Austin was launched on a tide of promise and self-congratulation. It started out named Waterloo in 1839 (the era of Napoleon still loomed large in the imagination, as evidenced by Lamar's middle name, Buonaparte) but was changed to Austin, which stuck. Just about every early visitor dilated upon the beauty of the natural surroundings, and the idea of Austin being a city of Nature emerged as a dominant theme in the rhapsodies and paeans to the hills and rills, the streams and trees. As if in tribute to its natural beauty, the first streets were named after the rivers (north-south) and trees (east-west) of Texas. Had this pattern continued, Austin could have embodied the full iconography of nature. Thus there would have been streets named after birds, animals, plants, stones, geological formations, creatures of the sea, continents and their animals and plants and topographical features, and so on through the rich, astounding plenitude of creation. But frontier towns tended toward the practical rather than the aesthetic, and although in the beginning Austin streets bore natural names, a numerical system was later introduced for the east-west running streets, and the tree names were history.

Two decades on, we get a glimpse of the city on a hill from a distinguished observer, Frederick Law Olmsted. The foremost landscape artist of the nineteenth century, the man responsible for, among other urban wonders, New York's Central Park, Olmsted stopped in Austin for a few days during a journey through Texas in 1854. He had come to inspect the conditions wrought by slavery and to see what was what in this remote province. Austin, he declared, reminded him of Washington "*en petit*, seen through a reversed glass." The city occupied a "fine situation" with "many agreeable views of distant hills" and a country around the town that was "rolling and picturesque." Closer at hand, the city did not fare so well. His hotel room was "extremely dirty" and the food execrable (Olmsted did not find anything palatable to eat in Texas until he reached New Braunfels, where cooking was still tied to the Europe the emigrants had recently left). As for literature, he noted, "There is a very remarkable number of drinking and gambling shops, but not one book-store." What is surprising, however, is how much he admired the Texas Legislature. Repeated visits there moved him to proclaim that he had "seldom been more impressed with respect for the working of Democratic institutions." Moreover, the lawmakers, he said, were marked by "manly dignity and trustworthiness for the duties that engaged them." He even said that they spoke with "honest eloquence." This may be the only time in recorded history that anybody had anything good to say about the Texas legislature.

Another early observer of Austin was Amelia E. Barr, who lived in the city during the Civil War era and later penned a number of novels, including *Remember the Alamo!* In her own account of those years in Austin—the rather flamboyantly titled *All the Days of My Life: An Autobiography (The Red Leaves of a Human Heart)*—Barr described her first entrance to the city in rhapsodic terms: "Then we mounted a hill, and a scene of unwritable beauty was before us on every side. Other portions of Texas are lovely as Paradise, but nowhere had I ever seen such exquisite and picturesque arrangement of wood and mountains, grassy stretches, and silvery waters, and crowned hills. From every mouth, there was an instant and spontaneous cry of delight." She continued, "The city was built on hills, surrounded by a rampart of higher hills, crowned with the evergreen cedar, and the shining waters of the Colorado wound in and out among these hills, and then swept grandly round the southern part of the city."

Elizabeth Custer, wife of George Armstrong Custer, later famous for that bloody debacle at Little Big Horn, accompanied her husband to Austin during a posting following the close of the Civil War, and wrote about the experience in her memoir, *Tenting on the Plains*. In the chapter "Life in a Texas Town" the town referred to was Austin. Mrs. Custer described the place as "a pretty town of stuccoed houses that appeared summery in the midst of the live-oak's perennial green." She seems to have been more interested in the general ambience of Texas, calling it a "'go-as-you-please' State . . ." where "the lawlessness was terrible." She also put into circulation a new explanation for the origin of the state's name: "I have read somewhere that Texas derived its name from a group of rascals, who, sitting around a fire on their arrival on the soil that was to protect them, composed this couplet:

If every other land forsakes us,

This is the land that freely takes us (Texas)."

A bit later in the century, the humorist Alex Sweet wrote a piece comparing Austin and San Antonio, in which, like just about every other commentator, he declared that "Austin is most emphatically a pretty city—perhaps the prettiest in Texas." The basis for this judgment was, once again, the "beautiful mountain scenery" and the "location of the city on a number of hills . . . calculated to please the eye, particularly at those heights crowned with family residences."

Modern Austin was pretty much in place by 1885. By then it had a state capitol of pink granite with a Goddess of Liberty statue on its dome. It had a new institution of higher learning (two years old), located on a hill north of the capitol, and charged with fulfilling Lamar's original vision of becoming a first-class university. It had a college to educate African-Americans (Tillotson Collegiate and Normal Institute, 1881), and a charter for a third college had been granted (St. Edwards). It had just lived through a sensational, and still to this day unsolved, set of grisly serial murders that a young pharmacist who would later become a convicted felon and the author O. Henry, would dub the work of the "servant girl annihilators."

Government, education, and natural beauty remained the three dominant features of Austin far into the new century.

Writing under the name James Oak in a 1948 piece for *Holiday*, J. Frank Dobie described the city in familiar terms: "Its character is mainly derived from containing the state capital and the University of Texas, and from its location. Nature has made its site one of the most beautiful for a city on the North American continent." Here Dobie encapsulates what many observers have said about Austin. Degrees of depth, detail, and emphasis may vary, but the chorus is remarkably consistent: government, education, and nature are the hallmarks of the Austin experience.

It is through the words of its writers, both those who live here and those passing through, that the inner life of Austin is perhaps best revealed. In the following pages the places and faces of Austin as a literary capital are much in evidence. This anthology is loosely conceived as an impressionistic "history" of Austin, a series of snapshots in prose and poetry of people and places. Many site-specific works have been included.

The material follows a roughly chronological, historical method of organization, from the founding of the city to the present—from wide-open frontier to urban gridlock. The selections include a wide spectrum of genres: journalism, belletristic essays, poetry, autobiographies, biographies, and fiction.

All anthologies are like photograph albums, moments in time, and all anthologies that I am familiar with invariably leave out pieces overlooked, undervalued, or unknown by the anthologist/editor. The very day this book appears, somebody may well publish a fine essay or poem or novel dealing with Austin. The city continues to generate writing in all genres—and at about the pace of new loft apartments going up in downtown Austin—at a steady rate with more to come.

There are also some very fine writers living in Austin who have never written anything set in the city or about the city. Site-specific work is one of the general principles underlying the series concept of literary cities in Texas, and this explains the absence of some writers from these pages.

It is also the case that many novels set in Austin do not contain the kind of detachable descriptions of place that make for good entries in an anthology of this kind. In such novels the city is more of a background ambience than a distinctive place described in detail. This is one reason I have included a list of Austin novels at the end, for those readers who wonder why their favorite Austin writer is missing from this collection or for those who want to read more widely in the novels that are set here. The list, I think it goes without saying, does not pretend to be definitive. And that list is ever growing. At least a half-dozen Austin-based novels have appeared on bookstore shelves since I began work on this project.

But one thing this book does show, and the bibliographical addendum further shows, is that Austin has been the site of far more fiction than anyone has previously noticed. I refer in particular to an article in the *Austin-American-Statesman* by Russell Cobb. In "Austin Often Overlooked as a Setting for Books" (October 30, 2005), Cobb mentions a grand total of five writers who have set their works in Austin and focuses mainly on Billy Lee Brammer's *The Gay Place* (1961) and Karen Olsson's *Waterloo* (2005). What I find among newcomers to Austin—and the city remains, as in the past, a place of newcomers—is a very thin view of history. History started when they arrived and ends with what they can find that's in print. Localized narcissism is a standard and long-familiar feature of the Austin mindset.

A city focused on government and education would have to produce reams of journalism, and Austin certainly has. I have no doubt that buried in the back numbers of local magazines and journals are some wonderful pieces, but those will have to await some future anthologist, because I confess to not having read all the back issues of all the local magazines and journals in order to find that lost masterpiece from the world of daily reporting. Much excellent journalism is time-bound, so that no matter how good it seems at the time, just a bit later it seems dated; the world has moved on. Major personalities and cultural figures, along with articles dealing with particular, recognizable Austin icons, have governed my choices instead. I aimed for the stars, as it were, of Austin culture, both literary, political, and otherwise.

In any event I have tried to cast my net pretty wide. As for now, in the summer of 2006, I am pleased with the variety, quality, and sheer interest of the materials here assembled.

For me, one of the real pleasures was digging up literary works that I had never read before. This was especially true of poetry, and I am happy to resurrect, as it were, some quite unjustly forgotten poems. It was also pleasant to discover previously unknown—to me, anyway—creative work by colleagues of mine past and present, in the Department of English of the University of Texas. Indeed, as I was walking along the corridors of the second and third floors of Parlin and Calhoun buildings the other day, I realized that within a hundred feet of my office are the offices of eight living authors included in this book and two deceased.

Although Austin is ever changing, most people have their own mythological version fixed in a particular time. There are those who believe it has great restaurants, in my view a dubious claim. There are those who believe it is an idyllic place without the problems of modern urban life, but I do not share this brand of local utopianism. In 2005 Austin, for the fifth year in a row, led all mid-size cities nationwide in traffic congestion. It is also among the nation's leaders in the percentage of automobile accidents. On average each citizen in the city can expect a collision every seven-and-a-half years. This puts Austin ahead of New York, Detroit, and Houston in this unenviable category. And I am not even going to talk about allergies and 108° temperatures near the end of September's annual extension of summer heat.

The city that emerges in the writings gathered here is one that most people who have lived here will recognize. For many, the book will be something of a nostalgia trip. For others, it will be, I hope, a revelation. In any event, just about everybody's Austin appears somewhere in these pages.

PART ONE

The Seat of Future Empire

WILLIAM SIDNEY PORTER (O. HENRY),
   Austin. A Brief Glance at Her History and Advantages 2

A.C. GREENE,
   The Founding of Austin 6

EDWIN SHRAKE,
   from *The Borderland* 8

DAVE OLIPHANT,
   from *Austin* 11

WILLIAM SIDNEY PORTER

Born in North Carolina in 1862, William Sidney Porter came to Texas in 1882, where he herded sheep in La Salle County for a couple of years before moving to Austin in 1884. For the next few years he worked at the General Land Office, then as a teller at the First National Bank. In 1887 he married seventeen-year-old Athol Estes, with whom he fathered a child. In April 1894 he started a humorous newspaper called the *Rolling Stone* that lasted a year minus one day. In 1898 Porter was sent to federal prison in Ohio on a five-year sentence for bank fraud. While in prison he began to write the stories that would make him famous as O. Henry. In 1903 he moved to New York City, where he wrote steadily and with great success until his death in 1910. In an early story, "Tic Tocq, the Great French Detective, in Austin" (*Rolling Stone*, 1894–95), Porter described Austin in a luminous phrase that has echoed down through the years: "City of the Violet Crown." The humorous history of Austin reprinted here appeared in the June 9, 1894, issue of *The Rolling Stone*. The unusual word "kourmiss" in the first paragraph is, as best I can determine, a version of *kumiss, koumiss, or koumiss,* a term for the fermented milk of a mare or camel, used as a beverage by Asian nomads. The term "cocaine store" seems self-evident and suggests a certain continuity in Austin culture from the nineteenth century until last week.

AUSTIN. A BRIEF GLANCE AT HER HISTORY AND ADVANTAGES

IN THE YEAR 18— STEPHEN F. AUSTIN, DANIEL BOONE, Davy Crockett, Ed Morris, Ponce de Leon, and Ben Thompson, together with other prominent citizens, while navigating the Colorado River in a canal boat, stopped to feed the mule and tap a fresh buffalo skin of *kourmiss* at the foot of what is now known in the guide book as Congress Avenue.

Those were early times in Texas.

After lunch the explorers took a fresh chew of jerked Indian and went ashore.

Suddenly an idea struck Stephen F. Austin, and he was too generous a man to conceal it.

"Boys," he said, "let's start a town site here and call it Austin."

"Just as you say," they all replied.

Then they got a gun and killed off all the Indians between the lunatic asylum and the river, and laid out Austin.

It has been laid out ever since.

Colonel Austin made a map showing all the streets just as they are seen, without the banana peelings and other unsanitary matter.

All hands then went down to W. B. Walker's store, where Ponce de Leon spread down a blanket and started a Monte bank.

This was the first industry ever begun in Austin.

At the time Austin was laid out it was a very young town.

As soon as people began to arrive the population increased.

Nothing so much adds to the age of a town as for it to grow older.

The people were of a hardy and vigorous nature and presented an Iron Front to the dangers that surrounded them.

Most of them were emigrants from other States, and their names were mentioned often in the wanted columns of the Eastern papers.

Sometime between June and the year 1870, the city organized and began to receive subscriptions for the widows of men who tried to walk down the Avenue with a plug hat on.

About this time, a shooting tournament was held, and the prize was won by Ben Thompson, who kept it for a number of years.

Austin has undergone a great many changes in the last 200 years.

Where the buffalo once roamed you can now get twenty-two pounds of sugar for a dollar.

Where the early settlers once lived you can now buy a cocktail, which is pretty much the same thing.

A man who has lived in Austin today and fifty years ago, cannot truthfully say anything.

Time brings many changes.

On the Avenue, where Dr. Taylor's stores now stand, as well as they can, a good many years ago were to be found real comfortable and weather-proof buildings.

Forty years ago the vacant square north of Christian & Crooker's lumber yard had nothing on it.

Today the business men of Austin point to it with pride and show you a baseball game there almost any afternoon, between two nines, one called the Bankers, because made up from men who work in banks, and the other called Gentlemen, which they do not attempt to explain.

The scholastic advantages of Austin are promoted almost entirely by the schools.

Austin has one soap factory, one electric light works, one cemetery, one dam, one racetrack, two beer gardens, one capitol, two city councils, one cocaine factory, and will probably some day have a newspaper.

If you had taken a man by the hand forty-five years ago and pointed out to him the wonderful changes that would take place in Austin in fifty years, you would still have five years in which to save your reputation as a prophet.

But Austin is rapidly coming to the Front.

One hundred years from now intrepid spirits will explore the capitol yard and make known its mysteries. Perhaps from its fastnesses will be brought forth the shrinking form of Charley Ross, John Wilkes Booth, or the Longview bank robbers.

Who can tell?

In the meantime let us each one put our shoulder to the wheel and try and get somebody else to advertise the town for us.

A brighter day is dawning.

Even now, by the judicious use of liquids, good food can be procured that can be readily eaten without lodging for a stated sum of money per month.

Any laboring man can do well in Austin if he receives steady work and good wages.

Austin holds out exceptional advantages to professional men.

4

Nowhere in the world can a good barber, who does a credit business, receive a better patronage.

We have the finest public institutions and asylums in the country, and a jail crowded day and night.

Look at our public troughs and parks. Some of the finest wild cat hunting in the State can be had in Pease park.

Austin is bound to become a summer resort for people who can't get away for a vacation.

Some of your most prominent merchants are already stirring themselves and have distributed several hundred dodgers on the streets, calling the attention of northern and eastern capital to our advantages.

We are the people. ★

1894

A. C. GREENE

A. C. Greene (1923–2002) was born in Abilene, Texas. He started out as a newspaper writer and for many years worked as a columnist for newspapers in Dallas. His books include *A Personal Country*, a memoir, and *The Highland Park Woman*, a collection of short stories. Greene lived in Austin for a time during the 1960s when he was in the American Studies program at the University of Texas. "The Founding of Austin" is typical of the brief columns about Texas history that were a staple of Greene's work. It appeared originally in the *Dallas Morning News*.

THE FOUNDING OF AUSTIN

AUSTIN ALONE AMONG TEXAS CITIES WAS FOUNDED ON beauty, the inspiration of Mirabeau Buonaparte Lamar, an impulsive poet who later became President of the Republic of Texas.

In 1837, when he was vice president under Sam Houston, Lamar decided to take a vacation from both President Houston and the new capital city named for him. There was no love lost between Old Sam, the doer, and Lamar, the dreamer. Someone suggested that Lamar hunt buffalo up on the Colorado River above Bastrop, so the Vice President and his private secretary, the Reverend Edward Fontaine, set out for that Indian-haunted frontier. They got an escort of six rangers from Fort Colorado and rode west beside the Colorado to where Jacob Harrell had created a little stockade settlement he called Waterloo at the mouth of Shoal Creek. Harrell welcomed the hunters and early on the morning following their arrival, his young son woke everybody up shouting that the prairie was full of buffalo.

The Vice President and his party were soon in the saddle and the chase began. Lamar brought down the biggest bull any of the hunters had seen, dropping the buffalo in a valley where Congress Avenue and Seventh Street would someday cross in downtown Austin. Later the party was assembled by the bugler to the hill where the capitol now stands, and Lamar, stirred by the magnificent surroundings, exclaimed to Fontaine, "This should be the seat of Future Empire!"

Lamar was elected president in September of 1838, and one of his first official acts after assuming office was to appoint a commission, early in 1839, to locate a site for a new capital nearer the center of the Republic—nobody but Old Sam and the local merchants liked Houston. It is not surprising that when the commission reported back in April, Waterloo was the unanimous choice. The commission's account of the proposed site was poetic in its praise: "The imagination of even the romantic will not be disappointed on viewing the Valley of the Colorado and the fertile and gracefully undulating woodlands and luxuriant Prairies at a distance from it . . . and the citizen's bosom must swell with honest pride when, standing in the Portico of the Capitol, he looks abroad upon a region worthy only of being the home of the brave and the free."

The Republic paid $3 an acre for 7,700 acres of land to contain and surround the capital. The Texas Congress had taken care of political egos, stipulating that the new capital, wherever located, would be named for the late Stephen F. Austin, the father of Texas. Edwin Waller, who was later elected Austin's first mayor, began surveying the town site and locating and erecting government buildings on May 21, 1839. On August 1 he conducted the town lot sale, disposing of 306 private parcels of land. The 640-acre town site was laid out north of the Colorado River, between Shoal Creek on the west and Waller Creek, named for the surveyor, on the east. East-west streets were originally named for Texas trees (numeralized in the 1880s), while the north-south streets, save for Congress Avenue in the center and East and West avenues, were named for Texas rivers. Lamar and cabinet arrived October 17, 1839, to find an instant city awaiting their use. ★

1985

EDWIN SHRAKE

Born in Fort Worth, Texas, Edwin (Bud) Shrake began his writing career as a sports reporter for newspapers in Fort Worth and later in Dallas. In 1962 he published his first novel, a paperback Western, and in 1964 another novel, *But Not For Love*. He was on the staff of *Sports Illustrated* for a number of years, and in the early 1970s moved to Austin, where he has resided ever since. Among his numerous books, one that stands out is *Strange Peaches* (1972), a novel set at the time of the Kennedy assassination. *The Borderland: A Novel of Texas* (1999) is based in part on the founding of Austin. The excerpt enlivens the historical record.

from THE BORDERLAND

THEY STOPPED TO LET A DOZEN PIGS TROT ACROSS PECAN Street, followed by two large white hogs. Cows roamed the streets, and chickens were clucking everywhere. At least three dogs were barking at any given moment, day or night. Pole pens were being erected on Congress Avenue to restrict the passage of domestic animals. There was a constant clamor of saws and axes. Buildings of pine and cedar were going up fast as the craftsmen could manage. Many newcomers lived in tents, most of them waiting for a house to be built. Because of the crowds and the difficulty of supply—shipments of hardware and staples and condiments came by ox wagon from Houston City or San Antonio—flour was a hundred redback dollars a barrel. But there was no shortage of food. As well as holding many domestic animals, the fields and woods of the valley were crawling with deer and birds and other game. The creeks were full of fish. Tonk and Lipan Indians—enemies of the Comanches—loitered around the edges of the city with stacks of buffalo hides and beaver and raccoon pelts for trade. It was unthinkable for Comanches to fight each other, but they fought everybody else. The Tonks and Lipans moved closer to the men with hats.

The city was laid out from south to north, beginning at the Colorado River. At what became Congress Avenue and the river had been a settlement named Waterloo—five families at a confluence with Shoal Creek that always disappeared in the regular floods. Waterloo was swallowed by the growth of Austin. Congress Avenue was being beaten out of the ground, its springs buried under rocks, its ravine filled with earth, to run north from the river's edge, called Water Street, to Capitol Square, the site that had been selected for the first capitol building. Because of a dispute between contractors, a temporary capitol building was in fact being constructed several blocks to the south and west.

Doc and Cullasaja enjoyed walking in Austin. Twenty streams flowed through the town. The north and south streets were named for the biggest Texas rivers—Rio Grande, Nueces, San Antonio, Guadalupe, La Vaca, Colorado, Brazos, San Jacinto, Trinity, Neches, Red River, and Sabine. Congress Avenue ran up the middle. The southern boundary was marked by the river and Water Street, and the northern by North Avenue, two blocks north of Capitol Square. The west to east streets were named for native trees—Live Oak, Cypress, Cedar, Pine, Pecan, Bois d'Arc, Hickory, Ash, Mulberry, Mesquite, Peach, and Walnut. West Avenue was the western boundary of the city and East Avenue was the eastern edge. College Avenue—on which land was set aside for the building of a university—went east and west from either side of Capitol Square. Waller Creek defined the eastern boundary, and Shoal Creek ran along the western. Both creeks flowed steadily year after year, even during times of no rain. Doc and Cullasaja could see the framework of the new French legation under construction on a hill east of East Avenue.

Cullasaja knew the names of the wildflowers abloom in the fields in their spring colors—bluebonnets, winecups, redbuds, Indian blankets, honeysuckle, wild verbena, Indian paintbrush, sunflowers, goldenrod, agarita berries, and purple sage. The twenty streams that flowed through the city were lined with cypress, cottonwood and sycamore trees. Oaks, hackberries, chinaberries, elm, and willows grew in abundance. Evergreen cedars were being chopped down to make fence posts and rails. In and around the city were rabbits, possums, squirrels, raccoons, foxes, armadillos, roadrunners, pigeons, pheasants, wild turkeys, coyotes, wolves, panthers, otters, beavers, hawks, and often a bear or an eagle would be seen.

The caravan of eighty-four wagons, drawn by oxen, that bore the archives of the Republic of Texas, made a steady pace of nine miles a day for the journey that was moving the capital from Houston City to Austin.

Two companies of Texas army regular infantry walked guard, dressed in new blue jackets that had been furnished them by the Secretary of War on the command of President Lamar. He wanted his soldiers to look utterly professional when they marched into the new, temporary capitol building, which was being called Fort Austin because of its surrounding stockade fence that was in turn surrounded by a moat six feet deep.

President Lamar traveled on horseback with the archives caravan. His aim was to ride into Austin as the head of government in a most tangible and symbolic fashion. He was nostalgic for a view of the violet hills that he recalled from an earlier visit to the place that had become Austin. Then he had been shooting for sport with buffalo hunters, and they had come across this hilly location that had plenty of flowing water and so many lovely vistas that Lamar had been inspired to jot poems in his notebook. At that time the local settlement had been called Waterloo. It was Lamar's inspiration to locate his new capital on the north side of the river in the valley with the crown of violet hills—he loved the image of "violet hills"—and used it often in writing about Austin—and his request to the Congress to move the capital from Houston City to Austin had started people swarming into the Colorado River valley and caused the sounds of saws and hammers and wagon wheels to become the dominant noise of the town, much louder than the piano playing at Dutch John's or cattle bawling in their pens. The President yearned to see his new mansion, the White House, built to the specifications he had drawn up and sent to Mayor Waller, his agent in the matter. On the night before the Fourth Texas Congress would convene for the first time at the new capitol, the President would hold the grandest party ever known in the new city. He would open his White House to members of the House and the Senate, to all local citizens of repute, to his cabinet and government workers to visitors who were looking for investment opportunities in the Republic. The White House would be a beacon that shone for all friends of Texas. ★

1999

Dave Oliphant

Born in Fort Worth, Dave Oliphant first came to Austin to enroll at the University of Texas in 1960, transferring as a junior from Lamar Tech in Beaumont. Leaving in 1966 with an M.A., he returned in 1976 with a Ph.D. from the University of Northern Illinois, and taught at the University of Texas until his retirement in 2006. The author of numerous volumes of poetry and criticism, Oliphant is one of the closest observers of the poetry scene in Texas, past and present. The following reproduces the opening pages of his long poem *Austin*, which appeared originally in 1985. Clearly influenced by William Carlos Williams' *Paterson*, *Austin* is quite allusive and very site-specific. "Estevan," of course, is the Spanish for Stephen (F. Austin).

from Austin

    at the center at the heart
    of how & why have been & are
    gardens of wrongs must still recall
    the seat of law & a greed feeds on
    site come true from the "academy scheme"
    Estevan's dream in '33
    of a campus of where to sit & listen
    at the feet of a Bedichek Dobie or Webb
    professors of a faith in a frontier way
    vouched from that time of toughing it out
    have longed somehow to touch
    without a loss of here & now
    their talk of cutting-horse lariat & brand
    sixshooter axe & bowie-knife blade
    windmill "bull wheel" cable or bit

simple tools proved so titan in hands
of men & women grown heroic-wise
in a prose of writers but rarely known
sensing none alone if not all together
might reach so deep to the meaning sought
no wildcatter logging the signs so well
could read the core & tell for certain
he had come to salt or sand
have awaited still the drill can strike
right for singing in stratum or source
will not so soon run dry
a lease longer than cattle or crude
will return Estevan's lay of the land
when he mapped its channels & bays
nearer his call for courses to take
in English Spanish & French
his belief in a credit line based
on what each man has said he'll do
at the very least to avow the debts
to summon up & render accounts
to name keepers among teachers & mates
dividends from a rented room
a class attended
memorial halls
memoried haunts
wins & losses
at stadium or court
the leaf- & creek-veined hills
of pecan cedar & oak
have soaked like rain
have burned like sun
remembered rays now magnified

held to the page to blaze for him
started upon the straight & error
paved the way for bones & blood
laid the slab & cornerstone
for every feeling & thought
paid the toll & utility bill
for these 300 yearly shining days
in a dank Inquisition cell
paid with the coin
of a gnawing doubt
with visions sired
these daily scenes
east & west on 11th Street
of blacks still down & out
of hooker bars & liquor stores
at a mere two blocks' remove
from a final resting place
from his Peach Point grave
the remains uprooted
interred in this the State maintains
his statue in bronze by Coppini
its right & dark-green outstretched hand
extended still toward all he hoped
would be achieved
to ills he'd not conceived
in its left a scroll
unrolled for all to read
epic of an entrepreneur
while at his back
the cape in folds
drapes to his founding feet
as he stares away

to the bier in white
the barred encased & sculpted corse
of Albert Sidney Johnston
commander fell at Shiloh
directing Confederate troops
whose ears
were it not
for that stronger stop
than glass's pane
than ironwork grates
would yet take in
the humble hymns
from the Shiloh Baptist choir
rise now & never falter
as Estevan stares to where
his indecision led
to the racial slurs & bloodied fields
to where his insight failed
to where if now he looked behind
with eyes at the back of his head
could spy across in littered yards
his slavery's kids ride metal scraps
roll tires or toss their airless balls
yelling jive in a grammar broken
as half their project homes
where just next door
his Mexican heirs
will ever insist
he stole it all
down their beers to polkas
corridos blasted out
on stereo tapes in lowered cars

in blouses loud
with red & pink
in frayed work shirts hung out to dry
from a dead mesquite (or so it seems)
a chinaberry with its inedible fruit
a weight of wetness swings on plastic lines
has sagged them down
lives of those
must still bear up
strive at greening deep within
with a sap will flesh
the yellow seed
these saging lines from seeing him
dragged in dirt
though each has need
of knowing earth
the bitter taste
of where it is he's
gotten off
deserves no greater blame
no stain for what was tried
tarnish *sí* on his "violet crown"
O'Henry's phrase
for this city's sunset sky
LBJ on tour down 6th
in full view then
of the legislature's lawns
in '38 had seen them there
40 families to a single lot
watched as from one faucet
each carted water a hundred yards
one leaky tub to wash them all

an eyesore in Lyndon's House report
a crying shame so near he said
to this tallest capitol dome
its very edifice set
on a chalk named after & for
Estevan's patient steady ways
no shale that swells when wet
shrinks when dry
& by geologist Flawn's account
the cause of most
foundation cracks
his holds firm
won't shift about. . . . ★

1985

PART TWO

City of the Violet Crown: 1900s-1940s

JOHN A. LOMAX,
     from *Adventures of a Ballad Hunter* 18

FREDERIC PROKOSCH,
     from *Voices: A Memoir* 23

RALPH YARBOROUGH,
     The Music of Running Waters 27

MARGARET COUSINS,
     from The Beatific Memories of an English Major 30

WILLIAM A. OWENS,
     from *Three Friends* 34

ROY BEDICHEK,
     [Letters on Sculptures] 40

LIZ CARPENTER,
     from *Getting Better All the Time* 44

LYNDON B. JOHNSON,
     from Tarnish on the Violet Crown 50

JOHN A. LOMAX

John Avery Lomax (1867–1948) was born in Goodman, Mississippi, but grew up in Central Texas in rural Bosque County. Lomax entered the University of Texas in 1895, later attended Harvard University, and eventually pursued a very distinguished career as a folklorist and collector of folk music. His first book, *Cowboy Songs and Other Frontier Ballads* (1910) is an American classic. Lomax, with his son John Alan, toured the U.S. in the 1930s, recording such important folk artists as Lightnin' Washington and Huddie Ledbetter (Leadbelly). The culmination of Lomax's efforts to preserve the music of the past was the collection of more than ten thousand recordings for the Archive of American Folk Song at the Library of Congress. In his autobiography, *Adventures of a Ballad Hunter* (1947), Lomax recalled his entrance into the University of Texas, his studies there, and the failure of professors in the English Department at UT to recognize the significance of the cowboy songs that he wanted to collect.

from ADVENTURES OF A BALLAD HUNTER

I BECAME DESPERATELY AWARE OF MY LACK OF ANY SUB-
stantial education. The years were passing, and I saw no way out of the coil of circumstance that surrounded me. At first my salary had been forty dollars a month. Now it was seventy-five, but I had spent all my savings in abortive, futile efforts to educate myself. Moreover, I had assumed a security debt that, at the end of fifteen years of paying, cost me four thousand dollars. I was terribly unhappy, in a frenzy of apprehension as if some awful calamity was about to swallow me, as desperate and undecided as when making up my mind to sell my pony, Selim. For years I had read a catalog of Vanderbilt University, thumbed it until the pages were frazzled at the edges. The specimen entrance examinations

printed on the last pages were beyond my ken. I couldn't solve the mathematics problems. Even with a pony the Latin passages were beyond me. I didn't have the heart to write and ask if the officials would relent for a Texan. Too late I was told they sometimes did. One day, in the Fort Worth Union Depot, I met Joe Etter of Sherman, Texas, then a student at the state university. "The University of Texas is the only place for *you*," he said. Instantly my mind was clear. To "Texas" I would go. All doubt was gone. Since that day I've stubbed my toe against many, many flinty rocks; I've blundered into frequent by-passes, but the main road over the horizon has always been plain if only I shifted my eyes and looked ahead. For many years thereafter, the University of Texas was the core of my life.

&

In Austin Miss Mignonette Carrington (afterward Mrs. J. E. Pearce), brilliant and fun-loving, taught me enough grammar to get me over the stile past Dr. Morgan Callaway, Jr., head of the English Department. How she managed the other subjects I can't imagine. I only know I took no entrance examinations. During the summer I had met President Leslie Waggener at evening gatherings of a group studying Shakespeare, my first introduction to the dramatist. President Waggener afterward suggested that I enter his senior class in Shakespeare during the regular session. Soon he asked each member of the class to prepare an essay on *Richard II*. I had never in my life written an essay, not even a one-page theme. When I set myself the task of tearing apart the machinery of Shakespeare's play, after the plan of Dr. Waggener (attempting to see the parts and how they fitted together, what made the whole thing tick), I got so excited that I forgot to sleep. I wrote on and on, into the dawn, twenty-five closely packed pages or more. One other time only—and years afterward—did I study all night.

Dr. Waggener did not return my paper when he handed the marked essays back to my classmates. Instead, he asked me to come to his office. I felt that the end had come, that I was to leave his class or to resign from the University. He asked me to sit down, and then looked at me gravely. I remember how dry my mouth felt, that my hands were shaking. "I called you in to tell you," he said, "that I have credited you with three full courses in English. Look at the corner of your essay," he added, smiling.

When I could see, there shone in red ink, written in his small copperplate handwriting, an E. Afterward, when I had stumbled speechless from the room, a friend told me that E meant "excellent," the highest mark. Those few minutes in Dr. Waggener's office were the high-water mark in my entire college career.

Dr. Waggener was a Kentuckian, Harvard '61, a gifted teacher. He was also a bred-in-the-bone Southerner, who had been shot down and left for dead on the field of battle in the Civil War. To me he had seemed like a god, far removed, reserved, stately. But now he had bent down and pinned an accolade on me. His large gray eyes had softened in kindness. I knew now how a serf felt when the lord of the manor called him from the ranks and knighted him. With credits also in mathematics, I had really started on my way, more than a fifth the distance to the magical A.B. degree dangling down the road ahead of me.

An A.B. degree! Never before would I allow myself to dream that I could earn such golden acclaim. I didn't want a Ph.D. or a B.S. or any other chaffy group of letters. I wanted only the majestic A.B., Artium Baccalaureus. To me the words brought visions of philosophers strolling among Grecian pillars, of senators discussing grave matters of state in the Roman Forum. So, in addition to English and mathematics in my freshman year, I plunged into beginners' Greek and Freshman Latin—I had had little Latin and no Greek at all, not even one letter of the alphabet. To these four subjects I added chemistry, history and Anglo-Saxon—twenty-three recitations a week when the normal number was twelve. Never was there such a hopeless hodge-podge. There I was, a Chatauqua-educated country boy who couldn't conjugate an English verb or decline a pronoun, attempting to master three other languages at the same time—Anglo-Saxon, Latin, Greek!

But I plunged on through the year, for, since I was older than the average freshman, I must hurry, hurry. I don't think I ever stopped to think how foolish it all was. Through the following summer I only increased the tempo of my haste. I went for the three summer months to the University of Chicago, doubling in Latin and Greek, and tackling French for good measure. I got a bit of pleasure from a class sight-reading Plato's *Dialogues*. Otherwise, for sixteen hours a day, I grubbed doggedly at the roots of three languages the same way I had grubbed at the pecan stumps in the Bosque County river bottom.

The beginning of the second year in the University of Texas found me over the hump in the number of credits. Still ahead of me was more Greek and Latin and French, more government and history and philosophy. But I had got my second wind and could swing along steadily and surely. I felt many "rosy-fingered" dawns in Homer and found satisfying beauty in the lyrics of Horace and Catullus. Dr. Waggener taught me to appreciate Browning, even "Sordello" and "The Ring and the Book." Otherwise, the maze of this jam-packed two years of ill-advised and fruitless hurry seemed only dust and ashes. When the diploma was handed to me the luster of the golden A.B. had faded to dull lead. I had won a coveted bauble, but there had been little joy in the working. I had given myself no time to look around me or to plan for the future. I had been blindly rushing somewhere, I didn't know where.

But in the University of Texas I had come in contact with a few genuine scholars, somewhat fewer who could really teach what they knew. For my blunder in tearing through my undergraduate years I could blame only myself. No longer was I forced to live in a world of make-believe. In some degree I had acquired intellectual independence. The little I knew, I knew that I knew. I was no longer ashamed.

The day after I was graduated I went to work for the University of Texas as secretary to the president, as registrar in charge of all admission correspondence, and as steward of the men's dormitory, etc., etc., all for $75 a month. On the side I was supposed to take enough studies to complete a Master of Arts degree within two years. . . .

When I first went to the University of Texas in 1895, I had carried in my trunk the tightly rolled batch of manuscript of cowboy songs. They were written out on scratch pads and on pieces of cardboard. I had not included certain songs that Bob Hanna was fond of singing to groups of workers resting in the shade of a threshing machine while repairs went on. I had listened intently, but I never dared to write out the words of "The Keyhole in the Door," "Winding Up Her Little Ball of Yarn," "The Oaks of Jim Darling," "The Transom over the Door," "Her Apron So Neat," and other favorite songs current in Dodge City, the end of the cattle trail. Nor can I recall any plan or purpose in making my collection of cowboy songs, or why I should wish to show them to Dr. Leslie

Waggener, who was then teaching me Shakespeare. But one day I did take my roll of songs to his office. Never before had I shown them to anyone.

Dr. Waggener referred me to Dr. Morgan Callaway, Jr., a Johns Hopkins University Doctor of Philosophy, whose scholarship is reflected in three studies, "The Absolute Participle in Anglo-Saxon," 1889; "The Appositive Participle in Anglo-Saxon," 1901; and "The Infinitive in Anglo-Saxon," 1913. Timidly I handed Dr. Callaway my roll of dingy manuscript written out in lead pencil and tied together with a cotton string. Courteous and kindly gentleman that he was, he thanked me and promised a report the next day. Alas, the following morning Dr. Callaway told me that my samples of frontier literature were tawdry, cheap, and unworthy. I had better give my attention to the great movements of writing that had come sounding down the ages. There was no possible connection, he said, between the tall tales of Texas and the tall tales of Beowulf. His decision, exquisitely considerate, was final, absolute. No single crumb of comfort was left for me. I was unwilling to have anyone else see the examples of my folly, or know of my disappointment. So that night in the dark, out behind Brackenridge Hall, the men's dormitory where I lodged, I made a small bonfire of every scrap of my cowboy songs.

Years afterward an associate of Dr. Callaway in the English faculty, Dr. R. H. Griffith, asked to examine a first copy of *Cowboy Songs and Other Frontier Ballads*. The following morning he brought the book to my desk, thanked me for the loan, turned on his heel, and went away with no word of comment about my first venture in the field of folksongs. The disfavor of my Cowboy Song project still survived. ★

1947

FREDERIC PROKOSCH

Frederick Prokosch was born in 1906 of German/Bohemian parents in Madison, Wisconsin. His first novel, *The Asiatics*, was published in 1935. His oeuvre consists of fourteen other novels; *The Missonlonghi Manuscript*, a "meditation" on Byron; *Voices*, his memoir; and four collections of poetry. He died in Grasse, France, in 1989. His father, Eduard Prokosch, a renowned philologist, was chairman of the German Department at the University of Texas, 1913–1919. Prokosch's memories of Austin suggest a lush landscape that is intensely Southern in its associations and culture.

from: VOICES: A MEMOIR

FROM WISCONSIN, WE WENT TO TEXAS AND SETTLED IN the town of Austin, which rose from the banks of the Colorado River. I was only eight years old and I was terrified of Austin. I was frightened of the scorpions and the cactus and the dragonflies, which flew in fiery zigzags, as though they had a poisonous sting in them.

We lived on West Twenty-third Street, just off Rio Grande Street, with two fig trees in the back amid an orgy of sunflowers. Beyond our house rose the Cochrane Mansion, which was said to be haunted and was draped with shawls of ivy and beards of Texas moss, and still beyond lay the fields of bluebonnets, which sloped down to the creek. I sought refuge from the heat and the cactus in the musky shadows that hung over the creek.

Here I prowled in the afternoons, chasing the gaudy Texas butterflies, such as *Papilio cresphontes*, a giant of black and cream, and *Dione vanillae*, a crimson beauty flecked with silver. My father taught linguistics and philology at the university. He was a finely profiled man with keen black eyes and a fondling voice. He had fled from Austria many years ago because of a scandal involving a duel, and he had sailed to America, rebellious and penniless. One evening in Milwaukee (or so he told me one day), he had a vision of a vast multiplicity of ancient languages, which blended into an all-engulfing panorama. After this he devoted his entire soul to a single end: to disentangle from this intricacy the history of the Indo-European tongues. His vision was fulfilled in a philological masterpiece of heroic proportions and of a saintly lucidity. It was called *The History of the Indo-European Languages,* and it was published after his death by the Yale University Press.

I still remember sitting in a fig tree as he walked in the garden and listening in secrecy as he uttered his consonants and diphthongs. These little fragments of vanished dialects traced in the air, like the calls of birds, the mysterious journey of the human tongue from the depths of the jungle into its modern complexities. He groped for the sounds and structures of strange, vanished languages as a diver gropes for pearls in the depths of the ocean. And when I finally read his masterpiece after his death, I detected, in those labyrinthine migrations of ancient diphthongs, the strains of an epic poetry more meandering than *The Odyssey* and even more interminable than *The Mahabharata.*

One day Anna Pavlova arrived in the town of Austin. "It is strange," said my father, "that Pavlova should come to Austin." "And why shouldn't she come to Austin?" said my mother rather plaintively. "It seems entirely natural. It's a logical place to visit. Remember, please, that Austin is the capital of Texas, and Texas is the biggest state in America." My mother sat at the piano and played the mazurkas of Chopin.

I used to crouch under the piano and listen intently to the music of Frederic Chopin, with whom I felt a mysterious kinship because of the identity of our names. I have never loved anyone as much as I loved my suffering mother, and I still, in my dreams, can see her staring at the album and spreading her fingers into the melodies of Chopin. "Very well," said my father. "Go and look at Pavlova." So we went one afternoon to a small stucco theater near the university campus, where they showed the films of Fatty Arbuckle, Mary Pickford, and Douglas Fairbanks. This little theater, with its gilded angels, was now given to Pavlova. The curtain went up on a pastel-tinted forest. The violins and cellos whined gently, insidiously. I leaned forward in my seat as the row of ballerinas entered, gliding mothlike on tiptoe through the twilit woods.

The trees grew brilliant, the music quickened. My mother gripped my elbow. "It's *The Glow Worm!*" she whispered. I grew tense with delight. The corps de ballet started to sway with a feverish delicacy. Pavlova surged skyward, more a ghost than a woman, and the curtain fell down on a ripple of applause.

After *The Glow-Worm* came a fantaisie impromptu by Chopin, a short bacchanal by Glazunov, and an adagio from *The Sleeping Beauty*. The last dance of all was *Le Cygne* by Saint-Saens. Pavlova went gliding over an imaginary sea, more a bird than a ballerina, more a specter than a woman. The curtain swung down on a spellbound silence, and my mother said softly, "What a revelation for Austin!"

On the following afternoon, Pavlova came to our house for coffee. Some Machiavellian stratagem of my mother's had succeeded. The great ballerina stepped out of a "jitney" and floated into the parlor amid a scent of violets and a flurry of fox-heads. "How very primitive," said my mother as she poured out the coffee, "our little Austin must look to you after the velvet of St. Petersburg!"

Pavlova lifted her coffee cup and gazed at it discreetly. There was a portrait of the Emperor Franz Josef on the side of it. It was the finest thing in the house, aside from my father's set of Goethe. She leaned forward. I still remember her quicksilver voice.

"Je suis absolument enthusiastisch for your beautiful state of Texas!"

She spoke in a mixture of fluttering French, hissing German, and gurgling English. I was already developing a fascination for curious words and mellifluous phrases, and Pavlova's utterances still linger in my mind with a strange precision. Her words danced through the air like many-hued butterflies; her fingers kept drumming vivaciously on the coffee cup. She spoke of Chicago and Oklahoma City and Boston. The names of these cities, in her gay, mercurial voice, took on the luster of Paris and Vienna and Monte Carlo.

My mother said, "My little Gertrude has an exquisite talent for dancing. Come, darling, dance your lovely mazurka for Pavlova."

She placed a record on the scratchy old Victrola, and we listened to Vladimir de Pachmann playing Chopin. My sister spread her arms and deftly raised her leg, and the mazurka grew alive under her swift, childlike movements.

Pavlova kept gazing at her with a sly, gentle malice. She said: "*Sehr charmant!* She is *absolument reitzend!*" Then she spoke of the cowboys of Oklahoma and the gangsters of Chicago. She fixed her luminous eyes on me with sinister intimacy.

"And what do you plan to be, my boy? A cowboy or a gangster?"

She rolled her eyes luridly and glanced around the room, as though detecting a lurking threat in the bowl of roses and the bust of Mozart. Her sunlit fingernails danced about under her chin, capricious as fireflies.

I kept peering at her face out of the corner of my eye. She looked surprisingly angular, after the undulations of *The Swan*, and disenchantingly opaque after the translucencies of *The Glow-Worm*. But I saw in her glowing eyes, which looked suave yet strangely agitated, a hint of realms and passions immeasurably remote from Austin.

One morning we were eating our pancakes in the shade of the honeysuckle and my father said sadly, "We are leaving Texas. We shall live in Pennsylvania."

He said it in his gentle but inexorable voice, which gave to the word *Texas* an air of desolation, in which the chanting of the Negroes rose from the aisles of hanging moss and the fields full of bluebonnets shone with a huge, savage innocence.

My fear of Texas and of Texans had turned into a wild leaping love. Every day after school I'd run down to the creek and watch the tadpoles wriggling in the coiling red water. The glory of the butterflies with their wings of red and silver hinted at a bright, bloodthirsty grandeur in the airs of Texas. The smells of Texas held the scent of rocks and horses and salamanders. I felt a cold stab of grief at the thought of leaving Texas. ★

1983

RALPH YARBOROUGH

Ralph Yarborough (1903–1996) grew up in Chandler, Texas, and graduated from the University of Texas Law School in 1927. He entered politics in the 1930s and eventually was elected to the U.S. Senate in 1957, serving until 1971. Yarborough prided himself on being a New Dealer and a liberal in a conservative Southern state. On November 22, 1963, Yarborough was in the motorcade in Dallas, riding with Vice-President Lyndon Johnson when the President was shot. A long-time resident of Austin, Yarborough valued Barton Springs and late in his life wrote about his earliest memories of the famous watering hole in "The Music of Running Waters."

THE MUSIC OF RUNNING WATERS

MY FIRST REMEMBRANCE OF BARTON SPRINGS CAME in June of 1917, when I was fourteen years of age and came to Austin with my father and other members of the family to visit my father's oldest sister and her husband, who was a clerk in the General Land Office. We left Chandler, Texas, at five A.M., knowing that would be a long, slow trip because the roads were unpaved, but we had a guidebook of roads, which were a patchwork with no connecting highway named for the area between Waco and Austin. Entries would say, "Jog to the right a mile and turn left at a fencepost; go 3 miles." Such was the state of roads in up-to-date guidebooks in 1917.

My father had a new Maxwell sedan automobile with all new tires. After we got out of the mud and sand of East Texas, the roads were paved for only eight miles in Navarro County, where the oil-field traffic was heavy. Once we passed Waco and got on the caliche and rock roads south, our tires were cut to pieces. Over and over we stopped on the side of the road to repair them. It was after dark, even with the long days of June, before we finally reached our destination in Austin on that torturous unpaved 225 miles of generally unmarked roads.

We saw the University of Texas and the Capitol and were told of Barton Springs. That was before radio, and Barton Springs was not as well known statewide as it became after the advent of broadcasting. We went on to San Antonio, stopped to see the wonderful springs in New Braunfels, and by the time we got back to Chandler we had utterly destroyed the four new tires in addition to the patched ones.

In 1921 I entered the University of Texas at midterm, and, staying with students, I formed a greater acquaintance with Barton Springs than on the brief stay in 1917. I recall going out to them one day, and I felt I was about to freeze in that cold water. To obtain the loans to stay in school, I had to maintain a B average, so all the time I was not working, I was studying and could not go often to the Springs. But I was listening to talk of Barton Springs and I was thoroughly grounded in the wonders of being there by students who did have the time to go. When I could go to Barton Springs, I usually dodged the cold waters and went upstream on the trails that paralleled the streams on the north side, looking for Indian arrowheads and watching the converging of the waters into rivulets and then into larger streams. I was listening to the sounds of the waters, the musical waters.

Later, I practiced law in El Paso, during which time I married, and I returned to Austin, on April 1, 1931, as an assistant attorney general. I worked on the land desk, suing for recovery of Permanent School Fund and Permanent University Fund monies. I heard more about Barton Springs, as radio had by then spread the news of it to many areas of Texas.

While most people went swimming, I still preferred to walk along the narrow paths up the creek, looking for the scarce Indian arrowheads, occasionally finding one after a rain. I admired not only the pool—smaller than before the dam was built—but also the bubbling waters that ran down from the Springs into it. . . .

So I became more and more alarmed by what could happen to Barton Springs and to the creek, whose fate increases in importance to the people with every passing year . . . It is a part of the living land of Austin. The streams from the springs on which branches I walked while a student in the university flow down in rivulets, the limpid waters rippling noisily over larger rocks, making pleasant gurgling sounds in the falls, singing a melody of sounds of running waters as they converge for a time into one connected pool en route to their search for the seas.

In *Goodbye to a River* John Graves has lovingly described the Brazos before it was cut up by dams; let it not be said that we are about to say good-bye to Barton Springs, or any free-flowing river.

Barton Springs is a dual natural treasure, the quiet scenic lands with that umbrella of green growth and the musical harmonies of the running waters, which combined soothes the soul of man and becomes the soul of the city eternal. ★

1993

MARGARET COUSINS

Margaret Cousins (1905–1996) was born in Munday (Knox County), Texas, and graduated from the University of Texas in 1926. She earned her living writing for magazines such as *Good Housekeeping, McCall's, Cosmopolitan*, and *Mademoiselle*. She was a senior editor for Doubleday & Co. from 1961 to 1973. One of her stories, "The Life of Lucy Gallant," was made into the film *Lucy Gallant*. She also published numerous books, including the memoir, *My Own Story* (1956) and *Big Spring: The Casual Biography of a Prairie Town* (1942). In the section below, Cousins remembers her days as an English major. One of the professors that she profiles is known today only for the fact that the building that houses the Department of English is named after him; the other is one of the most famous teachers in the history of the University.

from THE BEATIFIC MEMORIES OF AN ENGLISH MAJOR

MY EXPERIENCES WITH DR. PARLIN'S "ADVANCED Composition" course were productive. This class, which lasted only one semester, was composed of A students from various college departments who were interested in learning to write. It was a very small class. Members of the class were expected to contribute writings, on whatever subject matter and in whatever form of English composition they chose—when they were satisfied with what they had written. Since anyone who gained admittance to this section was likely to be an eager beaver, there was no necessity for insistence on contributions. They poured in, and competition was keen.

Dr. Parlin usually read favored examples of the students' works aloud to the class and invited criticism while you sat there. I lived in mortal terror that something of mine would be read aloud, for I was afraid I would cry. I was too much of a novice to live through the sort of criticism I heard in that class, though Dr. Parlin usually wound up each session with remarks of his own, often criticizing the critics more harshly than the writers.

I was in no position to compete with my cohorts, except when it came to poetry. Dr. Parlin read several of my sonnets to the class without giving my name, and I came off very well—at least my skin remained intact. He then introduced me to various verse forms: French forms such as triolets, ballades, villanelles; Japanese Haiku; Latin quatrains—a whole world of playful possibilities, which I adored. I became fairly expert, especially with the complex rhyme schemes of the French forms. He encouraged me to write variations of the sonnet forms and often read my poems to the class while keeping me anonymous. He was remarkably sensitive about the feelings of others.

Dr. Parlin was a man of middle height, compact in figure, with an aristocratic head, balding, and a squarish face and hooded eyes. He was always sleekly tailored, in excellent conservative clothes, and it was impossible to imagine him in any relaxed or recreational stance. I never saw him outside his office or the classroom. He did not, like most professors, stroll the campus or fraternize with the student body. He sometimes gave me the impression of an all-knowing Buddha, regarding with cynical patience the foibles and gyrations of lesser beings. At other times, he reminded me of a Roman emperor.

He was a brilliant lecturer. When he spoke, the sound of his voice, his choice of words, the depth of his knowledge were all mesmerizing. Nobody ever wanted his classes to end. He had a special sympathy for the authors of this world, which enabled him to see through the fabric of their works to their troubled souls or aching hearts, and to recreate them for his listeners. Not only did Dr. Parlin make an indelible impression on us as a teacher, he introduced us to all his friends—the great writers of English prose—so that they, too, became unforgettable.

Dr. Parlin handled a demanding deanship with finesse, and he had minimal time for teaching, but whatever course he taught always found its lecture audiences enormous and over-populated. He had little contact with his students and was not noted for his charity or even his popularity as a person. There was a coldness about him and it was possible to emerge from a conference on a term paper in tears. But whenever I had a few electives, I would sign up for one of his courses. His lectures on turn-of-the-century writers in England and America gave me such a fondness for the period that I became conversant with its art, music, and design, as well as its literature.

ᔍ

One of the impressive younger members of the English faculty was J. Frank Dobie, better known at the time as a folklorist. He wore cowboy boots and a Stetson hat to meet his classes and usually kept the hat on the back of his head while teaching. He taught advanced composition and his methods were unconventional. We never knew what to expect. Sometimes he would spend the whole hour reading aloud a few chapters from the works of Andy Adams. At other times he recited or chanted the rustic lyrics of ranch life, then being collected and preserved by John A. Lomax. Occasionally he would entertain us with tall tales or just spin yarns. We found everything he said and did enthralling.

It was only when we handed in our quiz papers or our feeble efforts at short stories and other writing assignments that we came to know his mettle. Of all the teachers I had, Mr. Dobie was the hardest to please. He did not care for mistakes, beginning with the mistake of calling him Dr. Dobie, on the presumption that he had attained a doctorate. This mistake could get you a genuine tongue-lashing. A mistake in grammar was unthinkable; he could not imagine how you had managed to matriculate in The University, much less arrive in his classroom. A mistake in punctuation simply marked you as hopeless. Any idiot could learn to punctuate.

Dr. Morgan Callaway, the Anglo-Saxon specialist of the English Department, was rumored to have broken his engagement because his fiancée wrote him a letter that contained a comma blunder. In my experience, this legendary strictness was equaled only by Mr. Dobie's threat to give me a failing grade for my major the last semester of my college career, which would have prevented me from graduating. I was already selling my work to such magazines as *College Humor* and the new *Mademoiselle* when he advised me that I was likely to fail "Advanced Composition" if I did not do something about my sloppy habits, especially in punctuation.

Mr. Dobie shared an office with Dr. Lloyd Loring Click, a whimsical tweedy professor who taught Victorian poetry and was appropriately genteel. When I came panting down the English Channel that April day to reason with Mr. Dobie about my plight, we soon got into a shouting match. Dr. Click (whose favorite quotation was: "If they hand you a lemon, make lemonade!") put up with this noisy encounter for quite a while. Observing that I was about to break down and snuffle and that he would indubitably have to comfort me, Dr. Click stood up behind his desk and said: "For Heaven's sake, Frank, give the girl her just desserts. You *know* she is going to write for money. And you know she is going to earn enough to hire somebody to punctuate for her!"

Mr. Dobie exhibited no sign of being impressed by this assessment, but he did stop hollering. In the end, he gave me a passing grade. So I graduated, wondering whether he had been nagging me for his own amusement. Shortly thereafter his great books began to be published: *Vaquero of the Brush Country*, followed by *Coronado's Children*—the first in a long line. When I read these books, I concluded that he was harder on himself than on anybody else, for there was no way to cavil at the quality of his "advanced composition." Many years later, after Mr. Dobie had become a celebrity, I went to hear him deliver a literary lecture. After the lecture, I stood in line to speak to him. When he took my hand he shook his head. "Never could punctuate!" he said, and grinned from ear to ear. ★

1984

WILLIAM A. OWENS

William A. Owens (1905–1990) was born in cotton-farming country, in Pin Hook, Texas, and received a Ph.D. from State University of Iowa in 1941. Owens' early work grew out of his interest in folklore. His first book, *Swing and Turn: Texas Play-Party Games,* was published in 1936. Following his service in the Philippines in World War II, Owens became Dean of the Extension School at Columbia University. His books include four memoirs, the most notable of which is *This Stubborn Soil: A Frontier Boyhood* (1966), and novels such as *Fever in the Earth* (1958). In *Three Friends: Bedichek, Dobie, Webb* (1969) Owens recalled the help given him by these men when his work in folklore brought him to Austin. Owens visited Austin many times during his long career.

from THREE FRIENDS

MY ASSOCIATIONS WITH THESE THREE MEN BEGAN ONE AT a time, and as much by chance as by design. Dobie came first. In 1933, I had completed a Master's Degree in English at Southern Methodist University. We were deep in the Depression and there were no jobs; I was trying to find out what to do next. Henry Nash Smith, with whom I had studied writing, suggested that I go to see J. Frank Dobie at the University of Texas and ask his advice. Smith had already encouraged me in my interest in collecting Texas folklore and writing fiction about Texas life. He had also assigned me to read *Coronado's Children,* Dobie's best-known book at the time. After reading the book, I needed no urging to go see Dobie.

Austin is two hundred miles from Dallas and I had no money for a fare. With no other way to go, I hitched a ride on a freight truck, with a driver who went down one night and returned the next. We left Dallas at dusk and arrived in Austin after daylight. About eight o'clock I found Dobie's office at the university on the ground floor of Breckenridge Hall. The door was open and I could see him at his desk, writing. I had not warned him that I was coming, and as I saw him there I knew I should have. He was then past forty, with a wide reputation as teacher and as editor for the Texas Folklore Society. He would not have time for every student that came by.

I was there and I waited for him to look up. When I told him that Henry Nash Smith had sent me, he asked me to come in and sit down.

I sat on a wooden bench and leaned against the hairy side of a tanned cowhide. He faced me, his arms on the desk, his shoulders broad, his eyes blue and sharp, his face round and friendly. He asked me why I had come and I began telling him: I wanted to study more and Southern Methodist University had no more to offer me. I wanted to come to the university, but I would have to work. Of the next three hours I know nothing, for I leaned over on the bench and went to sleep while I was talking.

When I woke up, Dobie was still sitting at his desk, working at his papers. I wanted to sidle out the door and get back to the freight station. He did not let me. As if nothing unusual had happened, he took up the conversation again and we talked until he had to leave the office, mostly about the folk songs and games I knew, a little about what I could expect if I came to the university.

I asked about jobs at the university; I asked at stores along Congress Avenue. No luck. Then I walked to the freight terminal for my ride back to Dallas. Nothing about my future had been resolved, though Dobie had been as helpful as he knew how to be. Over the long miles, stretched out on boxes of freight, I had plenty of time to think over the meeting. It was easy to know that something of Dobie had stayed with me; it took me years to find out how much.

Eight years later Dobie sent me to Bedichek. In the meantime, I had been teaching, studying, and collecting Texas ballads and songs on aluminum recording discs. Dobie had convinced Homer Price Rainey, President of the University of Texas, that the folklore of Texas should be collected. At the same time he envisioned a series of folk festivals as free and easy as old fiddlers' reunions. On Dobie's recommendation, I was hired to record the folklore and aid communities interested in running folk festivals.

As there was no office on campus to manage such a project, I was attached to the staff of Roy Bedichek, who was then Director of the Interscholastic League, in the Division of University Extension.

On January 2, 1941, I reported to a dun-colored building in what is called "The Little Campus," early enough to find Roy Bedichek alone in his office. Through the open door I could see him bent over his typewriter, intent on whatever he was putting down on yellow copy paper. He stood up, a tall man, and leaned forward to shake hands with me. His face and hands had the brown-burned look of a farmer; his voice and manner were friendly. There was something hawklike in the tilt of his beak, the purse of his lips, the rising inflection of his laugh.

Details of my job had to be worked out, but they had to wait while we talked folklore and books, birds, and the Interscholastic League. Our conversation got interrupted from time to time, but it went on most of the morning. At times I felt he was testing me for the job; more often he was talking because he loved to talk, not in chitchat but in wide gleanings from history, philosophy, and literature; not in pretentiousness—his words and anecdotes were too earthy for that.

Our talk went on as long as I was with him, and he never ran out of anything to say, though there were times of silence because he also appreciated silence. He also listened when he knew it was time to listen, as I soon came to know.

One of the early collecting trips he sent me on took me to the state prison farm near Sugar Land, to a field where white guards with shotguns and on horseback watched over Negro convicts hoeing. I went out to hear work songs of prisoners at work, but there was no singing. Their downcast faces, their sullen eyes showed there could be no singing in those fields. There was too much fear. Too upset by what I had seen to wait for night, when the convicts might feel free enough to sing, I headed for Austin, driving faster than the law allowed. I had to talk about what I had seen.

It was dark when I reached the edge of town. Bedichek would be in bed or on his way to bed. I telephoned him anyway and he met me outside his office. I told him what I had seen and felt, and apologized for my failure to get into what we both knew was one of the richest areas of Texas folklore. Except for details, I did not have to tell him. He knew enough of Texas prison life in general; he knew that the will to keep the Negro in his place was stronger in prison than out. I had never heard anyone so sympathetic to the Negro, or so concerned over the Negro question. He helped me understand a lesson I had begun to learn that day: To a collector, people must be more important than their folklore. Bedichek's work with the Interscholastic League required him to travel all over Texas. At times I went with him. The trips I remember best were those that took us hundreds of miles into west Texas, where roads stretched ahead over flat, sparsely covered earth. New words like "pencil bush," "greasewood," and "caliche" came into my vocabulary; into my consciousness, the cadences of English poetry sounded above the hum of tires on concrete.

On the highways, we belonged to the out-of-doors; in the towns, we took part in the entertainment provided for us. After one of those trips he wrote me:

> The day we had together during your last trip left me on a considerably higher level of spiritual well-being than I had been on in months, and I have always found you with that curious power. I think it is the depth and drive of your emotional make-up, your humor which is one phase of the emotions, and a keen intellect, and the instincts of a good healthy animal. Of this last, I shall never forget your dancing folk dances on the platform of the country club at Odessa. You seemed a kind of incarnation of Pan, not wicked, or wilful, but in fun-loving mood, and not in lust, but more as a mere joke, "ready to twitch the nymph's last garment off."

It took me less than a month to regard him not as boss but as friend. My job with Bedichek lasted only from January to September. The work was not finished, and I was still as interested in folklore as on the day I started. Bedichek wanted me to continue; so did the university. But times were against the project. The war was close upon us, and communities that in normal times would have been interested in their folklore and culture were already embarking on projects related to war and defense. The German armies rolled east and west; Churchill's voice rolled across Texas, with every radio turned on. Bedichek understood that it was impossible for me to go on at that time.

My work yielded for the University of Texas some recordings of rare Texas songs, including a new one made up by "The Gray Ghost" and called "De Hitler Blues." For me, it yielded a great deal more, especially in the close association it brought me with Bedichek, Dobie, and Webb.

It was Bedichek who arranged my meeting with Webb. There was to be a meeting of junior historians at Hillsboro, and Bedichek wanted me to attend. He called Webb and got him to take me up and back in his old coupe. It was more than a hundred miles each way on a rainy night. At first I wondered why Bedichek had stuck me with Webb. He sat hunched over the wheel, his round-ish face under the wide brim of a Stetson, his roundish eyes following the road through roundish glasses. He seemed to lack entirely the easy conversational manner of Bedichek and Dobie; at the time I would have described him as taci-turn, a quality I would not have expected in a man who had expressed himself so well in *The Great Plains* and *The Texas Rangers*.

The trip up was not a total loss, but almost, from my point of view. The return was much better. He had the same rough exterior I had come to know in Bedichek and Dobie, but he was much shyer; talk did not come easy to him, with strangers or in groups. On the way back, when we were shut in by a wet night, he opened up a little, enough for me to see why Bedichek had sent me.

Webb talked about Texas history in a way I had not encountered before. In sixth grade I had been forced to memorize names of men and battles and important dates. They remained in my mind as that and little more. With Webb, the history of Texas was the history of people opening new frontiers, bringing a part of their past with them, acquiring a different character through the kind of living they met. Consciously or not, he was opening to me new ways of thinking about folklore and the people from whom I collected it, and clearer understanding of overlappings from people to people as well as from past to present.

I knew that Texas had attracted many nationalities, many cultures, to a land that went from timbered in the east to desert in the west. I knew the people of the timbered east: Anglo-Saxon, Cajun French, Negro. He knew the people from east to west, and how and when they got there, the ones I knew and others: Germans, Swedes, French, Englishmen direct from England. All were shaped in some way by what we called Texas, from cotton farmers in the river bottoms to nesters living in dugouts on the plains before barbed wire was invented.

I left Austin in September 1941. For the next ten years I saw these three friends with some frequency, except when I was a soldier overseas. With Bedichek I maintained correspondence, but irregularly, as his chidings often show. Then in 1952 I was on the university staff for the summer as Director of the Oral History of Texas Oil Pioneers, and we spent much time together, some of it looking at the papers in his garage.

At the end of that summer, as I indicated earlier, Bedichek began transferring his papers to the Archives. Fortunately, Dobie and Webb also made gifts of their correspondence to the university.

One stipulation in Bedichek's letter of gift to the Archives Library is explicit: "The editing of my letters and documents will be assigned to William A. Owens." In this one sentence he opened to me intimately these three minds. ★

1969

ROY BEDICHEK

Roy Bedichek (1878–1959) was born in Illinois but grew up in Texas. When he was a young man he had a cotton-field conversion, a well-known Texas phenomenon, and left agricultural pursuits for those of higher education. He took two degrees from the University of Texas at Austin and for many years was director of the University Interscholastic League. At the age of sixty-nine, Bedichek was compelled by his friends J. Frank Dobie and Walter P. Webb to write a book; the result was *Adventures with a Texas Naturalist* (1947). Other books include *Karankaway Country* (1950) and *Letters of Roy Bedichek* (1985). Bedichek was a wonderful letter writer, and two of his best are reprinted here. The interested reader will note who is copied on the second letter, and this was in the days when copying—by means of typed carbons—was no easy task.

[Letters on Sculptures]
[to Dan Williams] *January 20, 1943*

Dear Dan:

... My appreciation of architecture is stunted. Some things in architecture have always impressed me, but I have never analyzed these "impressions" as I have in literature, for instance. Indeed, I do not know the language of architecture. The dome of our capitol building has given me for fifty years a great feeling of satisfaction, not only during my residence in Austin when I may look out and see it any time, but when I have been away. It is the one thing that gives Austin a sort of unity in my mind. Austin is clustered around it, so to speak, as fuzzy, string stuff gathers about a nucleus. I have often wondered if it impressed anyone else the same way.

Since the re-building of the University, of course, my attention has been drawn from time to time to various buildings on the campus. I find my mind takes this sort of attitude towards buildings which have any individuality or distinction: "It reminds me of" something or other. For instance, the immense Main Building reminds me of big business. All the Greek letters in gilt over the windows, and all the fancy mottoes, learned and beautiful, as "Ye shall know the truth," etc—all these marks and tags of learning and culture seem to me to be superficial, and that basically, this huge pile represents big business. It might be the home of Montgomery Ward, or of a great railroad (station and executive offices), or it might be the nerve center of the A&P. The vast wasted spaces inside instead of impressing me as they should, oppress me with a sense of pretension. Now I suppose someone learned in architecture could put all these ideas into the language of the art, and be able to tell why they arise in my mind.

I was in the old Littlefield home with Dr. Battle one day, and I called his attention to the massive and expensive interior decorations, and asked him to what period in art they belonged. He grunted, "Hum, seems to me EARLY PULLMAN." This struck me as a peculiarly apt description, or characterization.

Downtown, the Scarborough Building, the first skyscraper of Austin, reminds me of a good, sober, clean workman, rather athletic, in freshly laundered and rather close-fitting work-clothes. He seems ready for business. The Littlefield building diagonally across the corner of 6th and Congress, reminds me of an over-dressed whore. The newly completed and, I understand, classical Music Building on the campus, reminds me of a trim, sweet girl, with her bangs trimmed too short. And so it goes—this "reminds me" business. I wish I knew enough to talk intelligently about this basic art—really the incestuous mother and father of all arts, or rather, more accurately, the parthenogenic ancestor of all arts.

P.S. Speaking of art, enclosed is a letter I wrote Lomax a year or two ago upon a discovery of a statue in a third-rate tombstone-yard out on East Sixth Street. Such stuff as this should never be committed to paper, much less to *carbon* paper, but there has always been in me something of Pan . . . "Pan, ready to twitch the nymph's last garment off." R.B.

Yours,
Bedi

[to John A. Lomax] *November 13, 1941*
Replying please refer to "Obscenity File No. X342"

Subject: *Fireman's Statue*

Dear Lomax:

Away out East Sixth Street yesterday afternoon in the early twilight I beheld a dingy ghost of long ago. In an obscure corner of a run-down tomb-stone-yard, still grasping firmly the nozzle of his marble hose, stands the fireman's statue which, once topping the shaft to the left of the Capitol grounds' south entrance, caused such a scandal in our student days at the University.

Do you remember how this hideous figure of gigantic size, drawing a hose over his hip, appeared, at least from a certain point of the compass, to be holding not the nozzle of a hose, but something else, stiff and straight, protruding at an angle of about 45 degrees from an inguinal region? Do you remember how we dirty-minded boys insisted that he was really a part of a sculptural group, representing a very tense and dramatic moment, the other two members of the group being, (1) The Goddess surmounting the dome of the Capitol, and (2), the alert minute-man on the Alamo monument who, with fixed bayonet, stared threateningly at the fireman? In short, we figured it this way: This fireman was really the god, Priapus, in disguise, and the noble minute-man was determined to prevent the carrying out of his dishonorable intentions towards the Goddess.

The elm trees have now grown up so as to spoil our lewd interpretation entirely, since the three statues can no longer be seen as a group. But long before the decent elms obliterated our obscenity, the D.A.R. or some other association of patriotic women, heard these nasty rumors, and sent a committee to investigate the grounds for the same. The Committee studied the problem from *all angles,* and solemnly reported that from *one* angle, there did seem to be some justification for the University students' interpretation.

The proper authorities were then duly, discreetly, delicately memorialized, and in due time—say, a year or two—the offending statue was removed.

In its place appeared another statue identical with the one removed, except that in place of the hose, he carries a baby in the curve of his arm. To any but a group of boys determined to see evil in everything, this baby was apparently just rescued from a burning home at the risk of the fireman's life, probably at the cost of his life. But we refused to accept this heroic legend. Instead, we said, "I told you so; the damned minute-man went to sleep, Priapus accomplished his fiendish purpose, the terrible violation had indeed occurred, and now, as a penalty, imposed by Zeus, he had to *support the baby*." For proof, we pointed to the cherubic infant nestling against the father's stony breast.

I have often wondered in the intervening years where the old statue was, and whether or not the suggestive portion of it had been sawed off. Now I know. He stands in the monument yard of Backus,* 1016 East Sixth Street. I tried out the angles on him, and Lo! As of old, from one point of the compass the same extension appears, the same threat to virginity, the same eternal erection.

> "Cold Pastoral!
> When age shall this generation waste,
> Thou shalt remain, in midst of other woe
> Than ours. . . ."

As Keats once melodiously remarked anent a more innocent depicted upon a Grecian urn.

Yours truly,
Roy Bedichek

cc Walter Prescott Webb
J. Frank Dobie

*Probably a corruption of Bacchus—this thing has to be 100% classical. ★

1985

LIZ CARPENTER

Liz Carpenter grew up in Salado, Texas, and in 1942 graduated from the University of Texas with a degree in journalism. She moved to Washington, DC, in 1942 and covered presidents from FDR to LBJ. In 1960 she went to work for Vice-President Lyndon Johnson, and during his years in the White House she served as press secretary and staff director for Lady Bird Johnson. In the 1970s she moved to Austin and began lecturing and writing. Her books include *Ruffles & Flourishes: The Warm and Tender Story of a Simple Girl Who Found Adventure in the White House* (1970) and *Unplanned Parenthood: Confessions of a Seventy-Something Surrogate Parent* (1994). In her memoir, *Getting Better All the Time* (1987) she recounts her undergraduate years at the University of Texas.

from GETTING BETTER ALL THE TIME

I WAS ONE OF TEN THOUSAND STUDENTS ENROLLED AT THE University of Texas in 1938, and it was the most broadening experience I had encountered. Leslie Carpenter and I, both freshmen, headed for the journalism school as fast as we could and worked on the campus paper, *The Daily Texan*.

Our group of college journalists all fancied ourselves as characters in the movie *Front Page*, which was the rage then and influenced my era and profession as much as *All the President's Men* made Woodwards and Bernsteins out of reporters today. Starring Pat O'Brien, *Front Page* added to the glamour, typecasting, and romance of reporting. I can see it still: the sob sister with the big heart and cigarette dangling from her mouth as she perched on the desk of the city editor; newsman Pat O'Brien, hat on head and press card in the hat's wide band, writing frantically with the "hunt and peck" system of typing while someone "held the presses" on the story. Soon there would be extras on the streets.

Radio finally killed off the extra editions carried by small newsboys up and down the streets with the flashy headlines on disasters: "*Extrraaaa*, read all about it! Hauptmann guilty in Lindbergh trial!" "*Extrraaaa*, *Hindenburg* explodes over New Jersey!" "*Extrraaaa*, Hitler marches into Poland!"

It was a far simpler world than now: black or white, good or bad. It was a prepill world. "Nice girls" didn't "go all the way" with boys. We would lose their respect, and ultimately, they wouldn't marry anyone but a virgin. We danced, held hands, and kissed our dates good night, but heavy petting was out, especially for those from the Bible Belt. The innocence of my college days seems unreal now.

Throughout my school years I was drawn to people who were doing things, the girls active in campus activities, the boys and girls at work in campus politics, the students writing skits or campus plays. Les and I took a typewriter to the campus hangout to write a competition play for "Time Staggers On," the annual student spoof on itself. He was becoming a fixture in my life.

Dreaming aloud was as much a part of life as being a reporter-in-the-making. We avidly read Richard Halliburton's *Royal Road to Romance* and *Seven League Boots*, and they sparked our imaginations. We, too, wanted to swim the Nile by moonlight, see the Taj Mahal under the stars, and wind through the Casbahs of Morocco. Our classes in play-writing made us sure that one day we would produce a Broadway show together, and as we sipped Coca-Cola in the Texas Union, we dreamed of our names in lights. College was a place for dreaming. The day of counselors, aptitude tests, resumes, and college interviews had not yet dawned. We had every confidence we could make it to the top.

Campus politics at UT was, in those times, political campaigning with all the high jinks. I was the first girl to run for vice president of the student body and get elected. My two male opponents were millionaires, both delightful and imaginative, and it took ingenuity to keep up with them. One, Jimmy Craig, owned his own small airplane and a convertible. His campaign slogan was "Free Airplane Rides with High-Flying Jimmy Craig."

In answer, I brought in an attention getter to spice up my campaign, a mother duck and her babies, and I put them on the main mall along with the slogan: "Keep Your Feet on the Ground with Liz." I also had a set of sorority sisters in Alpha Phi who went serenading the dormitories each evening after dinner. Their spokesman was Joe Kilgore, then a law student and later a congressman, a marvelous speaker who would, after a song or two, step forward and say, "Ladies of Scottish Rite dormitory, I come here to boost the candidacy of Liz Sutherland for vice president of the student body." The dormitory windows would fill up with eager coeds cheering our performance.

I was blessed with energy and curiosity, and I am grateful that I've never lost either. I was in love with the freedom of thought a state university offered, and although it was a time of great problems worldwide, we were reaching for answers. We believed in government because we saw it working to lift people into opportunity. Roosevelt and the New Deal had put a leash on the Wall Street robbers. Hope abounded, and so did freedom.

Many future Texas politicians cut their political teeth—or fangs—at the University of Texas. We turned out governors, congressmen, senators, and judges for Texas. People often ask why I never ran for public office. Public office was not something many women sought then, but more important, I was swept up by newspapering. I took a side job on *The Austin American,* and it was there that I found politics.

I got my first political assignment by chance. No one else was in the city room of *The Austin American* when the AP and UP tickers rang, signaling "Flash! Big news!" Not just any news—Senator Alben Barkley was breaking with Franklin Roosevelt over the War Revenue Bill. It was noon, and everyone was gone except for the city editor, Weldon Hart, and me. He looked around for someone to send out to round up reaction. Our Democratic National Committeewoman, Clara Driscoll, was over at the Driskill Hotel, and someone had to interview her about whether she would side with FDR or Barkley. I was there, so I was dispatched to the hotel.

I had never been in a hotel in my life or even walked through the lobby without my father. You didn't want to be seen there in those days: Hotels had a negative connotation. But I bravely walked down to the Driskill, went up to the suite, and, knocked timidly. As I stood waiting nervously, "Miss Clara" opened the door, and she was . . . *smoking a cigarette!* I had never seen a woman smoking a cigarette before except in the movies. She was quite an imposing lady who carried a cane with a diamond in it. There was also a man there, Mr. Frank Scofield, the IRS collector and a political figure in Texas. And the two of them were . . . *drinking*—Manhattans, or something with a cherry in it. I had never been around people who drank, not even eggnog at Christmas. I was too nervous to sit, so I just asked my questions—Miss Clara sided with Barkley—and then I said good-bye and went back to the office. I had seen my first smoke-filled room and felt the intrigue. I couldn't put that scene out of my mind. They were in the know, they had power, they got interviewed by reporters. I've been in a thousand smoke-filled rooms since and have learned something in all of them.

Years later, after the landmark Woodward and Bernstein Watergate investigation, I look back and laugh. I guess if I had been an investigative reporter, I would have asked, "What is the Democratic National Committeewoman doing having a drink with the IRS collector? Is it sex? Is it a payoff?" But I didn't ask, and I suspect that it was just as it appeared to be, two old political friends enjoying each other's company and talking politics. Maybe I missed a Pulitzer. I doubt it, but if I did, I don't regret it.

By 1941, I was a senior in college. I remember a Sunday—December 7, 1941, to be exact. On that early afternoon, I was having a hamburger and Coke with Les at our favorite campus meeting place, "Triple X." A student wandered in with news heard on his car radio: "The Japs have bombed Pearl Harbor!" How young we were! We knew it was important, but little did we know how it would shape our world. We even had to ask where Pearl Harbor was. No one was quite sure.

In the next two months, most of the boys on campus enrolled in ROTC units. Les joined the naval ROTC. Washington became the news capital of the world. My oldest brother, Tommy, moved his young family there and began working for the Board of Economic Warfare. War clouds began to hang over our lives. Ration books were issued for everything from butter to safety pins. Tin cans disappeared for the war effort. We saved the tinfoil from Hershey's bars and cigarettes, rolled it into tight balls of silver, and turned it in to a central collection station. Graduation ceremonies went on as usual. Our speaker was Lord Halifax, the British ambassador to the United States, who came down from Washington to make a plea for freedom, for a united front against the enemies, Germany and Japan. The United States was now in the fight.

It is strange how many details one remembers, the high points or the first impression of an event or place. In assembling all my albums, clippings, and scrapbooks for this accounting of my life, I have come upon a line here, a memento there, that takes me back in time. My memory is often at odds with what actually occurred. One marvelous "find" is a suitcase of letters and cards which I wrote in the full flush of my girlish enthusiasm and romanticism. I am shocked at my bravado in a letter to my mother on Mother's Day, May 1942, written as I was about to graduate.

> I went to rehearsal for graduation today. It is hard to realize that only four years ago I stood gazing at the University tower in awe. I look around also at those seniors I started out with four years ago. For instance, Nancy, who has made Phi Beta Kappa, and achieved recognition in bacteriology, but who will probably marry this summer to be with that lazy poet. And there are scads more, some who've probably given and gotten far more from the University than I have. Nevertheless, I feel so much luckier. I don't know of anyone I'd trade shoes with. I ordered twenty invitations to graduation today, and I hope you'll give me a list of who to send them to.
>
> My plans for the summer I shall now state. I hope to heaven I can carry them out. After all, I deserve to get to do one thing I want after going through four years of hard labor. Jean, Elizabeth and I want to purchase a used car and travel all over Texas writing features. Dr. Reddick thinks we could make expenses. The experience and fun would be worth a million, and I know if we don't do it now, we never will. I don't see any difficulty in selling stories. The time is ripe and I certainly want to get in and do something I am inspired to do.

It's a shot in the dark, but it may be a chance to become famous. . . .
So I don't give a hang about coming to the capital where the rate is
twelve women to every male and everyone is grabbing for a hunk of
glory out of the national garbage can. Give me the wide open spaces,
a Model T, and a typewriter, and I'll see you in the hall of fame.

I can't believe I ever called my Washington, which I love and whose
every heartbeat I follow avidly, a "national garbage can." But there it is in my
own handwriting. As it turned out, by mid-June I had my typewriter and was
headed to Washington. ★

1987

Lyndon B. Johnson

Lyndon Baines Johnson (1908–1973) was born in Stonewall, Texas, and graduated from Southwest Texas State Teachers' College (now Texas State University) in 1931. Johnson taught high school briefly, and later, in 1937, was elected to the U.S. Congress, serving until 1949, whereupon he was elected to the U.S. Senate. He was elected Vice-President of the U.S. in 1960 and became President following the assassination of President John Kennedy in Dallas on November 22, 1963. He served as president until 1969. He fought two wars during his administration: one against poverty and one against the North Vietnamese. He was one of the most powerful men of his era. In a radio address of 1938, Johnson offered a sketch of shocking poverty in the capital city of Austin. The piece stylistically is reminiscent of American muckraking journalism of the 1890s.

from TARNISH ON THE VIOLET CROWN

LAST CHRISTMAS, WHEN ALL OVER THE WORLD PEOPLE were celebrating the birth of the Christ child, I took a walk here in Austin—a short walk, just a few short blocks from Congress Avenue, and there I found people living in such squalor that Christmas Day was to them just one more day of filth and misery. Forty families on one lot, using one water faucet. Living in barren one-room huts, they were deprived of the glory of sunshine in the daytime, and were so poor they could not even at night use the electricity that is to be generated by our great river. Here the men and women did not play at Santa Claus. Here the children were so much in need of the very essentials of life that they scarcely missed the added pleasures of our Christian celebration.

Typical Slum Family

I found one family that might almost be called typical. Living within one dreary room, where no single window let in the beneficent sunlight, and where not even the smallest vagrant breeze brought them relief in the hot summer—here they slept, here they cooked and ate, here they washed themselves in a leaky tin tub after carrying the water for 100 yards. Here they brought up their children ill-nourished and amid sordid surroundings. And on this Christmas morning there was no Santa Claus for the ten children, all under sixteen years old, who scrambled around the feet of a wretched mother bent over her washtub, while in this same room her husband, and the father of the brood, lay ill with an infectious disease.

Should Your Congressman Close His Eyes?

But why do I tell you this? Why, some may ask, should one who is elected to represent this district take note of such unattractive spots when our city has so much to be proud of? To those people I will answer that no one is more proud of the beauty and attainments of the city of Austin than I. But for that very reason I am unwilling to close my eyes to needless suffering and deprivation, which is not only a curse to the people immediately concerned, but is also a cancerous blight on the whole community.

Good housewives do not seek to hide the tarnish on their silver, nor can any good mayor or other public official afford to try to hide spots of tarnish on his city. Certainly our fine major, Tom Miller, is not one to look away from the facts, and when confronted with them he does not hesitate to apply the polish. Right how he is taking bold and effective steps to remove the slum tarnish from our community—the community O. Henry gave the appellation "The City of the Violet Crown." ★

1938

PART THREE

This True Paradise on Earth: 1950s

MARY LASSWELL,
    from *I'll Take Texas* 54

JOHN HENRY FAULK,
    from *Fear on Trial* 59

ROLANDO HINOJOSA-SMITH,
    '50s Austin: A Variform Education 64

WILSON M. HUDSON,
    from *Bedichek's Rock* 71

WALTER P. WEBB,
    J. Frank Dobie 73

DAVID RICHARDS,
    from *Once Upon a Time in Texas* 76

ANN RICHARDS,
    from *Straight from the Heart* 80

WILLIE MORRIS,
    from *North Toward Home* 87

CELIA MORRIS,
    from *Finding Celia's Place* 91

Mary Lasswell

Mary Lasswell (1905–1994) was born in Glasgow, Scotland, but grew up in Brownsville, Texas. She enjoyed popular success with her first book, *Suds in Your Eye*, published in 1942 and made into a Broadway play in 1944. Most of her work was in a humorous vein. In 1958 she published *I'll Take Texas*, an engaging, vernacular account of the state that had been her home. The Townsend Miller whose poem she quotes from is unknown to me. He is not the Townsend Miller who wrote music criticism for the *Austin American-Statesman* and was a world-record-holder gar fisherman.

from I'll Take Texas

Austin is the heart of Texas, geographically, politically, and culturally, I thought.

Townsend Miller's narrative poem, "A Letter from Texas," has this description of the capital:

> There lies the central city, the westering wall beyond
> Rising out of the plain under the blue plateau
> Naked by morning to the incredible sun
> Shielded and shadowed in the long afternoon—
> Austin, the central city, and she is crowned with sun
> And twice-crowned westward with the violet hills.
> John, the thick roses swarming over the wall
> The moon in the white courts, the quivering mornings!
> John, the girls and the young men walking in the streets
> Tall, splendid, easy, as wind over the prairie

Wind in their blue eyes and in the afternoon
They shake the day off in the cold shadowy pools,
By night on the great starlit river, the Colorado,
Their hands open and their hearts. This is the central city
And they walk in it and their hearts high.

Evocative and accurate, the lines convey the stately beauty of Austin, water-rich, solid, and steeped in tradition. This is a Texan city, not a cut-rate Chicago nor a reprint Rochester. No smelly industry mars the natural beauty that attracts so many retired persons to her hospitable hills and lake shores.

Within ten minutes' drive I could be in the fragrant hills looking down on Austin's links in the chain of six Highland Lakes within a sixty-mile stretch, man-made lakes that had appeared as if by magic during my absence. I could look at the sapphire sky reflected in their waters, and watch, with approach of night, the myriad twinkling lights that bejewel the bosom of the city that wears the Violet Crown. This was the beginning of Texas' "Hill Country," at the Balcones Fault, that great escarpment that separates the Edwards Plateau in the west from the Coastal Plains.

ॐ

I was almost afraid to turn the page of my memory when I came back to Austin in November of 1954, but old friends had changed not at all. All the rest had changed almost beyond recognition. . . .

Four blocks from the campus of the University of Texas, under the wide eaves of the white house with the hundred-year-old red cedars, I began to take in the heady blend of the strange and the familiar. The curious sensation of observing the "now" through the eyes of the "then" resulted in a kind of double exposure. I began to understand that all Texas is an eternal synthesis of past and present, superimposed one upon the other. It produces a feeling of being in two places at once. Skyscrapers for pigeonhole parking in one block, and a few blocks away an ancient wooden store with a false front high above it bears the crudely lettered words RAW FURS BOUGHT. The frontier past and the urban present of Texas are separated by a very short span of time. . . .

Out of my south window I could see the dome of the Capitol, high above the building made of red Texas granite, shaped like a Greek cross in Doric architecture. That study structure was completed in 1888 at the cost of 3,000,000 acres of Texas land, valued at that time at one dollar per acre. Sixteen oxen hauled the 18,000-pound cornerstone from the quarries near Marble Falls to Burnet, and on to Austin by a special railroad built to handle the granite for the Capitol building. The "Goddess of Liberty" stands sixteen feet tall on top of the dome, and holds aloft the Lone Star of Texas with her left hand, while her right hand holds a sword pointing down. At night a rosy glow comes from the dome, reminding me of the warm red earth of Texas' fruit lands.

From my east window I could see the University Tower, new and a little strange to me, an ornament whose charm has been much debated. Its height caused Frank Dobie to say: "If they'd lay the damn thing down on its side and run a gallery around it, it would look a lot more Texan." On victorious nights the tower is lighted with brilliant orange, the University color that stands out in startling contrast to the deep navy blue sky.

&

Here at the heart of the state, I realized that Austin had become "occupied country." Outlanders of every description had invaded the place and infiltrated the familiar scenes. Foreign faces, unknown tongues, outlandish dress and costume were everywhere on the streets and the now unrecognizable campus. Saris and sarongs. Turbans and togas. Blue jeans and boots. And most startling of all, very pregnant girls were much in evidence about the campus, lugging stacks of books uncomplainingly. It was hard for me to reconcile the present with the past, to conceive of the enormous number of married students I should find enrolled in the University, when during my student days marriages were carefully kept secret, and if discovered meant certain expulsion for both students. Now the University owned many special housing units for married students, they formed clubs and associations, had meetings to solve baby-sitter problems, and even elected a wife of the year: Mrs. Co-Wed.

I was surprised at the decline in the number of "Queens." There had been "Queens" of practically everything on the campus, but now most of them had been changed to "Miss." My all-time favorite is "Miss Service Station of Austin," who went right to the top as "Miss Portable Appliance of Texas," with a two-week, all-expense paid vacation in Hollywood!

There was no way to figure out what brought them—maybe the climate, or Texas' legendary advantages—but there were students here from nearly every state in the Union. A Texas accent was now almost a rarity on the campus. The tower might well have been likened to the Tower of Babel. During one lunch hour at the Commons I heard seven different languages spoken—and that was counting only those I could identify. During the twenties, I remember only one Chinese co-ed, who was stared at everywhere she went. A man from Belgrade, then Serbia, was a popular engineering student. With his roommate, a Belgian, these students made up our United Nations of that day. I am not including Latin Americans because there were always quite a few of them. A treasurer of the Republic of Mexico worked his way through the University of Texas and married an Austin girl.

I was struck by the desire of many of the foreign students to be assimilated into the American way of life. A Japanese chemistry-fellow had finished his course of studies and was returning to Japan. His friends in the lab noticed that he got through school in two nylon sport shirts. When he was leaving they took up a collection and bought him "a pair of Ivy League pants, and an Ivy League shirt, the kind with the little button in back of the collar, you know. There was even enough money to by him a belt! He wanted that outfit more than anything!" The fact that the *sine qua non* of the Ivy League, a coat, was missing marred his bliss not at all.

The influence of the automobile is felt strongly at the University and the parking problem is serious. I heard that 18,000 students owned 24,000 cars. To anyone trying to park his car in front of his house in the University neighborhood, the remark is less facetious than it seems.

೨ಎ

As I studied these startling additions to Texas' university life, I tried to be a Disinterested Observer. I was no longer enrolled in the University, and I had no children to attend it. One fact stood out above everything else: The University was alive.

What counted with me was the change, the yeasty upsurge of independent thought and action on the part of the students, a decided departure from the dogmatic, ironclad years I had known.

The school was demanding—and getting—the right to make its own mistakes. For years it had asked for bread and been given a stone . . . by the keepers of the cash, the Available Fund. Money for impressive buildings had been forthcoming, but little for faculty and great visiting teachers. Now I saw evidence on every side that the Powers That Be were well on the way to distinguishing brains from bricks. The University of Texas is entering its Golden Age. ★

1958

JOHN HENRY FAULK

John Henry Faulk (1913–1990) was born in Austin and attended the University of Texas in the 1930s. There he met Dobie, Webb, and Bedichek and, under their guidance, became a collector of folklore. In his M.A. thesis he recorded and analyzed African-American sermons from the Brazos River area. After service in World War II, Faulk went into radio, where his storytelling abilities could be featured. "The John Henry Faulk Show" ran on WCBS Radio from 1951 to 1957. The show ended because Faulk was blacklisted by a McCarthyesque organization called AWARE, and although Faulk won a libel suit in 1962, CBS would not rehire him. From 1975 to 1980 he appeared regularly on the television show *Hee Haw*. Faulk's subsequent years were spent traveling the country speaking out against infringements of constitutional rights. In 1964 Faulk published *Fear on Trial*, an account of his persecution during the blacklisting period. In the section reprinted here, Faulk describes his return to his hometown. The note of concern for social and racial justice was a constant theme in Faulk's life.

from FEAR ON TRIAL

As I DROVE SOUTH, EACH MILE FOUND THE WOODS AND fields turning greener, as though spring were moving north to meet us. And it seemed, too, that each mile I drove toward Texas, my spirits lifted. In my mind, I turned over the prospects before me. Austin was an interesting town. Besides, it was home. I had lived there all my life until I came to New York in 1946.

Austin is as near the dead center of the state as the founding fathers could put it. Although it's only on the western fringes of what in this country is called "the South," it is by background and social custom a Southern town. It has a large Negro population, which, until recently, was rigidly segregated by law and tradition. The University of Texas and the state capitol are located there, the former lending a mild intellectual atmosphere to the town, the latter a political air. However, the predominant influence in Austin life during my childhood and youth was a sort of Bible-belt Protestantism.

Flowing down through the wooded limestone hills to the west, the Colorado River runs along the southern border of the business section of Austin. The portion of the town lying south of the river is called South Austin. That is where I grew up. The fashionable and well-to-do citizens of the town all lived north of the river. During my childhood days, South Austin was a rather self-contained community, more rural than urban. Most of our neighbors maintained their own milk cows, chickens, and a garden. Churchgoing was by far the most popular activity.

In those days, the population of South Austin was about equally divided between Southern Methodists and Southern Baptists. There were a few stray Southern Presbyterians about, and among the very poor there was an exotic sect called the Holy Rollers. There was one family in South Austin known to be Catholic, the Gillises. Mr. Gillis was such a charitable and worthy citizen that he was respected and well liked by one and all. His name was seldom mentioned in conversation, however, without his being identified as a Catholic.

My family were all Methodists. Not only religious Methodists, but social Methodists. I was in my adolescence, in fact, before I came to realize that people met in social gatherings not connected in one way or another with the church. My parents were what the community called "pillars" of the Fred Allen Memorial Methodist Church in South Austin.

My childhood was that of any other churchgoing middle-class child in South Austin, with the exception that I was considered something of a sinner rather early in life. This was because I used profanity and knew the facts of life. My nearest and most constant companions from infancy to the first seven or eight years of my life were the children of a Negro family who lived on our place, the Batts. Together we frolicked about the cow lot and barn, through the woods and the fields, finding bird's nests, investigating hay stacks and cedar thickets, and climbing the live oak trees to see the world around us more clearly.

Daddy had been reared a sharecropper. However, he arranged to get an education, was graduated from the University of Texas Law School, and became a lawyer in Austin in 1900. He was a popular young lawyer and had a thriving clientele. However, he had discovered Emerson, Thoreau, and Thomas Jefferson. From them he went to Spinoza. He had long been an avid student of the Bible. His childhood experiences with poverty and deprivation weighed heavily on his mind. He began to move slowly but surely in his philosophy away from orthodoxy toward the wide world of the free-thinker. Mama, who married Daddy in 1902, was a pious Methodist. She was only mildly disturbed when Daddy undertook to explain to her that he loved and believed in the teachings of Jesus Christ but did not believe in the divinity of Jesus. Mama said she accepted his opinion because she accepted Daddy completely. Daddy became concerned with matters of civil rights and social justice. He formed a friendship and correspondence with Eugene V. Debs, who strongly influenced him toward socialism. He began to envisage the unlimited joy and happiness that could come to mankind through achieving a liberated mind.

Yet Daddy identified so completely and affectionately with his Texas surroundings that he was not regarded as alien in the community. I suppose few of them understood what he really believed. He was held in respect and admiration for his ready wit and good humor. In spite of his unorthodox beliefs, he was very active in the Masonic order and a faithful member of the Methodist Church. In fact, for as long as I can remember, he was the teacher of the Adult Bible Class at our church. He mixed a strong brew of Spinoza and Emerson with the scriptures and served it out to his nodding listeners every Sunday morning.

By the time I was a senior in high school I had come to appreciate and listen closely to the things that Daddy said and the observations he made. He had a sure and firm grasp on the history of the United States. "We've come a long way, Johnny, and we've got a long way to go. But America has the juice and the power to get there." The "there," to Daddy's way of thinking, was a state of freedom and justice, complete democracy. He was not so vain as to regard himself as a self-made man. On the contrary, he knew that many forces in our society made it possible for him to come from the life of a sharecropper to that of a comfortable and enlightened citizen, and he felt because he had been successful in his climb, that he had a lifelong obligation to assist others who were less fortunate than himself. One of his favorite themes was: "Jesus said, 'As you do unto the least of these, ye do unto Me,' and in a democracy like America, Johnny, as we do unto our least privileged citizen, whether he's Catholic, Jew, or Protestant, Native or foreign born, Negro or white, you do unto America."

Daddy was convinced that bigotry was a two-edged sword that punished the wielder as much as it did the victim. It was during this period that I first heard from him that racial integration would be an accomplished fact, probably within my lifetime. He believed this firmly. He told me that Negroes would go to the University of Texas just as white students did. He also told me that I, as a privileged white Texan and southerner, had a great responsibility to help in hastening that day when the terrible injustice of racial segregation would end.

It was always more or less taken for granted that I would become a lawyer. I took a prelaw course at the university. However, my chief interest had been literature. I was an avid reader and the world of books was my greatest joy. In my junior year I took J. Frank Dobie's "Life and Literature of the Southwest." Since that time many of my interests and activities have been influenced by Dobie.

Dobie was not only a scholar, he was a humanitarian and a thinker. He gave generously of his time and thought to me. Two other men at the university shared his love for free, searching intellect: Roy Bedichek and Walter P. Webb. The three of them have been my mentors since my university days.

J. Frank Dobie, Roy Bedichek, and Walter P. Webb lived in Austin. As I drove along, a warm affectionate feeling crept over me. I would join their circle again, go out to the Webb or Dobie ranch, sit out late at night talking.

Dobie and Bedichek had, perhaps, the greatest influence on my life, aside from my parents. Their conversation, their interests, their observations on the world around us had always fired my spirit, my imagination. Their respect and affection had meant a lot to me, particularly the last three years. . . .

My heart was pounding with excitement as we drove up dusty West Live Oak Street, and turned into our old home place. My sister Mary, with her husband, Chester Koock, and their seven children, were lined up, waiting for us. Texana and her husband, John T. Conn, and their three children, my niece, Anne McAfee, and her husband Bill and their five children, and my brother, Hamilton, and his wife, Bernice, were all on hand to greet us. My other sister, Martha, was teaching school in Houston. Their children had made "Welcome Home" signs of cardboard and brown wrapping paper, lettered in red, green, blue, and yellow crayon: "Welcome New York Cousins" and "Back Home at Last." A great hugging and kissing and general jubilation took place. This was followed by a washing up and a sumptuous meal. Everybody, including the children, babbled at the same time. The scene resembled a Sunday school picnic more than a family gathering.

I had a long visit with J. Frank Dobie and Roy Bedichek the next day. I recounted all of my experiences with the trial up to that point. I wanted to resume our regular sessions again, but my first order of business would be, of course, to find something to do in Austin. My resources were about depleted. But the problem was not so simple. I had to have a logical reason for my homecoming.

The most politic explanation would be that I had come to my senses and moved back to this true paradise on earth, Austin, Texas. I decided that the wisest course for me was to let it be thought that, having made some money in New York, I had now retired, as any sensible individual would, to Austin to spend the rest of my days. ★

1963

ROLANDO HINOJOSA-SMITH

Rolando Hinojosa-Smith was born in Mercedes, Texas. After serving with the U.S. Army in the Korean War, he attended the University of Texas in the mid-1950s. Hinojosa-Smith received his Ph.D. from the University of Illinois in 1969, and in the early 1980s joined the Department of English at the University of Texas, where he teaches, among other courses, Life and Literature of the Southwest. He is the author of numerous novels linked together under the series title *Klail City Death Trip,* a number of which have been translated into French, German, and Italian. His recent novels include *The Useless Servants* (1993), *Ask a Policeman* (1998), and *We Happy Few,* published in 2006. In the piece below Hinojosa-Smith recalls his undergraduate years at the University of Texas.

'50S AUSTIN: A VARIFORM EDUCATION

TWO WEEKS AFTER MY HONORABLE DISCHARGE AFTER A three-year sentence defending the country from the evils of Communism, I drove to the Hidalgo County Courthouse to meet with the Veterans' Affairs adviser. The rumor was he was actor James Stewart's father, (something he didn't deny) but I was as unconvinced then as I am today.

A nice enough man, though, and I told him of my plans to attend The University of Texas. An older brother, René (Class of '50) attended the University and I visited him and other Valley friends during my one furlough home; the army gives one two-and-a-half days of furlough time for every month served, (that's thirty days a year) and I was planning ahead; the Cold War planners had other ideas, but that's another story. So, I enrolled and put in for Cliff Courts as my place of residence. Cliff Courts must have been leveled over forty years ago and in their place is a gigantic parking lot just south of Jester dormitory; named for Beauford, a member of the Board of Regents during the building of the Tower and later a popular governor who died in office and in harness and was thus succeeded by a wise man: Allen Shivers. Wise because he married one of the Shary women, a native of the Valley, and a Catholic; Shivers was an East Texas Baptist and thus the two largest denominations in the state ganged up to reelect him for life, if he chose.

He also named my brother-in-law's brother as a district judge after my brother-in-law, O. B., turned down the job. Governor Shivers was a year behind O.B. and H.A. García at Pearce Hall, the old law school building. It too has disappeared to be replaced by the current one for which the then U.S. Attorney General, Herbert Brownell, delivered the inaugural address.

During my delay en route overseas, I went home for a few days and visited my brother at the University. He lived on 26th and Guadalupe at the Alhambra (aka the H(ispanic) A(merican House). A good-sized bunch of us, all Valley boys, went to Sixth Street then a wild and wooly place, some phrase that. I remember one bar in particular, the Hong Kong, which reminded me of some bars I'd been to after basic training. The Hong Kong, of course, is million light years away from the current Sixth Street, a source of pride of many Austinites and well-attended by Baylor students who brave the two-hundred mile round trip on occasion. That part of Sixth Street, obviously, was the Texas Mexican section, but not far from my favorite men's stores: Scarborough's, Merritt, Schaeffer, and Brown, and Reynolds Penland. Stores which today would go into immediate bankruptcy considering the attire of our current undergraduates, many of whom major in conspicuous poverty.

After my discharge and subsequent enrollment, I took the normal sixteen hours (and, yes, I also worked as did and do many UTers), but sixteen hours, (counting the hour lab) and four years were, in those halcyon days, the number of years one took to graduate although some of us finished in three and, in my case, three-and-a-half; I loved electives and took as many as I could. I worked at the Reserved Reading Room (which is now the Admissions Office) and it stands facing the Registrar's Office which has always stood on the extreme east of the Tower's rotunda, as it was called, incorrectly, too, since it isn't a rotunda at all; there's northing round about it unless one considers the run-around one can expect with bureaucracies, no matter how efficient they may be.

Working at the Reading Room (jammed with master's theses and doctoral dissertations, as UT calls its doctoral theses) was the one and only job I held and held on to it dearly; three reasons: I was born into a family of readers and the main library was in the Tower; the Room had its own elevator and was operated by Henry, who, surely must have been a veteran of the Spanish War. I'm sure he had a last name but I never asked. For me, working there was akin to putting a rabbit to guard the cabbage patch. The second reason was social, I met any number of co-eds there, and the third, since we had classes on Saturdays in those days, and the English Department demanded an essay a week during the Freshman year, my roommates Fred Kyle (Sherman), the late T.O. Wilson (Rosenberg), and John Dalrymple ((Little Rock) would fold their books and we'd walk to Memorial Stadium after closing time, one o'clock. All Southwest Conference games started in the blistering heat at two P.M. Student seating was excellent, on the sunny side, of course, but our seats went from one 30-yard line to the other. We could sit anywhere, up or down, and we all owned the blanket tax, a multipurpose card which served as an I.D. at the library and as entry to all, that's *all,* athletic events.

These, the four of us attended religiously; well, as religiously as T.O. and I attended St. Austen; Kyle, a fine Scottish name, was a Presbyterian, and Dalrymple, from Arkansas, a Baptist; no surprise there.

A disappointment, the *F* I received in Geology. This is what happened: The professor, a man named Stafford who affected a British intonation, said, during the first day of classes, that no hourly tests were to be missed, that no excuses would be accepted, and if one missed an hourly, this would result in a failing grade.

Well, my father died at two in the morning on the day of the exam. My oldest brother, Roy Lee, called me at Cliff Courts. There were no phones in the hutments; one went outside to a public telephone which some students abused by inserting a coin in the nickel slot and, using a screwdriver, would spin the coin down the chute to make the Southwestern Bell ring. The tool was kept by a junior student called Willie the Lion, not to be confused with the great stride pianist since there were no Black Texans enrolled at the time. While I'd been away in the Army, Heman Marion Sweatt had fought to be enrolled and had done so through the courts. Now there's a building on campus named for him; the word irony comes to mind.

Friends from home had arranged for a pilot and his Piper Cub to pick me up at what passed for Austin's airport at the time. We buried my father, and I rode the bus back to Austin. I believed Stafford's dictum about failure if one missed the exam, and I didn't go to his office. Hence, the F. I signed up for Geology again and, with help of a friendly co-ed, whom I helped with her advanced Spanish course, I earned a B both semesters. That was the only F. I was on the G.I. Bill; (confession time) I enjoyed seeing my name on the Dean's list and imagined my mother's smiling face when she received the grades sent by the university, which is the way it was done in those days.

The Co-op was where the Co-op is, without its many additions and subtractions; one could listen to music in the basement in any of the three booths so provided. The Co-op also carried more books at the time when slide rules, the contemporary computers, were put to good use.

I represented my college in Student Government one year (we were called Aldermen in those days) and there existed deep social and political divides in the student body between MICA and WICA (Men's Independent College Association and the Women I.C.A.) and The Clique, as the social organizations were called and so referred to in *The Daily Texan* under Ronnie Dugger and later, Willie Morris.

I was also a member of the Tejas Club and later became a Pike, a card-carrying member of the Pi Kappa Alpha fraternity; the use of *frat* was frowned upon in those days and no fraternity man used it; at least not in public. My good friend and fellow Tejas man, Lynn Beason (who later, after service in the Philippines as a marine lieutenant, attended law school and joined the old Coke and Coke firm in Dallas) became a Deke while retaining his Tejas membership. I remember talking about these relationships with Jack Holland, Dean of Men (now called something else, I believe) and he said he saw no problem if Beason and I didn't, and that was it. The other dean, Arno Nowotny served, I believe, as Dean of Student Life, whatever that meant. A native of New Braunfels, if I'm not mistaken. Typical of the times of *loco parentis*

I loved my classes except those I took in the College of Education; I did my practice teaching at the old Austin High on 12th Street, and I earned a B as I did in all my classes where an A was the usual order of the day whether one slept during class or not. I wanted to teach and my high GPA suffered on account of the Bs. Unlike today, an A was worth three points, a B two, and so on. A D was a passing grade but carried no points.

Talk about a lack of grade inflation in those times.

Biology was something else; we worked in two-person teams and began with a fetal pig; my partner, first name Barry, wanted to be a naval aviator but he wasn't about to touch a dead fetus. After this came a sheep's heart, a cow's eye, and we would wind up with an earthworm. I found this fascinating while Barry, hands in pockets, entertained me with jokes and stories. We passed with flying colors and took our lectures and lab work at the old Biology Building now called Painter Hall and named for Theophilus Schickel Painter, the man who, as President, signed René's diploma; mine was signed by Logan Wilson, a recent acquisition from Chapel Hill.

My brother wore his ring proudly but neglected to pick up his diploma. I solved this by walking across from the Reading Room into the Registrar's Office, said hello to one of the students who worked there who then led me to a sizable wire cage full of unclaimed diplomas stuffed in those round, hard-cover mailing containers. I mailed it to René who placed it next to his USS *Mississippi* shipmates' group photograph.

My diploma? Someone broke into my car at the Brownsville High School parking lot and took it. I imagine the thief saw no value in it and threw it away. I discovered it in a muddy pond in front of the football stadium. Ruined, of course, and that was it.

Movie houses. Four, as I remember: the Texas, in front of the Texas Union, and the Varsity, both on Guadalupe. The Texas exhibited many foreign films to packed houses; one had to read the subtitles and I suppose this may be too much for some students who have better things to do than to sit through English, French, and Italian movies. The Texas also showed operas on film; I remember *Rigoletto, The Marriage of Figaro*, and *Madama Butterfly*. The Varsity stuck to Hollywood films.

Faculty. I, along with my fellow undergraduates, had no idea of professorial rankings: teaching assistants, assistant professors, and so on. On the first day of classes, and this was common, someone would ask if we were to address the instructor as Dr. or Mr. (Few women in UT's faculty then.) The proper title must've been a touchy subject. The following occurred in American History, a sophomore class and a legislative requirement: The class included two students who enrolled with René in '46. Not to brag, but I earned a 100 in the 100 identification questions; the two, each, made a 12. One, and I forget which, but remember exactly what he said, asked me, "Do you think they'll curve the grades?"

The legislative requirement also held for the sophomore government class. One registered at Gregory Gym where, at the entrance, stood boxes filled with small pieces of paper asking if we were or had been, at one time or another, a member of subversive organizations. The Black Dragon Society is one I remember well. One was supposed to sign the chits. Ha! The boxes either remained filled or emptied on the steps of that fine old building. Gregory also served as the site for global examinations as did Hogg Auditorium where we sat in alternate seats and in alternate rows; the old honor system. In Hogg, the cement floors served as pencil sharpeners. One held up one's stub, the proctors gave the okay, and thus the pencils were sharpened. Rumors regarding wholesale cheating were common. A favorite myth centered on Freddy Phi Gam, a St. Bernard, said to wander casually into a classroom and 1) carry the answers in his collar, or 2) walk out and take the answers home when someone complained of Freddy's presence. Interesting if true, but I thought that anyone who believed that whopper must've fallen off a turnip truck.

Aside from basketball, Gregory was also used for dances, plays, and invited speakers, Hogg, too, but for smaller crowds where one enjoyed the San Antonio Symphony and a riot of a comedy show written and acted by students, *Time Staggers On*. One of the actresses was a Corpus Christi native who played the role of Lungs Bedlow and who much later played Barney Miller's wife in the popular TV sitcom. Varsity Carnival, alas, has disappeared. It was held in the intramural fields, which also housed sixteen high-fenced tennis courts and next to them, three 80-yard long football fields which also served as soccer fields or three softball diamonds.

Fame being a fleeting thing, I doubt the majority of Texans remember Jane Holcomb who, I was told, was a Miss Texas. Her seat, next to mine in Geology usually went unfilled (the class numbered some 300) but someone would sit in her place, and she would then be marked present. The teaching assistants took roll by looking at their seating arrangement charts and at the row number; later, the Geology building housed the Hogg Foundation for Medical Health. By the way, Miss Ima's name is pronounced Eema. And there was no Ura.

Yes, it was a small campus, and the women's swimming pool, named for professor Anna Hiss, stood behind the new Experimental Science building. The men's Olympic-sized pool was in Gregory. In those days, one took a foot bath before diving in, tight-fitting swimming caps were de riguer, but swimming trunks were not allowed. And how's that for the uptight '50s? ★

2006

WILSON M. HUDSON

Wilson Hudson (1907–2002) was born in Flatonia, Texas, and took two degrees from the University of Texas and his Ph.D. from the University of Chicago. Following service in the Army Air Force in World War II, Hudson joined the Department of English in 1947. Hudson studied and taught world literature, but he also taught the course made famous by J. Frank Dobie, Life and Literature of the Southwest. In 1964 he published an important contribution to Western American studies, *Andy Adams: His Life and Writings*. From 1951 until 1971 he edited the annual book publications of the Texas Folklore Society. In the piece below Hudson recalls the fondness of Bedichek and Dobie for the swimming pool at Zilker Park.

from "BEDICHEK'S ROCK"

DURING JULY AND AUGUST FROM THREE-THIRTY TILL five-thirty every day Mr. Bedichek would sit on his rock and talk to his friends. When he felt himself getting too hot he would interrupt the conversation for a quick dip in the bathtub. In a big flood of two years ago the sycamore tree was snapped off. Its upper branches became filled with driftwood and the force of the water was too much for it. Mr. Bedichek had hopes that the tree would grow out again, and it has sent out new shoots. He thought that if all the shoots but one were trimmed away, the tree might make a comeback.

Once I said to him, "Mr. Bedichek, when you and I are dead and gone, this rock will still be thought of as Bedichek's rock." Everyone seemed to regard the rock as his, and only a stranger would take his place while he was cooling in the bathtub.

In *King Lear* there is an allusion to an old rhyme, "Pillicock sat on Pillicock hill." Taking a hint from this, I made up a couplet for Mr. Bedichek's amusement.

Bedichek sat on Bedichek's rock,
The water was cold but Bedi was hot.

One of the most regular visitors to Bedichek's rock was Mr. Dobie. He did not alternate between the rock and the bathtub; he had his own way of cooling off. He would swim around in the deep water until he felt chilled; then he would go up on the hot cement and lie down. He said the heat of the sun above and of the cement below would drive the cold deep down into his bones.

In the course of an afternoon ten or fifteen of Mr. Bedichek's friends might come over at different times for a chat. If there was such a thing as a literary salon in Austin, its location was Bedichek's rock. This is not to say, though, that the conversation was limited to literary matters; it ranged far and wide, for Mr. Bedichek was ready to talk to anybody about anything. He had a very large store of information on a great variety of topics and he was willing to acquire more by listening. . . .

Almost every afternoon someone was sure to ask Mr. Bedichek a question about birds. "I saw a bird the other day that I've never seen before. It was smaller than a redbird and larger than a wren. It was gray all over and had a topknot. What was it?" Then Mr. Bedichek would consider all the possibilities and arrive at what he thought the best answer. "The only small gray-backed bird with a crest is a titmouse. Yes, it must have been a titmouse." So he told me on that last afternoon. . . .

I did not go to Barton's for a week after Mr. Bedichek's passing. When I did go, I swam over to Bedichek's rock and stood in the water before it. How many hours had he sat there over the years with his friends, talking about birds, quoting poetry, telling anecdotes, recalling passages in his life, analyzing politics, and speculating on the questions of existence! Let Bedichek's rock remain, unaltered in any way, unmarked by a bronze inscription. ★

WALTER P. WEBB

Walter Prescott Webb (1888–1963) was Texas' foremost historian. Born in East Texas in 1888, he was raised in West Texas, and his experience with the arid plains shaped his view of Texas—and Western—history. Webb's most famous books are *The Great Plains* (1931) and *The Texas Rangers* (1935). A long-time member of the Department of History at the University of Texas, Webb was the most distinguished Western historian of his era. He was killed in a car wreck in 1963. His roast of his friend J. Frank Dobie was delivered at a meeting of the Texas Folklore Society held at the Driskill Hotel in Austin on April 23, 1955. Webb follows the traditional rhetoric of the roast, in which the speaker says the opposite of what is meant.

J. FRANK DOBIE

I HAVE KNOWN FRANK DOBIE FOR ABOUT THIRTY-FIVE years, maybe a little longer. There are many sides to him, more facets than I know, and I suspect more than he knows or suspects. He cannot be confined, and is not subject to definition. All I can do is to describe some of his attributes as I have known them. Some of them may surprise you, but if they do, that will only illustrate how impossible it is to understand him.

The first thing to which I call your attention is that Frank Dobie dislikes Texas. He is never happy when he is here; he is never miserable when he is away. The happiest years of his life he spent in an Oklahoma agricultural college where he said he felt completely at home. The thing he likes best about Texans is their boastfulness. He said that the only thing he disliked about Oklahomans was their modesty. He never quite got used to it.

A second characteristic is his unfailing spirit of obedience, his submissiveness to authority. He likes all the people in high places, and he is especially fond of regents. He is always anxious to please them, and they never gave an order that he did not obey with alacrity. There is not any instance where they said come, that he did not come running. He can anticipate their wishes. He was never known to keep galloping around on the prairie when he was ordered in to the campus. The regents often cite him as an example of what a university would be like made up entirely of Dobies. A thing of undisturbed beauty and a joy forever. A very quiet place it would be.

Mr. Dobie is a great defender of architects and sculptors. He is particularly fond of the architects who designed the University buildings, those who put all the windows on the west side so as to incubate the heat, make life in them intolerable for seven months in the year, and make expensive air conditioning imperative. He once expressed his unstinted admiration for the Tower on the Main Building. Dobie said that Texas had plenty of length and breadth, and that it should also have height in proportion. No sense in spreading out over all this space, with shaded walks to fend off the sun. What we need, he said, is buildings imported from other regions, and that are comfortable only when they have snow on the roof. Dobie said you did not need a porch, that the only use for a porch was to put saddles on and provide shade for the dogs. He is not the critic who said of the University Tower that it would look better laid down on its side with a porch around it. That was another fellow who is to Dobie as Bacon to the English Bard.

His admiration of Texas sculptors surpasses that for the architects. He thinks the cenotaph on Alamo Plaza in San Antonio is the very embodiment of the artistic spirit of Texas, and that the sculptor who made it should be proclaimed an honorary Texas Ranger. He might add a few horses, but otherwise he approves of all the best Texas art.

Dobie is the best camp cook, I know, excepting one. He does not want any of the conveniences. He would prefer to build the fire out of cow chips, but since the drouth has burned them up, he will compromise with green brush, and the harder it is to gather the better he likes it. He will grudgingly use wood that others have gathered, but I have never known him to set the woodpile on fire rather than drag off a few chunks. He will not use a griddle to broil a steak. He wants a green stick with the steak speared on it. He likes the fire so hot that he can burn the steak up on the outside and have it raw on the inside. If he can drop it a time or two in the ashes, he considers the flavor improved. Some of his customers have said it didn't hurt.

Dobie is a total abstainer. He never drinks whiskey except on social occasions, and Dobie is really socially inclined. He does not know the difference between good whisky and bad whiskey, and really shows a strong preference for the more vicious brands. He cannot tolerate Jack Daniels or Old Forrester.

Dobie is quite fastidious in his tastes. He believes that everybody ought to dress for dinner, and he never misses a chance to put on tails or a dinner jacket. This is the influence of a year in England. You can tell by his stiff formality that he has departed far from his Texas heritage.

Dobie is one of the famous gardeners of Austin. His home on Waller Creek is set in grounds that are the envy of all his many visitors. He does all the planning himself, and any time you go there after five o'clock you will find him working near a table that is well equipped with what it takes to stimulate the artistic imagination of a gardener. It is generally assumed that Mrs. Dobie contributes something to this beautiful garden, but this is an error. Frank does it all.

There he is, ladies and gentlemen, and with all those simple virtues it is no wonder that we love him as much as we misunderstand him. ★

1964

DAVID RICHARDS

Born and raised in Waco, Texas, David Richards attended the University of Texas and practiced law for many years. He lived in Austin for much of his career. He is the father of six children and the author of a memoir, *Once Upon a Time in Texas: A Liberal in the Lone Star State* (2002). Currently Richards resides in California. In this passage from *Once Upon a Time in Texas* Richards describes a typical enthusiasm for Austin that is held by many graduates of the University of Texas. Scholz Garden, a German beer hall founded in the 1860s, is located at 1607 San Jacinto Blvd. It was Austin's most celebrated watering hole in the 1950s and '60s. Richards, incidentally, is absolutely correct when he says that Scholz's is not the same as it once was. In fact, Scholz's seems to have little awareness of its once important role in the cultural and literary life of the city.

from ONCE UPON A TIME IN TEXAS

ANN AND I, LIKE MANY OF OUR GENERATION WHO HAD gone to college in Austin, spent our Dallas years pining to return to the capital city. Dallas was a pinched-up, buttoned-down wasteland for the soul. Austin, on the other hand, seemed an oasis for mind and body, with its lakes, rivers, and a host of madcap adventurers. The lure finally became overwhelming.

For years, as we had discussed getting back, I had stumbled over the traditional litany of what will I do and how can I support my family. Finally one day, I was able to divide the inquiry in my mind and address each question separately. Do we want to leave Dallas? Yes. Do we want to move to Austin? A thunderous yes. Having made those decisions, the fog cleared. Now the only question was what to do, and that proved quite simple. I ran into Sam Houston Clinton at a political party in Austin, and he asked whether I might be interested in joining him in his Austin law practice. Instantly, it was a done deal.

&

Austin was also a natural fit for Ann and me. We already had a pool of friends there. Our dearest friends from Dallas, Sam and Virginia Whitten and their children, had earlier moved to Austin when Sam joined the UT Library School faculty. George Schatzki, with whom I had practiced law in Dallas, was now on the UT law faculty. The writers Bud Shrake and Gary—sometimes known as "Jap" because of his resemblance to a sumo wrestler—Cartwright were wending their way down to Austin from Dallas. These Dallas refugees, coupled with our political acquaintances and river-running buddies, gave us a ready-made social network of some magnitude—a network that had at its core political dissent and an abhorrence of prevailing Texas social taboos.

We purchased a somewhat frayed house on two acres in Westlake Hills that had spectacular views of Austin in the distance. There was a grand swimming pool that sat at the head of a small canyon and managed to leak hundreds of gallons of water at irregular intervals. The contrast with our Dallas Lovers Lane house was as dramatic as the contrast between the lifestyle of Dallas and Austin. For those who know Westlake now as an upscale white-flight suburb of Austin, the Westlake of those years would be unrecognizable. The school system, known as Eanes, only had one tiny school with six grades, so for the upper grades, children went to Austin. The population was divided between cedar choppers living in tumbledown quarters and those occupying the occasional somewhat grander digs, but all were scattered down gravel roads bearing little resemblance to today's orderly middle-class environs.

&

The center of our social life in those first years, our country club if you will, was Scholz Garden. The children claim they were raised there, which is a slight exaggeration. They did, indeed, spend many a Friday romping around the garden with the Whitten kids. Bill Brammer made it immortal in *The Gay Place* as the "Dearly Beloved Beer and Garden Party." His description remained apt for many years:

There were twenty or thirty others, mostly young people sitting at the unwashed tables, and through the windows of the building the boiled faces of some of the longtime customers were visible.

As he said, "the garden was shielded on three sides by the low yellow frame structure, a U-shaped Gothicism, scalloped and jig-sawed and wonderfully grotesque."

The garden itself covered probably a half-acre and was devoid of greenery except for the old elms that sheltered its many tables. In those years, the underfooting was white caliche, with the result that if you went to the garden in your lawyer's blue suit, there was no concealing that fact, for your pant legs would be splotched with white dust up to your knees. The old tables covered with their red-checked cloths could easily be moved as one's group expanded, and it seemed that no matter what the hour, a stop by the garden always produced an acquaintance whom you really wanted to see. There was an accepted notion that contributed to the sense of congeniality: If you chose to sit in the garden, as distinguished from the inside bar area, it signaled a welcome to be joined at your table.

In those years, liquor by the drink was to be found only in private clubs, to which none of us could or would belong, and beer was the drink of choice. The food was marginal at best, but some evenings the conversations were so stimulating one forgot and lapsed into ordering the sausage and kraut or some other filler.

It seems strange to write about a beer garden as if it were anything more, but it was the sum of its parts—the hundreds who found nourishment under its elms . . . Every progressive politician, state and local, would have at least one fund-raiser at the garden, and as victories became more numerous, it was also the site of happy victory celebrations. But the soul of the place was found in conversation; something about the place engendered leisurely discourse.

Despite the politics, the beer drinking, and the chatter, there was ample time for romance in this extended crowd of Texas liberals. We used to joke about creating a wall chart of marriages and liaisons in order to better understand the interplay, but the task was too daunting. The degrees of separation were not many. Bob Eckhardt was one of our great heroes of the era, serving with distinction in the Texas house and the U.S. Congress. Bob, along with Willie Morris, was reputedly one of the principal figures of *The Gay Place*. When I first met Bill Brammer around the tables in the mid-1950s, he was married to the ravishing Nadine. I looked up one day, and Nadine had become Bob Eckhardt's second wife, and Bill had married the equally stunning Dorothy Browne. The next thing I knew, Eckhardt had divorced Nadine and was married to Willie Morris's first wife, the lovely Celia. In the meantime, Dorothy and Bill had split, and Dorothy was married to the Houston legislator and Scholz habitué Arthur Vance. My patient and equally lovely wife Sandy, whom I did not know in those years, got her introduction to Austin as a waitress at the garden during the late 1960s. Too much can be made of this, but the fact remains that the Texas liberals of that era all seemed to know one another one way or the other.

&

On reflection, those Scholz years were a time of innocence. Our politics were pure—we did not win much in the way of elections. Our enemies were gross and obvious. The state of Texas, the city of Austin, and the University of Texas all were run by smug old-guard conservatives who perceived their role to be to preserve the status quo—in other words, to maintain racial segregation at the University and everywhere else, to stifle labor unions across the state, and to harass the antiwar movement at every turn. As a result, our job was fairly simple, as it required no great sophistication to oppose this old order. Somewhere along in the mid-1970s, the old Scholz scene dissolved. Liquor by the drink and pot smoking probably contributed, as neither were available around the tables of the garden. An old Scholz regular, the feckless Fletcher Boone, opened a joint called The Raw Deal in the grungy part of Sixth Street, and as many of us drifted off to this more happening place, our community began to fracture.

The garden still survives and is the site of periodic fund-raisers, victory celebrations, and birthdays, but the old mood seems to have deserted it, as has the old crowd. . . . I suppose we would all be better served if we could reclaim the spirit that animated the old dearly beloved garden. ★

2002

ANN RICHARDS

Dorothy Ann Willis Richards (1933-2006) was born in Lakeview, Texas. After receiving a bachelor's degree from Baylor University, she earned a teaching certificate from the University of Texas at Austin. She entered electoral politics in 1976, became State Treasurer in 1982, and Governor in 1991, serving until 1995. After leaving the Governor's office, she served on numerous boards and participated in Democratic party politics. In 1989 she published a memoir about her early days in Austin, *Straight from the Heart: My Life in Politics and Other Places*. Like many another Austinite of those years, she recalled with gusto the nights spent talking and drinking at Scholzgarden's.

from STRAIGHT FROM THE HEART

WE GRADUATED IN JUNE 1954, AND THERE WAS A LOT OF mulling over the question of what David was going to do when he grew up. He had majored in history and there was some talk of his going to business school, maybe Harvard or Wharton, but finally we went to Austin and David enrolled in the University of Texas Law School while I took graduate level speech and education courses toward my permanent teacher's certificate.

After some practice teaching I got a job teaching social studies to the seventh- and ninth-graders at Fulmore Junior High School. I believe the reason I got that job was that Austin's superintendent of schools, Ernest Cabe, had been the principal of my high school in Waco.

I was barely older than my students. I was twenty, they were about thirteen, though some boys were older. The school system at that time still indulged in "social promotion," which meant that no matter what a student's capabilities, he was promoted. This was to avoid a problem we certainly had had back in

Lakeview: Some kid can't pass and he gets left back a couple of years and then you have trouble on your hands. If he's some big ol' raw-boned boy he's going to be a real difficulty; too big, too aggressive, more physically and less emotionally mature than the rest of the class.

I found that if you want to be a good teacher there are a thousand situations set up to keep you from it. Our notion of teaching is imparting knowledge. Well, you might get to do that—if you are lucky—twenty percent of the time. The rest of the time you are a referee. You are listening to parents complain, you are listening to students complain. Your administrators are usually guys who couldn't make it as football coaches, or who did make it as football coaches until they started having losing seasons and then got kicked upstairs.

The adjustment from one class to another was enormous. I taught the 7–1's (seventh-grade students with first-grade abilities) to the 9–12's (ninth-graders with twelfth-grade skills). In the 7–1's we would make salt-and-flour maps of Texas. We would mix salt and flour and water, making a gooey paste that we could spread out over the map's outlines. We'd put in the mountains in the Big Bend country and draw little river valleys running down from the Oklahoma border. Of course, with the 7–1's it was a total mess; they would ball up that salt and flour and throw it all over the room.

And I don't think I was equipped to teach the 9–12's. Ninth grade was European history, and while these kids deserved someone who would force their thinking, I was barely one step ahead of them. I would end up giving them rote assignments like memorizing the kings and queens of England, which may have been good enough for the school board but didn't satisfy me.

Teaching was the hardest work I had ever done, and it remains the hardest work I have done to date. The rewards are very subtle, and they are certainly not monetary. Seldom does anyone tell a teacher she is really doing a good job. She's supposed to get her satisfaction by some sort of osmosis, just by knowing it.

In my classes I had many children of migrant farm workers. They would come to school for a while and then it would be time to hit the trail again and they would move on north to wherever they were working. Even when they were in one place they worked hard after school.

I had one little boy who would leave school at three o'clock and go sweep and clean out the barber shop. He wouldn't get home until seven or eight o'clock at night, have dinner, try to do his homework, and go to bed. In class I would look up and he'd be half asleep. You knew the kids who had to work after school; they were simply not as quick, not as alert. There was nothing wrong with their brains, they were bright as could be—they were tired.

David and I were settling in to being married. We were inseparable and, except when we were in class or working, we were always together. The routine was that David would go to school, I would teach school, and every Friday night we would go to the Scholz Beer Garden.

Scholz Garden was a big outdoor drinking establishment with gravel on the ground and big trees shading everything. Rows of folding chairs sat around old wooden tables that had decades of initials carved in them. The place attracted old-time Austinite political activists and a motley assortment of beer drinkers. It had the feel of a real good-time closed fraternity, and we fit right in.

We'd arrive each and every Friday and head straight for the table informally reserved for a group of political folk known as the Horses Association. There would always be some intrigue going on. This was where all the events of any political significance, all the gossip, all the Byzantine political ins and outs were hashed over—and never resolved.

Chief among the Horses Associates were Henry and Mary Holman, Sam Houston Clinton, Marge Hershey, Fletcher Boone. Membership was pretty much a matter of whether there was a seat for you. There were by-laws created when the Horses was originally formed, and I believe Dan Strawn was elected the head of the Horses Association for a ten- or twelve-year term, with Henry Holman as Vice Horse. But there was nothing ever written about how you became a member. It was decided more by attendance than anything else.

In later years the issue became more complex. Wayne Oakes wanted to get in, but Sam Houston Clinton blackballed him. When Sam Houston went to the bathroom they took another vote and he was accepted, so the question remains to this day whether Wayne Oakes is really a Horse.

It was always noisy and raucous at Scholz Garden, with lots of big talk. It was the mid-fifties and the Lyndon Johnson forces were attempting to wrest the power of the Democratic Party from the Allan Shivers forces, the Shivers forces being the conservatives and the Lyndon Johnson forces being the liberals. We were a part of the Lyndon Johnson wing.

I would like to tell you that the conversation that went on around that table was weighty and noteworthy, but by and large it was about who had stolen what convention—all sorts of nefarious planning that never came to fruition. Sam Houston, a veteran of those wars, would be recounting what had happened five or ten years before. This was yarn-spinning; any serious political planning would take place on the side; it would not go on around the table at Scholz's.

David had become interested in the University of Texas Young Democrats and had hooked up with a man named Marion Shafer. Marion Shafer had been a Young Democrat for all forty years of his life. (In those days there was no way you became an Old Democrat, there was no age cut-off.)

You must understand, often in politics being the kingpin of a political group offers you a portion of power that may not be backed up by anything in reality. Even though the Young Democrats had no clout, being the kingpin of the Young Democrats gave you quite a bit. This is the way young people were trained and brought along within the party structure.

The work wasn't fabulously complex. One time Marion Shafer had enlisted David's help in reproducing some flyers to be distributed on campus. The Young Democrats' duplicating machine was a relic that involved putting a piece of paper between two panes of glass and holding it out in the sun to make a print. This would fall to David as his task in the struggle, and he would come home with his head blistered by sunburn for having done his bit for democracy.

Sometime that autumn David was approached to take over the UT Young Democrats, which meant pulling a palace coup against Marion Shafer. We were twenty years old, and the thinking was, "We are the young Democrats and as the young Democrats we should run the show." So, at the first meeting of the Young Democrats we attended, the coup was performed. David was elected president of the University of Texas Young Democrats.

The problem was, David had never run a meeting before. Here he was president with a full agenda and work to get done. I had taken a course in parliamentary procedure at Baylor, so I became the parliamentarian. I don't remember what we did at that meeting, but I do remember that we carried it off.

Our first precinct convention at Brykerwood School was the confrontation between the Shivers and Johnson forces. Governor Shivers had endorsed Dwight Eisenhower for president. In fact it was predictable; every four years Shivers forces would head Democrats for . . . whoever the Republican nominee happened to be.

The University of Texas has a Homecoming celebration each fall called Round-up. Round-up was an occasion of great float-building on the part of all the campus clubs and sororities and fraternities, pretty women riding on flatbed trucks, and all the extravagant festivities that go with Homecoming parades. The Young Democrats agreed that we should bring attention to our cause with a Round-up float.

David and I were living in a house on West 31st Street that backed up to Shoal Creek, and the float was to be built in our garage. Being a woman, I was the only one who knew about papier-mâché. But I was also the only one who worked, so the float-building had to go on without me.

Our float was to be an apple. One side was going to look like a good apple, and the other side was going to look rotten. Our message was: "One rotten apple can spoil the Democratic barrel." Meaning, of course, the non-loyalist Democrats.

First we fashioned an apple out of chicken wire. Then we dumped great sacks of flour and some salt into a tub, put the hose to it and created this gooey gunk into which we were going to dip strips of newspaper and build this float. Dave Shapiro was involved, and Ann Klempt, and some others. We put this gooey paper stuff on the chicken wire, and of course it would just slide right off. We had a terrible time getting it to stick.

Round-up was rapidly approaching and the rotten apple was not progressing. It reached the point of fish or cut bait.

The good side never made it; we had to make the whole apple rotten. But that was okay, the message would still make sense. Unfortunately, there were these big gaping holes where the papier-mâché wouldn't adhere. We fixed that by putting worms in each of those holes. We made these worms out of chicken wire, but we didn't have time to cover them with papier-mâché, so we put brown paper sacks over them. There were these square-headed worms sticking out of the apple. The whole thing looked more like a blazing Benjamin Franklin stove that someone had beaten with a sledgehammer and stuck in a lot of stovepipes.

This was our first experience at building a float and we were not the best organized in the world; no one had thought to arrange for a truck to haul our creation. We found out quickly that, this being Homecoming, flatbed trucks were in short supply. We sent someone out to try and scare up a truck to put our apple on, and he came back with a truck the bed of which was eighteen feet long. So we've got about a three-and-a-half-foot apple sitting in the middle of an eighteen-foot truck.

We walked the apple to the trailer, which was parked at a filling station, and then hoisted it up. We were standing there looking at this dinky little class project resting forlornly in the bed of this great big old long trailer. Henry Holman and Jean Lee, the grande dame of Austin Democratic politics, were trying hard to be delicate about the disaster.

The next question was, Who will pull this thing? There were no volunteers. We all agreed that it should be pulled by a seedy-looking car—no sense in overshadowing a great political symbol with a shiny auto. Ann Klempt had a Hudson that was the worst-looking vehicle in our crowd, but she was having none of it. Not only was she not going to pull it, she wasn't going to let her car pull it, no matter who was driving.

About that time two eager-looking young fraternity men stopped and identified themselves as being members of the Round-up parade Float Committee. They had been driving down Lamar and happened to notice this trailer sitting here and just wondered if this was a float or what.

We got the picture. So, since we couldn't get anybody to pull it anyway, Henry Holman took our rotten apple home and put it in his backyard and his little boys played in it.

But it wasn't all papier-mâché. We took Young Democratic politics very, very seriously. We would hold state conventions and fight for the issues that concerned us just as hard as if we were choosing the President of the United States.

With David in law school I joined the Law Wives. The Law Wives met regularly at the Driskill Hotel to play bridge. We played like crazy for such prizes as corn-on-the-cob holders.

Heman Sweatt, a black man, had sued the University of Texas for admission to the law school, and attended classes in 1950. It opened the door for other black students, and the Law Wives realized that soon there might be a situation in which a black Law Wife might appear on the scene. I was president of the Law Wives David's senior year and I was astounded that there would be a suggestion that the Law Wives might not admit a black woman.

The selection of the next year's president turned on that issue. The woman who won was opposed to allowing a black woman to become a member. She later resigned and the turmoil of the fight reduced the organization to ineffectiveness. I think it ceased to exist shortly thereafter. ★

1989

WILLIE MORRIS

Willie Morris (1934–1999) grew up in Yazoo City, Mississippi, and attended the University of Texas from 1954–1958. He became well known on campus and beyond for his fiery editorship of *The Daily Texan*. After college, he studied history at Oxford as a Rhodes Scholar and returned to Texas where he edited the liberal weekly magazine, *The Texas Observer*. In 1967 he became editor of *Harper's*, and in the same year published an autobiography, *North Toward Home*. Morris's many other publications include the novel *The Last of the Southern Girls* (1973), a memoir, *New York Days* (1993), and a children's book *My Dog Skip* (1995), which was made into a film in 2000. The excerpt below is from "Texas," the middle section of *North Toward Home*.

from NORTH TOWARD HOME

WHAT WE BROUGHT TO THE UNIVERSITY OF TEXAS IN the 1950s, to an enormous, only partially formed state university, was a great awe before the splendid quotations on its buildings and the walls of its libraries, along with an absolutely prodigious insensitivity as to what they implied beyond decoration. Minds awakened slowly, painfully, and with pretentious and damaging inner searches. Where an Alfred Kazin at the age of nineteen might become aroused in the subway by reading a review by John Chamberlain in the *New York Times* and rush to his office to complain, we at eighteen or nineteen were only barely beginning to learn that there were ideas, much less ideas to arouse one from one's self. If places like City College or Columbia galvanized the young New York intellectuals already drenched in literature and polemics, the University of Texas had, in its halting, unsure, and often frivolous way, to teach those of us with good minds and small-town high school diplomas that we were intelligent human beings, with minds and hearts of our own that we might learn to call our own, that there were some things, many things—ideas, values, choices of action—worth committing one's self to and fighting for, that a man in some instances might become morally committed to honoring every manifestation of individual conscience and courage. Yet the hardest task at the University of Texas, as many of us were to learn, was to separate all the extraneous and empty things that can drown a young person there, as all big universities can drown its young people, from the few simple things that are worth living a life by. Without wishing to sound histrionic, I believe I am thinking of something approaching the Western cultural tradition; yet if someone had suggested that to me that September night in 1952, as I stepped off the bus in Austin to be greeted by three fraternity men anxious to look me over, I would have thought him either a fool or a con man.

I emerged from that bus frightened and tired, after having come 500 miles non-stop over the red hills of Louisiana and the pine forests of East Texas. The three men who met me—appalled, I was told later, by my green trousers and the National Honor Society medal on my gold-plated watch chain—were the kind that I briefly liked and admired, for their facility at small talk, their clothes, their manner, but whom I soon grew to deplore and finally to be bored by. They were the kind who made fraternities tick, the favorites of the Dean of Men at the time, respectable B or C-plus students, tolerable athletes, good with the Thetas or the Pi Phis; but one would find later, lurking there inside of them despite—or maybe because of—their good fun and jollity, the ideals of the insurance salesman and an aggressive distrust of anything approaching thought. One of them later told me, with the seriousness of an early disciple, that my table manners had become a source of acute embarrassment to all of them. That night they drove me around the campus, and they were impressed that I knew from my map-reading where the University library was, for two of them were not sure.

It was early fall, with that crispness in the air that awakened one's senses and seemed to make everything wondrously alive. My first days there I wandered about that enormous campus, mingling silently with its thousands of nameless students. I walked past the fraternity and sorority houses, which were like palaces to me with their broad porches and columns and patios, and down "The Drag" with its bookstores and restaurants, a perfectly contained little city of its own. On a slight rise dominating the place was a thirty-story skyscraper called the "Tower," topped with an edifice that was a mock Greek temple; the words carved on the white sandstone said, "*Ye Shall Know the Truth and the Truth Shall Make You Free*," causing me to catch my breath in wonder and bafflement. That first morning I took the elevator to the top, and looked out on those majestic purple hills to the west, changing to lighter shades of blue or a deeper purple as wisps of autumn clouds drifted around the sun; that, they would tell me, was the Great Balcones Divide, where the South ended and the West began, with its stark, severe landscape so different from any I had known before. I saw the state capitol, only a few blocks to the south, set on its sloping green acres, its pink granite catching the morning light, and away to the east the baseball field dug into the native rock, and the football stadium, the largest and most awesome I had ever seen. Then down again to the campus, where all the furious construction and demolition was going on, and where the swarms of students back for another year greeted each other with such shouts and screams of delight, war-whoops, and hoo-haws and wild embracing, and twangy "hello there's" with the "r's" exploited as nowhere else in the South, that I suddenly felt unbearably displaced and alone. Everything around me was brisk, burgeoning, *metropolitan*. It was bigger than Memphis when I was twelve.

&

I believe now that the University of Texas was somehow beginning to give me an interest and a curiosity in something outside my own parochial ego. It was beginning to suggest the power not merely of language, but the whole unfamiliar world of experience and evocation which language served. That world was new, and the recognition of its existence was slow, uncertain, and immature. Books and literature, I was beginning to see, were not for getting a grade, not for the utilitarian purpose of being considered a nice and versatile boy, not just for casual pleasure, but subversive as Socrates and expressions of man's soul. It took me years to understand that words are often as important as experience, because words make experience last, but here, in the spring of my freshman year, there were men who were teaching me these things, perhaps with very little hope that anyone in their classrooms remotely cared, and I think perhaps I may have been listening. Freshman English was the first step; it was often the first and last time that many young people, headed in a state like Texas for insurance or business or the Junior League, might have had for a kind of small internal salvation. ★

1967

CELIA MORRIS

Celia Morris, who grew up in Houston, came to the University of Texas in 1957. Years later she took a Ph.D. from City University of New York. Her books include *Fanny Wright: Rebel in America* (1984), *Storming the Statehouse: Running for Governor with Ann Richards and Dianne Feinstein* (1992), and *Bearing Witness: Sexual Harassment and Beyond—Everywoman's Story* (1994). She lives in Washington, D.C. In 2000, she published a memoir, *Finding Celia's Place*. Her account of the intellectual excitement generated by her experiences at the University of Texas is one that rings true for many students. Memoirs of that era, the late fifties through the sixties, often allude to the dynamic impact of John Silber, the charismatic philosophy professor and dean who was famously fired by Frank Irwin.

from FINDING CELIA'S PLACE

AND SO BEGAN ONE OF MY GREAT ADVENTURES—IN MIND, soul, and spirit. For the very air was crisper in Austin and the sky seemed a more pristine blue. The hills dotted with cedar outcroppings, along with the striated cliffs streaked ochre, rust colored, lavender, and gray that framed Lake Austin to the west gave the city a gentler tone than Houston in all its flat monotony. My spirits always rose with the land when we left the humid coast behind, and as we crested the hill at Bastrop thirty miles to the southeast, I would strain for a glimpse of the university tower and the capitol dome. In the 1950s, they were the town's only tall buildings, for Austin in those days had a manageable feel; it was drawn to human scale.

&

The most important outlet was Plan II. I was taking freshman English with Dr. Pratt, who introduced us to world literature, the life of the mind, and the precise use of language. "Miss Buchan," he would say, "it is not 'more or less.' It is either 'more' or 'less.'" Once he caught me spelling "basically" two different ways in the same paper and wryly called my laziness to the class's attention. I left his courses tiresomely insistent on the difference between "anxious" and "eager."

We started with Confucius and swept on to the Greeks—a bit of Homer, *Agamemnon, Oedipus Rex,* some poems by Sappho—and then to Vergil and the world-weary Aeneas. By the time we got to Chaucer, I was not only thrilled to find that I could recite the first twenty-two lines of the prologue as well as my father could, but I was also hooked for life on the study of what Matthew Arnold had called "the best that has been thought and written."

I discovered words for pain and the revolutionary notion that finding them mattered. I discovered words for anger and outrage and people to admire who expressed them. I found out that people had ideas that shaped the way they lived and that some ideas were more compelling than others. I got excited about the turn of a phrase and the shape of a sentence.

&

John Silber was a very handsome man at thirty—only ten years older than we—lean and wiry, with thick blond hair, a fine square jaw, fierce blue eyes, a wicked grin, and a presence that was electrifying. His right arm ended just below the elbow in a vestigial stump he used with great dexterity, and when he stood before that class, or stalked back and forth in a transport of intellectual glee, I forgot not so much that he had one hand but that most people have two.

A native of San Antonio, he spoke our language, though he'd gotten a Ph.D. from Yale. There was nothing arcane or esoteric about him, for philosophy to Silber was about how you know and what you do about it. The word "charisma" could have been invented for him, and if he ever had a down time, he certainly didn't show it to us.

On returning our first set of papers, he read mine aloud word for word, tearing it ever so slowly to pieces and holding it up as an example of an A student doing F work. (It was an English paper, he declared, not a philosophy paper.) He didn't identify the essay as mine, but now and then in the midst of this ritual blood bath, our eyes would meet and battle was joined. Whatever it took to win this man's respect, I was determined to do.

He was immensely patient, we discovered, with a student who was trying hard but didn't quite get it, and cutting only to those who hadn't done the work or were grandstanding. That year I never saw him mistake one kind of student for the other, and he invested the life of the mind with such urgency that every class was an adventure. We jousted with him. We explored. We dissected. We found.

I would also climb the stairs to his third-floor office, where he'd sit with his feet propped on his desk, his tie loosened, and his sleeve rolled up, and we'd talk about whatever outrageous thing was happening then on campus. The most memorable that fall was a motion from the faculty itself that they refrain from getting involved in campaigns for governor or lieutenant governor. The resolution was supported by the distinguished economist Clarence Ayres, a principal target for the legislature in the Rainey years but a rebel, it seemed, no longer. So in the faculty senate, after Ayres suggested that they draw a little circle around a small area of political activity, Silber jumped up to point out that this little circle happened to enclose 98 percent of his political interest.

I had *never* met anyone more defiant or persuasive—even when you were convinced he was wrongheaded, if not perverse—and he would sit in his office actually savoring the risk. With three small children and no tenure, he was taking on a lot more than any riverboat gambler did, and as far as an outsider could see, if he was convinced his cause was just, he wouldn't pull back even if nobody else supported him. On a campus in the 1950s where "working within the system" was the credo, John Silber by himself was an education in dissent.

I finally squeaked out an A in the introductory course and then signed up for his class in ethics, along with several friends as keen to take him on as I was. This was the class Silber would often refer to as the best he ever taught, and when a superb teacher is at the top of his form, the experience is breathtaking. He was a wizard with the Socratic method, and the tension could be mesmerizing as he sliced away at the intellectual ground under a student's feet until he or she was backed into a corner and saw no exit. Sometimes he was like a conductor—pointing to an urgent hand in the back, calling in a comment from the side, sketching connections, slowing us down, leaping forward, orchestrating harmonies, pulling things together.

He plucked analogies from the realms of music, sculpture, architecture, history, literature, psychology; he simply knew more than most people and could use what he knew more deftly. Once when I cited a dream to illustrate some point or other about perception, he grinned roguishly—I think he even blushed—and said, "I hope nobody here knows Freud." But we kept coming back for more.

Long afterward it dawned on me that several women in that class, including me, had been half in love with John Silber, who had probably never before been the object of so much concentrated female attention. Since Yale was still a men's college, his earlier teaching experience had not prepared him for Texas coeds, and more worldly men have had their heads turned by less. Though sex itself was out of the question, it is little wonder that he put in one scintillating performance after another, for the air had a sexual charge we were all too innocent to recognize, much less to acknowledge.

Not long after registration, Willis Pratt, arbiter of Plan II, called me in to say that in signing up for the ethics class I was taking a sophomore course when I needed senior credit to graduate. But if I read an extra book and wrote an extra paper, he said, all would be well. This was fine with Silber and fine with me, but as it was a busy semester, I didn't get around to the extra assignment. Then, as we parted for the summer, Silber said, "Why don't you read *The Brothers Karamazov* and write a Kierkegaardian interpretation of Ivan?" So I said "Sure!"

That summer I read Dostoevsky and came back, asking plaintively, "What have you done to me?" Silber grinned. So I read it again, and then read the "Pro and Contra" section over and over. Seven months late, I handed in a twenty-seven-page paper when I'd only been expected to turn in seven pages. I was auditing one of his courses when he gave it back with "A+ Excellent—You're on your way!" scrawled across the title page and "This was well worth waiting for. Thank you very much!" at the end.

Writing that paper was my most substantial intellectual adventure until well into graduate school and his response, the most gratifying. He had helped me know I could do good work, academically speaking, and that I loved the challenge. ★

2000

PART FOUR

An Oasis for Mind and Body: 1960s

J. FRANK DOBIE,
    For Years We Three Sat Together 97

BERTRAM ROTA,
    The Night of the Armadillos 110

JOE FRANTZ,
    from *The Forty Acre Follies* 116

BILLY LEE BRAMMER,
    from *The Gay Place* 119

LARRY MCMURTRY,
    from *In a Narrow Grave* 124

THOMAS WHITBREAD,
    Argumentative Poem Against Certain Articles 129

JONATHAN BRACKER,
    Garten of the Gods 132

OLIVIA DWIGHT (MARY HAZZARD),
    from *Close His Eyes* 134

CAROLYN OSBORN,
    The Vulture Descending Each Day 137

CHRISTOPHER MIDDLETON,
    The Armadillos 153

HARRY HUNTT RANSOM,
    Frontier Museum 155

MIGUEL GONZALEZ-GERTH,
    from Borges and Texas:
        Farewell To An Old Friend 156

HAZEL HARROD RANSOM,
    Quorum Pars Parva Fui 161

PRUDENCE MACINTOSH,
    from *Just As We Were* 165

JULIUS WHITTIER,
    from The Last Bastion 172

KINKY FRIEDMAN,
    The Left Bank of Texas 177

GARY LAVERGNE,
    from *A Sniper in the Tower:*
        The Charles Whitman Murders 179

WILLIAM J. HELMER,
    The Madman on the Tower 184

JAMES R. GILES,
    One August Day in Texas 197

J. FRANK DOBIE

James Frank Dobie (1888–1964) was born on a ranch in Live Oak County, Texas. In 1910 he graduated from Southwestern University in Georgetown and in 1913 took an M.A. from Columbia University. He joined the Department of English at the University of Texas in 1914, left in 1917 to serve in the field artillery in World War I, and returned to the University in 1919. In 1922 he became secretary-editor of the Texas Folklore Society, and in 1929 published his first book, *A Vaquero of the Brush Country*. Many books were to follow, including such well-known titles as *The Longhorns* (1941) and *The Mustangs* (1952). The best of Dobie can be found in the personal essays of *Some Part of Myself* (1964). His major contribution to the Department of English was the creation of a course that would become famous, Life and Literature of the Southwest. In 1963 he took time to remember his long-time friendship with two other influential figures during what might be called the Dobie Era in Texas letters.

FOR YEARS WE THREE SAT TOGETHER

WALTER PRESCOTT WEBB AND I WERE BORN IN THE SAME year, 1888. He belonged to one drouth-scarred part of Texas, I to another. His father was a country schoolteacher who homesteaded a quarter-section of poor land; mine was a rancher who rather expected that education would lead his sons to a better occupation. Webb came to the University of Texas as instructor in history in 1918, while I was a soldier in France, four years after I had come as instructor in English. We advanced concurrently, along divergent ways, as underlings at the University.

Our friendship developed more after about 1930, it seems to me, but I was never close to him as I was with Roy Bedichek, the dearest comrade of my life. Webb had sides never revealed directly to me. Bedichek died shortly before noon of May 21, 1959, while sitting in a chair waiting for his wife's cornbread to cook so that he could eat an early lunch and then drive me and Wilson Hudson in his pickup out to Paisano, my place on Barton Creek in the hills west of Austin. When he drove to where cedar stumps were available he liked to haul some in for his fireplace. As writers and men, Bedichek, Webb, and Dobie have been linked together—mostly by Texas people—many times in speech and in print.

On the evening of March 8, 1963, two other men and I sat down as guests with Frank Wardlaw in his home. He said, "Walter Webb thought he would join us, but he will be late." After conversation and "the better adjuncts of water," we went to a Mexican restaurant. Nobody knew where we were. Before we got back to our homes a number of people had tried to telephone Wardlaw and me. About 6:30 o'clock Webb and his wife had been found on the ground near their over-turned car, he dead and she so severely injured that she had to remain in a hospital for three months.

Bedichek was a kind of peg on which my happiest associations with Webb hung. For years we three sat together, with other men, at the same table during fortnightly dinners, "papers," and discussions of the Town and Gown club of Austin, but talk at our table was seldom so free and personal as it always was at prolonged picnic suppers in the country. Bedichek was the habitual planner of these supper parties, also cooker of the steaks. A vegetarian by philosophy in the later years of his life, he never threw off on his own steaks. The earliest of these picnic suppers that I remember were not far beyond the Rob Roy ranch, some distance off the Bee Caves road in the hills west of Austin. Bedi liked to camp high up. At one hilltop camp we looked down on bullbats (nighthawks) booming as they dived for insects. After Webb, in 1942, acquired Friday Mountain ranch, a location there on Bear creek became our supping and conversation grounds, though in the '50s we went several times to a place I then owned in Burnet County named Cherry Springs—on account of wild cherry trees growing by Fall Creek.

I got so that I took along potato salad prepared by Bertha Dobie as nobody else could prepare it. Someone might take something else, but Bedichek brought steaks, bread, tomatoes, lettuce, beer, and so on, and then saw that each man paid his share. Nobody was host and the drinking was moderate—one can of beer for Bedi. Webb did not really care for any. When he took whiskey, on other occasions, a jigger without water would do him all evening. He had not drunk at all until he was about fifty. Sitting with the dons after dinner at his college in Oxford, he had developed a mild taste for wine. He craved coffee, which Bedichek was particular in boiling and which he furnished, along with pot, tin plates, knives and forks.

Mody Boatright and Wilson Hudson, both of the University of Texas English Department, were regulars at these campfire suppers. After Frank Wardlaw came as director of the University Press, he added to talk and geniality. Any time that John Henry Faulk or Glen Evans was in town, he was there. One time, during World War II, Faulk brought an Englishman along and in capping limericks with each other both proved themselves bottomless artesian wells. I remember Coke Stevenson, then governor, saying at one supper—the only one he attended—that the American frontiersman carried a rifle, an axe, and a Bible. This was at Friday Mountain. We were by the same water when Homer Price Rainey, president of the university, told us that the regents were out to gut him. Ours was no club in any organized way and we never had regular gatherings, but all of us were liberal enough to be for Rainey and against the reactionary regents who for several years dominated the university.

While dismissing Rainey, the regents, in October 1944, elected Dr. T.S. Painter as acting president. Immediately thereafter he said in a letter addressed to the faculty: "I want it definitely understood that I am not a candidate for the position of permanent president, and I would not accept it if it were offered to me." The regents wanted an agent. Before long it was clear that they had what they wanted. When, in May 1946, they elected him president and he accepted the offer, a caucus of faculty men asked Webb to formulate their opinions. At a special meeting of the faculty a few days later Webb countered a resolution "assuring President Painter of our support and cooperation" with one "deep regret that Dr. Painter has not reciprocated the trust the faculty reposed in him, but has, on the contrary, broken faith and violated his pledge." The Webb motion of disconfidence failed to carry by a vote of 160 to 186.

His *Divided We Stand* (1937) was a stand for fairness. Based on figures in *The World Almanac* and the United States census, it made out a case against the prospering North for keeping the South in poverty as a colonial dependent until Franklin D. Roosevelt and the New Deal reversed the trend. Later Webb made clear that vast oil fields and rising industrialism in the South resulting from World War II advanced the region's prosperity.

Few other men of his stature and intellectual power had experienced so intimately the choke of poverty. The extremity of it is set forth in his essay, "The Search for William E. Hinds." As prosperity made him aware of the independence that it gives to an individual, he became, it seems to me, more actively considerate of that basis of freedom for other individuals and for Texas and the South.

In his later years Webb drew a good salary as distinguished professor. Beyond salaries (and motion picture rights amounting to $10,000 on his book, *The Texas Rangers*), he prospered through investing earnings from teaching and writing—especially from two textbooks—in real estate. A few years ago he drew up a plan to enable faculty members of the University of Texas who so wished and who had the money to invest in real estate. This plan, as far as I know, never got into operation.

Several times I heard him speak of the influence of L.M. Keasbey on his life. Before World War I, Keasbey, a professor in the university, gave a course of economics—though it was entitled "institutional history"—in which he emphasized one way to get rich: invest in land that the activities of an increasing population will make more valuable, very valuable if the land be chosen judiciously. At the time Webb was absorbing directions to the "unearned increment," an Austin peddler and then wholesale shipper of vegetables named M.H. Crockett took the Keasbey course. He, as I observed and as I heard him tell with pride, became expert in anticipating traffic routes of the city; he died one of the richest property owners in it.

Webb wrote little on civil rights. A few years after the decision of the Supreme Court of the United States on the desegregation of public schools, he could write and speak on the South's advancing economic prosperity without touching on the Negro economically or otherwise. Yet he did not ignore the subject. In a paper to have been delivered at Rice University shortly after he died, he said: "The southerner is so concerned with the racial issue that he has no time for anything else. This is the first issue that has plagued the South since 1820…The racial issue is too heavy to move; it is too green to burn; the best we can do for the present is to plow around it and cultivate the rest of the field."

Friday Mountain Ranch, in the hills seventeen miles southwest of Austin, consists of approximately a section of land that was, when Webb acquired it, eroded, devoid of humus, bare of vegetation beyond trees, cedars on the hills, and broomweeds in the valley. He had wastage accumulated at cotton gins east of Austin hauled out to spread on the ground. He applied commercial fertilizer to plots no longer tillable. While he was Harmsworth professor of American history at Oxford University, 1942–43, he gave his address to the English Who's Who as Friday Mountain Ranch, Austin, Texas. He belonged to it. During the terrible drouth that began late in the '40s and did not end until 1957 he made slow progress in restoring the soil and growing a turf of grass—a turf that reached its climax the spring he died.

He figured that the land should some day pay for the expenses he had been out on it. It did, by increase of real estate prices. Beyond all, he valued and enjoyed grass for itself, beautiful on any land, the mark of bounty on ground once impoverished. Several times when I was with him where grass flourished I saw him gather seeds of sideoats grama, little bluestem, Indian grass, and switch grass to take to Friday Mountain and scatter around. I suppose he bought seeds by the bushel also. In planning near the end of his life to transfer title to the land, he chose as purchaser a friend, Rodney Kidd, who would maintain the turf.

He was not a naturalist in the way that Bedichek was, but he observed. Twice at least he told me that we had missed much out of life by not learning botany while growing up in the country. One time as four or five of us were riding in a car along Fall Creek in Burnet County he called out to halt. He had spotted a hackberry about twenty feet high, growing up through the hollow trunk of a big dead live oak. He did not swim, but the pools of water impounded by dams he had constructed across Bear Creek gave him as much pleasure as any swimming hole ever gave any swimmer.

His brief book *Flat Top: A Story of Modern Ranching*, printed and published by Carl Hertzog of El Paso in 1960, is on grass and a man of grass names Charles Pettit. In 1938 Mr. Pettit bought 7,000 acres, to which he added 10,000 of worn-out, eroded farms. Year after year he combated weeds, prickly pear, and other competitors of grass. Year after year he applied fertilizer, planted clover, put out seeds of native grasses. He impounded over 3,400 acre feet of water, brought back a turf of grasses waist-high. After living with the land for a quarter of a century, he made the ranch pay. "The man really loves grass," Webb wrote. If Webb also had not loved grass, he would never have written this account of a model ranch in conservation practices.

About the time I was leaving for England late in 1945 to teach in a G.I. university, a civilized man of wealth who demanded anonymity granted a sum of money to relieve Roy Bedichek for a year from his duties as director of the Interscholastic League of Texas. He had a book to write. Webb invited him to take over a big upstairs room with a fireplace in the old Friday Mountain rock house, originally built for a boys' academy. Here, eager in his liberation, Bedichek made shelves of apple boxes to hold his books, carried water by bucket from a dug well, brought up wood, cooked over the fire. Through the year 1946 he worked at a table in front of the fireplace.

Chickens mechanically grown in rooms downstairs did not bother him. In fact, he based one of his richest chapters on "Denatured Chickens." Associating with himself, letting his richly-stored mind play, adding meanings to long-accumulating observations on people, birds, wild flowers, trees, and other forms of life, he achieved *Adventures with a Texas Naturalist*. Published in 1947, it was fourteen years later taken over by the University of Texas Press, an institution that Webb, more than any other man in the faculty, had furthered. "The Bedichek Room" remains, through Webb and Rodney Kidd, a feature at Friday Mountain.

Webb's *The Great Frontier*, officially published December 8, 1952, won the Carr P. Collins Award of a thousand dollars given annually by the Texas Institute of Letters. His response to the presentation was the after-dinner address to the institute—and mighty fidgety he was before the dinner. He asked me, also others, to notice how people received what he had to say, something so intimate to him that he shrank from making it public. He read his say. It was the most moving I have heard any man utter. It moved deeply all who heard it. He waited a long time to publish it, with some added details, under title of "The Search for William E. Hinds," in *Harper's Magazine,* July 1961. *Reader's Digest* published a condensation of it the following month.

The subject of autobiography came up several times among us while Bedichek was still on hand, iterating that he lacked the genius of Jean Jacques Rousseau for confession. As Webb was leaving my room one day in 1960, I again spoke about autobiography. He volunteered that he had written one while at Oxford University, 1942–43. He did not go into detail. The whole cannot, I believe, have anything else so intensely, so poignantly personal as the chapter in which he tells of a response received in 1904 to a letter he had written to the letter column of the *Sunny South*. It was from William E. Hinds of New York, an utter stranger, not only commending his ambition to be a writer but offering to send him books and magazines. Later this William E. Hinds urged him to get a college education and loaned him money while he was attending the University of Texas. Hinds died forty-five years before Webb's obligation to him became a chapter in published literature.

It resulted in many letters from unknowns, some sending money to help students as Hinds had helped Webb. For years he had been concerned over some way to requite Hinds and had given financial aid to able but needy students. He now set up the William E. Hinds scholarship fund at the University of Texas. After his death a check donating money to it was found in his pocketbook; it is an ultimate beneficiary in his will. The Hinds-Webb scholarship fund is now the official name.

I have no recollection of having heard Webb speak at any time of his soul, his religion, or God. He belonged to no church, ignored churches, liked some free-thinkers, some churchmen, especially Dr. Edmund Heinsohn, long pastor of the University Methodist church in Austin. After Heinsohn became a member of Town and Gown years ago, he often sat with Bedichek, Webb, and Dobie. He conducted Bedichek's funeral services, reading into them an interpretation of the man's character. At Webb's funeral he read an interpretive sketch of Webb's life. "I remain an agnostic," Somerset Maugham wrote in *The Summing Up*, "and the practical outcome of agnosticism is that you act as though God did not exist." As far as I can see, Walter Webb's positive goodness bore no relation to what is called God. His conduct was not determined by Biblical injunctions or by expectation of reward in some sort of post mortem existence. His mother is said to have been a fundamentalist, his father a skeptic who read the Bible in order to refute more specifically some of her credulities. I cannot imagine Webb's "praying for guidance," but at one time he believed in something beyond. After he married in 1916 he was teaching in San Antonio and became so low-spirited over the future that he, as I recall his story, was about to take a job in a jewelry store. . . . He consulted a noted fortuneteller known as Madam Skirls. She said: "The child will be a girl. I see nothing but books." With books he continued.

If the radical right appeared unjust and undemocratic to him, the radical left increasingly annoyed him. He was not a crusader and was not contentious. He sometimes wished, he once told me, that he did not have to think. He hungered after brightness and cheerful talk. His sense of humor tended to progress from anecdotes of rusticity to sharp wit. He loved stories, especially of people, and told them well. He held—at one time, at least—that a certain strengthening of the mind comes through playing poker. He liked to play poker and played with skill.

One time while we were walking along the railroad about Third Street in Austin, we stopped beside an old-time locomotive, stationary, throbbing with power. Webb said, "That is the greatest manifestation of power in the world." I told him that out of respect for its symbolism of power, Doctor Sanders, professor of Latin and Greek at Southwestern University about the beginning of the century, would remove his hat in salute to a steam engine pulling a train past him.

Whether Webb actually ever hated anybody I cannot say. I never heard him express hatred of any kind. He could be caustic, as when he wished that birth control had been in practice before a certain individual was born. He was more inclined to set forth the facts about a man than to praise or condemn. He inclined to the policy of Governor Jim Ferguson, who said, "I never use up energy hating." He was tolerant of human vagaries. He had developed as professor and historian under the late Dr. Eugene C. Barker, for years the head of the history department of the University of Texas. Barker's directness and his integrity were admirable. I myself owe considerable to him. The older he grew, the more conservative, even reactionary, he grew. He seemed in his later years to think that the masses of mankind need a kind of dictatorial direction in religion, politics, and other regions of life. While Dr. Barker became hostile, in his acrid way, to the New Deal and a strong bolster to the by-no-means-intellectual regents who deposed Rainey, mainly for being a New Dealer, Webb was strong for Franklin D. Roosevelt, as he was later for Truman. But he was never against Barker. "I did not understand him," I heard him say, "but he was my friend and supporter. He was open, generous, fearless. I remember him with respect."

Webb maintained a dim view of certain English teachers under whom he had studied in the University of Texas. He acknowledged no debt to them in mastering the craft of writing. Some time in the 1920's he was avidly reading O. Henry and trying out his own hand on short stories. I remember one based on an electric sign above Joske's store in San Antonio that every night flashed on the picture of a cowboy roping a steer.

I wish he had written more on the craft of writing. I quote from his essay "On the Writing of Books," published in *The Alcalde*, June 1952, (and repeated with changes and additions in his presidential address to the American historical association, reproduced in the *Texas Observer*, January 24, 1959):

It takes a good deal of ego to write a book. All authors have ego; most of them try to conceal it under a cloak of assumed modesty which they put on with unbecoming immodesty. This ego makes itself manifest in the following ways: (1) The author believes he has something to say. (2) He believes it is worth saying. (3) He believes he can say it better than anyone else. If he ever stops to doubt any one of these three beliefs, he immediately loses that confidence and self-deception—that ego, if you please—so essential to authorship. In effect, the author, to write a book, spins out of his own mind a cocoon, goes mentally into it, seals it up, and never comes out until the job is done. That explains why authors hide out, hole up in hotel rooms, neglect their friends, their family and their creditors . . . they may even neglect their students. They neglect everything that may tend to destroy their grand illusion.

The longer Webb jousted with words and thoughts, the finer-tempered his blade became. His use of the specific to bring home an idea suggests in style Jesus' application of the parable. His "The American West, Perpetual Mirage" (*Harper's Magazine*, May 1957) is as brilliant as any historical essay I have read. With what economy does he set forth the core!:

> The overriding influence that shapes the West is the desert. That is its one unifying force. It permeates the plains, climbs to all but the highest, mountain peaks, dwells continuously in the valleys, and plunges down the Pacific slope to argue with the sea.

Webb's generalizations are conclusions drawn from and supported by the concrete:

> Western history is bizarre because of the nature of what it has got. The historians and other writers do what men have always done in the desert. They make the best of what little they do have. Westerners have developed a talent for taking something small and blowing it up to giant size, as a photographer blows up a photograph.
>   They write of cowboys as if they were noble knights, and the cowmen kings. They do biographies of bad men, Billy the Kid, the Plummer gang, and Sam Bass, of bad women like Calamity

Jane, of gunmen like Wyatt Earp and Wild Bill Hickok . . . They blow the abandoned saloon up into an art museum, and Boot Hill into a shrine for pilgrims. In Montana Charlie Russell is better than Titian, and in the Black Hills Frederick Remington is greater than Michelangelo. Custer, who blundered to his death, taking better men with him, found a place in every saloon not already pre-empted to that travesty on decency and justice, Judge Roy Bean.

Some commentators have characterized Webb as "a great Texan." "We Texans," he wrote me in 1957, "have been as insular as Kansas—God save the mark." I remember well, with a certain personal shrinking, a period when his boundaries and my boundaries were to an extent circumscribed by the boundaries of Texas. Each of us in his way passed to a perspective beyond geographical lines, though each remained deeply marked by the land he lived in and by the inhabitants of that land. The greatness of Webb was as a man. "Man thinking"—Emerson's definition of a scholar—does not have around his head a band welded there by the confines of a province, by clerical ukases, or by any other mundane restrictions. Webb was not "finely suited" to life at Oxford University. He belonged to and marked the University of Texas. Only a few months before the end he published an opinion that it now had "within its grasp" the long sought-for status of "a university of the first class." All the while he maintained the critical judgment of "man thinking:"

Men at Oxford are free to follow their compass of truth wherever the needle points without looking over their shoulders to see what hounds are pursuing them. Professors are not even under suspicion. An Oxford man can attend a mass meeting in London and participate without jeopardizing his job. England is not afraid to have views expressed. England, with all its apparent stupidities, seems to know what a university really is.

In "For Whom the Historian Tolls," in *An Honest Preface and Other Essays*, with an introduction by Joe B. Frantz (1959), Webb provided this economical illumination:

> [Articles by historians in historical journals] are correct, the sentences usually—after the editors get through with them—are grammatical, and the footnotes are properly right at the bottom of the page. But one finds in them little charm, few vivid figures of speech, and practically none of that soft luminosity—an indefinable quality—which suffuses good writing. The reader may be informed, but he is rarely lured, enthralled, or captivated by the art of the performance.

Webb's chief research was for facts to lead to understanding. His superiority as an historian lies in his perception, his power of thought, his mastery of language, his interpretations of the land and the ever-evolving currents of human affairs. Not long after his first major book, *The Great Plains*, came out in 1931, Clem Yore of Colorado reported on a gathering of Western fiction writers who had been unaware of the meaning of barbed wire, windmills over wells drilled into the ground, the treeless plains themselves until Webb enlightened them. In his last big book, *The Great Frontier*, he interprets the western hemisphere as a frontier for the expansion of Europe. He says plainly and emphatically that America has been consuming irreplaceable natural resources and that prosperity based on such procedure cannot continue. He even questions the continuance of democracy. This book came out during the outrage of McCarthyism and of the House Un-American Activities Committee's blackguard betrayals of human rights. Some fanatics, without reading the book, slammed it as an "un-American" rebuke to "free enterprise." Webb never considers boosters as exemplars of patriotism.

The first Mrs. Webb, Jane Oliphant, after having been married to Walter for more than forty-three years, died in the summer of 1960, survived by a daughter, Mildred, of whom father as well as mother was very fond. In December of 1961, he married Terrell Maverick, widow of the late Maury Maverick of San Antonio, vivacious in mind and body, delightful and sensible too.

Considering his love for her and considering her marrying him, he said, "This is an unexpected dividend from life." He was openly naïve in expressing joy in her being. He had, as it were, been born again. His happy ardency made his friends rejoice. During the summer of 1962 while he was lecturing at the University of Alaska, she unable to accompany him as both had planned, he airmailed a letter to her every day. He had never seemed so eagerly active over the publication of one of his own books as he was over publishing *Washington Wife*, by Ellen Maury Slayden, the manuscript of which Terrell Webb had inherited and which both of them foreworded. They autographed the book in a San Antonio bookstore the last afternoon of Webb's life.

Any man who has seen and been a part of life wants to leave it before decomposing into a juiceless vegetable. Webb died standing up, as Caesar considered it meet for a man to die. In a flash he passed from wisdom and happiness to the finality of death. No person who has added as much to the heritage of human life as Walter Webb added ceases to be. His thinking, his writing, and his standing up will surely continue as elements of his projected shadow. ★

1963

BERTRAM ROTA

Bertram Rota (1903–1966) was an English dealer in rare books and manuscripts, and as such he did business with the Harry Ransom Humanities Research Center at the University of Texas at Austin. A member of the Anglo-Texan Society, he always enjoyed his visits to Austin, where he and Frank Dobie quickly became good friends. In "The Night of the Armadillos" Rota presents an interesting account of a visit to Dobie's Paisano Ranch, about fifteen miles southwest of Austin. Since the late 1970s the Texas Institute of Letters, along with the University of Texas, has sponsored Paisano Fellowships for two writers or artists who live on the Ranch for a term of six months each.

THE NIGHT OF THE ARMADILLOS

WE SWUNG OFF THE HIGHWAY ABOUT A DOZEN MILES OUT of Austin and headed for Barton Creek, down a deteriorating road which soon became a winding track, testing the springs of the Ford Falcon.

Avoiding only the potholes deep enough to bury a sizeable corpse Franklin drove as if axle-deep ruts and knee-high boulders were commonplace, as they probably are on some of the byways of Texas. He did swing sharply when cattle-grids over a stream could be by-passed by open gates and he even stopped for closed gates. At these, Warren (barely recognisable in leisure clothes as the Associate Director of the Humanities Research Center of the University of Texas) descended smartly, opened the gates for our passage and religiously closed them behind us, for which piety he was compelled to chase us and leap perilously aboard as the station-wagon gathered way again.

At length we slithered down a bank, rounded a bend on perhaps two of the four wheels and found ourselves at Bee Cave, within sight of the long, low ranch-house of Paisano, country retreat of that beloved doyen of Texan, South-western and indeed all-American authorities on natural history, folk-lore and ranching, J. Frank Dobie.

The Master was there. We could see him, seated on the porch in the evening sunshine. His gay plaid shirt and his worn jeans proclaimed him at ease. His white hair tumbled over his brow as he gazed intently through the longest-barrelled field glasses I ever saw. Even when we drove within a few yards, climbed out of the car, and stood mute around the porch, Frank remained glued to the glasses as if spell-bound. At length he lowered them and motioned to the nearest of us.

"Take a look," he said. "I've been watchin' the grass wavin' on that bluff over there. That's po'try. And look at the mockingbird on that wire fence."

Then the grand old man climbed to his feet, standing four-square on legs forever bowed by half a lifetime on horseback. His blue eyes twinkled at us as he bade us welcome and called for his Mexican boy Tomas to bring us chairs and drink.

"Are you-all whiskey men or beer men?" he asked. Thirsty from the drive we opted for beer.

"Then are you bottle men or glass men?" was his next question.

Two Texans and the Londoner confessed, almost shamefacedly, to a preference for glasses. Frank forgave us and heaped coals of fire on our heads by calling for cold stone mugs, beaded with frost from the refrigerator. The light beer gurgled, the mugs rose lip-high and the amber fluid did its refreshing work.

Then we were sitting, lounging, or heel-squatting in the Texan style; a relaxed, contented group. As the conversation eddied I stole a glance at my companions. Doc Roberts, guardian of one of the richest rare book and manuscript collections in the land; Bill Ferguson, attorney and book-collector (I suspect in the reverse order); John Henry Faulk, erstwhile New York broadcaster, returned to his native Texas; Franklin Gilliam, Austin bookseller (*the* Austin bookseller) and Frank Dobie himself, whose house and head are stuffed with books. It was easy to see what brought us so naturally together.

They were talking of books, winking out from the old man's memory the name of some barely-known pamphlet with an early El Paso imprint. "I don't know exactly," he said (giving them the author, title, printer, date, and quick précis of the contents, with the authority of a Library of Congress card), "but you can look for yourselves after dinner. I've got it inside. Got it in New Orleans in 1910."

Was there an almost imperceptible chuckle in his voice? Why shouldn't there be?

I told them of a snippet I had found, from a Paris newspaper of 1869, recording that the leader of a party of Polish labourers had passed through New Orleans en route for a site on the banks of the Trinity River, where he had acquired fifty thousand acres of land for one dollar, to set up a colony. Even in those days it must have been cheap, or a generous Texan gesture.

As the light fell and the air cooled a little it seemed to me that the loud susurration of crickets which had filled my unaccustomed ears throughout became even louder and more insistent. I remarked that at home in London a stray cricket was not uncommon and that in the English countryside one might hear scores, in a babel of tiny chirpings, but that I had never before encountered the strong rhythmic beat which I heard here, as if the whole chorus was taking its time from a leader.

"That's just what they do," Dobie told me. "And as it gets cooler they get quicker. There was a fellow who worked out a formula—I've got it some-where—so that by counting the number of chirrups in a minute and applying the formula you can tell the temperature."

This time no suspicion of a chuckle in the voice suggested that a tender-foot Limey was having his leg pulled, and I shall believe forever in the wonder of Nature's thermometer.

Now the Master rose and led us to a dining table splendid with appetising sights and aromas. Crisp salads, fruits and cheeses, great bowls of pimentos, hot breads, and the piece-de-resistance—a sizzling roast lamb, served with baked yams and the traditional Mexican dish of frijoles. With these Pinto beans our host had cunningly mixed some small onions and a few tiny green

Chili peppers of astonishing power. He warned his uninitiated foreigner of their perils, and we fell to.

Never has a meal gone more happily, as good stories, strange facts, and purple lies were washed down, and all the world wondered at the mounds of lemon meringue pie which, having surely been made by magicians disappeared by equal magic.

Now, like Anadyomene from the foam, hoary-headed Frank Dobie rose at the head of the table.

"Gentleman," he said, "I want to give you a toast."

I shrank back in my chair as inconspicuously as possible, anticipating a courtesy to the visitor but a little abashed at the prospect of having to respond, however informally, to these good fellows.

"I want you to drink with me," said Frank, with a telling pause, "to Anthony Rota."

Astonished, delighted, and relieved that I could join in the toast, I had to swallow hard to hide my emotion at the thought that the warm goodwill was this moment reaching five thousand miles across half a continent and the wide Atlantic.

"Had a lovely letter from him this morning," Dobie confided. And this time there was an undisguised chuckle in his voice.

Now it was Franklin Gilliam's turn. He somehow produced, as if from his vest pocket, a large and handsome volume. We craned. It was "Buck Schiwetz's Texas," a newly-published album of delightful drawings of quiet corners of the State; old missions, court-houses, forts, graceful homes and remote towns.

Had Mr. Dobie seen it yet? No, Mr. Dobie hadn't. Obviously it was the ideal gift for him, and the sort of thing which Franklin thinks of first. The other guests inscribed the book in turn, but as it reached me, pen in hand and frantically composing my contribution, old Frank leaned over and took it from me. Bemused, I watched him write—and then hand back to me a book inscribed by all, not to the Master, not to my son, but to the luckiest and most grateful British bookseller who ever set foot in Texas.

Out on the porch again in the velvet night we sipped Jack Daniels, the Tennessee "sippin' whisky" and watched the fire-flies glittering in the buses and the brilliant Evening Star. Dobie quoted me Keats on the Evening Star and then moved on to Wordsworth. Here was my chance.

"Mr. Dobie, Sir," I said, "with your memory you may be able to put me right about some Wordsworth lines which I suspect I may be misremembering."

"I doubt it," said he, "but let's see."

Tongue in cheek, I began:—

"She dwelt among the untrodden ways . . ."

He nodded, and I continued:

"Beside the River Wandle."

"No!" he exploded. "Beside the springs of Dove."

"But that doesn't rhyme," I complained. "Because my version goes on:

A maiden in those far-off days

Whom there were very few to praise

And fewer still to fondle.

She had a rustic, woodland air

That was extremely hard to bear."

The Master put back his head and rocked with laughter. One up to Harry Graham and his delightful parody "Elsie Bloy"!

Now Franklin needed cigarettes and went to his car. He stepped off the foot-high porch and recoiled with a shout.

"Mis' Dobie! Look what's here"!

We rushed to the edge and peered at a white shape. Franklin switched on the headlights. An armadillo! As large as life, and twice as natural in the eyes of a Londoner who had never seen this prehistoric survival outside the London Zoo. With the poet I could sing:

"I've ne'er seen an armadillo

Nor yet a daffodil

A-dillowing in his armour

And I s'pose I never shall."

But now I had! A good two feet long and armoured like a tank the creature quietly nibbled grass, quite unruffled.

"Dang it," said old Frank, "I don't know that I've ever seen one by night before. I've seen 'em by day occasionally. They're supposed to have come up here from South America through Mexico, but I'd like to chase 'em back. They root up everything I plant. Done more damage than I can bear."

Looking along the beam of the headlights I saw a movement. Then a whitish-grey shape. Another armadillo! Then another! And another! Six in all! A school of armadillos!

This was too much for Dobie.

"Drive 'em off!" he shouted. "Drive 'em into the creek!" Without creaking himself, he leapt from the porch and charged the herd. Short-sighted creatures, they did not see him until he was amongst them, thwacking away. Then they scattered and ran.

"Hold 'em!" yelled Dobie. "Head 'em off!"

We plunged through knee-high grass, whooping frenziedly. I chased one monster who seemed to be a little slower over a hundred yards than I am myself, even now. I passed him and turned in his path, but with something near a leer he slipped sideways under a barbed-wire fence and was gone.

John Henry was doing well, feinting at his adversary, both poised for a dart either way. Bill Ferguson seemed to think that his prey had climbed a tree. Franklin was in the car, manoeuvring so that his lamps would light the scene. Doc Roberts was on all fours, pretending to be an armadillo himself. Napoleonic, the Master stood in the glare of the car's headlights, directing the battle. It was a fair fight, six to six, but the armadillos won. In a sudden scurry all were gone and quietness reigned.

Six chastened men puffed their way back to the porch and to the solace of Jack Daniels. Probably only one of them, sippin' again, could barely believe it was all true and that he had not merely dozed for a moment at his desk in London, over a story by W. H. Hudson, soon to awake amongst the books at Bodley House. ★

1960

JOE B. FRANTZ

Joe B. Frantz (1917–1993) was born in Weatherford, Texas. In 1938 he graduated from the University of Texas with a degree in journalism. Later, following distinguished service in the Navy during World War II, he returned to the University and received his doctorate in 1948, working with Professor Walter P. Webb. His numerous books include *Gail Borden: Dairyman to a Nation* (1951); with Julian E. Choate, Jr.; *The American Cowboy: The Myth and the Reality* (1955); and *Texas: A Bicentennial History* (1976). The sketch of the funerals of Roy Bedichek and J. Frank Dobie is a typical example of Frantz's lively narrative manner.

from THE FORTY ACRE FOLLIES

AT BEDICHEK'S FUNERAL BERTHA DOBIE WAS MORE uncomfortable than the widow, for Frank Dobie attended and sat beside her. Bertha was a devout Methodist, and Frank was an equally devout and evangelical atheist. Although the service was conducted by Edmund Heinsohn, pastor of the University Methodist Church, and he had the good taste to soft-pedal orthodox religious dogma in speaking of Bedichek, whose religious beliefs were strictly his own and had little in common with traditional teachings, Dobie grunted and heaved through the whole service. Without bothering to lower his voice, he kept a drumfire going throughout the service:

"Cant! Pure cant!" he would say in a voice that could be heard several rows away.

"Hush, Frank!" Mrs. Dobie would jab him, as if he were a kid who wouldn't behave in church.

"Mummery!"

"Hush, Frank!"

"I don't care," he'd whisper. "Ed Heinsohn ought to be ashamed for saying such things when Bedi can't answer back."

On the way from the church, Dobie announced to all who would listen: "When I die, I don't want my body inside any damned church where some preacher can insult my mind!"

"Frank, hush!"

It was a bad day for Mrs. Dobie.

Heinsohn, an old B Haller who practiced law successfully for eleven years before turning minister of the gospel, had the dubious honor of officiating at the funerals of all three men. He was about the only preacher that any of them looked on as a friend. Webb once snorted to me when another local preacher's name arose, "Hell, he's the kind who, if he ever visited a whorehouse, would ask for a ministerial discount!" I never felt the preacher's holiness again.

It may have been that same preacher who was forever filling his pulpit with guest speakers. Webb maintained that the minister was too lazy to prepare his own sermons. Eventually the preacher got around to Webb, asking him to preach on religion among the cowboys. Webb accepted.

On that particular Sunday morning, Webb arose in the pulpit, looked out over the congregation, said that he had been requested to talk about the religion of the cowboy. Then he grinned his rail-splitting grin and said, "The cowboy didn't have any religion." And sat down. He never had to fear another invitation.

When Dobie died, in 1964, Frank Wardlaw, director of the UT Press, and I converged on Mrs. Dobie's home to help with the burial arrangements. First, we called the White House, where Dobie had recently been a guest to receive the Medal of Freedom from President Johnson, got the president out of a state dinner, told him the news, and let him say the proper words to Mrs. Dobie. Johnson had a rural man's ability to comfort at the time of death.

Then we faced a dilemma: how to bury Dobie without offending his spirit and without offending his widow. Dobie had left clear instructions how he was to be buried. He preferred to be placed on a loft of sticks, Indian fashion, whence the buzzards and animals could gradually return him to the earth he cherished. Mrs. Dobie thought that was brutal. He had an alternative—to be wrapped in a wagon sheet and allowed to disintegrate and fuse into the soil at his beloved ranch, Paisano, west of Austin. That contravened state and county health laws. Under no circumstances did he want to be embalmed or fussed over by a preacher in a church.

Dobie also wanted a case of Scotch (for non-Texans or folks from Dallas) at his feet, a case of Jack Daniel's at his head, and a couple of dozen friends to toast his departure. They would gather to exchange Frank Dobie stories as they quaffed his last hospitality, and recount all the good and the bad. He wanted no eulogy, but memories. Mrs. Dobie thought that was pagan.

Wardlaw and I contacted an understanding friend, Harry Ransom, who persuaded the Department of Drama to vacate Hogg Auditorium for a couple of days so we could hold a mammoth memorial service there. We had only two speakers and no prayers. One speaker was Dr. Heinsohn, who knew Old Pancho well enough to stick to the Bible, which Dobie loved for its rhythms; while Wardlaw, a Presbyterian minister's son with a gift for brush arbor oratory, gave an appreciation of Dobie's spirit. If you had wandered in off the street not knowing either of the principals, you would have been unable to say which of the speakers was a minister and which was a layman. In fact, several people from out of town asked me later to identify that fiery preacher with the South Carolina accent, meaning Wardlaw.

Mrs. Dobie got her preacher, and Pancho didn't stir uneasily in his new grave in the Texas State Cemetery from being exposed to the confines of a church. ★

1983

BILLY LEE BRAMMER

Billie Lee Brammer, a journalist and novelist, was born in 1929 in Oak Cliff, Dallas, Texas. After graduating from North Texas State College, he worked as a press aide for Senator Lyndon B. Johnson from 1955 to 1959. During that period he wrote *The Gay Place* (1961), a novel that cast an LBJ type as the governor of Texas. Brammer worked briefly for *Time* magazine and taught writing at SMU in 1970. He died in 1978. His novel is saturated with the texture and atmospherics of Austin in the 1950s. The excerpt below includes the opening panoramic description of the countryside from the Gulf Coast to the capital city, and a typical scene set at Scholzgarten's, every liberal's favorite watering hole in that era.

from THE GAY PLACE

THE COUNTRY IS MOST BARBAROUSLY LARGE AND FINAL. It is too much country—boondock country—alternately drab and dazzling, spectral and remote. It is so wrongfully muddled and various that it is difficult to conceive of it as all of a piece. Though it begins simply enough, as a part of the other.

It begins, very like the other, in an ancient backwash of old dead seas and lambent estuaries, around which rise cypress and cedar and pine thickets hung with spiked vines and the cheerless festoons of Spanish moss. Farther on, the earth firms: Stagnant pools are stirred by the rumble of living river, and the mild ferment of bottomland dissolves as the country begins to reveal itself in the vast hallucination of salt dome and cotton row, tree farm and rice field and irrigated pasture and the flawed dream of the cities. And away and beyond, even farther, the land continues to rise, as on a counterbalance with the water tables, and then the first faint range of the West comes into view; a great serpentine escarpment, changing colors with the hours, with the seasons, hummocky and soft-shaped at one end, rude and wind-blasted at the other, blue and green, green and gray and dune-colored, a staggered faultline extending hundreds of miles north and south.

This range is not so high as it is sudden and aberrant, a disorder in the even westerly roll of the land. One could not call it mountain, but it is a considerable hill, or set of hills, and here again the country is transformed. The land rises steeply beyond the first escarpment and everything is changed: texture, configuration, blistered façade, all of it warped and ruptured and bruise-colored. The few rivers run deep, like old wounds, boiling round the fractures and revealing folds of slate and shell and glittering blue limestone, spilling back and across and out of the hills toward the lower country.

The city lies against and below two short spiny ribs of hill. One of the little rivers runs round and about, and from the hills it is possible to view the city overall and draw therefrom an impression of sweet curving streets and graceful sweeping lawns and the unequivocally happy sound of children always at play. Close on, the feeling is only partly confirmed, though it should seem enough to have even a part. It is a pleasant city, clean and quiet, with wide rambling walks and elaborate public gardens and elegant old homes faintly ruined in the shadow of arching poplars. Occasionally through the trees, and always from a point of higher ground, one can see the college tower and the Capitol building. On brilliant mornings the white sandstone of the tower and the Capitol's granite dome are joined for an instant, all pink and cream, catching the first light.

આ

The two young men sat out under the trees in straw-bottomed chairs, barking their shins against the wooden tables. They sat waiting, looking glum. Record music came from a speaker overhead, somewhere in the trees. The music was turned loud so it could be heard above the noise from a next-door bowling alley. There were periods of relative quiet when the bowling slacked off and the records changed, during which they could hear halfhearted cheers from a lighted intramural field a block away, near the college, but the record music predominated. The sounds from the bowling alley ruined only the ballads.

Roy Sherwood looked around and groaned.

"You don't like music?" Willie said. "And a gay party atmosphere?"

"I like music fine," Roy said. "I just don't like these gaptoothed teddy boys raping some old favorite with a chorus of ex-truckdrivers behind them going 'ooh-ah, oom-ah, ooh-ah.'" He looked around the beer garden impatiently. "Can't they turn it down?"

"That would be a violence to the whole idea of the Dearly Beloved," Willie said.

"Exactly," Roy said.

Willie said: "It's not so bad. What was it Rinemiller was saying the other day?"

"Rinemiller's a sewer," Roy said.

"He said it was genuine. Simple and alive and—"

"A sod and a sewer," Roy said conclusively. He looked around for the waitress.

They sat talking. There were twenty or thirty others, mostly young people, out under the trees, sitting at the unwashed tables, and through the windows of the building the boiled faces of some of the old-time customers were visible. It was still very early in the evening: The lights had just now come on, and the Dearly Beloved Beer and Garden Party was only partly filled.

A waitress finally appeared. She was a pretty girl, wearing a white uniform with a faded checkered apron. She smiled and said: "Ike and Mike—my favorite customers."

"Stop calling us that," Roy said. "Think of something else." He did not look at the waitress, but gave his attention instead to a group of undergraduates and their dates just now arriving.

"You don't like Ike and Mike?" the girl said.

"It's just that neither of us wants to be Ike," Willie said.

The girl nodded. "You want menus?"

"Some of the light," Willie said.

"How about a pitcher?" the waitress said. The two young men hesitated, looking at each other, numbed momentarily by the weight of decision. The bowling eased off some next door. A singer's voice came to them through the trees:

Tew . . .

Spen' . . .

One . . .

Naaaht . . .

Wishyew . . .

"Let's get a pitcher," Willie said.

"We wait for Huggins, he'll buy pitchers for everyone," Roy said. The waitress swayed slightly to the music, looking away, her eyes foggy.

"You strapped again?" Willie said.

"No. Trying to avoid it, though. I'm budgeting myself. Watch the pennies, the dollars take care of themselves."

The waitress leaned down and rested her elbows on the table. She looked at the young men closely. "It's only seventy-five cents," she said.

"It mounts up," Roy said. "And I'm out of work."

"You make thirty dollars a day, for God's sake," the waitress said. "I read it in the paper."

"Only when we're in session," Roy said. "And that money's got to last me the year round. Otherwise, I'd have to practice the law. Or live off lobbyists. You tryin' to corrupt me?"

"Two glasses of the light," Willie said. "And when you see Huggins come in, ask if he wants to order some pitchers."

The waitress nodded. "I'll get your lousy fifteen-cent beers," the girl said.

She turned, walked across the garden and up the stone steps into the building.

The beer garden was shielded on three sides by the low yellow frame structure, a V-shaped Gothicism, scalloped and jigsawed and wonderfully grotesque. The bar, the kitchen and dining spaces were at the front; the one side and the back were clubrooms for the Germans who came to town once or twice a week to bowl and play cards. The Germans had bought half the block years before and built the bar and clubrooms. During the hard times of the 1930s they had begun leasing out the front part as a public bar, an arrangement that had proved so profitable that it was continued through the war years and was now apparently destined for the ever-after.

Just prior to the war there had been rumors of German-American Bund meetings in the back rooms. People in town talked about seeing goosestepping farmers through the windows, their arms raised in fascist salute. But nothing was ever proved; no one ever came forward to substantiate the claims, and after Pearl Harbor it was nearly forgotten. There was even a little plaque got up to honor certain of the clientele gone off to war; there were waitresses who boasted of being Gold Star Sweethearts. Business—and the beer—had always been good, before, during, after the war, and even in recent years when some of Roy's and Willie's friends had petitioned for a change in names: when they wanted to call it the *Weltschmertz*. ★

1961

LARRY MCMURTRY

Born in Wichita Falls, Larry McMurtry grew up on a ranch near Archer City, Texas. He attended Rice University and took his B.A. in English from North Texas State University. Later he took an M.A. from Rice University. By that time, in the early sixties, he was well on his way to becoming the most significant Texas writer in the history of the state. His first novel, *Horseman, Pass By*, was published in 1961, followed by *Leaving Cheyenne* (1963) and *The Last Picture Show* (1965). Many more were to follow, including *Lonesome Dove* (1985), for which McMurtry won a Pulitzer Prize. In 1989 *Lonesome Dove* was turned into a notable TV miniseries. McMurtry has continued to turn out novels about the Old West and novels about Modern Texas for going on forty years. He has also published distinguished volumes of essays and authored many film scripts. In 2006 McMurtry and Diana Ossana won a Golden Globe and an Oscar for Best Adapted Screenplay for *Brokeback Mountain*. The excerpt below is from *In a Narrow Grave: Essays on Texas* (1968), McMurtry's highly insightful commentary on the Lone Star state. McMurtry lived in Austin for eight months, in 1963, just long enough to take the measure of the capital city about as accurately and acutely as anyone has. The sightings of J. Frank Dobie represent one of the great non-meetings in Texas cultural history.

from IN A NARROW GRAVE

I SAW MR. DOBIE ONLY TWICE, ONCE AT A LITERARY PARTY in Dallas in 1962, and the second time on a hot street in Austin only a month or two before he died. In Dallas he was a joy to watch, though in Dallas any happy man would be. It was February, but Dobie wore his white suit, and with that, his white hair and his roguish grin he seemed amid that somber, wintry company to project the combined appeal of Buffalo Bill and

Dylan Thomas. In five minutes he had reduced the matrons to twinkles, giggles, and coos.

In Austin, I was walking down Travis Street toward noon of a hot summer day, on my way to visit a bookshop, when I saw Mr. Dobie starting up the hill below me. He had a book in his hand and had probably just emerged from the shop I was meaning to visit. As he approached I debated speaking, but the day was broiling, I was carrying my young son, and Mr. Dobie was obviously concentrating on getting up the hill and into the shade. He didn't look up, and I said nothing, but when I crossed the street at the foot of the hill I saw him at the top, his Stetson pushed back and his white hair fallen on his brow, resting a moment by a parking meter. Though I did not know him and at that time did not care for his books I felt that catch in the heart that always comes when I see that one of the Old Ones of this land will soon be gone, no more to ride the river nor follow the Longhorn cow.

&

Austin is a happy place, sort of; foreigners and easterners surrender their affections to Austin more readily than to any other place in the state. They come reluctantly, drawn by the fragrance of our cash, and a great many of them stay. It is a pretty, sunny town, the climate warm, the sky blue and unsmogged. The sun sets plangent and golden into the purple of the Austin hills at evening, and the moon, whiter than a breast, lights the Colorado River. The students, those darlings, return year after year like the swans of Yeats, unwearied by passion or conquest, young, clean, beautifully limbed, and, as often as not, innocently promiscuous. If, for some reason, the students fail to gather at one's bed, there are certain to be Wives, legislative, academic, or miscellaneous, some of them long in the tooth and lean in the shank, others graceful and nervous as does, but all of them, it sometimes seems, dedicated to the principle that the horn is always greener on the other guy.

Year after year literary celebrities descend on Austin, and, one by one, year after year, the Wives ambush them at the first bend in the party and hasten them off to bed. The results have been known to make sexual pessimists of both Wives and celebrities, but they also provide the indispensable raw material for the Southwest's most productive gossip mill.

My own period of residence in Austin was blessedly short. I lived there for eight months in 1963, and I feel no impulse to write at length about the city since there exists a lively and accurate book about it, William Brammer's *The Gay Place*. Mr. Dobie, Mr. Bedichek, and Dr. Webb lived in Austin for many years, but the city never became their spiritual property to the extent to which it is now the spiritual property of Mr. Brammer. How he may eventually improve the property we must wait to discover, but I am of the opinion that his slow-growing second novel *Fustian Days* will treat the Austin of the sixties as well as *The Gay Place* treated the Austin of the fifties.

During the last two months of my stay in Austin it was my good fortune to be thrown much in the company of Mr. Brammer. We were both, at the time, in respite of wives and money, and shared a house on Windsor Road. Mr. Brammer was at that time the local culture hero, *The Gay Place* having been published only two years before. He was thus a natural target for anyone in Austin who was aspiring, frustrated, or bored. The inrush of Wives threatened to wrench the hinges off the door, and Mr. Brammer faced it with the courteous and rather melancholy patience with which he would probably face a buffalo stampede. In the wake of the Wives came a sweaty and verbally diarrhetic mass of bored or bitter professors, broke or bitter politicians, protohippies with beach balls full of laughing gas, and broke-bored-bitter young journalists who looked like they had been using themselves for blotters.

In time I sealed off my part of the house and left Bill to cope with the crowd as best he could, but during the brief weeks when I spent my nights opening the door I got, it seemed to me, an adequate glimpse of Austin. It had, among other adolescent characteristics, a fascination with its own pubic hair, and a corresponding uneasy fear that its sexual development might stop just short of adequacy. Groupiness was endemic. No one might be missing from the group, lest he turn out to be somewhere better, with a wilder, more swinging group. In such a town the person who is sure of himself is apt to be literally crushed by the surging mobs of the insecure, all rushing to confirm themselves by association.

I am told that my view of Austin is too limited, that higher on the slopes, in secluded dells, the significant political and intellectual work of Austin goes on, serious, responsible, mature. Maybe, and again, maybe not. There are indeed a fair number of first-rate people on the faculty of the University, but for the most part these are all people whose accomplishment guarantees them the freedom to leave Austin frequently—a freedom most of them take full advantage of. Habitance there is occasionally convenient for them, but they scarcely alter the tone of the community. Indeed, it could even be argued that Austin has begun to work against them intellectually by encouraging them to think of themselves as a group.

Cliquishness can be especially insidious in a town the size of Austin, where those in favor seldom if ever receive any strong-minded local criticism. This same factor, as I have said, worked against Dobie and Webb and Bedichek.

The emotional activity most characteristic of Austin is, I think, the attempt to acquire power through knowledge. Accordingly, Austin is the one town in the state where there is a real tolerance of the intellectual; and yet one's final impression of Austin is of widespread intellectual confusion. Perhaps the phenomenon most expressive of this paradox is the University's rare book program. For the last decade, rare books have been sucked into Austin like particles of dust into a vacuum cleaner; the University's enormous and almost amorphous acquisitiveness remains the wonder, joy, and despair of the rare book world. No one can doubt that an extraordinary library is being formed in Austin, one whose potential usefulness is very great; yet the manner in which it is being formed leaves one a trifle abashed. The Humanities Research Center, for all its riches, comes too close to being a kind of intellectual's Astrodome. The University's almost frenzied acquisitiveness seems to stem not so much from a vision of the needs of future generations as from its own immediate intellectual insecurity. A successful acquisition brings a temporary sense of intellectual power, and it is the acquisition of books and manuscripts, rather than their use, which seems to be the dominant concern; that and the creation of a symbol of prestige (the Center) which the scholarly world cannot ignore.

This megalomaniacal acquisition of books, like the equally megalomaniacal boosterism which afflicts almost all our cities, might serve as a reminder that in an assessment of Austin (or Texas) there is yet a greater megalomaniac to be considered. Austin is Johnson's town, and before long the king will be returning to the counting house. What he will do there is not, at the moment, an especially fruitful subject for speculation, but it will not be likely to decrease the insecurity of Austin's intellectual community. Austin intellectuals have always been frightened and awed by Johnson's force, and, though the imagery differs, they accord him the sort of respect that Milton accorded Satan. ★

1968

THOMAS WHITBREAD

Thomas Whitbread was born in Massachusetts, and educated at Amherst and Harvard, where he earned his Ph.D. in 1959. That same year he joined the Department of English at the University of Texas in Austin. Here he continues to profess literature and poetry. He is the author of two books of poetry, *Four Infinitives* (1964) and *Whomp and Moonshiver* (1982). A third will be published in 2007. His "Argumentative Poem Against Certain Articles" expresses the kind of exasperation felt by many Texans—and Austinites—at having their state and city misrepresented by outside observers who don't take time to get the facts right before launching into preconceived generalizations.

ARGUMENTATIVE POEM AGAINST CERTAIN ARTICLES*

I am tired of articles against railroads and
against Texas.
Just last night, in the current *Harper's*, I read
An article against both. For sure against
railroads:
The dining car was a desert, the roomettes
empty
On the Texas Eagle (inferred), and the Texan
scenery
An unending sparse and level barrenness,
But why does she say that when she got to
Austin
She had to wash off "three days' worth of soot?"
I assure her

*In particular, "Days and Nights in Texas," by Barbara Probst Solomon, *Harper's* Magazine, November 1963.

The Missouri Pacific is dying (if it is, which
it isn't)
With a large fleet of diesel engines pulling it.
Now, she does have some things good to say of
Texas,
But gets mixed up, referring to "Lake Mansfield"
(There's a Mansfield Dam, and behind it a
Lake Travis,
Currently low to the anguish of boat dock
owners
And residents, but there's been little rain this
year, and water
Was drawn off to some blankety-blank rice
paddies),
And mixed up again in her list of happy roads,
Putting Bridle Path, a staid residential street,
Beside Bee Caves Road and Red Bud Trail,
real rovers
Through the hills west of town across the
Colorado,
And where are the "new motels" along old
Speedway?
That amusingly no longer aptly named dull
street?
There are no new motels on Speedway: you
can find them
On Interregional, mostly, or down on Town
Lake,
But she was only here nine months, and makes
some good
Points about Texas. What I really hate, what
deeply tires me
Is the ease, the uncaring, with which she

patronizes

The train. I can take, without liking, the sloppy
seeing

That lets her say nothing exists in Austin

Between "flat, somnolent countryside" and "the
station."

No suburbs? streets? homes? They are there by
the railside

And were there in '61, when she saw Saxton.

I can take, as faulty seeing or remembering,

Her reporting a sign, "EL PASO 585 miles,"

When the sign that was read "EL PASO 592."

Period. Bleaker, truer. Trivial?

I do not think so, though I am gullet-tired

Of inaccuracies. But what really galls

Is the uncaring ease with which this writer,

Partly reporter, partly distorter, says

"Empty," "vacant," "deserted," "menu cut to
the bone,"

Of the train I have been on six times, seen
arrive

In Austin fifty others in four years,

Including the nine months she was here, and

Even at non-

Holiday seasons seen actual people in!

"Well, railroads belonged to another time."

That's true,

In that passenger service is not what it was,

But I'll not have this writer tell me so.

If there are to be obituaries, let them

Be from elegiac people who can see

    With accuracy and report with sense. ★

1964

JONATHAN BRACKER

Born in New York City in 1936, Jonathan Bracker grew up in Louisiana and Texas. He studied creative writing at the University of Texas and taught English in Amarillo and Wichita Falls. His poems have appeared in many magazines and in three chapbooks. Bracker has lived in San Francisco since 1968. "Garten of the Gods" celebrates an experience enjoyed by many patrons of the old German beer garden. Scholzgarten is still a popular place on UT football home-game days, but the old-time charms it held when there were few watering holes in the city, are not much in evidence today. For a period in the 1980s the management was actively hostile to all young men wearing white baseball caps (frat boys mainly). It would seem that the gods have departed.

GARTEN OF THE GODS

Good people one has known
are like real bread
after supermarket stuff, water
after a strawberry shake.
With them one can walk.
Among them, two can talk.
In their company,
content to be contented,
one can sit afternoons under the trees
at Scholz's Garten, where a little breeze
alternates with sunshine on the back of necks.
I hope that you have such a place.
There
Lanza's voice

scratchily encourages all
to "Drink, drink, drink . . ."
There too much intellect's suspect
and if one thinks at all
it's of which leaves fall
on red checkered tablecloths
and which do not.
There blood may flood to faces, causing smiles.
Well, maybe it is the beer,
but with good people I have known
I was somehow changed; I shone. ★

1964

OLIVIA DWIGHT

Olivia Dwight is the pseudonym of Mary Hazzard, author of four novels and numerous plays under her own name. Hazzard graduated from Yale Drama School and has received fellowships from numerous prestigious organizations. Hazzard lives near Boston, but in the early 1960s she lived in Austin where her husband, Peter Swiggart, taught in the Department of English at the University of Texas. It was here that Hazzard, writing as Olivia Dwight, wrote a novel about the death of a famous writer who jumps from the Tower—or is pushed. (It's a mystery novel, after all.) The scene below is a marvelous comic sequence built around two of the campus's most famous structures. One detail that might be puzzling to some readers is that we are told that the professor-narrator—named John Dryden, another literary jest–has six eight-o'clocks. In those days there were no Tuesday-Thursday classes, and as a result classes met on MWF or TTS. This schedule was nothing to laugh at.

from CLOSE HIS EYES

I FINALLY FOUND WHAT SEEMED LIKE THE IDEAL PLACE for the trivial but arduous work I had to do. There was a cafeteria near the campus, one of those large, dark places that seem to have almost no customers but a few shabby old men sitting alone with coffee and pie. Not at meal times, of course; then it was crowded with students. But in the mornings there was no one there but the old men. Students going out for coffee between classes preferred the smaller, livelier places. I found that I could go there at nine after my class (they had given me six eight o-clocks), get a booth and a cup of coffee, and work till noon without feeling that I was unwelcome. I discovered the place in the first week, and by the second it had become my regular morning working place. Some of the waitresses got to know me and had sense enough not to disturb me with unnecessary table-wiping.

I was there as usual one morning in early March, with student papers and red pencils spread out on the table. I remember I was rather distressed at the moment because my coffee cup had made a brown ring in the middle of the first page of a theme on Beauty, and I was trying to scrub it away with a paper napkin but not succeeding; the coffee mixed with the ink, and my scrubbing wiped away more ink than coffee. I didn't want the student to think I had used his paper as a placemat, but there was nothing to do about the situation.

The Beauty assignment was turning out to be a better one than I had thought it would. One day in class my students had somehow got into a discussion of the meaning of the word "beautiful" and someone of course had wanted to know whether truth was really the same thing as beauty. I said I doubted it but allowed the discussion to go on. I knew what they were doing. They were trying to avoid a quiz they thought I had prepared for the last ten minutes of the class. I hadn't got around to preparing it, so I let them talk. Then, just before the bell rang, I told them that since they were so fascinated by the subject, why didn't they write a theme for me on Beauty, defining it as exactly as possible and giving as an example some object that they found beautiful. They were angry and felt that I had tricked them, but they had to write the themes. They would have had to write about something else anyway if that subject hadn't come up. I made them write a theme a week, not much compared with some colleges, but I couldn't deal with more than that, and I didn't have a wife to do it for me.

The reason these themes were interesting lay in the students' choice of beautiful objects. I saw for the first time how much loyalty the University had already managed to instill into its first-year students. The campus had two main sights, things to be proud of. One was the library tower. There is a wide pavement in front of the library, made of blocks of stone about a yard square. This pavement is very broad and very deep, but if you stand at the far edge of it in front of the library, you still have to crane your neck to see the top of the tower. The library part of the building looks like an ordinary, fairly modern campus building. It is long and made of cream-colored stone, has two stories besides the basement, and is full of tall windows. It looks like the physics building or the social science building or most of the other structures on campus.

Except for the tower. That, as I think I've said, has fourteen floors. Each floor holds quite a few offices, but the tower looks tall and thin from the outside, like an unusually large chimney sticking out of the library roof. Then, on top of the chimney part, above the fourteen floors, is perched a little Greek temple. I'm not making this up; it is a real temple, with Ionic columns all the way around. It's where they keep the bells. The whole tower is flood-lighted every night. It would have to be, I suppose, because of airplanes. But on the nights of great football or basketball victories there are special lights that turn the temple red (one of the school colors).

The other campus attraction is the fountain on the green below the library. You can get to it by walking along the path between the rows of statues and benches. It is large too, though nothing to compare with the tower, and represents Neptune and his sons going swimming (I think the inscription says, though it sounds wrong now that I think about it) on Sunday morning. Neptune is fat and covered with scales, and there are lots of small bronze dolphins frolicking around him and the sons. I am told that when one of the history professors first saw it after its unveiling, he exclaimed, "Ye gods and little fishes," and that is what it has been called, informally, ever since.

The reason I am telling you about these two things is that they turned out to be the Beautiful Objects described by more than half of my students. But it was worse than that; most of the girls chose the tower, and the boys chose the fountain. I have done only enough reading in Freud to hope that he was wrong, but I was embarrassed. I wondered if any of the students would remember this assignment next year when they hit Sophomore Psychology. ★

1961

CAROLYN OSBORN

Carolyn Osborn, who hails from Tennessee, has lived in Austin since 1951. In 1969 she received an M.A. in creative writing from the University of Texas. Her stories have appeared in many literary magazines, and she has published three collections of short fiction: *A Horse of Another Color* (1977), *The Fields of Memory* (1984), and *Warriors and Maidens* (1991). Approximately a fourth of her published work has been set in Austin. "The Vulture Descending Each Day," an excerpt from an unpublished novel, first appeared in The *Texas Quarterly* in 1968. The action takes place at the Elizabet Ney Museum, located at 304 E. 44th Street.

THE VULTURE DESCENDING EACH DAY

IT WAS USUALLY QUIET AT THE MUSEUM ON SATURDAYS when Mr. Issacs was there. An obscure place even in Austin, a small city where there were few obscurities, it was seldom visited. Located in a block of parkland, well back from the streets, surrounded by straggling cedar trees and high bushes, protected in front by a low rock wall, the Elizabet Ney welcomed the general public with an open gate and a path leading to the front door, but the general public, Mr. Issacs had observed, did not often come to see what Miss Ney had left them.

Saturday was Mr. Issacs's day to serve as the museum's keeper. All week long he looked forward to the one day he would be impeccably dressed in his only black suit with his gold watch chain stretched opulently across his vest instead of crumpled in his side pocket. He walked to the museum, a small, neat man doing his civic duty in his funeral clothes. He thought of his part-time job as a favor he could do the city although he took the dollar per hour pay they gave him. At the end of each month he donated his salary to the upkeep of the museum. It was not an outright bribe. He put the bills in the iron box in the front hall with the sign Voluntary Contributions posted above it; if he wanted he could always donate the thirty-five dollars to some other institution. The city, however, needed someone at the Elizabet Ney on Saturdays, and he needed something to do.

Mr. Issacs settled himself at the small desk behind a glass display case. Directly behind him double wooden doors were shut against March drafts; above the doors the only daylight in the room filtered through a wide north window rapidly being overgrown by a jungle of pot plants on the sill. In one corner the cut-stone fireplace had been boarded up to enclose an electric heater still buzzing and glowing. Though the ceiling was high and the stone walls must have been cold early in the morning, the place was now much too warm. He felt like a wizened plant in a dry greenhouse. Straight across the room in his line of vision was a bust of one of the governors of Texas, a rather grim looking old man. Mr. Issacs preferred to shift his eyes to the pleasant ringleted head of the daughter of another governor. All the Europeans except Miss Ney, who had been German, and her husband, a Scot, were segregated in an adjoining room. Mr. Issacs was encircled by Texas governors, judges, and heroes and oil portraits of Miss Ney and her patrons. He surveyed the room, acknowledging, as he usually did, that if his part-time job did not provide much human companionship, it did give him the company of some distinguished ghosts. He led, he reflected, a part-time life. He was a part-time sleeper, a part-time cook, a part-time dog walker—a continual mourner. His wife had been dead for two years and his recurrent wishful dream was that she was still alive. Yet, she'd died a miserable death. Cancer ate her up and when she was gone everyone said it was a merciful death. He agreed at the time, knowing it was better for her anguish to die, but he would have given the days he had left to him to hear her voice calling his name, her plaintive voice calling him to come to her room and turn her over.

"Who is the man handcuffed to the rock?"

Mr. Issacs, jolted out of his daydream by the intensity of the question, twisted around in his chair to look at a Mexican boy.

"How did you get in?" He was a small boy with a jagged haircut and old but well-shined shoes. His clothes were as clean and neatly pressed as Mr. Issacs's. Evidently his mother cared how he looked. A smudge of dust on his forehead showed he didn't pay much attention to himself. Probably he'd been running his hands over the sculptures. Some of them were not very well dusted.

"The back door." The boy pointed to the room where the Europeans were collected. "It was open." He walked around to Mr. Issacs's side and braced himself with one dirty hand against the glass case. Yes, he must have been touching the statues. Good sculpture should arouse the tactile sense, though he did not think Miss Ney's figures often did. Who wanted to pat an old baron's stony head—not the children dragged in by culture-conscious mothers. The only thing that ever interested them was Stephen F. Austin's plaster gun, and the fact that it didn't shoot was always a disappointment to the little machine-age monsters.

"Yes, I remember. I unlocked the door this morning." Mr. Issacs tapped the glass top with his dry fingers. The child had asked him something. What was it? He should answer. Visitors hardly ever asked him anything. When he had first started working he'd followed people around from room to room commenting on Miss Ney and her work, chattering, he soon perceived, mostly to himself. He retired to the desk to sit as mute as the rest of the statues . . . the child had asked about a statue, the man handcuffed to the rock.

"It isn't a statue exactly. It's a cast, a plaster cast taken from a statue of Prometheus, the god who brought fire to men."

"Why is he handcuffed to the rock?"

"He is being punished. Those old Greek gods knew how to punish. Because he gave the fire away Zeus had him chained to a high mountain and—" The child was too young to know anything about mythology. He could not tell him about the vulture descending each day.

"Does it hurt him?" The boy looked at his own skinny arms. "What is your name? Is he real? Does it hurt him?" He stretched his arms out by his sides.

"Yes, it hurts. He does not complain though."

"Where is the mountain at?" Mr. Issacs sucked in his lower lip in an effort not to correct him.

"What is your name?"

"I am called Ricardo. I am eight. Where is the mountain at?"

"Between the a and the t," Mr. Issacs snapped, the pedagogue in him overcoming caution. He sighed; another one demanding to be taught. He used to see children like that in his classes. They couldn't be stopped and neither could this one. Why, after all, should he be? It was a brutal story, no more brutal than many fairy tales though, nor half as vivid as a television murder.

"If you are eight, Ricardo, you are old enough to read. Go to the library and ask for a book about Prometheus. Here. This will tell you all about the museum." He lifted a folder from the top of a large pile and slid it across the case toward the boy.

Ricardo's hand closed over the paper; he crunched it into a ball and stuck it in his pocket. "Where is the library?"

Mr. Issacs opened the drawer to the desk and pulled out a city map. "You are here at the museum. Do you see?"

Ricardo nodded. "Here is the library down here near the city hall. Can you get down there from here?"

"I can go anywheres on my bicycle."

"Good. Go to the library, then come back and tell me about Prometheus."

"You already know." The boy left Mr. Issacs's side and ran out, the front door. The museum keeper waited a moment, then got up and followed him. Ricardo was riding away on a bicycle much too large for him. He had to throw all his weight from one side to another in order to reach the pedals. Mr. Issacs shook his head. The child was determined, but he seemed so wary. Of course, he could have told him about Prometheus, but if he'd told him, he would have forgotten. Perhaps he wasn't even on his way to the library. Children were often intensely interested in something they forgot in five minutes. It was better sometimes to be stingy with knowledge. They used to argue about that, he and Kate. Give, she would say, give all you've got. No, you must withhold something unless you want parrots uttering your own thoughts. It's a long way to the library, miles, and that child has to struggle with his enormous bicycle.

I know it, Kate! Don't exaggerate!

"Tim!" he called, turning away from the door. There was no answer. Where was he? He was part of the upkeep Mr. Issacs helped pay for, a Negro man who cleaned and dusted; he'd been maintaining the museum years before Mr. Issacs had started to work there.

"Tim?" His voice wavered, a thin echo preceded him through the hall.

"Up here." Tim's answer rolled down. He seemed to be somewhere outside, but there were no repairs needed on the tiny front balcony which, with its storeroom, comprised the second level. Plenty of dusting should be done in the big sculpture-filled rooms downstairs, by the look of Ricardo's hands.

Mr. Issacs started up the narrow wooden steps. "What are you doing?" They were always shouting, he and Tim, like two small boys delighting in the noise they could make in the vacant rooms. Tim's muffled voice roared again. "Washing winders. I'm settin' here on this winder sill and I'm about to fall off."

Mr. Issacs sighed. Terrible things were always about to happen to Tim, and they never did. "Which room are you in?" He stood at the top of the stairs. A winding circular fire escape led to a tower room on the third level. He hoped Tim wasn't up there. He didn't like to make the stiff climb, and the anatomical studies stacked on shelves, hands without arms, feet without legs, mortally depressed him.

"I'm in the storeroom, part way in anyways." Mr. Issacs entered the storeroom. Tim's body filled the window in one corner. As the frames were mounted on hinges allowing both halves to be swung inside like French doors, it was completely unnecessary for anyone to perch on the sill while washing them. Mr. Issacs eyed Tim narrowly, wondering if the simple idea of imminent danger made life more exciting for him. Then he glanced around the room. The entire place had been emptied and cleaned, the walls covered with white burlap, and all the woodwork painted white. "What's going on up here?"

Tim stood up, being careful not to catch his starched white jacket on the sill. He wore the jacket for every job. Mr. Issacs didn't know who had provided it, some former employer maybe. It made him look more like a butler than a janitor, perhaps his reason for wearing it all the time.

"Don't you know? We are having a art gallery in here. I been cleaning all week."

"An art gallery? But we have that downstairs!"

"Yes, sir, but this one's going to be pictures."

"What kind of pictures? Whose pictures?"

"Modren artists are going to send some." Mr. Issacs sucked in his lip and closed his eyes. It wasn't Tim's destruction of the language he minded; he'd grown accustomed to that. Since he'd decided from the first never to play the officious white boss, he had never attempted to correct him. The thing that outraged him was the thought of contemporary paintings at the Ney Museum. They would clash terribly with the nineteenth-century sculpture, making Miss Ney's work appear more outdated than ever. He shuddered at visions of bright gashes of color across the walls.

"It do seem funny to me," said Tim, "but I guess it will bring more people in."

Mr. Issacs opened his eyes and looked at Tim's comforting face. All his life one Negro servant or another—a maid, a yardman, a janitor—had been telling him things were going to be all right. They knew and he knew things were not going to be anywhere near right . . . still, he appreciated the soothing voices. "I grow old . . . I grow old," he murmured to himself. "I am hardly growing old anymore. I am old."

"Well," Tim shrugged, "so am I."

"This must have taken you all week." Mr. Issacs waved his arm to indicate the room.

"Yes. A whole lot of old junk had to be moved to the cellar. I nearly broke my hip on them stairs."

"Did you do the painting, too? Yes, you did. You've got paint on your glasses. How can you see with them all spattered like that?"

"Used to the spots now." Tim grinned. "The whole world's gone polka dotted."

Mr. Issacs surveyed the room again. "It looks good."

The Negro man touched the wall with his outspread hand. "Yes, it looks so good I hate to think of anybody nailing a nail in it, and I'm probably the very one that'll have to do it." His hand slid off the wall. "Nobody told you?"

Mr. Issacs shook his head. "No reason for anybody on the board to call me and tell me what they're doing. I just work here." He began walking about the room peering out the windows. The original glass, bubbled and wavy, was still in some of them. Through these panes the flowering quince looked like soft pink streaks and the surrounding park, a haze of green, but the new glass showed the trees should have been trimmed in the fall and the grass was patched with brown spots. By the end of the summer the lawn would be brown all over. Decay was not pleasant to see even though he felt at home in the middle of it.

"When are the pictures supposed to arrive?"

"Anytime from today on. The show's not going to be for a month. They need a lot of notice, I guess."

"Yes . . . well." Mr. Issacs pulled out his majestic gold watch. "It's eleven-thirty. I'm going back downstairs and get my lunch."

Harder on the heart going down, they said, than going up . . . Mr. Issacs walked slowly down the stairs. There were no restaurants anywhere near the museum so he brought some sandwiches and a vacuum bottle filled with tea with him in a brown paper sack he saved from his weekly visit to the grocery store. Kate had gone to the store every day. She was always running out of something or deciding, at the last minute, to try a new recipe. He went only once a week. The other old people there bothered him, the widows who continued to go every day to buy one frozen potpie and to begin a conversation with anyone who'd listen. It was cowardly to go to the grocery every day out of sheer loneliness. When he did go, Mrs. Dickens, the widow of a college professor (she never ceased reminding him), was always pecking around the green vegetables, an old hen in search of another rooster.

He leaned over the glass case to get his lunch out of the desk drawer, pushing the pile of folders into a sprawling heap. "Lord God in heaven most high!" He drew out the curse, turning it into a supplication before he was finished. At least once every Saturday he knocked over the folders. Stacking them up again, he wondered what it would have been like to have been married to Elizabet Ney. The picture of her on the front of each folder, taken from a painting done in 1859, showed her standing by the bust she had made of King George V, the last king of Hanover. Part of the king's profile was shown, a brooding mustachioed shadow. Elizabet's left arm rested against the stand holding the figure. She had a long face, a long straight nose, dark eyes, dark curly hair, and a determined expression. In her right hand, against the soft folds of her long dress, she held a curved claymodeling tool. Born in Germany in 1833, the daughter of a master stonecutter, she became a sculptress. Somehow she made the Art Academy in Munich accept her as a student, a young woman demanding to be taught an art open only to men. While she lived in Europe, she made busts and statues of a lot of famous people: Jacob Grimm, Schopenhauer, Garibaldi, Ludwig II, the mad king of Bavaria. She ended in Texas making statues of state heroes, governors, and friends.

A formidable woman—she cut her hair short, wore trousers to mount her scaffolds, kept her maiden name, and called her husband "my best friend"—one of those nineteenth-century heroines who hammered and chipped until the strictures of convention left her free to hammer and chip. The museum had been her studio and her home. From the outside it resembled a small stone fortress.

Her best friend and husband, Dr. Montgomery, stayed over a hundred miles away at their farm, Liendo Plantation, making various scientific experiments and writing philosophical treatises. They had two sons, one who died young and another who volunteered for the Spanish American War. When the children were little, Miss Ney stayed at home with them, but after the first child died and the second grew older, she built her fortress. There was a lot of conjecture about whether she and Dr. Montgomery were really married or not. They were—it had been proved by some busybody who looked up the certificate—but compared to the quiet life he and Kate had lived together, Elizabet Ney and Edmund Montgomery were a dashing pair. Mr. Issacs thumped down the collected folders. Had he ever done anything dashing?

He'd broken off a branch of his mother's prize flowering peach tree when he was fifteen and carried it like a banner before him to give to a girl. The blossoms had fallen off by the time he was halfway to her house. He had volunteered for World War I, more out of a desire to see France than from patriotic motives, and all he saw was the inside of a hospital. He caught influenza two days after his ship docked at Le Havre. He had followed the regular course of a man's life: married, fathered sons, had a profession, retired, lost his wife. His life had been filled with commonplaces, the usual virtues, the general sins, and there was very little time left for anything unusual to happen to him. Perhaps he should develop some amazing eccentricity? He could wear his coat backwards, throw his garbage over the neighbors' fence, call Mrs. Dickens an old bitch to her face . . . but wearing his coat backwards would be uncomfortable, he liked his neighbors, and Mrs. Dickens was only a lonely old widow. He could dye his white hair blue. That wouldn't hurt anyone. Cake coloring would probably do the job. He would be forgiven for his blue hair because of his age, here comes Mr. Issacs, he's harmless really, an old man with a passion for blue. It would be a nuisance. He'd never wanted to be stared at. Why, at seventy, was he thinking of reverting to adolescence? The mind played tricks. Was his failing? Preposterous! His body would fail him before his mind was gone!

Carrying his sack, Mr. Issacs climbed the stairs once more, passed through the new art gallery, and came out on the balcony. He sat down in a folding chair welcoming the sunlight. The balcony, with its dark red painted floorboards and two enormous green tin stars between the railings, was his favorite part of the museum. Under a live-oak tree in the back Tim was eating his lunch. When he got through he would remove his white jacket and lie down in the sun for a nap. Mr. Issacs would have joined him, but he did not want to take off his own jacket and sprawl on the grass; he might get grass stains on his vest and trousers. He preferred his rooftop view where he could watch the birds rummaging in the branches and smell the strong purple flowers of the mountain laurel below, a funeral smell, a funeral tree. No, it was too weak to hold dead weight. He approved of the Comanche burial; they flung their dead in trees to be picked clean by buzzards . . . better than rotting underground, but who could stand the odor of corruption or the bloody sight of the feast? He shuddered at his morbidity . . . forty years of teaching American history, forty years of trying to form an orderly civilized pattern, and still he fell back to savagery. A car stopped in front of the gate and a young woman in white slacks and a loud yellow shirt bolted out of it. She opened the back door, pulled a canvas, and came hurrying across the lawn with it in one hand. Looking up she caught him staring down at her from the balcony.

"Hello. Are you open?"

"Closed for lunch." Mr. Issacs poured himself some tea and took a sip.

"Can I leave this here?"

"What is it?"

"A picture for your opening."

Mr. Issacs bit into his sandwich . . . ham. He'd made it himself at seven that morning and five hours later had already forgotten what he'd packed for lunch. He couldn't understand why he brought ham sandwiches. They made him so thirsty. He looked over the railing again. The girl was still waiting.

"The door isn't locked. You can leave it in the hall," he said grudgingly, annoyed at himself for his forgetfulness and the girl for her persistence.

"I'd like to see where it's going to be hung."

"The gallery's up here."

"I'll bring it up then," the girl said cheerfully.

Before he could answer he heard her running up the stairs. He threw the rest of the sandwich back into his sack and drank his tea. The girl popped out on his balcony.

"Oh! How beautiful it is up here. I'm sorry I've never been out before. I'm Melrose Davis." She sat down on the railing facing him.

Mr. Issacs glared at her. Her hair was almost as yellow as her shirt, dyed probably, and her slacks were too tight. He took one furtive downward look at her canvas and recoiled. It was a picture of a flat tire, realistic, enormous, and terribly flat, lying on a highway going from nowhere to nowhere. A useless, purposeless object, it made him feel older and more worn out than he actually was.

"Why this?" He made his voice as colorless as he could.

"I don't know—épater le bourgeois, I guess. I wanted to see if I could do that sort of thing."

Mr. Issacs could feel indignation rising like steam inside his head.

He had to let a little of it out. "It's rather depressing."

"Do you think so? One of my teachers thought it was funny, but he thinks all pop art is funny."

"Ah," he breathed, not knowing how to tell her why her picture depressed him or if she cared to know. He led her into the new gallery. Melrose leaned her picture against one wall, then straightened up to give the room a quick professional once-over.

"The light's fine, now, but you're going to have to get some supplementary spots for the late afternoon."

"This was Miss Ney's bedroom. It was never intended for a picture gallery. She built the light she needed for her work into the house. You'll see nothing but north windows in the studio rooms downstairs." He continued on down in silence, half listening to Melrose chatter about the importance of indirect lighting, the best-lit museums she'd seen, her desire to see the effects of light on snow in the mountains of Greece or did it ever snow in Greece? Mr. Issacs couldn't remember. They went into the first studio room.

"They're all plaster!"

"Most of them, yes. After all, she was working on commission. You can't expect people to give their marble statues back to the museum."

He left her to confront the Texans. The past, by sheer weight of history, would vindicate him. What was a flat tire on a lonely road—nothing. Retiring to his desk he watched her circling the room. She paused for a moment in front of Dr. Montgomery and said something about his beard. Terribly talkative girl. Kate had been a quiet woman. They had a lot to talk about though, married forty-three years and still had a lot to say to each other . . . both of them sitting in the living room remembering their sons, their students, their summer vacations in Mexico, the year abroad when he had a research grant, their long mutual pasts, and in the end, during the last week of her life, all she said was his name, Theo. He dozed and Melrose, seeing him asleep, tiptoed past him on her way out.

Mr. Issacs did not hear her; he was dreaming of two empty rocking chairs on either side of a fireplace filled with ashes. He entered the room and pushed first one chair then the other so they were rocking gently to and fro. When he quit pushing they both stopped absolutely still. The sight of the stilled chairs frightened him, and he ran from the room. He awoke knowing fresh grief—he did not mourn his wife's death as much as he feared his own.

When he was well awake he looked over the visitors' book. Ricardo had not signed it, but Melrose had printed her name in big letters. Didn't they teach handwriting anymore?

Who are they? Mr. Issacs raised his head like an old hunting dog sniffing the wind. A couple holding hands entered the door, letting their hands drop to their sides as they passed. He had seen the woman before, but not the man. She lived in his neighborhood; he was certain he'd met her out walking with her children. She and the man could have been brother and sister; both of them were young and fair, the tops of their heads streaked lighter by the sun, and they had similar expressions on their faces . . . hunger. No, they were not kin, couldn't be, and the man was not her husband. He had seen the husband going in and out of the house. So, she had a lover. Mr. Issacs was delighted. He'd caught a glimpse of a marvelous secret; he was warmed by the aura enveloping them. Oh, he was a disgusting old man, warming himself at someone else's fire . . . probably take up window-peeping next. What was he to do with himself? Did Kate have a lover? No, she wasn't the sort of woman for that. What is the sort? She was not a sensual woman, but she might have been warmer for someone else. Who? Was he jealous of the dead? He'd never questioned her faithfulness while she was living. Perhaps some other man had made her happier than he had. He couldn't begrudge her that. He had been faithful . . . forty-three years he'd been faithful in body if not in mind. He'd looked at other women but he'd never done a thing . . . kissed them on New Year's politely on the cheek and never even patted a passing fanny. He'd been a ninny, a nambypamby, a respected member of the faculty.

There was Ricardo again. The smudge of dust was still on his forehead and he'd ripped the edge of one pants leg at the bottom, caught it on his bicycle chain. "What have you got?"

"A picture. See." He held it up to Mr. Issacs's face.

Mr. Issacs frowned. It was a picture of Christ, showing his bleeding heart. A cross was glowing in the middle of the heart. "Why have you brought me this?"

"His insides are showing, like Prometheus."

"Hmm," Mr. Issacs murmured and placed the picture face down in front of him. Did the child love the bloody thing or was it only that insides fascinated him? "You went to the library?"

"Yes, on my bicycle I went. I rode fast. I have never gone there before, but I seen it."

"Saw," Mr. Issacs corrected automatically. "And you found the book?"

"A lady found it for me. She let me hold it, and I sat down there and read. They have chairs and tables."

"Yes. You could have taken the book home with you if you wanted.

"I know," the boy said scornfully. "At home my baby sister tears up books." He picked up the picture and put it in his shirt pocket. "The statue in there. It is not true."

"It is a myth," said Mr. Issacs carefully.

"A vulture came every day and pecked his liver out, and it growed back every day. The statue isn't right. His liver don't show. Why don't they show his liver? They don't show it in the book either, and they don't tell me where the mountain is."

"Not they, she."

"She?"

"The lady who made the statue."

"A lady made that?"

"She made everything in this museum."

"How could she?"

"With a hammer and a mallet, a chisel, some talent, and a lot of time."

"Could I do it?"

"Perhaps, if you had the proper training."

"If I made a statue of Prometheus, I would make it better than a woman. I would not be afraid to show his insides."

"That statue was important to Miss Ney, Ricardo. She always wanted to do Prometheus. Come, let me show you something she was also interested in." He got up intending to take him into the next room and show him the figure of Ludwig II, but he could hear the voices of the young couple. They were quarreling. He delayed entering and began talking to Ricardo again. He was sure the young woman knew who he was. That was good, to be known when he was so old he hardly believed in his own shadow any longer. He had been recognized; he had to be avoided. Negative recognition was better than none at all. He wished he could tell her she need not avoid him. Her secret was hers to keep, but there was no way he could tell her except to stay where he was and talk loudly enough so they could hear him and leave.

"Look," he indicated a bas-relief of a young boy's head.

"See how carefully this has been done. It's cut in hard stone, but see how soft the cheeks and curls seem."

"How old is he?"

"I'm not sure. What do you think?"

Ricardo stared at the child's face. "Five, maybe. He is a baby still."

Mr. Issacs heard the voices in the next room diminish to silence, then footsteps. They had found the back door. He took Ricardo past the statues of Travis and Austin to Ludwig.

"Here is a king who went mad."

"He has a lot of clothes on. Why is he so dressed up?"

Ludwig, arrayed in a richly patterned doublet and flowing cloak, stared over their heads, frozen in his frippery and fine nonchalance. "He admired the king of France, Louis XIV, and he tried to copy everything he'd done. Louis was extravagant in his dress so Ludwig dressed up also." He looked at the boy, who was gaping at him in astonishment.

"Like Halloween?"

"Somewhat."

"Can I go up there?" Ricardo pointed to a raised platform built into the south corner. A hammock hung from the ceiling above it.

"Yes, but don't try the hammock. It's old and the rope is rotten by now."

"She sleep up here?"

"I'm told she did, but I doubt it."

"This high up I see everything."

"She could have a different view of her sculptures from there. It's important to be able to see from all angles."

Mr. Issacs walked over to the side of the cast of Prometheus and touched the plaster leg, stained and worn smooth where many others had touched it.

"This was not a commissioned piece . . . no one paid her to do it." He stumbled in his explanation not knowing how much the child could understand. "You are looking down on it, but I think she intended for people to look up to him. She cared about the gift of fire Prometheus gave to man. She never intended to show his insides."

"Do you know where the mountain is?" Ricardo started down the stairs. He had not touched the hammock.

"In the Caucasus, I believe." He thought of telling him the mountains were in Asia but did not. All the child wanted was a name; the mountain could be anywhere.

"There is another name for him, for Prometheus. I read it in the book."

"What is it?"

"Forethought, a funny name you think?"

"It didn't help him much, did it?"

"No, he got caught anyway." Ricardo stopped at the bottom of the steps and pointed to the open back door. "A man and a woman are out there. Bra-aagh!" He snorted. "They're kissing."

Mr. Issacs suppressed the beginning of a smile. "Some people do that in gardens."

"Why?"

"I don't know why."

"I will go to the library and ask for a book about gardens. Then I will tell you."

"Yes," Mr. Issacs nodded, "look for a book about gardens."

Ricardo leaned over the stair rail and looked down at the figure to his right.

"Albert Sidney Johnston, 1803 to 1862. Poor Albert Sidney Johnston, only fifty-nine when he died. The card says he's in the State Cemetery. He has a flag for a blanket. Why did they wrap him in a flag?"

"He was a Confederate general who was killed on the battleground of Shiloh. That's a Confederate flag draped over him . . . You'd better get a book on the Civil War. It will interest you more than gardens."

"Was poor Albert Sidney Johnston a hero like Prometheus?"

"Prometheus brought the gift of fire to man and endured the torture of the vulture without complaint until Hercules set him free. That is the myth. Judge for yourself."

"His liver growed back, didn't it?"

"It grew, yes. Every day it grew back, and he provided a new feast for the vulture."

"Albert Sidney Johnston was lucky. He didn't have no vulture."

"A vulture," said Mr. Issacs. ★

1968

CHRISTOPHER MIDDLETON

Christopher Middleton, who was born in Truro, Cornwall (Great Britain), studied at Merton College, Oxford, and taught at the University of Zurich and King's College, London, before becoming a professor of Germanic languages at the University of Texas, Austin. He retired in 1998. A poet and translator, especially of German literature, Middleton has published numerous volumes of poetry and prose, including *Faint Harps and Silver Voices: Selected Translations* (2000) and *The Word Pavilion and Selected Poems* (2001). The poem "The Armadillos" was written before that creature became an icon of Austin's counterculture.

THE ARMADILLOS

You suddenly woke and saw
on the bedroom hearth an apple green
puddle of moonlight. It was the armadillo,
sitting on top of the chimney, put it there;
with his long snout for a siphon, I suppose.
More often the armadillos
perch in the trees. They stare
at each other, count the rings
which buckle them in; or—
they discuss things.
Don't fall, Harriet! Arthur, don't fall!
We can't help it if the armadillos
drop like bombs and catch only
in the lower branches with their claws.
Falling like that, they can't be lonely.

Winters, they leave the trees and trundle
to the end of the valley. In twos and fours
they cluster there and comfort each other.
The frost feels them under their bucklers;
they taste it happening in their jaws.
But in the trees where they build hides
of cardboard boxes and paper bags,
their main concern is believing summer.
For my friends broken by special committees
I hang out armadillo flags.
They run fast and go underground
where silence is, for sending signals.
Or they climb to the tops of telephone poles
and jam the exchanges of political assholes
with the terrible sound of knitting.
If you wake again, do not scare,
but wonder at the armadillos;
they'll be watching us from up there,
winking their neat eyes, arranging their faces,
hoping that something shows. ★

1966

HARRY HUNTT RANSOM

Harry Huntt Ransom (1908–1976) was born in Galveston and received his Ph.D. from Yale University in 1938. He joined the English Department of the University of Texas in 1935, rising through the ranks. Following distinguished service in the United States Army Air Force in World War II, Ransom returned to the University and began his administrative career capped by his service as chancellor from 1961–1971. But Ransom's major, lasting, and world-class contribution to the University was building up special library and archival collections culminating in the Harry Ransom Humanities Research Center, which opened in 1974. Unbeknownst to many people, Ransom also wrote poetry, collected and published posthumously in *The Song of Things Begun* (1998). Given Ransom's interest in historical preservation, "Frontier Museum" seems the most appropriate poem to reprint here.

FRONTIER MUSEUM

We brought prim order out of old wild living;
It made more sense that I would have surmised.
The spinning wheel is polished, ready, threaded . . .
Even the longhorn spoons are sterilized.
No trace of years appears upon the labels,
We note their pristine wording as we pass;
The lighting's indirect upon the tables . . .
The bright estate of muskets under glass. ★

1998

Miguel González-Gerth

Miguel González-Gerth was born in Mexico City, the son of a Mexican army general. He received a B.A. from the University of Texas in 1950 and a Ph.D. from Princeton University in 1973. He taught in the Department of Spanish at the University of Texas from 1965 until his retirement in 2000. From 1972 to 1978, he edited *The Texas Quarterly*. His books include *T.E. Lawrence, Richard Aldington, and the Death of Heroes* (1994), *The Musicians and Other Poems* (1991), and *The Brandywine in Winter* (2004). In the remembrance printed here, González-Gerth recalls his friendship with the great Argentine writer, Jorge Luis Borges, who often visited Austin in the 1960s.

from Borges and Texas: Farewell To An Old Friend

Jorge Luis Borges first came to Texas in September of 1961, because he had been appointed Edward Laroque Tinker Visiting Professor of Spanish American Literature at the University of Texas at Austin for the fall semester of that year. Not being married at the time, he came with his mother, Dona Leonor Acevedo de Borges, a lady of much character who affectionately called her genius son "Georgie" in English. In the months that followed, both Borges and his mother had occasion to meet socially with my parents, who were then living in Austin. It was through them that I first became acquainted with Borges, the human being. I heard all about how he talked, what he said, how he behaved, and it seemed amazing to me that the man who wrote these mystifying works, whose mind could only be described as dazzling, turned out to be such an easy going and affable fellow.

Because he had a peculiar sense of personal history, with a deep pride in his military ancestors who took active part in the Spanish American wars of independence from Spain, Borges became interested in my father who, as a young cavalry officer, had led a charge that assured the success of a subsequent major battle won by Mexican revolutionary forces in 1913. On the other hand, since literature was most often on his mind, Borges listened as my mother told him of having known in various degrees the likes of Salvador Díaz Mirón, Alfonso Reyes (a friend of Borges), and José Gorostiza, among Mexican poets, but above all the intense pre-van-guardist Ramón López Velarde, who was born in the same state as my mother. By the time I got to be on speaking terms with Borges myself, he remembered few details of those conversations. Yet, when he occasionally confused my name, he would call me "*el mexicano*."

That there is any connection between Borges and Texas beyond his visiting teaching sojourn may come as a surprise. Later he would say in print that Texas was his first physical encounter with North America (see *The New Yorker*, September 19, 1970). Borges had been nearly blind since 1965, and that fact substantially must have influenced his perceptions concerning Texas. To begin with, he found in Austin, San Antonio, and other Texas cities, a very hospitable environment. It was natural that he would imagine Texas to be the way he wished it. I remember well his good humored bewilderment when, now and then, I managed to stop the flow of his speech in order to dissuade him of unimportant though mistaken conjectures regarding Texas history and customs or to explain something he had not already anticipated about the Texas landscape. There is, after all, a vague parallel between Texas (actually the whole Southwest) and Borges's native country. Both were discovered and first colonized by the Spaniards, both have considerable flatlands with access to the sea, both at one time had Indian populations that had been dealt with perhaps too harshly, and both have agricultural and social milieus that produced colorful epic types and situations.

It was logical for Borges to counterpose the cowboy and the gaucho, the Comanche and the Kiowa to the Araucano and the Guaycurué, the battles for Texas independence in 1836 to those for Spanish American independence beginning in 1810, the fast gun of the West with the skillful knife of the *compadrito*. Borges, in fact, mentions Texas in an early sketch dealing with the legend of Billy the Kid. . . . Surprisingly enough, the early image of an unemotional killer, so much at odds with the apparent nature of the author, will turn out to be significant. All one has to do to prove this is to read some of his detective stories like "Death and the Compass" and "The End."

I suppose that the best example of the impact of Texas on Borges is his sonnet, first published in 1964, which bears the name of the state. As Don Graham says in his *Texas: A Literary Portrait*, this poem by Borges "seeks to define the spiritual essence of Texas, searching to divine among the origins of the state some elemental moral quality." Recognition of this intent and its accomplishment was immediately given by the institution where Borges was teaching when he conceived the poem. The Harry Ransom Humanities Research Center of the University of Texas at Austin (the HRC) printed a limited edition of the translation by the American poet Mark Strand, who later conducted a videotaped interview with Borges. During Borges's last visit to Austin, he experienced the intellectual pleasure of seeing his own work surrounded by manuscripts in the hands of Baudelaire, Proust, Joyce, and others, shown to him by Carlton Lake, executive curator of the HRC.

The year 1961 was pivotal for Borges's reputation as a world writer. He shared with Samuel Beckett an international literary prize awarded in Paris. Also, while he was in Texas, the translation of his work into English gained substantial impetus. Four pieces from *El hacedor (The Maker)*, then recently published in Argentina, appeared in the winter issue of *The Texas Quarterly*, along with a critical article on Borges and two poems dedicated to him. The magazine was edited at the time by Dr. Harry Ransom, founder of the now world famous Humanities Research Center and later chancellor of the University of Texas System. This sort of publication was vital for both Borges's future in English and for the future of Texas's higher culture. There was here at that time a scholar and administrator in higher education with sufficient vision to establish "in the capital city," as he himself put it (*TQ*, Winter 1958), "a research center to be the Bibliotheque Nationale of the only state that started out as an independent nation."

Ransom realized the appropriateness of publishing translations from Borges, himself director of the National Library in Buenos Aires, and critical evaluations of his work; this at a time when only a handful of prose pieces and a handful of poems had been translated into English and had appeared in Eastern magazines and anthologies. Only Spanish American literary specialists knew Borges in this country, people who frequented the literary circles and, perhaps, traveled to Buenos Aires and the capital cities of Europe. Borges was invited to Texas at the suggestion of the late Professor Miguel Engueídanos (later at Indiana and Vanderbilt), who had studied his work. Two others of Borges's best academic critics were also Texans: James Irby, at Princeton, and Carter Wheelock, at the University of Texas at Austin.

&

Borges would pay us four other much briefer visits. I met him in 1971 when he took part in a wonderful poetry reading which also included Robert Duncan, Alberto de Lacerda, Czeslaw Milosz, Octavio Paz, and Dionisio Ridruejo. He returned the next year to lecture on Cervantes. Our acquaintance developed, and he wanted to know about my own writing and, above all, my reading. We had many preferences in common: Cervantes, Shakespeare, Tennyson, Browning, Edward Fitzgerald, Poe, Hawthorne, Whitman, Mallarmé, Valéry, Leopoldo Lugones. But he had read a hundred, maybe a thousand times more than I, and so the conversations usually turned into lectures or soliloquies to which I listened in awe and with inexplicable pleasure. His last two stays in Austin were in the spring months of 1976 and 1982. They were, I think, despite his relative physical decline, the most satisfying of the short visits for him. He had come with Maria Kodama and seemed happy and calm. There was no hint then, that I could observe, of the incurable malady that would end his life. He lectured in an enormous auditorium filled to overflowing. The entire audience was spellbound; except for his voice, there was silence. Borges, the frail old man, was like a conquering hero, a demigod. . . .

At its 1983 annual meeting the Modern Language Association of America devoted a whole program to Borges. His American readership was now widespread, spurred on by critical praise such as that of George Steiner in his article, "Tigers in the Mirror" (*The New Yorker*, June 20, 1970). Donald Barthelme, another dislocated Texan, early on had become interested in Borges. Among "real" Texas writers, John Graves admits admiring in Borges's fiction "a distinctive cleanness and spareness of style," often finding "the insights that illuminate it quite moving." A. C. Greene concludes that Borges's writing is "more Europeanized than I had expected of a Latin American writer." These are not idle observations. Latin American writers are not known for their laconism, and it is natural that in present times their works are less representative of European models than of their native ethos. Borges is not an exception; he is an anomaly. Rolando Hinojosa-Smith remembers reading Borges in graduate school and later seeing him in Chicago, where Borges spoke on *Huckleberry Finn*. "Something he said that cold winter day," Hinojosa muses, "became internalized in order to become useful in my own fiction." So an Argentine writer speaking in English about Mark Twain influenced a Mexican-American writer.

&

Borges was not an old man when he first came to Texas; he was old the last time he came. His work, however, will never be old; it is timeless. He came to Texas, to Austin, particularly, and later remembered it in his poems. And both during his life and after his death, Austin remembered him. At the University of Texas, the flags flew at half-mast in his honor. ★

1987

HAZEL HARROD RANSOM

Hazel Louise Harrod (1920–1993) was born in Mart, east of Waco. She earned a B.A. from the University of Texas in 1942 and an M.A. in English in 1944. In 1951 she married Harry Huntt Ransom. After his death in 1976 she devoted herself, in part, to collecting and editing the articles and speeches of Harry Ransom for publication. In 1996 a collection of her own writings, *A Vacation in the Sun and Other Stories*, was published. The Latin title of the piece printed here may be translated as "of which I was a small part" or "in which I played a small part." It is adapted from the *Aeneid* and refers to the destruction of Troy. The full translation from the original is: "Such misery I myself saw, and of which I was an important part." Here Hazel Ransom describes a dinner party and the part she played in honoring the principal guest, Jorge Luis Borges.

Quorum Pars Parva Fui

BEFORE DECIDING ON THE TITLE OF THIS TEXT, I MUST confess that I did not know exactly what I was going to write. All I know is because of that night I harbored for a while and on the back of my mind something like a very old and incomplete recollection. I cannot describe to the full its nature or implications. It was as if a series of events I either witnessed or experienced and had forgotten for a very long time suddenly, through some inexplicable mental quirk, had been recaptured but only partially. If my narrative lacks coherence, I trust it does only because whatever lay on the back of my mind, that incomplete recollection itself, definitely lacked sufficient coherence and obvious meaning.

In any case it seemed to have been triggered by something that was said one evening after dinner. Adding to the vagueness of it all is the fact that the restaurant in Austin where it took place no longer exists as it did then. It has changed hands, perhaps more than once, and when I have returned there its appearance and ambience are not in the least the same.

I had arranged a dinner in honor of Jorge Luis Borges, who had been invited for the fourth or fifth time to lecture at the University. Besides him, his companion, Maria Kodama, and me, there were present Ellen Clayton Garwood, who had once had Argentine connections, my friend Miguel Gonzalez-Gerth, and two or three other friends. As might be expected, the conversation was lively, exhibiting a combination of sophistication and simplicity. Borges, of course, was the center of attention. Everyone deferred to him. Eyes and ears turned to him whenever he began to make a statement or reply to a question someone else had asked. Our constant consideration of him stemmed not so much from his being a famous writer or even from being now elderly and almost completely blind (two facts not without importance) as from his quietly generating a sort of magical presence.

The table talk turned on numerous topics including our city and Texas (which Borges admitted liking), the University, recent travels by members of the group, and, of course, literature. I was seated to Borges's right and Miguel to his left. Though Borges, Maria and Miguel could have spoken to one another in Spanish, the conversation remained totally in English, to Borges's delight. During a moment when the others became engaged in a certain discussion, I approached Borges on whether he had thought of leaving his personal papers to some institution for posterity. At the time I assumed that his answer would involve the Argentine national library in Buenos Aires. To my surprise, he replied by saying that several of his manuscripts were on loan to specific individuals in the United States. Indeed, to my knowledge, Borges's progressive blindness had allowed him to compose many of his earlier works in his own hand, eventually with the aid of a magnifying glass. And then came a reason for our sudden excitement: If the University of Texas would find the means to retrieve those manuscripts, held by the borrowers no longer with the author's consent, he would gladly donate them free of charge to the Harry Ransom Humanities Research

Center. And Borges said this with unequivocal determination. I never will forget that night Borges's signing a letter of bequest at Miguel's suggestion under what seemed to be the curious façade of the Driskill Hotel, with Maria and me acting as witnesses. (That letter, I am told, remains on file at the HRHRC, although the Borges papers were not acquired, due to incompetence in administrative and legal pursuit or the skillful dissembling by those in possession or both.)

But I digress, as it is sometimes said. While still at the restaurant, having finished dinner, our conversation continued in the barely lighted alcove which contained our table. Borges spoke almost continuously, stopping only now and then as if to muse to himself. He made lengthy commentaries on English literature of various periods. Then, for some reason I do not remember, he referred to *Floris and Blanchefleur*, a medieval romance composed in French and English. Nothing surprised his listeners, for we took for granted the great man's vast knowledge of the world of letters. But it was at that point that a feeling struck me in a way so strange that it was difficult for me to follow the remainder of the evening's discussion.

That night, after dropping off Borges and Maria Kodama at the Driskill, I went home and had trouble going to sleep. I lay in bed and thought little about the very pleasant evening I had had or even about the possible coup of getting Borges's manuscripts for our library. Instead I was overtaken by a kind of anxiety caused by wanting almost frantically to remember something and not being able to do so. What could it be, I wondered. It was a state I had never previously experienced. Though not an obsession, it seemed on the brink of becoming one. I decided to take a sleeping pill, something I never do. Finally, in the wee hours I fell asleep from sheer exhaustion, only to wake up suddenly with this thought: Had Borges at some juncture in the conversation cited the phrase *"Dilecti quoniam?"* If he did, what was the context?

I had enough presence of mind to discern that, given my distraction toward the end of the evening, I could have missed a number of things and not even guessed it. Needless to say, Borges was capable of embroidering any number of literary and linguistic topics. But, if he had quoted that phrase in Latin from, say, a breviary containing the daily prayers for the canonical hours, why had he done so, and was it addressed to me? And then I found myself saying, half-asleep and also lacking explanation, "*habere in deliciis aliquem.*" How utterly strange that was, for Latin is a language I scarcely studied in college.

Before daybreak I had a dream. In it there were three people, clearly delineated. The female protagonist had a tyrannical older husband, who imprisoned her in a tower after their wedding, and a daring younger suitor, who dug an underground passage so that he and the lady could meet from time to time. It was not, however, an erotic dream; the lovemaking was totally implicit. Nevertheless, the dream was permeated with a sort of passion. And that passion seemed to focus on a book, an old medieval book which, when seen from different angles, would multiply itself until it became many books, a veritable library. Furthermore, a peculiar aspect of that book was that it had been handed to the lady by her young suitor during a religious ceremony.

Late in the morning and completely awake, I looked up the meaning of what I recalled saying in my half sleep: to love someone tenderly. I have not been able to interpret the narrative in my dream nor my somnolent thinking in Latin. Therefore, and most importantly, I do not know how it all might apply to the dreamer. All I know is that I have ceased being anxious about events which might have happened to me long ago, perhaps in another life, but which I can no longer remember. ★

1996

Prudence Mackintosh

Born in Texarkana, Prudence Mackintosh grew up in a newspaper family and attended the University of Texas, graduating in 1966. She is the author of four books, including *Thundering Sneakers* (1981), *Retreads* (1985), and *Sneaking Out* (2002). She has lived in Dallas since 1969. In this piece, from *Just As We Were: A Narrow Slice of Texas Womanhood* (1996), she details one of the cultural staples of the University of Texas, the hopes, dreams, and epiphanies of women in sororities.

from Just As We Were

It was the fall of 1962, and I had just hobbled in ill-fitting stiletto-heeled shoes from the Chi Omega house on Wichita to the Tri Delt house on Twenty-seventh Street in Austin. Word had not reached Texarkana that during rush week, regardless of the University policy that forbade freshmen to have cars, it was unseemly to walk from sorority house to sorority house. Socially astute and ambitious mothers from Houston and Dallas had willingly stranded themselves at the Villa Capri motel near campus, so that their daughters could drive the family car and arrive poised and oblivious to the beastly Austin September sun in their de rigueur dark cottons. My dark cottons were severely circled under the armpits and the humidity made me regret the tight permanent wave that my mother had felt was necessary to keep my already naturally curly hair out of my eyes. The lengthy walk had made me late, and I half hoped that I could sit this one out. But before I could blot the sweat from my upper lip, a vivacious girl costumed like Judy Garland's dog, Toto, pinned a huge name tag on me and led me down a cardboard yellow brick road into the cool interior of her sorority house.

Like young Jay Gatsby, I had seldom been in such beautiful houses before. Although F. Scott Fitzgerald never mentioned Daisy's sorority affiliation, these houses—particularly the Tri Delt and Pi Phi houses—could have been hers. Like Gatsby, I suspected that these houses held "ripe mystery . . . a hint of bedrooms upstairs more beautiful and cool than other bedrooms, of gay and radiant activities taking place through its corridors." I was much too naive to recognize voices "full of money," but I did marvel at the inexhaustible charm of these breathless beauties. I wrote to my parents after that first day of parties with Pi Phis, Tri Delts, Zetas, Chi Omegas, Kappas, and Thetas that I had never seen such a gathering of beautiful girls in my life. "High in a white palace, the king's daughters, the golden girls" in Pappagallo shoes.

Sororities at the University of Texas in 1962 were large by national standards. If all pledges remained active, a UT sorority could usually boast close to 150 active members. Even if only half of them were really beauties, the effect was overwhelming when you saw them—exquisitely groomed—in one large room.

After what seemed interminable non-conversation and punch that never really quenched one's thirst, the lights dimmed at the Tri Delt house, and Toto gave me a quick squeeze. "You just sit right here on the front row. I'll be back when the skit is over." My naivete once again kept me from being impressed by this privileged front-row position. Being squired around by a costumed sorority personality, I would later learn, also might indicate favoritism. The skits blur a little in my mind, but they were nothing less than major musical productions, often with professional lighting and costumes. We were the tail end of a generation raised on Broadway musicals and consequently were prime suckers for lyrics lifted from *Carousel* or *South Pacific* and altered for sorority purposes. I distinctly remember a green-eyed Tri Delt named Kay dressed as the carnival barker from *Carousel* sending shivers down my spine with "When you walk through a storm, hold your head up high . . ." It was that unflinching eye contact that got me every time, and by the end of the week, if you were a desirable rushee, someone might be squeezing your elbow by the time Kay's voice reached the final "You'll never walk aaalone." Although the songs varied, that was the pitch at most of the houses. The girls locked arms around the room and swayed gently as they sang, all to remind you that it was a big University and that joining these self-confident beauties meant not having to face it alone.

As I watched these sorority girls flash their perfect teeth and sing and dance, I surmised that they possessed secrets that they might share if I managed to get out of the foyer and into those upstairs rooms. They not only knew their way to class on the 150 acres that then composed the University, but they also knew appropriate retorts when drunk Kappa Sigs pulled their skirts up at parties and howled, "Look at the wheels on this woman!" I knew they could hold their beer and their cool when someone "dropped trou" or toga at a Fiji Island party. I was sure that they did not worry—as I did—about where one slept when one accepted an OU-Texas date to Dallas or when one made the bacchanalian pilgrimage to Laredo for George Washington's Birthday.

But the week was not all costumed escorts, squeezes, and front-row seats. Sometimes the carefully concealed rush machinery broke down and the party lost its air of graciousness. A survivor recalls that in the grand finale of the *Carousel* skit, performers tossed bags of popcorn to prize rushees on the front row. One player overshot the front row, but remedied her error by wrenching the popcorn bag from the second-row innocent's hand and restoring it to its intended mark. More often the embarrassing moments were brought on by a provincial rushee. It's probably apocryphal, but the story floated around for years that, on being passed a silver tray of cigarettes, a rushee at the Zeta house looked puzzled for a moment, then reached furtively into her purse, emptied her cigarette pack onto the tray, and quickly passed it on.

At the Pi Phi house I once held four "floaters" (sorority members who moved in and out of many circles at each party to get an overall picture of the rushees) captive with a fifteen-minute maudlin tale about the day my dog died when I was eleven. They feigned intense interest, their eyes brimming at appropriate times, but doubtless they collapsed in spasms of laughter and goose calls when I made my exit. The next day, to my horror, I was repeatedly introduced at the Pi Phi house with, "This is Prudence. Get her to tell you that neat story about her dog."

But despite our faux pas, my roommates and I had an easy time of it. We were under no parental pressure to pledge at all. Totally ignorant of the machinations of rush, we innocently perceived the whole rush week scene as one exhausting and bewildering but happy experience in which we were to decide whom we liked best. We had only the vaguest notions about sorority rankings on campus. Although there were twenty sororities on the UT campus in 1962, for many girls, accepting a bid from other than the "big six" was apparently unthinkable. We were aware of tears down the hall as "cuts" were made by the sororities following the first and second periods of parties, but we could not appreciate the pain of the "legacy" (the daughter of a sorority alum) whose mother responded to her daughter's rejection with, "Pack your bags, honey. SMU has deferred rush." Or the one who declared, "See, I told you you should have gone to Tech first"—where it was easier to make it into an elite sorority and then transfer to UT.

The third period of rush week consisted of two Saturday evening parties. It was tense, and girls on both sides were exhausted. Members had culled their rushee lists to approximately 100. Too many rushees at a final-period party could scare top rushees away. ("There were ten Houston girls at that party; they won't take us all.") In 1962 rushees were required to wear "after five" dresses to these parties. Members usually dressed in white or, in the case of the Kappas, in sepulchral black. Sidewalks were lined with hurricane lamps and the houses were candlelit. This was the party for sentimental tearjerkers. The Thetas were renowned for leaving no dry eyes. The Tri Delts put a string of pearls around your neck and instructed you to toss a wishing pearl in a shell fountain while an alumna with a haunting voice sang mysteriously from an upstairs window.

After two such parties (a first and second preference), the rushees departed for Hogg Auditorium to sign preference cards, which would be sorted by computer. Needless to say, no one folded, spindled, or mutilated her card. Sorority members would be up in all-night final hash sessions to determine their top fifty choices. On Sunday afternoon, the computer would print out the results. Panhellenic representatives sat with boxes of alphabetized envelopes. For appearances' sake, there was an envelope for every girl who had attended a final party, but some contained cards with the message, "You have received no sorority bid at this time. Please feel free to come by the Panhellenic office to register for open rush." Amid the squealing and squeezing that went on as envelopes were ripped open, perhaps it was possible to run unnoticed from the room with such an envelope and back to a lonely dorm room for a bitter cry. We were among the shriekers and squeezers and we did not notice. My three roommates and I had received bids to the same sorority, and our course was set.

Although we were to become somewhat aberrant sorority members, we had unwittingly chosen our bridesmaids, the godmothers for our future children, and access to certain social circles. Others in our pledge class already had this social entree by virtue of their birth; numerous legacies recall hearing Kappa songs as lullabies. I remember being fascinated by a framed family tree that hung in the study hall of the Kappa house. The genealogy was illustrated by linking Kappa keys (the sorority symbol) indicating that all of the women in this family had been Kappas for four generations. I distinctly remember feeling sorry for these girls whose choices were made inevitable by long family tradition. Still others had simply been born in the right neighborhoods and had distinguished themselves in the privileged big city high schools—which then were Lamar (Houston), Alamo Heights (San Antonio), Highland Park (Dallas), and Arlington Heights (Fort Worth). Small-town sorority members might have already joined these elite circles at expensive summer camps. Only one of my new Kappa roommates had done any of these things. She was a product of Camp Mystic, had attended a boarding school, recognized prestige clothing labels, and generally knew her way around the social scene into which the other three of us had stumbled. She was appalled at our ignorance. We had blindly selected our sorority because we liked each other and because we agreed that the Kappas' whole rush setup was pleasantly amateurish and not at all intimidating. Quite frankly, we felt like we might be able to help them out. In a smalltown high school, where rivalry was not particularly fierce, one tended to get an inflated idea of one's abilities and talents. In a competitive big-city high school, one might be a cheerleader or serve on the student council, but in a smaller pond like ours, it was entirely possible to be cheerleader, star in the senior play, be the editor of the school paper, participate as a member, and probably an officer, in every school organization, and still do well scholastically.

&

By the time we reached our junior year in college, however, many of us had begun to sense that something was amiss. There were strong conflicts between belonging to a sorority and trying to pursue an education. Why did we volunteer our time to help the Phi Delts gather wood for the Aggie bonfire when I could have been with my English class buddies hearing Tom Wolfe and Truman Capote? I missed Igor Stravinsky's visit to campus because I was the song leader at chapter dinner. In retrospect, the conflict was most apparent when the sorority pretended to serve academic purposes. The poet John Crowe Ransom joined us for dinner one evening, and the only sustained conversation we could handle was "How are your grandchildren?" Even worse was the night William Sloane Coffin, the activist chaplain from Yale, came for dinner. If I led the chapter in singing "Kayappa, Kayappa, Kayappa, Gayamma, I am so hayuppy tha-ut I yamma . . ." that night I have thankfully blocked it from my memory. Coffin, of course, was already condemning the escalating war in Vietnam and generally taking a few cracks at lifestyles like ours. We, who had spent the previous weekend parading around in initiation sheets and performing the solemn Victorian rituals required to initiate our pledges, were ill-equipped to defend ourselves. The chaplain so easily trapped us that we could hardly say no when he challenged us to follow him to the SDS (Students for a Democratic Society) meeting he was scheduled to address when he left our house. Slipping our pearl-encrusted Kappa keys into our pockets, we followed him with great trepidation down the alley to the University Christian Church, where the meeting was to be held. We had seen these humorless campus radicals on the steps of the Student Union. Some of us had given token support to slightly suspect University "Y" activities; others had at least signed the petition to integrate Roy's Lounge on the Drag, but we had never sat in the midst of such a group, and we shivered that our opinion on the Gulf of Tonkin might be sought. Fortunately the SDS was much too taken with Coffin even to notice us, much less explore our ignorance.

Besides the educational conflicts, the sorority could also be indicted for providing a womb like environment in which one could avoid practically all contact with the unfamiliar or unknown. Many of my sorority sisters now freely admit that they never even knew how to get to the Main Library, nor did they ever darken the door of the Chuck Wagon in the Student Union, where my roommates and I frequently drank dishwater-colored iced tea with foreign students or "rat-running" psychology lab instructors. This same narrow environment also kept the haves from developing much sensitivity for the have-nots. Sorority alumnae groups are generous philanthropists, but in college our philanthropy was usually limited to a Christmas party for blind children or an Easter egg hunt for the retarded. The only have-nots that sorority girls encountered on a regular basis were the servants in the house. I often wondered how the cook felt when the KA's rode up on horseback and sent a small black boy to the door with Old South Ball invitations on a silver tray. ★

1976

JULIUS WHITTIER

Julius Whittier was born and raised in San Antonio. He attended the University of Texas, where he majored in philosophy and played varsity football for four years. Later he graduated from the LBJ School and the UT law school. He practices law in Dallas. His essay recalls the days when African-American players were just beginning to be welcome at the University of Texas.

from THE LAST BASTION

THE NAME "ROYAL" HAD A CERTAIN MAJESTY TO IT that I am certain has left no small impression on many a Texas recruit. It certainly impressed me when I first heard it and found out exactly who he was. To be honest, I had no plans at all regarding college attendance after my senior year in high school, and had given it little or no thought. Thus, when Coach Humphreys told me with a big smile that Texas was interested in me, I didn't know how to react. Noting this, Coach Humphreys told me about the University of Texas and its head football coach, Darrell Royal. Royal had coached at Texas since 1957 and had been head coach the whole time. He had coached nine post-season bowl teams at Texas and had been named Coach of the Year several times. He had coached a National Championship Football Team and several Southwest Conference Championship Teams. Royal had one of the top winning percentages of all time among major college football coaches. With his record and his name, it was not surprising that he could field a team every year made up of the best athletes that the state, and the nation, could offer.

After lunch we went down to Memorial Stadium to look over the locker rooms and training facilities. At the time of my visit, the upper deck at the stadium was only in the planning stages. Waller Creek lay peacefully in the natural bed it had cut for itself, oblivious of the rapid changes the campus around it was going through. (Remember Waller Creek, and the important battle over it between the protectors of the Creek's ecosystem and Regent Frank Erwin, whose style was not appreciated, but who was backed by all the pro-Memorial Stadium expansion groups? The fuss was over whether Waller Creek should be moved twenty feet or so to the west in order to add the stadium's upper deck.) Before crossing Waller Creek, we walked past the prefabricated military barracks that constituted San Jacinto Men's Residence Hall to take a look at the huge, open grass-covered field called Freshman Field (now, after complete renovation, renamed Clark Field), located between Prather Men's Residence Hall and San Jacinto Boulevard. Leon informed me that this was where the freshmen football team practiced. Back in 1969, before the Southwest Conference established a limit of thirty scholarships per school, all freshmen played on the freshman team. We had our own schedule, coaches, and workouts. I remember asking Leon whether he knew of any other black players being recruited by Texas because, as we walked through the Freshman Field, I contemplated what the rest of my teammates would be like. He mentioned several names, but the only one I remember now is John Harvey. I remember being impressed that Texas was trying to recruit him, for he was not only one of the best running backs in Texas, but also one of the best sprinters. It was encouraging to think that I might get to play football with athletes of his caliber. I'm certain this helped me decide before I left that weekend that I would accept a scholarship to Texas. We then walked across Waller Creek and San Jacinto Boulevard to Memorial Stadium.

We looked over the stadium—the field was still a grass oval with a cinder track around it—and then went up to the T-Room and the varsity weight room, both of which are located on the ramps between the ground-level and the second-level entrances to the bleachers on the west side of the stadium. Having trained in high school with cheap weights stacked in the corner of a small utility room, I relished thinking of what I could do with the equipment in the varsity weight room. It seemed as if there was an exercise machine for every muscle in your body, with plenty of space in between. The T-Room is a lounge that is opened for lettermen during home games and on other occasions. It contains numerous mementos of UT's lush athletic history, along with a list naming everyone who has lettered in a varsity sport at Texas. The pictures of recent Texas football teams contained no black players. Leon had been speaking constantly about how important it was for people like me who were offered scholarships to accept them in order to get blacks on the rosters of Texas football lettermen. He emphasized, as I have to numerous prospects since then, how much of an opportunity playing at Texas is. Yet this opportunity was being overlooked by black athletes.

It was being overlooked because of fear—fear based on Texas' lily-white image. What was clear to Leon, and later to me, was that this fear was not based on the concrete experiences of black scholarship football players. There was no one to whom these things had happened. We both thought that it was time for someone to go through the Texas scholarship football program to meet this intimidation head on and either give it real life or destroy it. I knew when we left the T-Room that day that I would see to it that The University would no longer labor under the weight and embarrassment of white-boys-only scholarship football program.

&

That evening Leon and I went out to dinner at a steak restaurant and talked about what dorm life was like and what it would be like having all white teammates. Leon was honest in what he had to say about these things. Dorm life, he said, would be comfortable but extremely easy to get enough of. He said that with all of these different guys from towns all over Texas, there would be something happening all the time, from quiet studying and television watching to . . . well, just about anything. Getting along with the white football players would not be much of a problem, Leon said, because most of them did not have a problem with having black teammates. Of course, there would be some guys who would, but there would be guys like that anywhere I might go. Leon pointed out that what commanded the most respect was showing everyone, coaches and players alike, that you "took care of business" on the football field. Leon said that most of the players who didn't have cars, like himself, had no problem borrowing a car from one of the other players who did. Little things like this, he said, helped him to learn that getting along with whites at Texas is much like getting along with anyone anywhere: You must treat persons as individuals because they are all different.

The following morning Leon picked me up from the Villa Capri and took me to Coach Royal. On the ride over to his office, I remember thinking that the meeting would be a turn-off if it took the form of a hard sell. I thought this despite Leon's having told me that Royal was "pretty cool, and easy to talk to." When we got up to his office, a few other players were standing with the recruits they had shown around, waiting to see Royal. As we stood outside it occurred to me that Royal must be pretty intense to bring in all these recruits and give each of them a one-on-one hard sell about signing with Texas. The recruits coming out of his office before me didn't appear to have been pressured or intimidated. Finally my turn came. I went in and was pleasantly surprised by Coach Royal's approach.

Coach Royal was very poised when he greeted Leon and me and invited us in to talk. I imagine that his tactic of bringing Leon in with me was designed to help me relax, and it worked. My first impression of Royal was that he wanted me to be comfortable with my choice of college and that, while he wanted me to attend Texas, he would not be offended if I chose to go elsewhere. By questions he asked he made it clear that I should think about my choice of college as an important part of my future. Do you enjoy living in San Antonio and Texas? What kinds of things would you like to do if you do not make a career of football? What academic goals do you have? Instead of giving a hard sell, he really believed that this was a very important decision, because it affected my future, and he wanted me to give it careful thought.

Before I could broach my concerns about race Coach Royal brought up the subject himself. He said that he was aware of my concerns and that he wanted me to feel free to talk about them. He would answer any questions I had. He seemed to believe that Leon and Coach Campbell had told me all about what I could expect at Texas. He said he would stand by everything they had said. His openness and his confidence in his staff and his program won me over as a friend and admirer from that day on. Leon and I had explored most of the things that concerned me, so our meeting was rather short. Coach Royal thanked me for coming up for the weekend and, as we walked to the door, he shook my hand and said he hoped that I liked the program and the facilities. I wonder whether he knew that he had just recruited the person who would eventually be the first black to play, start, and graduate from Texas.

On February 11, 1969, I signed the Southwest Conference letter of intent, declaring that I intended to accept the scholarship offer from Texas. On August 22, 1969, I arrived in Austin to begin pre-season football training and to begin my freshman year at The University. In the fall of 1971 I received my first varsity starting assignment on the Longhorn football team as an offensive tackle. That season was ruined by a knee injury that caused me to miss the first five games of the season and to lose my starting position.

In the fall of my senior season in 1972 I received my second starting assignment as a tight-end and started for the entire season. During that season I caught *all* of the team's touchdown passes. The season ended with the 1973 Cotton Bowl game in which we defeated Alabama. And in May of 1974 I graduated from The University with a Bachelor of Arts degree in Philosophy. ★

1984

KINKY FRIEDMAN

Richard F. (Kinky) Friedman was born in Chicago and moved to Central Texas with his family during his childhood. Friedman graduated from the University of Texas in 1966, served in the Peace Corps in Borneo, and formed a progressive country-western band, The Texas Jewboys, in the early 1970s. Such Friedman songs as "The Ballad of Charlie Whitman" and "They Ain't Making Jews Like Jesus Anymore" earned him nearly undying fame. In the 1980s Friedman launched into writing detective novels with catchy titles like *The Love Song of J. Edgar Hoover* and *Elvis, Jesus and Coca-Cola*. Friedman's latest career move has been to run as an independent in the Texas Governor's race in 2006. Friedman lives near Kerrville, Texas, where he operates the Utopia Animal Rescue Ranch for stray, abused, and aging animals. In "The Left Bank of Texas" he performs a familiar ritual among Austin-lovers: remembering what used to be, in this instance the old Nighthawk restaurant on Guadalupe, near the UT campus.

THE LEFT BANK OF TEXAS

My FAVORITE PLACE IN TEXAS IS A RESTAURANT THAT closed almost ten years ago. It was known as the Nighthawk on the Drag. The Drag, of course, spiritually speaking, isn't doing too well either. But in the early sixties, when I was a student at the University of Texas in Austin, the Nighthawk, along with the Pancake House and the old Plantation restaurant, was where people went to stay up all night, drink coffee, and solve the problems of the world. Sort of the Left Bank of Texas.

It was a different world then. People didn't rent movies. Women knew their place. Homosexuals still hid in the closet. A scruffy guy named Bob Dylan had just put out his first album. Soon the SDS would be holding raucous meetings at the Y. Revolution was on the way. Coffee was a dime. All right, it was twenty cents.

It was an age of innocence. Barton Springs ran pure as it had since the beginning of time. Though Elvis was no longer driving a truck and Fidel was no longer playing baseball, Charles Whitman and Lee Harvey Oswald had not yet dreamed of ascending great heights and rearranging the local or national landscape. In a quiet booth beside a window looking out on the Drag and the world, I first contemplated joining the Peace Corps.

I think it must've been sometime later while I was riding Greyhounds and driving pickup trucks across America trying to find myself that the Nighthawk on the Drag disappeared. Just flew away in the night.

Today it's gone, the Drag's been sterilized of hippies, radicals, and riff-raff, and the campus hums along like a happy Volkswagen factory. There will always be Young Republicans in this world, but the phantom clientele of the Nighthawk may be an endangered species.

And there was a waitress there I remember . . . ★

1986

GARY M. LAVERGNE

Gary Lavergne was born in the Cajun community of Church Point, Louisiana, and earned a B.A. (1976) and M.A. (1981) from the University of Louisiana at Lafayette. He currently is Director of Policy Analysis and Research for the Admissions Office of the University of Texas, but moonlights as a crime writer. He has authored three well-received books on crimes in Texas: *A Sniper in the Tower: The Charles Whitman Murders* (1997), *Bad Boy from Rosebud: The Murderous Life of Kenneth Allen McDuff* (1999), and *Worse Than Death: The Dallas Nightclub Murders and the Texas Multiple Murder Law* (2003). In his job at the University he works in the very tower from which Charles Whitman rained down death that day in August 1966. The section below offers a brief history of significant crimes in the city leading up to the attack by Whitman.

from A SNIPER IN THE TOWER: THE CHARLES WHITMAN MURDERS

AUSTIN'S CRIMINAL HISTORY TENDED TO FOCUS ON A few infamous cases. In a case eerily similar to that of Jack the Ripper, the "Servant Girl Annihilator" terrorized Austin from 1884–85. The serial killer hacked young girls while they slept. At the time, City Marshal James E. Lucy had a police squad of fourteen men. The force, citizen patrols, and several posses with bloodhounds never caught the killer. The last two Annihilator murders occurred on Christmas Day, 1885, when two women were hacked and their bodies dragged from their homes. During the reign of terror thirteen women were killed. The crimes have never been solved.

In 1925 E. E. Engler, his wife, and their twenty-five-year-old daughter were victims of a brutal ritual-like torture and murder. They were found shot to death in their modest farmhouse near Del Valle, a small suburb south and east of Austin.

In all of 1965 Austin would have only nineteen homicides. James C. Cross, Jr., of Fort Worth, confessed to the two best known of the murders. He strangled two University of Texas coeds and dumped their bodies in a field in north Austin. Cross was sentenced to life in prison. The crime was still the talk of the campus when Charlie and Kathy Whitman returned to make a home for themselves. While the Austin community grieved the loss of the young coeds, Austin was still thought of as a good and safe place to live. Murder was seen as an infrequent crime committed by stalkers who crept up on their victims in the dark of night. Killing was done in private so that there would be no witnesses. Few could conceive of murderers who might make no attempt to escape and might be willing to pay for their crimes with their own lives. Shortly, more people would begin to accept those notions, not only in Austin, but in all of America.

The University of Texas at Austin had 25,511 students enrolled in 1966, but only 13,000 for the summer session. Its campus was comprised of 232 acres of Spanish-style buildings with red terra cotta tiled roofs and wide, tree-lined walkways called malls. Elaborate fountains greeted visitors at the entrance of each mall, and a consistent architectural style gave the campus character. The West Mall connected Guadalupe Street, also known as the "Drag," with the center of the campus. The larger South Mall ran from 21st Street to the center of the campus, past the famous Littlefield Fountain and statues of American, Confederate, and Texan heroes. Each mall led to the Main Building, from which rose the symbol of the university—the Tower.

The campus, located just a few blocks north of the state capitol, was very near the center of the city. In 1966, it already had serious parking and traffic problems. The Drag formed the western border of the campus. There, small shops catered to a student and faculty clientele. Bookstores, dress shops, music stores, theaters, and barber shops lined the street that by 1968 would also boast street vendors peddling cheap "stuff." Musicians played in doorways and on street corners with instrument cases opened, hoping pedestrians would throw in some change. But the Drag was not part of the campus—not officially anyway.

The University of Texas Tower, Austin's tallest building, rose 307 feet above an area of Austin which was itself 606 feet above sea level; the state capitol rose 311 feet above an area 600 feet above sea level. This meant that the Tower was taller by two feet, and for some Texans this was significant. Should any of UT's athletic teams win a national championship, all four sides of the structure were (and still are) lighted orange, and selected rooms are lit to form a "1." The top of the Tower is also lit to celebrate Texas Independence Day and other holidays. During World War II the Tower became a symbol of potential combat by housing Austin's air raid warning system, but on V-J Day its huge carillon played "America" while students and others in the area stood silently. After the war, people remembered the Tower as a source of melodious euphony emitted from its carillon as the world wept and greeted peace. War and peace! How much more diverse can a symbol be? Such diversity was very "Austin."

The genesis of the Tower was similar to that of many public buildings of the era. During the early 1930s, when university officials identified a need for a new main building and library complex, the Great Depression and Franklin Roosevelt's New Deal response provided an opportunity for the university to expand its physical plant. The Public Works Administration (PWA) allotted $1,633,000.00 for the project, but nearly a year would pass before W. S. Bellows Construction Company of Oklahoma City signed a construction contract. Foundation work began shortly afterwards, and by 1937 the building had been occupied.

The collaborative efforts of Robert L. White, the university's supervising architect, and Paul Cret of Philadelphia, created the Tower design in typical 1930s style, where colossal skyscrapers like the Empire State and Chrysler Buildings rose above cities to dominate urban landscapes. Smaller versions of the architectural style, like Huey Long's Louisiana state capitol in Baton Rouge and the UT Tower in Austin, became symbols of their locales. In the same way it became impossible to think of New York City without the Empire State Building, it eventually became impossible to think of the University of Texas without envisioning the Tower.

Its design and construction, however, were not universally lauded and in some quarters were derided. Self-appointed critics were uncomfortable because the style fit no convenient category; it has been called many things from "modified Spanish Renaissance" to the oxymoronic "Modern Classical." In a 1947 article, Thad W. Riker, Professor of Modern European History, called the Tower "a mongrel, a hybrid. It is partly classical, partly Spanish." Folklorist and Professor J. Frank Dobie became the Tower's best known and most vocal critic. He described the style as "Late Bastardian" and the crown of columns above the observation deck as the "Temple of Vestal Virgins." Dobie suggested that the Tower be laid on its side so that all rooms would be close to the ground. Speaking to a southwest literature class during the building's construction, Dobie was reported to have said: "It's the most ridiculous thing I ever saw. With as much room as there is in Texas and as many acres of land as the University owns, we have to put up a building like those in New York."

Defenders of the Tower had a simple response. So what if the Tower reached for the sky! It was big—like Texas itself. Professors Riker and Dobie could hardly deny the building became a source of pride for their students or for Texas. Almost immediately tourists began to visit the Tower in order to step out onto the observation deck on the twenty-eighth floor. By 1966 visitors reached the deck at an annual rate of about 20,000. University officials found the spectacular view useful; the deck became a convenient observation point to direct traffic by radio after UT football games. Some Tower visitors wanted a close-up view of the famous clock which served as the principal time piece for the campus community. First set when it arrived in 1936, its four faces, one on each side of the Tower, had a diameter of more than twelve feet. Quarter-hours were marked by four bells of the Westminster Chime, a bell weighing three-and-a half tons marked each hour, and a carillon of seventeen bells allowed musicians to ring out holiday music on special occasions.

The first death associated with the Tower occurred in the fall of 1935 during the construction of the building. Charles Vernon Tanner, a construction worker, accidentally slipped off a scaffold and fell twelve floors to his death. The first suicide did not occur until nine years later on 11 June 1945 when an English professor and faculty member, Dr. A. P. Thomason, leapt to his death after slashing his wrists, ankles, and throat. Four years later a UT sophomore named Edward Graydon Grounds leapt from a window on the nineteenth floor. Less than a year later Benny Utense Seller accidentally fell from a window ledge in an apparent attempt to regain entrance to the building. The 1950s was a safe decade for Tower visitors; the next death did not occur until 3 March 1961 when Harry Julius Rosenstein jumped from the twenty-first floor after learning he was three academic hours short of graduation. ★

1997

WILLIAM J. HELMER

Born in Iowa City, Iowa, William Joseph Helmer attended high school in Pharr, Texas, and obtained a B.A. in Journalism from the University of Texas in 1959. After working as a magazine editor in New York City, Helmer returned to UT in 1964 and in 1968 received a B.A. in American Studies. His M.A. Thesis was titled "Development of the Thompson Submachine Gun." In 1994 his book *Dillinger: The Untold Story* was published. In "The Madman on the Tower" Helmer, writing twenty years after the fact, recreated that day in August 1966, when the University of Texas became the scene of a bloodbath.

THE MADMAN ON THE TOWER

IT'S LIKE BELONGING TO A FRATERNITY THAT NEVER meets: You are talking with someone and learn he was living in Austin in 1966, and pretty soon the subject of Charles Whitman comes up. Then for a minute or so, it's where-were-you time—that Monday, August 1, under bright skies with the temperature approaching one hundred. I was a University of Texas graduate student supervising student publications as a part-time job. Walking from the old journalism building on Twenty-fourth Street to the Union to get a sandwich for lunch, I could hear loud reports that had the *boom, snap* quality of rifle shots. They were coming from the vicinity of the Main Building, but I didn't see any unusual activity there and shrugged them off as the sounds of a nail-driving gun, which had been periodically banging away on a construction project there. Later I discovered that everyone hearing that noise was running it through a mental cardsorter until it found a slot that offered a perfectly ordinary explanation. One person, also mindful of the construction, decided that it was the sound of large planks falling over and slapping concrete. Another, closer to the mark, decided the ROTC must be shooting blanks for some ceremonial reason on the mall in front of the Main Building with its twenty-seven-story Tower. Yet another saw a girl fling herself to the grass and assumed, having read a feature in the campus paper a few days earlier, that it was some kind of goofy crowd-response experiment being carried out by the psychology folks.

I was still operating on the nail-gun theory when some students standing behind a pillar of the Academic Center started shouting something about a guy on the Tower shooting people and how I should get moving. My first response was to resent being yelled at, so I just stood there in the middle of a grassy inner-drive area, squinting up at the Tower's northwest corner. Sure enough, I could see a gun barrel poke out over the parapet and emit smoke, followed an instant later by the boom I had been hearing. Now the computer was working a lot faster but still coming up with a bad read-out: *Just look at that! There's some fool up there with a rifle, trying to get himself in one hell of a lot of trouble!* From my angle, it didn't look like the man was shooting downward, but was just trying to create a commotion.

So I turned around and started walking (don't show fear, they can smell it) the two hundred or so feet back to the protective corner of Hogg Auditoriium, maybe trotting the last few yards. A student already there was pointing and jabbering about a girl who was hit in the side yard of the biology building, which I had just crossed coming from journalism. That bumped the alarm meter up substantially, and I joined him in yelling at a student strolling along the sidewalk past the old Littlefield Home, right behind us and to our left. We nearly got the guy killed, for when he stopped to look at us in puzzlement, the sniper opened up on him with a semiautomatic rifle. That sent him scrambling to the protection of an alley as bullets whacked into the low limestone wall behind him, popping like movie squibs. Since then, I've wondered if he knew how lucky he was that Whitman had evidently emptied his two other rifles and was using his little open-sight Army carbine. With his scoped 6mm bolt-action Remington, it had been strictly one shot, one man, in the old Marine Corps tradition.

That bit of excitement convinced me that something not only very weird but very bad was happening. I had a queasy feeling that returned later that day when the paper said one Tower office employee looked out and saw "two young boys laying face down in front of Hogg Auditorium," and it came back a few days later, when a *Life* magazine aerial photo showed X's where people had been hit along the route I had just taken.

I had been a little slow in switching over to emergency, but my wits were supposedly about me as I made my way around the back of the auditorium to the Union, where I knew of a stairwell window that afforded a good and, I thought, safe view of the Tower. The window was wide open, and a girl in a white blouse was already sharing the right-hand side with someone, so I went to the left where only one student was standing and looked over his shoulder. Everyone was talking, and I could hear people downstairs in the Union lobby, babbling in confusion. Someone had come in from outside and was running through the lobby, crying, "That man is *dead*! That man is *dead*!" as though such a thing were entirely impossible.

I could see the sniper fairly well; he would lean out over the parapet, bring the rifle to bear on a target, fire, tip the weapon up as he worked the action, then walk quickly to another point and do the same thing. It must have been about that time that he hit an electrician next to his truck at Twentieth Street and University Avenue, a quarter of a mile away. It was about that time, too, that the Tower clock started chiming and then, with coldblooded indifference, tolled the noon hour. And it must have been only moments after those echoes died that the sniper, evidently firing through one of the Tower's drain spouts, put a shot through the open window where the four of us stood gawking.

The bullet struck the edge of the window opening in front of the girl's face like an exploding stick of dynamite, filling the stairwell with glass, splinters, bullet fragments, and concrete dust. The blast put us on the floor, and the first thing I perceived was the girl, flat on her back, hands to her face, screaming. Which surprised me; I didn't think there could be any face left to scream with. I started crawling over to her, and my left hand slipped so that I partly fell forward into blood that was rapidly covering the floor of the stairwell. The blood wasn't hers; the bullet had fragmented, and a large chunk of it had pierced the right forearm of the guy on my side of the window. It had hit an artery that now, as he lay partly on his side, was pumping out blood in rapid squirts about three inches high.

It's strange what happens to time in situations like this. All motion slowed down and became dreamlike. I knew how to contend with arterial bleeding, but in the second or two it took me to get my hands to his arm it seemed as if I had ages to consider the neatness of the wound, the brightness of the blood, and its fountainlike behavior. I refused to think another shot might come through that window, because my legs were still exposed. I could still hear the girl's sobbing, and I could hear my own voice, squawking for someone to give me a handkerchief. The shooting victim used his good arm to pull one from his back pocket and hand it to me.

The girl had debris in her eyes but was otherwise okay. The guy would be okay once he was slid under the window and into the hands of other students who had come running up the stairs. I was okay but pretty blood-splattered and had trouble convincing one samaritan that the blood was not mine. Except for a tiny bit; while washing up in the basement men's room, I found that what looked like a shaving cut in my neck held a piece of the bullet's copper jacket, not much bigger than a pinhead. Realizing that that could have been the large chunk of bullet made it hard to breathe for a little while.

When I went back upstairs, no one had any real idea of what was going on—how many riflemen were up there or if the killings were part of something else that was happening. That feeling was enhanced by the absence of the police. Rarely does a person witness a car wreck or a fire or another emergency except in aftermath, when the scene is swarming with cops and firemen and spectators. To witness an emergency taking place is to realize that the cops don't come with it. After the first ten or fifteen minutes, I began hearing an occasional siren that ordinarily wouldn't have signaled anything more than a traffic problem here or an ambulance run there. But the shooting had been under way for nearly half an hour before the sirens of police cars and ambulances became obvious, blending into yelps and howls like a neighborhood full of dogs set off by a passing fire engine. That noise, punctuated by auto horns blown in panic and anger, blanketed the city. To that was soon added the garbled voices of newscasters blaring through more and more transistor radios. At least the radio reports were bringing things into sharper focus, describing a carnage far greater than anyone walking on campus could guess. Those early shots that had caused me more astonishment than alarm had, I now learned, hit their targets nearly every time, all over campus, up and down Guadalupe, at amazing ranges, killing people. Whitman hit running targets, bicycling targets, targets at ranges of up to five hundred yards; he even put a bullet through a light plane carrying a police rifleman. And his field of fire was so great that targets never stopped presenting themselves at distances they mistakenly thought were safe.

And something else incredible was happening. From about noon on, I had been hearing the occasional crack of return fire from the ground. I supposed it to be police, who at last were dashing around, revolvers in hand like pacifiers, looking helplessly officious. A couple of them had riot shotguns, which likewise could not have served much more than the psychological purpose of reducing frustration. But when I walked out the front door of the Union, staying out of Tower range, I felt the concussion of a high-powered rifle firing from somewhere nearby. I thought, "Ah, now we're getting someplace!" though I wasn't sure where. Minutes later I saw a man in street clothes with a scoped deer rifle in one hand and an Army surplus ammo can in the other, running in a crouch across Guadalupe toward the back of the architecture building, where he disappeared into bushes. I went back inside to find a safe route to the Academic Center, the only building between the Union and the Tower, and God help me if I didn't see a middle-aged man in a hunting cap and full camouflage hunting outfit, pockets bulging, standing in the Union's protected courtyard and squinting up at rooftops, apparently looking for a position from which to shoot. Later I heard some bizarre stories. A member of the Confederate Air Force antique-aircraft club in the Valley supposedly called the Department of Public Safety and offered to head north at full throttle in a World War II fighter, armed with privately owned .50-caliber machine guns. I somehow doubt that, but such a thing would not have been out of the question. Some friends of mine who were glued to a television set in the old San Jacinto Cafe a few blocks southeast of campus said that a man carrying a deer rifle rushed in, bought a six-pack of beer, and rushed back out.

About the only difference between police and citizens that day were uniforms and radios, and some cops had neither. Nobody seemed to know what to do except keep down, and I found out afterward that the officers on campus were angry and frustrated that no helpful suggestions were coming from headquarters, which had not even unlimbered the department's supply of fairly old .35-caliber rifles, which at least had the range. The only cops with useful weapons were those who went home and got them or those who came from home and brought them. One I knew, Lieutenant Burt Gerding, had headed for the campus with a .30–06 Army Springfield, scoped and sporterized from its World War I configuration, and several bandoliers of Army surplus armor-piercing ammunition. He took up a position on the roof of the business and economics building off the Tower's southeast corner and doesn't mind admitting now that before he got sighted in, the first shot went high and put the most conspicuous hole in the Tower clock's translucent glass face. After that, he hit a bag of cartridges that Whitman had set on the parapet and maybe one of Whitman's rifles, which appeared to have been struck by an armor-piercing bullet.

The ground fire was picking up, maybe a shot every five or ten seconds, which was causing me to think, "Just what we need—a bunch of loonies lobbing bullets all over the place, killing even more people." But I noticed that as the ground fire increased, the shots from the Tower came less often. Peeking carefully upward from a corner of the Academic Center, I could see puffs around the Tower's parapet that were not smoke from the sniper's guns but bullets striking the soft stone, sometimes knocking out sizable chunks that seemed to waft slowly downward. At one point the shooting picked up in much the same way that kernels of corn begin to pop sporadically for a time, then more and more often, until all of a sudden the popping blends into a roar before tapering off again.

I was trying to figure out what that barrage was all about when some-body pointed toward the mall in front of the Main Building, where a girl was stranded in the grassy area, squeezed behind the thick base of a flag-pole, her face in her hands. A man's body was lying out there in the sun, cooking on the intensely hot concrete. Through the space between some large shrubbery I glimpsed someone running across the mall, fully exposed to the Tower. I found out later that some students had dashed out into the open, distances of twenty, thirty, maybe forty yards, to pick up the dead and wounded and carry them back out of range. The sniper wasn't firing because the fusillade from the ground was hitting the Tower's parapet like a slow-motion discharge from a giant shotgun.

I was watching part of this on live television in the basement of the Academic Center. One of the school's TV cameras had been rolled outside the door of some building and had been left there, unmanned, zoomed in on the top of the Tower and feeding a TV monitor in the lower level of the Academic Center. That was eerie—seeing the observation deck close up, seeing the little puffs of dust kicked out of the limestone by bullets, with the sound coming not from the TV but from outside, where it all was hap-pening. A reminder of that was a wounded girl stretched out on a table in the same room. No one seemed to be looking after her when I walked in, so I asked if I could do anything or get her anything, and she shook her head no, as if she preferred to be left alone. I turned my attention to the TV and after a few minutes was perversely thinking that this show didn't have much action. Then, finally, something did happen—a piece of cloth waved briefly above the parapet, signaling the end.

I went outside to see maybe a thousand students emerging from every-where and stampeding toward the Tower, nearly overwhelming several cops who were trying to keep them back. It crossed my mind that if the signal were a trick, the sniper had just cleverly replenished his supply of targets. But it was over, and I could hear a transistor radio calling for a halt to the ground fire on orders of the police. And now I was on the Academic Center breezeway, watching the crowd trying to turn itself into a mob, some over-adrenalinized students starting to yell obscenities and words like "lynch" and "kill," as if more of that were needed. I found myself wanting to strike out at them as much as at whatever tortured creature had been in its death throes up in the Tower.

The accounts of Charles Whitman's death were pretty garbled at the time, and there was no way that those of us on the ground would understand what had just happened on the Tower. After the pilot of the small plane reported only one sniper, it seemed obvious to me that he had knowingly trapped himself, intending to die and to take with him as many others as possible. When the finale came, at about 1:25 P.M., it did so in a stroke that was at once a monument to official disorganization, dumb luck, and great personal courage.

The cops who had made it into the Main Building were trying to control the fairly panicky situation there, while others, deciding they were on their own, had taken the Tower elevator to the twenty-seventh floor, which gave access to the switchback stairs leading two more flights up to the observation level. There they encountered new problems. Whitman, after lugging his gear up to the central reception area, had first killed the middle-aged woman who was well known to the campus for her insistence that everyone sign the visitors' register and not make jokes about jumping; then he had not killed a sight-seeing couple who came in from the outside walkway. Those two went on out, assuming that the man holding a gun who had cheerily said, "Hi, how are you?" was a school employee preparing to shoot pigeons. But six members of a tourist family who next came up were received with blasts from Whitman's sawed-off 12-gauge and four of them, two dead, were now lying on the stairs on top of one another in a great bloody mess.

Efforts to help those people and to push through the sniper's hastily erected barricades of furniture resulted in four men reaching the reception room at the observation level with no plan of action. Whitman was outside and unseen, but the sound of his shots seemed to be coming from the northwest corner of the outside walkway that circumscribed the clock tower. Luckily, that was exactly opposite the doorway leading outside, which was at the southeast corner.

The first man through the door was twenty-nine-year-old Ramiro Martinez, an officer who without discussion turned left and began working his way north along the Tower's east side, armed only with a revolver. Following him was Officer Houston McCoy, twenty-six, armed with a revolver and a riot shotgun. Posted to guard the south side was a civilian, Allen Crum, the forty-year-old floor manager of the University Co-op bookstore who had asked to join the attack party; he was more or less deputized and given a rifle by a policeman downstairs. Joining him moments later was Officer Jerry Day, also acting as rear guard in case the sniper retreated in that direction.

Martinez and McCoy traversed the walkway on the east side of the building one after the other, hopping past drain spouts that were still funneling in bullets from the ground. Then, in a move of terrible courage that might now seem short on wisdom, Martinez leapt from cover and with one hand began firing his revolver at the young man with blondish hair who was backed into the opposite corner, about fifty feet away, holding a semiautomatic Army carbine. The carbine was swinging around to fire when McCoy delivered two bursts of doubleaught buckshot to Whitman's head and neck, making up for the .38 bullets that appeared to be missing their target.

Later, neither cop went beyond a few clichés in trying to describe how it felt to climb over the dead and dying victims of a mass murderer and then confront the madman and his rifle face to face, but the psychic energy it took to do that thing displayed itself in ways that were not fully recorded in police reports. McCoy remembers that his colleague gave a war cry when Whitman was knocked backward by the blasts and that Martinez then slammed his empty revolver to the tiles, grabbed the shotgun from McCoy's hands, and ran to the still-jerking body to fire point-blank into its heart. After that he threw the shotgun down too hard to suit its owner and ran, shouting for the shooting to stop, toward the others on the walkway, who recognized him in time. Martinez doesn't recall being so rough on the guns but admits he was a bit rattled at the time and needed a hand getting back to the police station. That night he hid from the press at his brother's house, drinking an entire bottle of gin without—he said later—feeling its effects. McCoy stayed crouched by the body, searching it for identification, and spoke to it, warning it that if its spreading pool of blood ruined his boots he was going to heave it over the side. He likewise avoided reporters and spent the evening drinking.

Since neither cop claimed personal credit for killing Whitman, it went by default to Martinez, who was found more newsworthy by reporters pleased to have a genuine minority hero. He was widely honored and ended up a Texas Ranger, now stationed in New Braunfels. McCoy quickly faded from the picture and today works at a Boy Scout camp near Menard.

It took time for the magnitude of August 1, 1966, to sink in and for the press to sort out what had happened. You don't get the biggest mass murder in the country's history very often, and whether this one qualified depended somewhat on definitions. Even the body count hinged upon the theological issue of a fetus that was killed but whose mother survived, and then there was the matter of Whitman's mother and wife, whom he had killed the previous night. Counting the latter and the fetus, the final toll came to sixteen dead and thirty-one wounded, though it was possible that one or two others were treated for minor wounds at the height of the confusion and did not make the list. That Whitman, a twenty-five-year-old architectural engineering student, was discovered to be a former altar boy and Eagle Scout provided delicious irony—the ugly duckling tale in reverse. That his marksmanship was astounding could be attributed to good Marine Corps training. Superficially he presented the image of a happily married college student and an all-American boy from the proverbial good family. But on closer examination, it turned out that his marriage wasn't happy, his family situation was thoroughly screwed up, and Whitman was a driven, pill-popping, self-flogging bully and all-around psycho with a talent for concealing it.

Exactly why Whitman snapped (and that seems to be the word) can never be known, but in the preceding weeks he had talked to a university psychiatrist about the emotional strain he was under, pressures that were building up, and his increasingly violent impulses, which apparently began to surface (or resurface) with the breakup of his parents' marriage a few months earlier. "I talked with a Doctor once for about two hours and tried to convey to him my fears that I felt come [*sic*] overwhelming violent impulses," Whitman wrote in a letter. "After one session I never saw the Doctor again, and since then I have been fighting my mental turmoil alone, and seemingly to no avail."

In fact, Whitman had told the psychiatrist that his urge was to go up on the Tower with a rifle and begin killing people. That was dismissed as fantasy, since thoughts of the Tower were not uncommon in the minds of troubled students, the doctor told a press conference the next day. I'm sure that's true, but I attended the press conference and was interested to see that the psychiatrist was the same one whom my wife and I had consulted independently a few months earlier when a pending divorce was causing us both some serious depression. My visit consisted mainly of listening to him talk on the telephone with the driller who was putting in a water well on his ranch, after which he gave me a prescription for Librium. My wife came back from her visit crying and said that after pretty much baring her soul, his advice to her was "Grow up." I won't hazard a guess as to what comfort and advice he gave Charles Whitman.

Whitman professed hatred for his rigid and authoritarian father in Florida, just as he expressed deep love for his wife and mother—feelings he described in remarkably lucid and introspective notes written the previous evening in the course of killing them both. In a letter dated "Sunday, July 31, 1966, 6:45 P.M." before his first step was even taken, the mixture of past and present tense suggests that a final decision had been made very recently by a compulsive man who placed great importance on following through:

> I don't quite understand what it is that compels me to type this letter. Perhaps it is to leave some vague reason for the actions I have recently performed. I don't really understand myself these days. I am supposed to be an average reasonable and intelligent young man. However, lately (I can't recall when it started) I have been a victim of many unusual and irrational thoughts. These

thoughts constantly recur, and it requires a tremendous mental effort to concentrate on useful and progressive tasks. . . .

It was after much thought that I decided to kill my wife, Kathy, tonight after I pick her up from work at the telephone company. I love her dearly, and she has been as fine a wife to me as any man could ever hope to have. I cannot rationaly [*sic*] pinpoint any specific reason for doing this. I don't know whether it is selfishness, or if I don't want her to have to face the embrassment [*sic*] my actions would surely cause her. At this time, though, the prominent reason in my mind is that I truly do not consider this world worth living in, and am prepared to die, and I do not want to leave her to suffer alone in it. I intend to kill her as painlessly as possible.

Similar reasons provoked me to take my mother's life also. . . .

At about that point in the letter, with his mother still alive in her apartment across town, Whitman remained true to his tightly scripted personality by scribbling in the margin, "Friends interrupted." The friends, a student and his wife, later described Whitman as acting "particularly relieved about something—you know, as if he had solved a problem." And he had. The exact nature of Whitman's madness is open to speculation—there were many family factors and possibly religious ones; there was a report of a small brain tumor whose possible effects are disputed. But most students of the mind would agree that he resolved some intolerable psychological conflict by turning over to his personal demon all responsibility for his actions and placing his skills at its disposal. With that came, evidently, the kind of relief psychiatrists and criminologists sometimes see in prisoners for whom a single but exceptionally brutal killing has been the safety valve gone pop! Afterward those people confront their fate with an equanimity bordering on apathy. For them, death is only a further release—possibly the one they unconsciously sought all along but without Whitman's ability to turn it all into a prolonged drama. He returned to the letter and scribbled the matter-of-fact notation "8–1–66. Mon. 3:00 A.M. Both Dead."

Whitman spent the rest of the night and the next morning readying himself to depart life in a style reflecting the pressures that had been building for months, maybe years. He had several guns but bought two more, plus ammunition, without arousing suspicion, chatting amiably with clerks. Then he dressed in overalls, parked his car near the Main Building sometime after eleven in the morning and, giving the appearance of a maintenance man, dollied a duffel bag and a footlocker crammed with ordnance and supplies to the observation deck of the Tower. His encounter with the receptionist and the tourists may have caused him to miss the changing of classes at eleven, when the campus below him would have looked like a busy ant bed. About eleven-forty-five he fired his first shot from the parapet. An hour and a half later, he was killed.

I saw Whitman when they brought him out. When the shooting was over, my journalistic instincts revived, and I went to one of the back doors of the Main Building to avoid the crowd. The police, likewise avoiding the crowds at other doors, wheeled out a stretcher bearing the sniper's body under a blood-soaked sheet. My sense of time may be off, but it seemed as if they brought their bundle out quickly, as if they wanted it out of there before the mob could get to it.

I finished school in 1968, left Austin, and since then have worked in other cities, but the memories of that day are as lasting as the proofmarks on the barrel of a gun. I come back to Austin to visit friends and family, and I visit the UT campus often enough that it no longer affects me to walk around there, though I occasionally find myself idly figuring out the least-exposed route from one building to another. I don't actually go that way, of course. And I don't give more than a moment's thought to the things I saw and did that day. But if I'm walking from the Main Building across that wide concrete mall, say, or along one of the inner-campus drives, I can't quite shake an ever so slightly uneasy feeling that the Tower, somehow, is watching me. ★

1986

JAMES R. GILES

A native of Bowie, Texas, James R. Giles received his Ph.D. from the University of Texas in 1966. He has been a member of the Department of English at Northern Illinois University since 1970. He is the author of numerous scholarly monographs on such writers as Irwin Shaw, James Jones, and Hubert Selby, Jr. His latest book is *Violence in the Contemporary American Novel: An End to Innocence* (2000). Giles was having lunch in the UT Student Center the day Charles Whitman began firing from the University tower, and later turned that episode into a documentary-style story.

ONE AUGUST DAY IN TEXAS

AUGUST 1, 1966–11:30 A.M. TERESE TELLICKA WAS standing with Abby, her child of four, at the magazine rack of a drug store-restaurant located on the fringe of the campus. Her desperate flipping of the pages of magazine after magazine typified Terese's approach to everything. She communicated nothing so much as the sensation that her every act, every movement, every gesture were struggles against an overwhelming and unrelenting foe; and, in fact, they were.

Reality had never been easy for Terese. Not since the time her father, gone from her life before she had a distinct impression of what he looked like, had turned to her and laughed and said: "Jesus, what a weird, ugly kid!" All the years of her childhood; constantly moving with her mother from one Southern state to another; staying for brief periods with one group of strangers, then with another related in no discernible way to the last; then on to a newer group, and a newer. . . . She learned the word "nomad" early. Her mother. Beautiful, Terese *thought*. She didn't remember for sure. After leaving her mother she realized that she had seen that aloof figure no more clearly than anything else in her life; but she did have an impression of long black hair, penetrating auburn eyes intensified by dark lashes, and high cheekbones covered by a skin which radiated beauty and passion. Her mother had left her often and for increasingly long periods with the strangers. She stopped crying after the first few times until the night when she was thirteen and a man with red hair and a bracelet of a design that frightened her came into the room where she was sleeping on the floor and pulled off her covers and jerked down her pants and did it to her. When her mother returned a week later she did not tell, but there was a scene between her mother and the man anyway, and they soon left that place.

She had hated what he did to her, and it was four years before it happened to her again. Her mother had given her a pill to "make her feel better about things," and there was a boy of about seventeen and a field below the house, and he didn't force her. Then her body started changing; and her mother screamed at her and asked who, and then gave her money and told her to get out. She had the baby, Abby, in Shreveport, Louisiana, and then worked as a waitress in one little Louisiana and Texas town after another until she received a letter from her mother postmarked "Miami, Fla." It caught up with her in Refugio, Texas, and read: 'Terese, I want you to have a chance for a life. Here is money. There is more. Whenever you need it." A check for $3,000. She and Abby arrived in Austin accidentally of course, but still they stayed. And almost instantly she became part of the University of Texas campus. The anonymity inherent in a "community" of 35,000 concentrated within a landscape of Spanish-brick buildings, countless fountains, and statuary ranging from lifeless, "traditional" images of Lee, Davis, Washington to grotesque abstractions ("Pioneer Mother," "Winged Victory") offered her security. Since childhood she had felt anonymous, and here everyone seemed intent upon submerging himself into the mass of students.

She especially enjoyed sitting in the lecture courses of fifty to 200, even though she understood little, if any, of what the remote figures on the stages were so earnestly talking about. After one such lecture, she was adopted by a group of English graduate students. It was not long before she was living with first one of them, then another; getting drunk or stoned at their parties; listening to their passionate, if incomprehensible, conversations; and finally attempting to read their books. She knew that her reactions to the novels, the poetry, and the philosophy amused them, but still they liked her being around and they took care of Abby better than anyone ever had. She was, in fact, a "personality" in the English department. Pathetic, ugly Terese (her mother had given her no more of her beauty than she had anything else, until the check in Refugio) with her strange child. Still it was an identity and had been for over two years.

She would meet a group of grad students in the union building for coffee in an hour; and now she was attempting to read, digest, memorize the new magazines so that she might better follow the conversation this time. She had not slept the previous night, reading *Notes from the Underground* instead. Abby was standing patiently waiting for her mother to move. It had been a long time since she had cried and begged for attention during moments like this.

Finally, Terese did move and walked out into the brutal August sun. The sidewalks radiated waves of unbelievable heat. She felt that she was walking in a capsule of perspiration. Her skull and her lungs were bursting. It was literally dangerous to be outside. Terese suddenly had a new comprehension of "sunstroke." Not a deadly assault upon the head alone, but a scorching violation of every cell of the body. Like the egg frying on the sidewalk. That was a good metaphor; it could happen to you. Objects appeared through a quivering mist. Nothing was distinct. Only outlines, forms which refused to remain stationary. With no conscious knowledge of how she got there, she was at the campus post office. There was a letter from her mother—postmarked "Atlanta, Ga." Four hundred dollars inside, and a "letter: "Terese, your life is yours. Let no one control it. Refuse submission to anything." She and Abby left the post office at 12:01 P.M. and started along the mall toward the union. Rising above the mall was the university tower.

JULY 31, 1966-Sometime during the night. Charles Whitman, twenty-five years of age, fired two shots into the back of his mother's head.

JULY 31, 1966–11 :00 P.M. Dr. Stanley Maxwell was very drunk. He was screaming at his wife who stared mutely at him: "You want what? Do you know? Have you ever known? Would you know if, it came up to you and said, 'Here I am, Bette, you bitch. What you lack, desire, require, urgently need. The fulfillment you've been robbed of. The self denied to you. The accomplishments you can't accomplish. Something to make you more known, respected, admired than even Stanley, your intellectual bastard of a husband. The. . . . '"

Then Bette was out of the room and his range of vision. For a minute, Dr. Maxwell stood, fondling his beer and gazing after her. He had a vague sensation that people were staring at him. Undoubtedly, the graduate students were shaking their heads sadly and sighing: "Poor Dr. Max. Always at every party. It's getting old, really old."

And it was. Had been for some time. Stanley Maxwell grew up in a slum section of Scranton, Pennsylvania; his father had been a night watchman, and his mother had raised children. In addition to which Stanley Maxwell was and always had been physically unattractive. For instance, he even had small feet—abnormally small feet. He felt that a great deal of his personal tragedy stemmed directly from that fact. But poor, ugly Stanley had done well enough in college to win a graduate fellowship to Cornell where he earned a doctorate in English literature (specialty: modern British poetry).

The best job he had been able to get then had been in the English department of the University of Texas. He had never considered the state of Texas or the University of Texas to be innately good or bad things until he landed one July night in Austin. Almost immediately, however, he had an attitude toward both—the state was a sprawling barbaric land inhabited exclusively by mentally retarded rednecks and oppressed minorities, and the university (most definitely including the English department) was run by failed Compsons and Sutpens from Mississippi and Tennessee whose concept of "the academy" was incurably ante-bellum. About the university he was not entirely wrong; and for three years, Stanley Maxwell did not fare well. He attempted desperately to cover his Scranton, Pa., childhood with his Ivy League education; but there were always moments (especially at the interminable English department cocktail parties) when the cover slipped. And he was poor, ugly Stanley with the abnormally small feet again. So he cultivated his contempt for the state, the university, and his colleagues and students.

He was doomed at Austin until he met Bette Schindler, a graduate student in sociology and a daughter of a university regent. The regent was a Dallas oil millionaire; otherwise, he would not have been a regent, of course. Soon he was also Stanley's father-in-law. Bette had always been a lonely, terrified girl; and she felt a familiarity and comfort in Stanley's bitterness and anger. He expressed always what she had never had the nerve to express. After their marriage, Stanley was promoted to associate professor, could do or say nothing wrong at departmental cocktail parties, and discovered that the graduate students whom he was now allowed to teach enjoyed his "Eastern iconoclasm." He, in short, had it made. So almost immediately he began making life hell for Bette. Telling her in private or in public about her own mediocrity and her sick jealousy of him. A scene like tonight had become almost mandatory at all parties. It wasn't a scandal anymore; it was, in fact, simply "getting old."

In realization of that fact and of the fact that all his "attitudes" were losing their novelty, Stanley threw his Pearl across the room and ran out of the house and fell into a clump of bushes in someone's backyard and passed out.

JULY 31, 1966—Sometime during the night. Twice in rapid succession, Charles Whitman plunged a knife into his wife's body.

AUGUST 1, 1966—11:30 P.M. Shirley Evans was sixteen years old, and until this wonderful weekend had never been out of Avoca, Texas (pop. 2,670). But now she had been "chosen out of all the girls in her high school" to come visit "the state capital" and "the state university." It was a reward for "outstanding merit." "It will be a wonderful weekend for you," her mother had said. Her father had beamed proudly and given her money. He nearly always did both things around her. Shirley Evans had had a fine sixteen years. She had exhibited "special merit" in the eyes of everyone—her parents, her teachers, and her fellow students. Now, as a reward, she, along with sixty other obviously special girls from "all over Texas," was on a tour of the very heart of her state. All sixty had, in fact, just stepped off buses at "the university" in front of an enormous fountain in the center of which was a statue of several men with odd helmets riding plunging horses. Even the heat did not bother Shirley. Two of the other girls had fainted earlier that morning, but nothing could spoil Shirley Evans' "wonderful weekend."

AUGUST 1, 1966–11:40 A.M. Tom Hendricks was the associate editor of an Austin-based "liberal political journal." Tom, like the journal, had long felt a special obligation to keep alive the flames of political reform and humanitarian values in Texas. The flame seemed always on the verge of extinction. So many outrages against the helpless by every segment of the establishment—the politicians, the press, and the millionaires who owned both the politicians and all of the press except "his journal"—occurred daily, so that one could not possibly report them all. Much less comment on them. Certainly not fight them all. So Tom had learned long ago that a Texas "liberal" had to battle injustice selectively—he had no choice but to pick the most outrageous examples of corruption, brutality, and mediocrity and scream about them in print. But all the screams were drowned by the daily papers of Dallas, Houston, and Fort Worth with their front-page pictures of little boys in bathing suits running through water sprinklers, and the accompanying implication that suffering was unknown, indeed against the law, in Texas.

But worse than all that were the betrayals. You heard a young member of the Texas legislature talking sensibly about basic reforms (minimum wage laws, racial and sexual equality laws, whatever) and you began to support him. And you supported him; and, if he really did go someplace (Congress or even the governor's mansion), he no longer talked sensibly about anything. They had gotten to him, and you had helped create him.

So why did he still try? Why had he continued to try for fifteen years? The few victories—really honest-to-god victories that you could count on the fingers of one hand? Senator Yarborough? No, because like an alcoholic, you had the habit. You had to have the struggle, knowing always in advance that you would lose somehow, someplace. But you had to have it. It was like the heat—it was deadly, but you got to needing it. The defeats and petty treacheries, like the rays of the sun, assaulted your brain until you would have felt strange in their absence.

All this was what Tom Hendricks was thinking as he sat in the student union building on the UT campus drinking his fifth cup of coffee. For over three weeks, he had been attempting to "investigate" one of the myriad aspects of racism in the university. But, as he would have predicted in advance, the "investigation" had led nowhere. It was no problem to point out instances of racism; but it was quite another thing to locate final responsibility for racist policies, or even to prove that such policies, in fact, existed. Every administrator in the university could, and, in fact, did point to his own helplessness in such matters; some nebulous higher power had always issued an edict that tied everyone's hands. The path led beyond even the regents to the external forces that controlled them. Ultimately, the suggestion seemed to be that every moral outrage in Austin could be blamed on Dallas and Houston and, in a very real sense, it could be. Tom drank his coffee and attempted to reconcile himself to the idea that once again his journal would be reduced to slightly hysterical protest against blatantly obvious outrages perpetrated by a nameless, faceless "they."

For some reason which he could not quite comprehend, Tom found such a position much more difficult to accept than it ordinarily was. This particular indecency had been no worse than a hundred others. He must simply be tired, and older. Much, much older than the time when, as an undergraduate in this same booth in this same union building, he had first fallen in love with liberal politics under the spell of an English professor whose life personified, in almost mythic proportions, total identification with a concept of Texas as a unique geographical region loved beyond all rationality, as well as the lonely struggle against that official greed and ignorance that morally perverted the beloved "part of space." Tom had heard the defiant old man say more than once, "Only a Faulkner could explain

Texas, but it hasn't produced one. I'm not it, maybe you'll be." Tom had long since discovered that he wouldn't be that he had no gift for words except as weapons in tangible, immediate struggles. He lacked "creative genius." He was, and ever would be, merely a journalist, and not the ordinary kind of journalist at that. But the kind that was right for journals like his journal and for nothing else—the master of a prose perennially outraged by oppression and injustice.

A nostalgia almost sweet in its sadness filled Tom's heart and mind as he slowly got up and walked out of the union. *It would have been nice to have creative talent,* he thought, *I would have enjoyed that. Really enjoyed it. My writing is dead before it hits the streets, and it never changes anything, not a fucking thing. So why not just say, screw it? Become a teacher, a bank teller, an insurance salesman, work for the federal government, anything. Since it is a habit and a bad one at that, I can kick it.* As Tom reached the door to the furnace outside, his eyes caught the headline of the daily student paper: TEXAS FOOTBALL COACH SAYS UT ATHLETICS NOT READY FOR BLACKS. *Goddam, another outrage while I was sitting there!* A few students glanced curiously at the screaming man in the hopelessly baggy suit pushing his way out the door and breaking into a less than athletic sprint beneath the blazing sun.

AUGUST 1, 1966–APPROXIMATELY 11:00 A.M. Leaving a trail of bloody mangled bodies in his wake, Charles Whitman climbed to the viewing platform encircling the top of the University of Texas library tower. Resting most of his artillery for the moment, he selected one deer-rifle and quite calmly began testing it for accuracy of sight.

AUGUST 1, 1966–12:01 P.M. Directly beneath the library tower is a concrete mall. This mall is the center of the university. It is virtually impossible to go anywhere on campus without crossing it. One climbs a flight of concrete steps to reach it from any of three directions. Abby Tellicka was walking beside her frantic mother when she heard an explosion. Then there was blood all over her dress, and her mother was lying facedown on the mall's blazing concrete and what she could see of her mother's head was an incomprehensible tangle of blood-soaked hair and flesh. Abby crouched down and began to scream. She screamed without stopping until she was picked up almost two hours later by a strange man.

AUGUST 1, 1966-SOMETIME BETWEEN 11:00 A.M. AND NOON. When Dr. Stanley Maxwell woke up that morning, he found himself lying for some unknown reason in a clump of bushes. He got up painfully and began to walk stiffly toward the campus. "Christ, it's hot!" On the way, last night began coming back to him in fragments, and he was just remembering the fight with Bette when he reached the campus. Then he was distracted by what sounded like incredibly loud firecrackers. While climbing the steps of the central mall, he saw people lying on the concrete. Crazy psychologists will conduct experiments in any kind of weather. Then his arm was torn by a searing pain and there was blood all over his suit. Somehow, and he never could remember how, he managed to get off the steps and beneath some shrubbery that surrounded the mall's base. Through teeth clenched by a nearly unbearable pain, Stanley Maxwell shouted: "I've been shot. Walking to my goddam office on the campus of a university in the United States in the twentieth century, I've been shot. For the love of god, I've been shot." He was still repeating this when he was rescued ninety minutes later. It was some time before he realized that he could incorporate this experience into his "attitude."

AUGUST 1, 1966–12:02 P.M. Shirley Evans' group had just reached the top of the mall when Shirley heard a series of explosions and saw a woman fall to the concrete and a little girl with her crouch down and begin to scream. Then more explosions and more people falling. Shirley Evans began to scream when the face of the girl next to her exploded. "Fall down!" someone yelled just as Shirley huddled on the concrete. She lay face-down sobbing uncontrollably for almost two hours of unrelenting shots and screams until someone picked her up and carried her to a hospital where she was officially diagnosed to be "in a state of shock." She is still alive and still "in a state of shock."

AUGUST 1, 1966–12:09 P.M. Tom Hendricks was running across Guadalupe Street—the "drag" that marked the boundary of the UT campus—when he began hearing shots. Close. Jesus Christ, damn close.

Where? Who? He saw a man buying a newspaper at a stand on the "town" side of Guadalupe suddenly fall to the ground. *Above my head! That one was right above my head!* The next one wasn't, and Tom Hendricks had fought his last hopeless battle against entrenched injustice.

AUGUST 1, 1966–APPROXIMATELY 1:30 P.M. After a ninety-minute barrage during which he killed fourteen people (including an unborn child) and wounded thirty others, Charles Whitman, twenty-five years of age, was himself shot to death by an off-duty Austin policeman. At 1:40 P.M. his body was carried down from the top of the tower. Later the bodies of Whitman's mother (shot in the back of the head) and his wife (stabbed to death) were discovered. Other facts gradually came to light: Whitman had killed his wife and mother sometime during the previous night; he had assembled an arsenal (three rifles, two pistols, a shotgun, a knife) and a locker filled with food and drink and, sometime between 10:30 and 11:00 P.M. on August 1, had reached the top of the tower, continuing his spree of killing while on the building. The autopsy revealed Whitman to have a small, nonmalignant tumor in his brain. The university psychiatrist stated that, earlier in the year, the young man had consulted with him and expressed a desire to shoot people from the tower with a deer rifle. ★

1975

PART FIVE

Austin is the Heart of Texas: 1970s

GREG CURTIS,
Austin, May 15, 1973 208

ALBERT HUFFSTICKLER,
The Ghosts of College City 209

MICHAEL MEWSHAW,
from *Earthly Bread* 212

PAT ELLIS TAYLOR,
Spring Water Celebration 215

ZULFIKAR GHOSE,
It's Your Land, Boss 220

JAN REID,
from *The Improbable Rise of Redneck Rock* 223

MICHAEL ADAMS,
Crossroads at the Broken Spoke 229

RONNIE DUGGER,
from *Our Invaded Universities* 237

GREG CURTIS

Greg Curtis grew up in Houston and attended Rice University. He served as editor of *Texas Monthly* from 1981 to 2000. In 2003 he published *Disarmed: The Story of the Venus de Milo,* and in 2006, *The Cave Painters: Probing the Mysteries of the World's First Artists.* Early in his writing career he wrote some poems, and "Austin, May 15, 1973" has a touching lost-in-time quality, as does the obscure little magazine, *Lucile,* in which the poem appeared. The poem succinctly limns the three defining elements of Austin's history: politics, education, and natural beauty.

AUSTIN, MAY 15, 1973

I. In the capitol
   Bulging suits perch awkwardly
   while florid jowls wobble in dispute.
   In the hallways buckled shoes
   creep into private offices
   to squeak at secretaries.
II. Near the University
   Jesus's people threaten souls
   and hare krishna missionaries
   peer around an incense cloud
   down the blouse of a college girl.
   Dogs beg for handfuls of brown rice.
III. Alone at Barton Springs
   Icy water pressed
   My skin against my bones.
   Agony, irony
   Oozed into the stream. ★

1973

208

ALBERT HUFFSTICKLER

Albert Huffstickler (1927–2002) lived in Austin for many years and wrote many poems about the city. His front-page obituary in the *Austin Chronicle* referred to him as the Poet Laureate of Hyde Park, an old neighborhood located just north of the University of Texas. He was in the true sense a coffeehouse poet, and many of his poems attest to his abiding attachment to the University and its environs. Although I did not know Albert Huffstickler, I realized upon seeing his photo that I had seen him around the campus going on twenty years or more. "The Ghosts of College City" is representative of his Whitmanesque sympathy for the lonely and unfulfilled who haunt such places as universities.

THE GHOSTS OF COLLEGE CITY

I *know* they do. I've seen them.
They come here as young men,
maybe with a little income,
start school, attend classes
meeting no one,
graduate and then,
realizing there's nothing
they want to do,
enroll in a new program
designed to last years
and be extended if necessary.
And they walk the evening walks
of the campus,
eat in the corners of the cafeterias,
hidden in a book
or peering furtively out

assessing the lives of their
fellow diners,
every one a stranger,
walk the streets of night home
to the apartment from whose walls
loneliness drips like pale blood,
rooms filled with odd mementos
recalling nothing but the day ahead,
and books, books, books.
And something inside these people
bleeding so silently they
no longer notice.
And, the seasons growing and passing,
the nights stacked like blocks
of ice in the corners of the
small rooms,
they walk their days
with a placidity unbroken
by any measurable crisis.
They belong to this scene:
the campus at dusk,
tree-lined Twenty Second Street,
the Varsity Cafeteria.
They have stamped themselves
like an undecipherable inscription
on the pages of our lives.
They are here.
We pass them, hardly noticing,
day after day after day.
They are here, patient and
enduring,
breathing our air, brushing our

elbows,
passing a small smile if addressed,
then vanishing.
And they keep alive a certain essence,
futile, inward, utterly essential,
defining for us what's buried
but inescapable,
shadows caught by a street lamp,
walking home through the dark
on any street in town. ★

Sept. 29, 1977

MICHAEL MEWSHAW

Michael Mewshaw is the author of ten novels and seven books of non-fiction, most recently *Do I Owe You Something? A Memoir of the Literary Life* (2003). Hundreds of his articles and reviews have appeared in the *New York Times*, the *Washington Post*, the *Los Angeles Times*, and other newspapers and magazines around the world. He divides his time between London and Key West. Mewshaw lived in Austin in the 1970s and early '80s and taught creative writing at the University of Texas. The scene below is another of those first sightings of Austin and the University by a newcomer. It is from his only novel set in Texas, *Earthly Bread* (1976).

from EARTHLY BREAD

TEXAS DIDN'T LOOK LIKE BIG COUNTRY OR ANY MORE like the west than Weehawken, New Jersey. True, a few palms and cactus plants struggled for survival on the median strip, but every other inch of the asphalt we sped over was lined by discount drugstores, cut-rate gas stations, barbecue pits, fortune tellers, wig outlets, warehouses, vast parking lots, and a dizzying assortment of fast-food chains. Nothing unusual about that. As American as the Golden Arches. What had I expected, adobe huts and cattle on the open range? Yet somehow the familiar scene didn't improve my spirits.

As we waited for a red light at a wide two-tier highway, soggy air, growing warmer, washed through the car. Where was the dry heat? Larry pressed a button to raise the windows, then crossed Interstate 35, and I spotted the Texas Tower and a stonehenge of tall, stark buildings done in what Larry called "a Mediterranean motif." Which meant red tile roofs. My eye was attracted to an immense football stadium, the omphalos of the

University of Texas campus, but Larry pointed right. "Over there's the LBJ Library. People say if you like Mussolini's Rome, you'll love it."

I smiled, although the white bunker of a building resembled no Italian monument I had seen, and it seemed more likely to contain prisoners than books. Its facade was webbed with scaffolding. "When do they expect to have it completed?"

"Oh, it's been finished for years. Started falling apart right after they opened it. They're putting a new face on it."

Swinging away from the University, he followed a cross street where other forbidding stone structures alternated with rubble-strewn lots over-run by weeds. Each building with its slabs of concrete and slotlike windows looked as if it had been designed with an eye to easy defense. Very few people were on the sidewalks.

"How far are we from town?"

Larry squinted at me through his wire-rim spectacles. "This is the town."

"This? Here?"

"Well, more or less." But he shot a quick look around, as if unsure. "There aren't many people around in August, so it looks a little deserted," he admitted. "We're between the summer session and the fall semester. But wait till next month." Larry took a right onto a street which was brightly lit and broad, yet again virtually empty. "This is Guadalupe. The students call it The Drag. And that's the plant over there."

St. Austin's bore the most rudimentary resemblance to a church, and could have been a false front from a movie set. The building had apparently been white before smoke or smog had discolored the concrete block walls. Making a U-turn, Larry stopped in front of the rectory, not far from a clump of red oleanders next to the entrance. If it hadn't been for that lovely bush, I doubt I could have brought myself to climb out and unload the baggage.

The temperature was still rising, but I had begun to perspire as much from nerves as from the heat. Larry must have noticed my fidgety mood. He kept up a constant stream of chatter about the liberal city government and the energetic parish and the mild winters and good country music as we stacked my black suitcases on the sidewalk. Then he paused and said, "To be honest, Tony, Texas takes some getting used to. It was months before I felt at home. But you'll like it here if you let yourself."

"I'm going to try," I said, drawing a breath. "It smells like they have dinner waiting for us."

"No, they eat early. It's always like that on The Drag because . . ."

His voice trailed off as he motioned in either direction to an all but unbroken row of restaurants, snack bars, fried-chicken stands, and pizza parlors, each one with an exhaust fan funneling out the odor of French-fried everything.

᪥

We drove past the Hillel House, where a sign had gone up for the oncoming semester: SHALOM Y'ALL AND WELCOME BACK TO U. T. GET YOUR FREE TICKETS FOR THE HIGH HOLY DAYS." The menorah under the message seemed to have lost its five middle branches. But no, that was the ubiquitous Longhorns symbol.

At Twenty-fourth Street we headed west, away from the clutter of the University, and coasted down past nine abandoned tennis courts where the green asphalt sent up wavering rays of heat. Though a parched wind shook the highest tree limbs, I couldn't hear it over the engine and the air conditioner. Then I sneezed explosively.

"Hey, you got it bad, don't you?" the driver said. "Sorry about the air conditioner. It's only got two speeds—off and on. That's better than the heater. It's got one speed—broken. Some days I freeze my butt off."

We crossed Lamar Boulevard and, soon afterward, Shoal Creek, no more than a trickle in its bleached gravel bed. Then we climbed uphill to an area of enormous tree-shaded homes where the lawns were broad, lush and close-cropped. This had to be one of the "nice neighborhoods" I'd been told about. Although I noticed no children playing in the streets or yards, I could imagine it as a marvelous place to be raised—here in the glittering suburbs that surrounded the emptiness at the center of the city like the honey-dipped crust of a doughnut. ★

1976

PAT ELLIS TAYLOR

Pat Ellis Taylor, who some years ago changed her name to Pat Littledog, was born in Bryan, Texas, and educated at the University of Texas at El Paso. She is the author of several books, including *Afoot in a Field of Men and Other Stories from Dallas East Side* (1983) and *The God Chaser: A Spirited Assortment of Tales* (1986). The first deals with poverty-level existence in Dallas, and the second contains numerous pieces set in Austin, where she lived for a number of years. Her work offers an insight into the old hippie counter-culture that was once so central to making Austin, Austin. The setting of "Spring Water Celebration" is familiar to just about everyone who knows the city: Barton Springs in Zilker Park.

SPRING WATER CELEBRATION

So it was getting close to springtime, a certain undercurrent of fever and bustle in everyone like I imagined was also happening with the seeds and roots and all underground getting ready to come rushing down and up and out. But it was heating up too fast, no rain for weeks, and the heat over eighty degrees one day after another, too hot for young plants. So I talked to the Austin goddess-followers to see if I could help them plan a spring celebration at a spring, and we decided on a little pool of water with a gravel bed called Sunken Gardens shaped like a womb three-fourths circled by tiers of earth and opening toward the Barton Creek side. Barton Springs, heart flow and center of Austin water where hippie women have bathed topless years before other parts of Texas ever saw a public boob, was only yards away but closed for the first time in any spring because of a too-high bacterial count from shopping center sewage runoff, running hot—Shit Creek, as they say, with no paddlers. The goddess-followers said we could have a picnic in a cedar grove nearby. We would parade ourselves over to the spring where we could all meet at 4:56 P.M. on March 20, clock-time for the spring beginning. There would be some dancers and musicians and we would wind around Zilker Park where the frisbee-people and the dog-walkers and barbequers and shadetree-poets and all would also no doubt be, who might then feel compelled, upon seeing us a-trooping, to join in for the walk to the springs. Then at the springs we would have a celebration.

Now I don't know exactly what kind of celebration there would be at the springs, and it seemed important that nobody knew what celebration there would be—so that whatever magic happened would be coming from this particular water joined for this particular springtime with these people who were naturally drawn together for whatever reason of their own. No borrowed rituals or ceremonies. No set words. The flyer sent out for the occasion said only that there would be a water celebration with one hour of spontaneous words. So I figured everyone would bring their magic stuff, whatever it was, and I started collecting mine. First a friend and I went around to the flower shops in town and got some big bunches of throw-away flowers—beautiful daisies, red gladiolas, yellow snapdragons, long-stemmed roses saved from the garbage piles. We put them in a basket, I tied on a goat-bell found by a friend in the West Texas desert, and I put on a long white robe embroidered with flowers my own pet-lover Chuck gave me after his last trip to the southern Rio Grande. My son Chico brought a flute, Chuck put a water poem in his pocket and brought a blue and white wind-sock; and so we started out.

The day was grey not sunny. And when we got to the goddess-followers picnic, they were milling around, unsure of what to do. So I started giving out the flowers. Two women-dancers got up and said they were going to lead the parade. But they said the parade should be silent, that no one should say a word, that we should make deliberate steps and breathe in and breathe out in a deliberate manner, concentrating on breathing in spring and breathing out winter, or something along that line. There were about twenty people in all. There was a guitar player and a fiddler and they had been playing some music when we first got there, but they put their instruments in cases and carried them quietly when the parade began.

Well, no one really gets much into following a silent parade unless it's a wake for a friend (an elegy for an unclean pool) so the rest of the park people ignored us as we paraded behind the two silent high-stepping dancers who were leading the breathing and the two musicians with their instruments encased. But the goat-bell slammed against the flower basket I was carrying, and I felt a little like a goat myself tripping along, Chuck's windsock floating above the procession, the path leading through buses and trees which were just beginning to leaf themselves out.

When we got to the spring there was another group of people waiting there for us. Grey Eagle from Dallas was there, also Ed Ward and Marsha with Passion the baby, Dorothy the goddess missionary, the sun mother Margaret, a woman with a feather-stick, several others ranging themselves along the rock and earth shelves. I got up on a ledge and started talking. I told about Balcones Fault, the long crack in the earth which Austin is built on, where Barton Springs comes up along, where people have lived for hundreds and maybe thousands of years, believing that it is a special and powerful place to be—putting out fumes of Austin mellowness in the air—appropriate place for legislators to converge upon trying to work out agreements. And then I said some things about the pollution, how sad it was that we should forget that our water is a reflection of our own state of health, and that it was time to give something more to water than our sewage. It wasn't a very coherent talk, and not very celebrational. But then there was a song, and the flute-player started playing his flute and the fiddler got her fiddle out and the guitar player began strumming, and people threw flowers into the spring and I threw in the rest of the basketful.

The water didn't look too good. It was the lowest I had ever seen it, not even high enough to flow out of its opening into the creek bed. I had bought a bucket in case people wanted to baptize themselves, but after so much publicity about the sewage, baptism didn't carry the weight of its cleansing and purifying metaphors too well. How could there be a water ceremony though without water? While everyone was chanting and singing, looking down from their dry perches into the water, this was the question which continued to come to my mind. So I kept peering into the water, trying to see something—how polluted it was or wasn't, and if it smelled at all, and what the stuff was mixing with the flowers floating on top of it . . . next year have a water ceremony at a local swimming pool maybe . . . in somebody's hot tub . . . back home underneath the shower. Then I looked around at everybody, looking beautiful and dry. No magic in a water ceremony without water; that was the strong message coming to me at the time. So I crawled down to the stone opening where the water would have been flowing out of it if it had been deep enough, took my bucket, took off my shoes and waded in. I walked out into the middle of the pool. The water was cool and it smelled good, like water, and there were flowers everywhere, and I thought well, water is polluted everywhere, water is polluted that comes out of the tap after all, and this water has just been blessed with dozens of flowers coming from dozens of good people, and if it makes me sick, it makes me sick, I don't care. Someone said take your robe off! And so I did. So there I was nude in the middle of the pool with flowers everywhere. I ducked down and ducked down again and floated around and it was cold but it wasn't too cold—so I called out to the people standing around, don't be afraid of this water! Then there was Marsha Ward at the spring opening, her clothes already shed, and she started splashing around, too, and after her came children wading in a little bit at a time and a young man who got his ankles wet and a woman to keep the flowers floating.

It was a grey day. No one really knew what to do without a printed program. We all come from different traditions when it comes to magic, and our songs and vocabularies are strange and unfamiliar to each other. I wasn't even sure the magic had come until I got out of the pool and someone gave me a shawl and we started walking to the car. Then I realized that there had been a message from the water: it was underneath my own skin now, my hands cool to everyone I touch, my body cool and calm. The message was SLOW DOWN; COOL OFF; PEOPLE EVERYWHERE THIS

SPRING SHOULD CONCENTRATE ON COOLING DOWN. The sky was grey and getting greyer, and a cool breeze was coming up, and while we were driving home, the first raindrops misted across the windshield, the first rain in weeks which would continue steady for seven days bringing the temperature down into the sixties, spring magic for the most skeptical, of the best kind. ★

1986

ZULFIKAR GHOSE

Born in Pakistan, Zulfikar Ghose moved to London in 1952. He obtained a B.A. from Keele University and supported himself as a cricket correspondent for the *Observer* in London. In 1969 he joined the Department of English at the University of Texas. He has published extensively, fiction, essays, and poetry. An autobiography, *Confessions of a Native-Alien*, appeared in 1965, and the *Incredible Brazilian* trilogy from 1972 to 1985. His *Collected Poems* was published in 1991. "It's Your Land, Boss" is his only poem set in Austin, and it well displays his international perspective.

It's Your Land, Boss

On a hillside in Texas,
digging the brown earth to deliver like calves
the limestone rocks with which it bulged, I thought:
The stubborn earth survives
more than the periodic drought
and the seasonal rainstorm; but how affects us
the word, O Earth, we call,
stooping, when like pilgrims we come to a land,
packaged across the turbulent air in the paths of jets!
A T.V. feature, canned
For syndication, that's
the prophet's dramatic way: to come home and fall
on his knees with an at last
finality, seeing salvation in a handful of earth,
I think of Israel and of the Jews who kill
and die for it, the land worth
the idea they fulfill

With their dying, an absolute belief and trust
that the earth has a mother's
claim to patriotic rites and sacrificial feasts.
The coarse, porous earth, toothy with flints,
casting out mythological beasts,
cynically hints
that it might actually be soulless. Let others
define whose perceptions
don't pickaxe the soil. I have more on my mind.
There's the grave mystique, too, compelling the youth
of America to find
primitive versions of truth,
to lose itself in flowery misconceptions,
wearing homespun cotton and beads;
or to stand before microphones on a college campus
and declare its own peculiar allegiance
to the earth. And thus,
whether it makes sense
or not, a revolutionary rhetoric breeds
a counter-rhetoric's pretentious
slogans: *America–Love It or Leave It,* and so on.
Earth-kissing Zionists aside (and each country
is an Israel for someone),
people don't really
care nowadays for sentimental gestures,
for sacredness is suspect,
the earth more a problem for conservation than
a banner across a jingoist breast, and the land
merely a real estate speculation.
Countries, countries! Brand-
names, faded and disfigured, on the wrecked
product that builds up rust

among the weeds and wild flowers growing behind
the idle farms. Worms and beetle-like insects
and the burrowing animals find
a home in the wreck's
corrugations. Old mother earth's a heap of dust.
My temporary peasant fervour
plays out its fantasy on the Texas hillside.
I'm not sure what this earth means to me.
I don't take the peasant's pride
in the quality
of the soil. I don't need to. But feel poorer
because of this loss,
this irrelevance. I rake aside the stones, push
at a rock that's too heavy to move. I throw
away tufts of grass. From this lush
land, too, I must go
towards horizons which the jet liners cross. ★

1972

JAN REID

Jan Reid was born in Abilene, Texas, but grew up in Wichita Falls. He received an M.A. from the University of Texas in 1972. He has written for many magazines and is the author of several books, including a novel, *Deerinwater* (1985); *The Bullet Meant for Me: A Memoir* (2002), an account of a near fatal shooting that occurred in Mexico City; and *Close Calls: Jan Reid's Texas* (2000), a collection of his journalism. "The Gay Place" is the title of the first chapter of *The Improbable Rise of Redneck Rock* (1984), Reid's first book, which depicted the exciting Texas music scene of the 1970s and its famed location at the Armadillo World Headquarters. That site, at the nexus of Barton Springs Road and South Fifth Street, is now a multistoried office building. A generic plaque commemorating the historic site was installed in 2006.

from THE IMPROBABLE RISE OF REDNECK ROCK

IN THE LATE SIXTIES POPULAR MUSIC WAS NO MORE than a dab of rouge on Austin's social cheek. Interest in music was healthy enough—record shops flourished by the score—but there were few reasons to believe Austin would ever be nationally known for its music. The state capital was often by-passed by major touring performers in those days, for the chances for packed houses were greater in the larger cities of Dallas, Houston, and San Antonio. When major acts came to town, they repeated the show they had played in Little Rock the night before, conceded to an encore or two after a sufficient period of clapping and foot-stomping, then caught the next plane out for Tucson. In the interval between those concerts, Austinites contented themselves with what was available locally. Folksingers strummed their guitars for nickles and dimes in the university area. Rock & rollers lived communally, tried to imitate their psychedelic heroes' best licks in free concerts in the park and paid for their new amplifiers by playing rubber-stamp dance music for the fraternities and sororities. Rhythm & blues bands played wherever they could, which was usually limited to the black east side. Country bands played in dimly-lit beer taverns as waitresses circled the room with tambourines in their hands, soliciting donations for the musicians. Any of those musicians might attract spirited local followings, but they knew, and their followers knew, that if they were going to make any sort of national impression, one day they would have to try their luck in the major music centers—New York, Los Angeles, Nashville.

In 1970 two developments changed all that. A number of musicians who were already battered and bruised by the major music centers began to settle in Austin. They were songwriters and singers of varied experience and potential, but they were good enough to land recording contracts with major companies. Many had backgrounds in folk and rock music that was not native to Texas, but the music they spawned in Austin was rooted in the forms young Texans had grown up with: fundamentalist gospel, black blues, and most important, country-western. That same year, a small group of young men and women launched a music-business enterprise with the unlikely name, Armadillo World Headquarters. It was a counter-cultural concert hall with adequate floor space but almost no furnishings. That first year the south Austin enterprise appeared particularly ill-fated, but it survived through the tenacity of its founders, who were goaded by a dream of a community center for artistic expression. Armadillo World Headquarters grew in community acceptance, if not profitability, and it became known as the forum for the unique music offered by the immigrant musicians. As the musicians grew in popularity they created an audience famous for its exuberant response to music, and performers from other parts of the country began to covet appearances at Armadillo World Headquarters. The success of the recorded Austin artists encouraged other local performers to return to the roots of their musical heritage, and the success of the Armadillo prompted other aspiring entrepreneurs to bid for a piece of the action. Soon

Austin was swarming with talented young musicians, and the most popular public spectacle was no longer football or political chicanery, but live music. Through the interest of a curious national press and word-of-mouth communication by touring musicians, Austin gained almost overnight a reputation as one of the most exciting centers of musical activity in the country.

A mild chill hung in the air one April night in 1973, a faint reminder of the harshest winter Austin had seen in years. But there was also a flowering smell of spring, a dance of light on the Colorado River. Trusting hitchhikers lined the curbs. Armadillo World Headquarters, an abandoned armory with a skating rink for a next-door neighbor, and the adjoining buildings were flanked by a parking lot riddled with chugholes. A muffled, metallic hum came from inside the skating rink. Leaning against the wall outside were a trio of young blacks whose leader watched the movement of loosely-clad white girls with long slow sweeps of his hat brim, turned a quarter over in his palm, and addressed every other male, "Hey brother, you got a dime?" On the other end of the parking lot, a German shepherd watchdog impounded for the night in an auto repair shop yard reacted to the stream of intruders with alternating bluff and bewilderment.

Inspiration had apparently visited the Armadillo staff artist again. He had started off on an outdoor wall with a mural that portrayed Ravi Shankar and band at ethereal work while in the background a nine-banded armadillo devoured the moon, but the mural on the new building housing additional toilets was more complex. It was a hazy landscape of the blue Texas Hill Country, enlivened by slices of watermelon, an ice cream bar, an old Chevrolet pickup parked near a stand of shade trees, an apple half with the Alamo for a core.

The interior sensation of the Armadillo was one of dark, airy space, at least until the cloud of smoke began to build. No one was onstage yet except a black cat which slept with one paw hanging off the piano, and elsewhere in the hall the look was barren. There were concrete walls, sparrows fluttered around the heaters and scraps of carpet suspended from the ceiling, a concrete floor partially covered with more patches of used carpet, a few tables, and folding metal chairs. Nothing of visual interest except another mural, this one depicting Freddie King in agonized guitar play while an armadillo burst from his chest, splattering blood. Freddie King recorded an album at the Armadillo once.

A group of young boys played touch football with a pillow on the carpeted section of the floor, hurdled toddlers in diapers, and taunted their young sisters. But then their football field began to shrink as the growing crowd ran out of tables and chairs and staked claims on the floor. The first band onstage was Whistler, a group that introduced Austin to country-rock in an east side barbecue dive in 1969 but disbanded shortly afterward because of nagging creditors. Whistler was together again for the first time in several months and the set was somewhat ragged, but the singer and piano player sounded a little like Linda Ronstadt, and they got a nostalgic reception.

Next onstage were Man Mountain & the Green Slime Boys, one of the more hopeful bands in town at the time. Man Mountain wasn't all that obese, but he sat down with a steel and dobro while his fellow San Antonians—individualized by a straw cowboy hat, a railroad cap and Jesus-length blonde hair-parodied Buck Owens, praised the legendary Chicken Ranch whorehouse in LaGrange, and brought the house down with a colored barbershop revival of the old Cadillacs' hit, "Speedo." The crowd got off to Man Mountain and brought them back for an encore, which left the boys a little abashed, considering who was waiting in the wings.

The next band began to drift out of the darkness after a short break: a woman with waist-length hair and a Barbara Streisand nose who walked over and sat down at the piano with her back to the audience, a long-haired young man who flapped his elbows as he tuned his bass, an older man in a Honolulu shirt with long blonde hair and a harrowed face who slouched over a pedal steel, and the drummer, costumed in a Machiavellian beard, Dracula cape and Pancho Villa cartridge belt. Finally he started a drum roll, and a white spotlight inspected each of the band members then settled on a short man in boots, beard, cowboy hat, and gold earring who walked to the microphone.

Willie Nelson and his band looked different, but except for the addition of some rock licks and lyrical references to Rita Coolidge's cleavage, it was the same time-worn music—the thumping bass, the rinky-tonk piano, the vocal steel, the same flat, sorrowful baritone. A Willie Nelson performance consisted of a tight, virtual medley of the songs he had written, but for those familiar with country top forty the list was astonishingly long: "Hello Walls," "The Party's Over," "Night Life," "Funny How Time Slips Away," "Me and Paul," "Yesterday's Wine." Nelson didn't record all those songs in hit-single form, but he sang most of them better than the artists who borrowed them. Yet the contagion of his performance derived more from the singer than the songs. Disembodied on record, Nelson was a good country artist, but in person he was a magician.

The guitar-and-song performance became the great American ritual well before Willie Nelson made his debut, but he was a master of the art. Young girls didn't scream when he walked onstage, and it was hard to imagine Nelson whanging his guitar against an amplifier, aborted voltage sparking all around him. He stood considerably less than six feet tall, his torso was beginning to belly out a little with age, and he cocked his hip and dipped his shoulder as he played his guitar and seemed forever in want of a comfortable stance. But he was always seeking eye contact with the people in front of him, nodding and grinning once it was established. Women flushed with pleasure when the skin around Nelson's eyes wrinkled in their behalf, but his look was just as direct and genuine when it fell on another male. He involved the audience with himself, his music, and they felt better for it. His songs might be sad, but he had the look of a happy man, a rare animal indeed, in these times.

As remarkable as Nelson's act that night was his audience. While freaks in gingham gowns and cowboy boots sashayed like they invented country music, remnants of Nelson's old audience had themselves a time too. A prim little grandmother from Taylor sat at a table beaming with excitement. "Oh lord, hon," she said. "I got ever' one of Willie's records, but I never got to see him before." A booted, western-dressed beauty from

Waxahachie drove 150 miles for the show, and she said, "I just love Willie Nelson and I'd drive anywhere to see him . . . but you know, he's sure been doin' some changin' lately." She looked around. "I have never seen so many hippies in my life." Be that as it may, she abandoned her date to dance a good part of the night away with one of them, a brawny thirty-year-old named Sunshine who used to ride broncs and play football for Texas Tech before he underwent some changes of his own. The crowd pressed toward the stage, resulting in a bobbing, visually bizarre mix of beehive hairdos, naked midriffs, and bare hippie feet. An aging man in a turtleneck stubbed out his cigar and dragged his wife into the mayhem, where she received a jolt she probably did not deserve: a marijuana cigarette passed in front of her face. She had heard about it, she had seen it on television, and she probably considered herself fairly enlightened on the subject, but that was clearly asking too much of her. A young girl observed the woman frantically fanning the air in front of her face, smiled, looked the woman in the eye, and took another hit.

But Nelson relieved any tension that developed beneath him. He played straight through for nearly two hours, singing all his recorded songs then starting over. They handed him pitchers of beer, threw bluebonnets onstage, yelled, "We love *you*, Willie"—a sentiment he returned when he finally called it quits: "I love *you* all. Good night." ★

1974

MICHAEL ADAMS

Born in Killeen, Texas, Michael Adams received his Ph.D. from the University of Texas at Austin in 1973. Adams is the author of two novels—*Blind Man's Bluff* (1982) and *Anniversaries in the Blood* (1988)—and a textbook on writing: *The Writer's Mind: Making Writing Make Sense.* He teaches English at UT and is Associate Director of the James A. Michener Center for Writers. In the essay reprinted here, Adams defines and memorializes the most famous country-western dance hall in Austin, the Broken Spoke, located at 3101 South Lamar.

CROSSROADS AT THE BROKEN SPOKE

IN THE EARLY '60S, JAMES M. WHITE DECIDED TO BUILD A honky-tonk that would provide people like him with a place where they could hear the kind of music he liked. What he got, eventually, was a dance hall honored by the state Senate, filmed by a Japanese camera crew making a documentary on American culture for its exchange students, rented out as a meeting hall by the National Historical Society, venerated by *Entertainment* magazine as the "Best Dance Hall in the Nation," and annually visited by a tour-bus load of western-dressed Germans on their "cowboy" club's pilgrimage to the heart of authentic Texas. How did this happen? Even James M. White isn't sure.

What is sure is that the Broken Spoke, as cited by *Texas State Highways* magazine, soon became not just the best honky-tonk in Texas, but something close to a shrine. Yet honky-tonk isn't exactly accurate. When Hollywood's in town, it's the chic place for their after-filming rap parties. When the Legislature's in session, senators and representatives meet there on Tuesday nights to dance, drink, and mingle with the salt of the earth. When NBC news was seeking an answer to their unknowingly provincial question, "What is a Texan?" they needed only three photographs—the Capitol building, The University of Texas campus (a studious book-reading coed below a bronze longhorn steer), and the Broken Spoke Saloon—the third in the trinity that makes up the Holy Body Texas.

What lured and lures the foreign, the popular, and the powerful to one of Texas' best and last honky-tonks is not just the love of country music and the simple pleasure of the Texas two-step, but the nostalgic lure of the mythic past. A good hat, rugged boots, and a fluid fiddle can carry you back to a simpler time—a time when there were clear distinctions between good and evil, right and wrong, up and out, love and loss, and where, in the lyrics, one could always find simple truths ("Every time you throw some dirt you lose a little ground"), simple fantasy ("Heaven's just a sin away"), simple psychology ("You're so good when you're bad"), and simple emotion ("Walk out backwards so I'll think you're coming in"). In an increasingly fragmented world, one could find simple tradition at the Broken Spoke.

The sense of tradition at "The Spoke" was a deliberate goal. When James M. White opened up the Broken Spoke as a café in 1964 and then added the dance hall in 1966, he wanted to create a sense of the past. After all, he was part of Texas tradition.

His great-great-grandfather arrived in 1836 to help fight for Texas independence. His grandfather was a Texas Ranger and Indian fighter, as was an uncle who was killed pursuing an army deserter in the Piney Woods of East Texas. Music was always a part of their life, his maternal grandfather clearing out the top room in his general store in Oak Hill, a community just south of Austin his grandfather helped name, and his friends carrying up their fiddles or guitars where they would play dance music all Saturday night. Men, being gentlemen, did their drinking outside in front of the buggies. Having heard country music all his life, either in bars where his father was a bouncer, or at places like the Moose Head, where his father now a deputy constable, would take his family, James M. White wanted to capture the atmosphere of the '40s and '50s and provide a place where people like himself could hear good Texas music every week. Without a blueprint and recapping what was left of a foundation sitting on a vacant lot, James and his wife Annetta built the Broken Spoke in a month and a half, holding their grand opening on November 10, 1964. Any dancing was done after serving hours in the dining area they would clear away. Two years later they christened the dance floor with the music of Johnny Rex, and, like Johnny's, the very connotations of the names of the bands to follow would suggest just what James White wanted to hear: Travis and the Westerners, Bill Darcy and the Melody Drifters, D. J. Burrows and the Western Melodies (paid $32 a night). Soon bigger names would follow: Ernest Tubb, Bob Wills, Tex Ritter, Ray Price, Roy Acuff, Kitty Wells, Willie Nelson, George Strait. If you wanted to hear real country music, in a real Texas dance hall, the place to be was the Broken Spoke.

Not insignificantly, the Broken Spoke dance hall began on the edge of town. It was a kind of swinging door right on the border between country and city, denizens of each needing a temporary peek into the other's world. The ranchers and farmers, tired or resigned by routine and conformity, arrived seeking escape or companionship, the pleasure of live music and, more personally, the lively dancing somehow more charged by the pull of gravity from a permissive city. The city man, worn down by pressure, deadlines, traffic, and surrounded by plastic and chrome, sought the simple, unpretentiousness of it all (sinking ceiling, raw wood, stale aroma of the past, the down-home gingham of the farm kitchen, the warm and easy crowdedness of a family of strangers). The same door swings a different way for each. In this sense, James M. White's place became something unintentional—As Ernest Tubb's rhythm guitarist Cal Smith might say—"a place somewhere between lust and sitting home watching TV."

The single country man or boy didn't need to change into a costume, only wash his rural clothes before he wandered into a dance hall with his hopeful fantasy hidden from his friends—and at times even himself. For the single city man, changing costumes was part of the need The Spoke satisfied. He could pitch aside his three-piece suit and tie, tug on his boots and jeans, crown himself with his store-bought hat and enter a different world, not just literally but metaphorically, for here the little boy who once dressed up like Roy Rogers and roamed the high sierras on a stick horse emerges from his Maverick or Pinto or Mustang as the Marlboro Man Incarnate.

But most of the clientele was not stray slacks but couples, even families—beer drinking Germans, Methodists, and other liberal religions that didn't see the Devil's hand in brew and dancing—that made it a kind of tribal outing. After chicken-fried steak (plenty of gravy) or Tex-Mex (plenty of grease), the parents and grandparents would dance while the children played bumper pool or pinball, or even danced a time or two themselves—usually reluctantly, usually with some old, age-spotted relative, or worse, a lower form of life, a brother or sister.

The very nature of the dances also held their lure, for within the honky-tonk moaning with the steel guitar, you did not find the anarchy of freedom in partnerless modern dancing, especially popular in the late sixties, but rather the specific and traditional movements of the two-step or polka, as you always moved the same counterclockwise direction around the floor. Any idiosyncratic style had to come within the sameness of movement. Thus, the dances gave the couples the security of conformity and the eccentricity of individuality—a safe and useful kind of pleasure.

It wasn't long, however, that the city grew past the saloon and the country moved farther away, and though everything changed around it, the Broken Spoke was still the swinging door on the edge. And into this crossroads dance hall kept pouring the society that surrounded it.

Eventually, in the early '70s, James White began booking country outlaw bands and local rock/country/folk bands like Marcia Ball, and for the first time cowboy hippies and long-haired cowboys made righteous by Willie Nelson began entering his doors, and to his surprise the unironed tie-dyed shirts and pearl-studded and starched western shirts crowded the dance floor with only a little friction now and then. The music was more Texas than Nashville now, but the image stayed the same. And The Spoke was becoming part of the Austin tradition of tolerance and good fun that would eventually and kindly be bumper-stickered into "Keep Austin Weird." Though more and more people who entered the swinging doors didn't sound like Texans (calling grocery sacks bags, selling inSURANCE instead of INsurance, buying ceMENT instead of SEEment, mispronouncing the city streets—Burr-Nétt for Burnet, Guadalupé for Guadalupe) and though many lacked the bone structure to give the proper slouch during the Texas two-step, such obvious outsiderness didn't matter inside these walls. And therein lay The Spoke's hidden therapy. Here anyone could feel safe.

The power of such an image, not limited to social hierarchy or geographical heritage, and the location of its shrine—amidst the state Capitol, the state's flagship university, a city beginning to swell with newcomers—inevitably drew a variety of pilgrims, making the Broken Spoke not just a haven for cowboys and cowgirls (urban or rural, drugged or drugstore), but a social crossroads that attracted Cadillacs and pickups, the rich and the poor, bankers and bikers, the white collar and blue collar, the brie and barbecue set. And this social crossroads in itself became another kind of lure. On any Saturday night, especially when a popular Texas band like Alvin Crow and the Pleasant Valley boys is there, you will see them:

FFA sweethearts poured like concrete into their jeans, beefy young bucks with big white hats, a doctor in turquoise bola, a state worker in satin blouse (a sequined scene of yellow cactus blooms), a professor in lizard-skinned boots and new jeans, a Jesuit priest with his name branded on the back of his belt—"Thomas" (Aquinas or the doubting one?), Dell computer suburbanites leading newcomers into this haven and pointing and whispering like the know-it-all tour guides they are, university students, both foreign and domestic, out for an evening of quasi-slumming and just unreflective, if noisy, pleasure.

And over there's an ex-Texas ranger bouncingly waltzing his fragile grand-daughter, his hawk eyes guarding her from the reckless high schoolers dancing the way they drive; and over there, a young couple from Manor doing all their special turns and twists among the more sedate dancers; and there a plump middle-aged couple in matching shirts—western piping of a tight-hatted cow-boy bucked high in the sky by the bronco with a belly full of springs. And there a covey of small-town young couples dancing as a group, smiling those incan-descent smiles not yet strained with age—or experience. And there, Fred Astair graduates lightly and swiftly floating around the sawdusted floor like Fred and Ginger, almost ethereal, too ideal and Hollywoodish for the earthly needs of the stumbling and graceless. And there some newlyweds (but Spoke old-timers) blowing minnow kisses and willfully giving into their publicly private smiles. And there some cocky high school boys and girls, obviously refugees from some more sanitary party, the boys in starched jeans and white shirts, the girls in floral dresses and high heels about to become instruments of acceptable torture. And over there a group of girls' night-outers, married women, some halfway from it, clumped in a back corner, their malelessness a magnetic pull for a few surveillant bachelors (faux or authentic) out on the prowl. And there an old couple, Friday night regulars, she with her eyes shut, her face as peaceful as a Madonna there on his shoulders, he holding her hand like a tiny bird as he leads her once more through the familiar pattern that lets them feel at once lost and loved. And there, the recent widower, sitting alone at "their" table (south side middle, closest to the dance floor), occasionally consoled (and even teased) by the waitresses who know him well, and he frequently retreating into nostalgia as he sips his beer and smiles poignantly at the color and movement of life on the dance floor. There are a few identifiables like these, but for the most part it's impossible to tell where someone comes from. And this is part of the comfort The Spoke unintentionally provides.

On occasion the real thing comes in. Some cowboy from a local rodeo, his number still on his back, his spine straight with pride (his cutting horse once more turning on a dime and giving back five cents in change), his young, wasp-waisted wife or girlfriend in silk shirt and designer jeans, sure to keep her eyes away from the many eyes she feels inspecting her—like judges at the day's livestock show. And from time to time some rich and handsome couple in tux and gown will wander in and find the darkest corner and, never dancing, sip beer, tip big, and watch the dancers—enjoying the simple pleasure of being there AND not having to be a part of "there."

All this cross-pollination has its effect in time. It's not unusual to see cowboy hat and tennis shoes, or evening dress with bright red boots, or baseball cap with ponytail dangling out the back, even straw hat and brown sandals in the summer. On Halloween you occasionally find the most bizarre mythic half-breeds—Werewolf under Stetson, Frankenstein in Tony Lamas, French maid in moccasins, clown-faced cowboy walking around with a knife in his back—is this costume or metaphor? But as diverse as the patrons are, they, ironically, come to represent another kind of truly "social" class—people from various social strata lured by a place where you can find both eccentricity and tradition.

The Broken Spoke crossroads has become such a lure that James M. White has cornered off a little museum to The Spoke itself. A kind of shrine to the myth. There under glass, you can find hats worn by Bob Wills, George Strait, Willie Nelson, and even LBJ. On the walls are plenty of photographs of James M. White with a famous crooner who's walked through The Spoke's doors—from Johnny Gimble to George Jones, from Kris Kristofferson to Dolly Parton. There's an American flag that once flew over the state Capitol building, and there are citations from Delaware to Germany, and displayed bumper stickers ("I Danced at The Broken Spoke") that, as a little note points out, have been distributed all over the world, plaques from our own state government offering its "highest esteem" and "profound gratitude" for entertaining such a "diverse clientele" and for creating one of the pre-eminent honky-tonks in Texas. And of course, the memorabilia: a 1968 menu (hamburgers .75 cents) and a half-smoked cigar, chewed on by Bob Wills on March 27, 1939.

Although The Spoke has seen the changes in the world outside waltz in and out of its more constant landscape—long-haired outlaw cowboys, cosmic cowboys, urban cowboys (John Travolta was brought here to see what a real Texas honky-tonk was like)—things are pretty much just as they were more than a quarter a century ago—same ranch curtains (grazing horses) in the restaurant, same chicken-friend steak, same bottled Thousand Island dressing on a wedge of lettuce, same pool tables and shuffle boards right there among the dining tables. And in the dance hall is the same low and precariously loose ceiling, the same metal folding chairs, red gingham table cloths, the same scattered neon beer signs, the Texas flag behind the bandstand, the same stagnant perfume of stale beer and smoke, the same collection of myths and mavericks. It's still a place where one can dance and actually feel both a sense of community and that self-reliant individuality of the cowboy on the open range. Too often for many, both seem to be lost in the world outside.

This sense of belonging is strongest during the dance that has become a tradition on Friday and Saturday nights—the cotton-eyed Joe. It's the moment when all the dancers lock arm in arm, or arm around waist in chorus rows and kick and shout their way around the dance floor. It is a time when you have permission to touch a stranger, and strangers have permission to touch you, and, even if it is transitory, just for a moment, as you shuffle around the floor, you have a sense of togetherness and tradition. The wheel is not broken here at the crossroads, behind the swinging door that still slaps back and forth on the edge—between past-present, city-country, us-them. Eternally on the edge. ★

1991

Ronnie Dugger

Ronnie Dugger was born in Chicago and grew up in San Antonio, Texas. He attended the University of Texas and was editor of the *Daily Texan*. In 1954 he was founding editor of the liberal journal of reportage and opinion, *The Texas Observer*. Dugger's first book was *Three Men in Texas*, a collection of essays in honor of Roy Bedichek, J. Frank Dobie, and Walter Prescott Webb (1967). In the same year he published *Dark Star: Hiroshima Reconsidered in the Life of Claude Eatherly of Lincoln Park, Texas* (1967). He has also written books on Lyndon Johnson and Ronald Reagan. Dugger has lived in New York City for the past couple of decades. In a free-wheeling case history of the University of Texas, *Our Invaded Universities, A Non-Fiction Play for Five Stages* (1973), Dugger described the recently opened LBJ Library and Museum. This site, located at 2313 Red River on the east side of the UT campus, remains a popular one for people in buses.

from OUR INVADED UNIVERSITIES

SO THERE IT IS, THE JOHNSON LIBRARY.

Before, one campus mall had run from the Tower westward past the student union and another stretched southward from the Tower toward the State Capitol. For the library a third axis was opened eastward from the Tower down to the Waller Creek valley and up to what may as well now be called Johnson Hill.

A walkway leads down the valley to a new fountain and thence, by a widened roadway, up the hill alongside the football stadium. Behind the library, the new Richardson Hall, which contains the new Johnson school, serves as a visual and psychological foundation for the monument to Johnson. As you walk up the hill past the stadium your gaze is cast upward to the memorial, the Johnson library, squatly resplendent, dominating the vista of the university spread-eagled before it. The effect is unmistakable and it was unmistakably intended.

Rectangular, eight stories high, with a heavy lid on the top, containing records and artifacts of Johnson's life and career, the edifice irresistibly suggests a tomb, a mausoleum. "He couldn't wait for death," said Representative Farenthold, upon the dedication of the place. The broad stairway's steps are canted, again inclining the gaze upward as one ascends them. Fifth-year architecture student Joe Freeman saw an Egyptian monumentality in "the grand axial vistas, the courts built on ascending levels, the ramps rising toward the holy of holies, and the sacred chamber housing the remnants of that now past dynasty." There has been a tendency to compare the place with the pyramids. It is more like an immense sarcophagus in pale beige Italian travertine marble. That it was erected with the democracy's tax money in the name of higher education under the direction and control of the seated president whom it was designed to perpetualize drives one to reflect upon what has been happening to higher education and to the United States.

Entering, you can believe it only because the new national capital is Disneyland. The Great Hall is the width of the building, eighty-five feet wide and deep and seven stories high, the encasement of space for show. There are no windows, which is just as well, since only birds could get up high enough to see out of them. You may eyeball at leisure on the west wall a presidential seal more than eleven yards wide. The Great Hall's only other feature, except air, is a stairway. At the top of it you may stand, feeling somewhat diminished, at the base of a twelve-foot-high granite obelisklike spire, craning your neck to read statements by Johnson or his ghost writers graven into each side of it. This activity leads you around to five murals, each one eight or nine feet across, each one etched in magnesium, showing, from left to right, Lyndon Johnson with Franklin Roosevelt, Lyndon Johnson with Harry Truman, Lyndon Johnson with Dwight Eisenhower, Lyndon Johnson with John Kennedy, and Lyndon Johnson. Moving either to the right or the left of this paneltheon you may watch a bank of five identical images of Johnson on five color TV screens uncritically celebrating, as Johnson's own, actual and alleged achievements during his presidency in education, health, civil rights, international affairs, the war on poverty, conservation, housing, and space. Spending a while in front of these machines, you can see what the evening news would be like if the president was the news editor. Showcases display Johnson's idealized life in photographs, his days in his life as the president, his daughters' wedding gowns, letters he wanted people to read, and gifts to him and to his wife when they reigned from political leaders and common people. On the next floor, there is a theater that shows films on Johnson's or his wife's trips, a month in his life when he was president, and the Texas hill country he came from. The exhibits were chosen by the Johnsons to sentimentalize themselves and the presidency, to romanticize Johnson's domestic and political accomplishments, and to minimize, almost by expungement, the Vietnam War. The place represents the collective national life personalized, ego on a tax-paid tear, self-serving in the name of a university, self-glorifying in the stacks of scholarship.

At the dedication Johnson said, "There is no record of a mistake, nothing critical, ugly, or unpleasant that is not included in the files here." That, one may believe if one chooses. The papers are packed in nearly forty thousand boxes, and we will learn a great deal from them in time. What the tourist sees now is the forty-two hundred red buckram boxes on the outside shelves and, glued onto each box, a small gold-colored replica of the presidential seal.

The eighth floor, that which from the outside looks like the lid of the tomb, contains a replica of the Oval Office in the White House with windows of bullet-proof glass. On the top floor there are also reading rooms, a research area, and an open patio onto which, at least at first, the people were not allowed. The helicopter landing pad, sixty feet wide, on the roof, and a sleeping area near the office were for Johnson.

The cost of the library and Richardson Hall adjacent to it is accepted to have been $18.6 million, paid by UT. Ransom said at the dedication that the Johnsons put in another $2 million. "The people of Texas built this library," Johnson said at the dedication. The federal taxpayers' maintenance and operating costs, $540,000 a year, are two-fifths higher than for any of the other presidential libraries.

The library contains about thirty-one million pages of manuscript materials; a still photograph collection of nearly five hundred thousand negatives, including the uncountable photographs Johnson had taken of himself almost constantly during his presidency; five million pages of agency records of the Johnson administration microfilmed for the library; more than a thousand motion picture films; more than three thousand reels of video tape and twenty-six hundred reels of audio tape; and semiofficial personal belongings of President and Mrs. Johnson, books, political cartoons, White House china, clothes, presidential office furnishings and equipment, pens used by Johnson to sign legislation, records of supposedly every phone call made to the White House, the lengths of meetings, and presidential time spent with visitors, conference notes, memos, a Persian carpet given by the Shah of Iran, a white sculptured porcelain horse, crocheted flags.

The first director of the library, Chester Newland, wrote that "the White House Central Files," containing the bulk of Johnson's papers, were transferred to the library as Johnson left office, the next largest block of the papers is "the White House Social Files," and there are separate files on Johnson's prepresidential papers and his presidential commissions, committees, and task forces. The fourteen task forces reports were made to Johnson only "off the record" and some were not made public, presumably because they displeased Johnson or contained recommendations he chose not to advocate. There were also, in the library, about two million "classified papers" locked in vaults.

Johnson, then, controlled his research depository on the campus, and he used it also as a place to meet the public and give autographs. When his book *The Vantage Point* came out, the library handled advance orders of autographed copies ("Advance orders . . . should be mailed with a check or money order to: The LBJ Library, 2313 Red River."), opened an exhibit containing several working pages of the manuscript, and served as the scene for Johnson's Sunday afternoon autographing party attended, it was announced, by about eight thousand persons.

When, then, Johnson died, his body lay in state overnight in the library, and seventy thousand people passed by.

What then is a university? *"Let us have a first-class university,"* Governor Roberts of Texas said in 1882, and *"then will this state have put on her armor to vie with other states and nations for superiority."* ★

1974

PART SIX

Austin Is a Happy Place, Sort Of: 1980s

ANDY CLAUSEN,
Conversation With a Lady I Took to
the Airport Who Loved Austin Texas 243

PETER LaSALLE,
from *Strange Sunlight* 247

JAMES HYNES,
from *Publish and Perish: Three Tales of
Tenure and Terror* 251

MAX WESTBROOK,
Bartons Creek 255

STEPHEN HARRIGAN,
[A "School" of Austin Writers?] 257

DAGOBERTO GILB,
From a Letter to Pat Ellis Taylor 259

KURTH SPRAGUE,
from *Frighten the Horses* 262

MARIAN WINIK,
The Texas Heat Wave 265

CHUCK TAYLOR,

Texas 267

BETTY SUE FLOWERS,

Being Imagined 270

JOSEPH JONES,

from *Life on Waller Creek* 272

TOM ZIGAL,

Recent Developments 277

ANDY CLAUSEN

Andy Clausen, who was born Andre Laloux in a Belgian bomb shelter in 1943, grew up in Oakland, California. After attending six colleges, he fell under the influence of the Beats and became friends with Allen Ginsberg, Gregory Corso, and others of the Beat Movement. In 1978 he moved to Austin, where he drove a taxi and wrote poems. These were collected in a volume titled *Austin, Texas Austin, Texas*, published in 1981. Clausen has published numerous other volumes of poetry. He lives in New York where he works as a stone mason, a troubadour, and a freelance teacher of creative writing in the NYC school system. The poem below typifies Clausen's Beat impressions of the Austin scene in the late 1970s.

Conversation with a Lady I Took to the Airport Who Loved Austin Texas

       another old lady
keep up–try–you gotta try–make her feel good
       "You've got a fine house."
       "It's not so nice; I have nice bushes
to hide it."
it's true–on second glance I see–
could use paint; needs repairs–
       "My husband's been gone 5 years. Our house
       used to be the only one out here.
       Exposition Blvd. Wasn't even paved; this
       was the country. I'm happy there, an
       old friend who's a doctor lives
       across the street. I'm happy behind
       my bushes. I'm just an old woman nobody
       wants an old woman."

No expressways from Deep West Tarrytown East
to the Airport the U. of Texas inbetween.
Now she's complaining her children
want to apartment her to senior citizen her.
But driving piece work, bare wired
To hustling nickels & dimes
With all the wounded wretched
paying me—I can't afford to not be cynical
With a 55 dollar a day lease.
  "Don't ever" she says "don't ever
  make someone move when they're happy."
I can see that
  happiness is more precious than gold
  "Oh, why did you drive thru the University?"
  "I think it's less distance, mam."
I answered true knowing most old folks
  would rather pay 20 cents less
  a slower way.
"I taught here 15 years; I hate it. I simply despise
  it."
"Look," I say surprised by her venom
for the economic main vein
of this youthful adult city
"Look, green lawns, what the literati
understand as verdure, trees,
squirrels, students, clean & probably not mean.
"Ah, it ain't so bad."
"Concrete," she snapped "concrete. It's
all concrete," becoming plaintive
"I hate Austin! If old Mr. Barton could see
what they're doing to his springs; he'd turn
over in his grave. He loved those springs.

He so loved those springs he wouldn't
leave that land to his own children
because he wanted it for us all; that's
why he gave it to the City. If he
could see what they've done and are
going to do, I just don't know. It's
horrible. It's the most beautiful place on earth!
Even if I can't get over there anymore
I'd like to think others could. Look
at what they've done to downtown.
It's so ugly, I hate it. I hate Austin.
One could walk down Congress Avenue
and see people they knew & loved
now all the faces are strangers
who want to stay that way."
Here it comes I figure
"So you think Yankees have
made it that way?"
"We were all Yankees when we came here.
Even the Indians & Mexicans came from
someplace else. Face it, we did it ourselves.
Why the American Bank was owned by an Austin man
who moved to Houston. He doesn't own it now;
he sold it to the Arabs. Oh he kept a percentage
& position. The old building was handsome,
longhorn door handles on huge oak doors
people would travel hundreds of miles just
to see & touch. Look at the sordid garish thing
now glaring its windows so ugly. He shouldn't
of done it. We shouldn't have let them do it.
They've sold half of Texas to the Arabs. We
Shouldn't have let them do it."

O the sad, the Plight, the Beauty
of Anger and permeating
sadness–I'm fighting my face
I can't let the airport cabbies
those Harlems and Roys & black porters
see me weeping
like a Canuck mother at a son's funeral
      "It still isn't such a bad place"
      I say remembering how the brutality
      & inexplicable misfortune
      of the people of my years
      never stopped tomorrow
      the tears locked in the recesses
      of my taxi eyes.
Her check hangs on my bulletin board
made out to Taxi Co.
      uncashed forever– ★

1981

PETER LaSalle

Peter LaSalle grew up in Rhode Island, graduated from Harvard, and worked as a newspaper reporter before coming to Austin to teach creative writing at the University of Texas. His books include the novel *Strange Sunlight* and two story collections, *The Graves of Famous Writers* (1980)and *Hockey Sur Glace* (1996). His work has appeared in many anthologies, among them ***Best American Short Stories, Prize Stories: The O. Henry Awards, Best of the West,* and *Sports Best Short Stories***. The selection below, from his novel *Strange Sunlight* (1984), tracks the archetypal encounter of someone from the East Coast encountering Texas, and specifically, Austin and the University of Texas scene, for the first time.

from STRANGE SUNLIGHT

NOT LONG AFTER HE HAD FIRST ARRIVED IN AUSTIN, Willington had met a displaced New Yorker in a bar. The New Yorker introduced himself as a retired postman. He had a bulbous rum nose and talked with a nasal accent. He wore a T-shirt advertising a local barbecue place, but he still conjured up a sense of flat-footing it around Bedford-Stuyvesant behind an aluminum cart and its leather sack, bundled up for winter in a government-issue gray twill uniform jacket and a Korean War-style postman's hat. He said he had studied cost-of-living statistics for over a year before he had left his job, taking a small but decent pension on the "early plan." He lived in a mobile home with his wife, who liked to call the state "the Republic."

"And that isn't bull crap. I mean, when they say the Empire State for New York, nobody ever thinks of an empire. But this is a republic, the Republic of Texas. Nobody here gives a shit or Shinola what the rest of the country is doing. It's something on its own."

Willington liked his accent. And he hadn't heard "shit or Shinola" since he was a kid. The guy did have a point. There were a lot of clichés lately about Texas, perpetrated by magazines and the couple of successful "Texas" television series. Most of them boiled down to telling you the kind of thing that was as old as any rerunning movie about the state, from *Giant*, with mean James Dean in his dark sunglasses, to *Hud*, with wild Paul Newman in his dusty boots and weathered chambray work shirt—those two stock stories (out of hundreds) about cattle versus oil as the maker of Texas millionaires. But the idea of "the Republic," though not a new one, was an interesting one, and a good way of looking at the place. And ever since the postman—his name was Haggerty or Rafferty—had planted the idea with Willington, Willington had applied it accordingly. Or he applied it specifically, by using the symbol of the Republic, that Lone Star, as a touchstone. Once you became aware of its five-pointed presence, you were amazed at its profusion.

There was a Lone Star under most every gable in the posh Driskill Hotel downtown. Each was chiseled out of the stone—and a little strange in form, due to artistic interpretation—in the nineteenth-century monster, the sides of which had recently been washed with pink. Willington thought that pointy-faced John Connally himself, who reportedly booked a huge suite of rooms there for his visits to the capital, could certainly take satisfaction in knowing that the Lone Star was above his head, like a halo, every time he looked from the glass to the street below. There was a massive Lone Star, either cast bronze or sculpted stone, on the façade of each of the new state office buildings that flanked the state capitol, an edifice for the meeting of an elected assembly second in size only to the Washington, DC, version (as every brochure emphasized) and located on an elm-covered knoll at the end of handsomely wide Congress Avenue.

There was a Lone Star on the red-white-and-blue flag, of course. And in that flag motif it turned up just about everywhere too. There were simple T-shirts like the flag with its Lone Star. There were more complicated nylon jogging shorts like the flag with its Lone Star. There were popular bumper stickers like the flag with its Lone Star—and below that a message of "Secede" or "Native Texan." There were so many police in the city—local, statehouse, and university, as well as the Rangers—that sometimes you found yourself strolling on a sidewalk through a sea of white short-sleeved uniform shirts, whistles attached to the left front pockets and a moving parade of little embroidered flags, with the Lone Star, affixed to the right shoulders.

There was a Lone Star in the carved mahogany bar facades in at least three new restaurants that were supposed to look like old restaurants on East Sixth Street. For those more literary, there was an enormous sign of glowing red neon spelling out "Lone Star" to advertise what was dubbed the National Beer of Texas; it sat perched on twin steel poles above the tallest buildings on Guadalupe Street, "the Drag," a long line of photocopy shops, bookstores, punk record places, typewriter rental stores, and the rest that bordered the rich university and its sprawling oil-funded campus—all handsome yellow limestone buildings with red Mexican tile roofs and terraced gardens cascading thick box-cut laurel and fresh fleshy flowers in beds with loam as rich as coffee grounds.

Willington's favorite was the Lone Star that you found underfoot, embossed on every cast-iron manhole cover. A couple of feet wide, each made sure that even if you were a bit low, you wouldn't forget the Republic. Around the periphery was some embossed rubric imparting information as to which proud local iron works was affixing its signature to this particular astral masterpiece.

And on this sunny Saturday, Willington walked through the parking lot of the university's Memorial Stadium. He noticed the Lone Stars, cast and painted white, on the side of the monstrosity. It wasn't a university game day.

Willington had never seen a stadium so well kept. The old poured concrete seemed as groomed as pressed gray flannel. The team's burnt orange shone in long vertical stripes between the facade's repeated arches. The new upper deck sat on the original construction gracefully, a sweep, streamlined and outer spacey, that appeared to hang there by the sheer belief alone in the eternal truth that there would be winning season after winning season for the nationally powerful Longhorns. Slim cigars of tall, trimmed evergreens added enough vegetation to keep it all from looking harsh.

Willington could hear Santa Rita No. 1. It was the original oil rig to produce a gush of crude on the university's land-grant properties in West Texas—what had once been thought to be worthless scrub land and now was a two-million-acre treasure that kept swelling the school's billion-dollar-plus endowment, the second largest of any institution in the country; Harvard was tops. The university had reassembled the creaky black-painted thing across from the stadium and hooked up a taped commentary system. The narration now was at the point where it told how the first wildcatters who leased some of the land-grant properties from the university had gone to New York to raise money for drilling in 1923. A Catholic charity there invested some funds with the stipulation that the well be named in honor of the patron saint of the long shot. The voice was loud and warbly through the speakers. Willington never caught more than a snip of it, though it was perpetual in its pitch, said to be known for scaring schoolchildren in their blue afternoons, and bums who wandered over from the Drag in their long hallucinating nights. ★

1984

JAMES HYNES

James Hynes is the author of three novels—*The Wild Colonial Boy* (1990), *The Lecturer's Tale* (2001) and *Kings of Infinite Space* (2004). A native of Michigan, he has lived in Austin since 1995, occasionally offering courses in creative writing at the University of Texas, and setting some of his fiction in an imaginary Austin named Lamar. The excerpt below, from "Casting the **Runes**" second novella in the collection *Publish and Perish: Three Tales of Tenure and Terror* (1997), introduces a young Midwestern academic to a university named Longhorn State. If any of this sounds familiar, it should.

from PUBLISH AND PERISH: THREE TALES OF TENURE AND TERROR

VIRGINIA DUNNING WAS A TALL, PALE DAUGHTER OF small-town Minnesota, and had lived the first twenty-eight winters of her life under the protocols of the upper Midwest: hand-knit sweaters and thermal underwear, long wool stockings and boots with rubber soles like tractor treads, six-foot scarves that came up over her nose, and wool hats that came down to her eyebrows. The worst thing that could happen to you, said her genes and her mother, was exposure, so you showed as little of yourself as possible, layering your clothes and keeping your opinions to yourself.

She had been a quiet, bookish girl in high school, proceeding dutifully to academic stardom at a small liberal arts college in the town where the flamboyant outlaw Cole Younger had been shot to death by tight-lipped Minnesotans. From there she went straight on to the prestigious University of the Midwest in Hamilton Groves, where she had been an improbable star of the history department. As shy as she was gifted, Virginia scarcely said a word in public for the first two years of graduate school. Even if she had, she certainly did not intend to tell anyone at Midwestern that her favorite book as a girl, and the seed of her interest in history, had been *Hawaii* by James Michener, or that she'd devoted a good deal of her early adolescence to imagining herself in the place of Julie Andrews, who'd played a missionary's wife in the film version. Regarding herself in the mirror after yet another viewing of the video, the young Virginia had even thought that she glimpsed a Juliesque paleness in her complexion, a similar astringent sharpness to her cheekbones. Hence, years later, her dissertation topic: a feminist history of Christian women missionaries in the Hawaiian Islands, modestly written but rigorous, and widely regarded as an important intervention in the study of the European encounter in the South Pacific.

But even as her confidence grew and she allowed herself to speak in the presence of her professors and the other graduate students, Virginia kept covered up. She wore her hair to her shoulders like a blond helmet, with bangs to her eyebrows and huge glasses like Gloria Steinem's, and she tiptoed through graduate school with a tall girl's stoop, hunching her shoulders and wringing her long-fingered hands. Even in the mild Minnesota summer, she wore a long-sleeved T-shirt, a skirt to her ankles, socks with her Birkenstocks, and a big hat to keep the pale Midwestern sun off her head.

Upon graduating, she received offers from several admirable institutions, including an Ivy, but she astonished everyone by accepting a tenure-track position at Longhorn State University in Lamar, Texas. From the cocoon of their progressive, Yankee rectitude, Texas seemed like a foreign country to her friends in Hamilton Groves, a semi-imaginary land made up in equal measure of old John Wayne movies, episodes of *Dallas*, and the last scene of *Easy Rider*. What about the heat? they all cried, recoiling from the thought of cool, pale Virginia shriveling up like a pepper under the wide Texas sky, as if she were some rancher's mail-order Norwegian bride. What about the scorpion in your shoe in the morning? The fire ants in the kitchen, the snake in the brush pile, the black widow in the grass? What about the tight-jeaned, potbellied bubbas in their pickups, shotguns in the rack behind the seat, cruising the backroads, flattening armadillos, flinging beer cans out the window, and looking for hippies to kill? What about the big-haired women with gaudy, expensive designer suits and matching nails and lipstick, who cruised the eight-lane freeways in pink Cadillac convertibles with a pair of longhorns for a hood ornament, on their way to spend Daddy's oil money on black sable at Neiman-Marcus? And what about the heat?

Virginia went anyway. Her graduate department at Midwestern had been a vipers' nest of big egos, empire builders, and campus politicians, a neo-Jacobean play in which the only thing that didn't run down the halls was actual human blood. Longhorn State was a step or two down the academic food chain from Midwestern, better known for its powerhouse football team than for its scholarship, but the history department was a young one, a lot of ambitious assistant professors with reputations to make. Maybe it wasn't the pinnacle of her profession at the moment, but given half a chance she could help put it on the map. And contrary to her friends' expectations, Lamar itself was one of the grooviest addresses in the nation these days, a slacker theme park staffed by long-haired singer-songwriters, buzz-cut cowboy novelists, video clerks turned indie filmmakers, skinhead neopunks, and the latest twenty-five-year-old billionaire software designer.

Indeed, the moment she arrived in Lamar, stepping out of the air-conditioned cab of her little yellow rental truck into the basting heat and whitish glare of a July afternoon in Central Texas, she knew she'd made the right choice. In a matter of seconds the heat soaked through to her bones and melted twenty-eight years of ice, and almost overnight she blossomed like a Texas bluebonnet. Lamar was a great place to be young, and Virginia wasn't even thirty yet. She straightened up and threw her shoulders back, she discovered sandals and tank tops and miniskirts, she learned to walk in long strides like a rancher. She gave away her assorted records by lugubrious Canadian folksingers and bought the Butthole Surfers and Bob Wills and the Texas Playboys on compact disc. She ate brisket with her fingers, she bought a tortilla warmer, she made her own fajita marinade. With her first paycheck from the university, she traded in her rusty, salt-eaten Dodge Colt and put a down payment on a little cherry-red pickup—Japanese, but enough of a truck to warrant the coveted "Texas Truck" license plate. Pulling out of the dealer's lot, she set the radio to a Tejano station, bopping behind the wheel to accordion music all the way home.

Without a trace of regret she ended by phone her moribund long-distance relationship with her patronizing, alcoholic British boyfriend, and took a new lover, Chip, a tall, wry native Texan like the young Clint Eastwood who worked in a hip video store by night and wrote television pilots on spec by day. She cut her hair into a pageboy and slicked it down on a Texas Saturday night, when she wore a little red dress and cowboy boots and went club hopping with Chip till dawn down on Sixth Street. She spent weekends in her pickup cruising the yellow grass and dusty green cedars of the Hill Country, opening the windows to the hot blast of air at seventy-five miles an hour as she dodged the armadillos in the road and drove with a cool, sweating, non-returnable bottle of Shiner Bock between her legs. She wanted to stay at Longhorn State for the rest of her life; she wanted to grow old under the hot Texas sun; she wanted her skin to bronze and thicken and crease up like an old boot, so she could age into a tough ol' Texas gal like Molly Ivins or Ann Richards, and say what she wanted and do as she pleased, a lover of good times and a sworn enemy of bullshit. ★

1997

MAX WESTBROOK

Max Westbrook (1927–2002) was born in Malvern, Arkansas, served in the Korean War, and took his Ph.D. from the University of Texas in 1960. He joined the Department of English at the University in 1962. During his career he published major critical articles on such writers as Stephen Crane and Ernest Hemingway, and an important book on the Western writer, Walter Van Tilburg Clark (1969). He also published two poetry chapbooks, *Country Boy* (1979) and *Confrontations* (1982). In "Bartons Creek" he writes of the most famous swimming hole in Texas, located in Zilker Park, on Barton Springs Road. I remain forever in Max Westbrook's debt for directing my dissertation on Frank Norris, and for his always enthusiastic support and encouragement.

BARTONS CREEK

In Travis County we play games with a sun
so fierce the air you breathe is on fire
and every secret hiding place and porch
is discovered, invaded, subdued.
But the water in Bartons Creek dances in sun
and we know it is so cold your body screams
in total, delicious shock as you dive below
having tricked the mad ambition of the sun.
Yet we are chilled by the grace of a king
who waits above in charge of the world
making it hot even in the shade of a live oak,
that dumb, perverse brute of a tree
that grows in rock, sucks a drink from the dust

and stays improbably green all year long
trying to offer relief from a sun so near
it would send most counties fleeing in terror.
But we like this immoderate land and learn
to walk the hidden trail, swim the water,
touch the oak and smell the mountain laurel
to let the blood remember what the mind forgets. ★

1982

STEPHEN HARRIGAN

Born in Oklahoma City, Stephen Harrigan grew up in Corpus Christi and attended the University of Texas at Austin. For years he worked as a writer/editor for *Texas Monthly*. He is the author of seven books, including several collections of essays and the novels *The Gates of the Alamo* (2000) and *Challenger Park* (2006). He lives in Austin. The piece reprinted here served as the introduction to an anthology of Austin-based writing that was published in 1980. In it Harrigan ponders the question asked many times by local writers and readers: Is there an Austin "school" of scribbling?

[A "School" of Austin Writers?]

TEXAS WRITERS ARE NOTORIOUSLY FOND OF EXAGGERATing the indifference and suspicion with which they are regarded in their own state, but I think it is true that a writer who lives in Texas cannot help but feel isolated and somewhat peculiar. The traditional cure for this malady has been to move to New York, where writers are as common as the sorghum farmer and petro-chemical workers back home. But for many this is a disillusioning adventure: They find that their newly discovered literary community soon degenerates into a forum for literary gossip, while their primary experience in Texas recedes farther and farther into the distance.

What saved me from this scenario was not foresight or a determination to stay on my own ground; it was Austin. Austin was the bar over which my little wave of migratory ambition broke.

When I came here as a student at the University of Texas I barely noticed the place. It seemed like a congenial, middle-sized American city, but hardly the environment I had in mind for myself. I would spend four years here, receive the college degree that I naively thought a writer must have to write, and then move to the sort of famous or exotic place I thought a writer must live.

But Austin began to work on me, as it works on almost everyone. It is famous within Texas as a cultural oasis, and it is equipped with the sort of facilities that aspiring writers in particular find highly useful and encouraging: libraries, bookstores, readings, a smattering of publishing enterprises, some of them very successful and credible. But while it is true that Austin's intellectual resources are sound, they do not lie at the heart of its appeal. In the last decade or so the city has changed nearly beyond recognition as a result of overcrowding and unconscionable development. But there is still something seductive and resolute about Austin. One believes, as one believes about few cities, that at bottom it stands for something besides chaos, that it possesses an almost organic sense of purpose and calm.

The city is situated along the Colorado River in South Central Texas, at the edge of a great geological fault called the Balcones Escarpment that abruptly separates the Hill Country from the Coastal Plain. The Colorado has been dammed to create a series of man-made lakes, and throughout the area there are clear-water springs, craggy, low-level vistas, and, in the spring, great swaths of wildflowers in the lowlands. It is beautiful country, without the burden of being spectacular country. The weather is temperate in the winter, but this is balanced by the almost debilitating heat and humidity of the summer. Consequently the average writer does not walk around in an exalted state, thrown into a creative stupor by the scenery, or by the quality of the air, or by a relentless and disturbing energy of city life. One of the main points about Austin is that it has no energy; it has charm, and it has power. Its rhythms are slow and deliberate; its citizens are simultaneously lulled and stirred.

I once picked up a hitch-hiker in New Mexico who, after he heard I was from Austin, told me he had stopped there once for the weekend, and stayed ten years. I merely nodded. I knew what he meant, since very much the same thing had happened to me. I have lived here for fifteen years—for all of my life as a writer—without ever seriously wanting to live anywhere else.

From time to time someone will make reference to the existence of an Austin "school" of writing. Perhaps there is such a thing, but for me the real revelation is how light a touch Austin has on its writers. For all of them, I believe, the effects of Austin are secret and ineradicable. ★

1980

258

DAGOBERTO GILB

Dagoberto Gilb was born in Los Angeles and graduated from the University of California at Santa Barbara in 1973, majoring in philosophy and religious studies. Three years later he received a master's degree in religious studies. He worked as a carpenter for the next fifteen years and eventually moved to El Paso. During these years he began to write short stories, and in 1985 *Winners on the Pass Line* was published. Other books include *The Magic of Blood* (1993) and *Woodcuts of Women* (2001). In 2003 he published *Gritos*, a collection of essays. Gilb lives in Austin and teaches creative writing at Texas State University in San Marcos. The essay below, in the form of a letter, is based on Gilb's stint as a visiting writer at the University of Texas, back in the late eighties. The professor that he describes near the end, the one in the white shirt and tie, would be me. As a point of clarification, I should mention that Rolando Hinojosa's course in Life and Literature of the Southwest also includes Anglo writers such as Larry McMurtry and George Sessions Perry, while my version of Life and Lit includes Mexican-American authors, namely Américo Paredes, Tomás Rivera, Rolando Hinojosa-Smith, Benjamin Alire Sáenz, Ray Gonzalez, Rafael Castillo, Sandra Cisneros, and Dagoberto Gilb.

FROM A LETTER TO PAT ELLIS TAYLOR

El Paso
January 13, 1989

A COUPLE MONTHS AGO I DISCOVERED AND THEN GOT bothered about the fact that one of the (if not *the*) most popular English-department courses at the University of Texas was the one that Mr. Dobie started, "The Life and Literature of the Southwest" (translation: "Fiction from and about Texas"), although there is not one writer of Mexican descent represented in that course. That struck me as Mighty Strange, and no less so because two of Texas's most important writers, Rolando Hinojosa and Américo Paredes (the movie *The Ballad of Gregorio Cortez* from his *With His Pistol in His Hand*), are faculty. I guess it struck Rolando so strange that he asked to teach the same course, though his uses an extra adjective in the title—"The Life and Literature of the Hispanic Southwest." As I understand it, a student can't even get two courses of credit for taking both.

Which gets me to a subject you brought up a few months ago, about your writing getting criticized for not striking Deep in the Heart of Texas. Let me tell you what I've learned—that "Texas Literature" is considered, uniquely to this state and from inside it, a national literature, one separate from the U.S.A., in the same way French or British literature isn't just called European (New Mexico is the only other state I know of where the same might be said, but I think there are considerable differences.) Maybe everyone else knows this, but I didn't. I realized this after I got back from Paisano, reading through a copy of a journal (*Southwestern Historical Quarterly*) whose page after page are reverent and nostalgic embraces of Frank Dobie and Walter Prescott Webb. Out on the Paisano ranch, I read quite a bit by and on Mr. Dobie, but I suppose I must have thought, naively, that interest in him was arcane—I mean, I know people from all over the West, even a few in Texas (though most of them are illegitimates or disavowed from here in El Paso), some are even educated, and I'd say many if not most haven't heard of the man. It occurred to me, in other words, that Texas takes its Texas Literature seriously. Surprise, right? Anyway, I think it was Dobie who established this Republic of Texas attitude—he went over to England as a Texan, not an American.

That's one observation. Another has to do with me saying that you're in a Janis Joplin tradition of writer, which explains why all the young people who like that kind of rock'n'blues like your writing a lot (your book was very popular in those classes I taught). But this fact doesn't bode too well for you with the chambers of (artistic) commerce in this republic. Janis wasn't very popular with them, either. Until she died—now they've got a monument to her there in Port Arthur. Writing tastes could be said to parallel music tastes (or at least that's a way to look at it, to make a point or two), and my impression has been that the trend in the country has gone classical. That is, go to school, be trained by and learn the skills at the proper conservatories from the proper teachers, play in one orchestra after another. In the writing world, that seems to be called "creative writing." Nobody'd deny that these people play skillfully or are talented, nobody'd argue that classical music isn't beautiful, and good for the senses, but what about rock'n'roll or jazz? Would Buddy Holly's or Roy Orbison's music be better if they'd "studied" guitar? What about BB King or Bobby Blue Bland or Chuck Berry? Duke Ellington? My feeling is that they played in garages and on porches and in nightclubs and that's why their music is like it is. I'd say the literary sound in the country is Classical Only, and it's no different here in Texas, though I think around here, it's expected that a little Bob Wills be mixed in some. Anyway, I think the belief is that good-boy and -girl writers should wear the proper literary attire in public, and your writing, Miss Taylor, gets too naked. Good writing has proper manners, and your writing has this bad habit of getting loud sometimes—really, decent lady writing must show more constraint and control of itself, Miss Taylor.

Here I can't remember how I planned to link this to Rolando Hinojosa teaching his own "Literary Tradition" course about native Texas writers like Américo Paredes and Tomás Rivera (and maybe even himself), but I'm thinking about Tex-Mex music, and about how I was thinking these things while I was wandering the lonely halls of UT. I mean, I don't know how a person is supposed to punch it out with that tough-guy cowboy-type heritage, especially when it's not even wearing a cowboy hat anymore, just a clean white shirt and tie. I sort of saw all my deep thinking there as halfbreed-like and short (next to all those tall, lanky siblings of cowboy thoughts)—you know, like that cook in *Lonesome Dove* who knows lots about critters to eat, those snakes and bugs, but doesn't have much to say about the Big Drive. Maybe next time I'll have it figured out and let you know.

Yours,
Dagoberto ★

2003

261

KURTH SPRAGUE

Kurth Sprague was born in New Jersey, grew up in Manhattan, and graduated from Princeton in 1956. In 1978 he received a doctorate in English from the University of Texas at Austin. He taught at UT-Austin from 1970 until his retirement in 1996. Sprague has edited two volumes of work by T.H. White, the subject of his dissertation. He has also published three volumes of poetry and *The National Horse Show: A Centennial History, 1883–1983* (1985). In 2003 he published his first novel, *Frighten the Horses: A Rusty Coulter Mystery.* The narrator, a trainer of horses and a Lecturer in the Department of English, combines two of Sprague's life-long interests. Although the university is called the University of the Southwest and Parlin Hall becomes McFarland Hall, the place and its atmospherics are very familiar. There have been several murder mysteries set on the UT campus; this is one of the best of them.

from FRIGHTEN THE HORSES

THE THIRD-LARGEST SINGLE-CAMPUS UNIVERSITY IN THE nation and one of the top ten research universities worldwide, The University of the Southwest (over 50,000 students, plus another 6,000 or so staff and faculty), occupies close to 400 acres situated just north of the complex of state office buildings and the capitol, huge, sprawling, yet possessing a rough beauty of jumbled architectural styles.

The Department of English is in MacFarland Hall, a vaguely Mediterranean, white limestone and red-tile-roofed building on the tree-shaded west side of the campus. Across the main drag separating town from gown were the usual university-area cottage industries. There were three churches—Baptist, Catholic, and Methodist—quiet during the week except for the odd funeral and each running its own day care center for harried university parents' children; now midmorning on a Sunday, halfway through their busiest day, having commenced with early morning mass at St. Michael's. There were a bookshop, a record store, a small restaurant run by a Vietnamese family, and a European-style coffee shop which sold battery-acid espresso and fey prints, and rented mailboxes. I drove onto the campus on Twenty-Fourth and wound around the inner campus drive until I found a parking space near MacFarland Hall.

The main door was locked and I had to let myself in with my key. Inside the building, although the air was, as usual for the summertime, dead and chill, I was aware of that crackle of ozone that tells you something's gone seriously wrong. It's the residual stench of danger, of undissipated tension. I've noticed it in lawyers' offices where couples have broken off bitter arguments as you enter the room; and out on a windy hunt course while you're waiting for the ambulance to arrive and everything is very quiet. Not quite the stink of burning insulation, but a hint of it. Just a whiff.

Spray-painted graffiti smeared the walls and bulletin boards. Papers were strewn across the floors. The work of rage and fury. I made my way down the hall to the mailroom and jiggled my key and opened the door. Triggering recollection, smell bypassed sight and overrode reason: mud and sun and swollen bodies; then, my mother's hospital deathbed.

By the subaqueous light from the window across from the door I saw Sebastian Roylert lying crumpled on the floor, his scalp showing pinkly through his wavy silver hair. Blood had leaked in rivulets from his ears pooling onto the floor. He was lying across the width of the mailroom from left to right resting more or less on his right side, his face away from me, his right arm and shoulder drawn up underneath and slightly behind him, his torso twisted so that his chest was almost square to the floor, his left arm stretched out toward the far right corner of the room. His blue-gray raw silk jacket was tucked up in back. I could see where his roughly-woven madras checked shirt was tucked into his gray slacks, now soiled with the final humiliation of incontinence. He was wearing soft Italian-style burgundy loafers. On the periphery of my vision I was aware of the bank of mailboxes filling the wall to my right, most of them stuffed with papers, while on the floor beneath were stacked a number of book cartons. Near the chairman's body in the far corner was what appeared to be a very large, thick book. On the left wall was a corkboard with the usual notices pinned above a table. Past Roylett's body to the left of the window was a small desk and rolling typist's stool and wastebasket.

I looked at him for a moment, lying there, and then, as I'd been taught to do, knelt to feel for the pulse in the juncture below his ear. I heard the door behind me being unlocked, and, in an instant later there was a ululation of genuine terror.

&

When I arrived on campus after dropping off my policy statements and syllabi to be duplicated at Kinko's, The University was already humming like a giant complex machine—irregular verbs chattering away down in the French department, Kant and Schopenhauer having a dialogue, I guessed, over in Philosophy, weird multi-hued potions frothing up cheerfully in chemistry, the dry insect voices of professors professing, and on the quarter-hour, the brazen-throated tower bells pealing. On the Drag, backed up by Japanese boom boxes, Hare Krishnas stood in their saffron robes chanting next to small, clean-shaven men in white shirts and blue trousers passing out miniature New Testaments. Railing like a madman in the hot sun, a large bearded man in cinctured monk's robe and sandals had reached that point in his diatribe where the campus police, experienced in such matters, were about to close in on him—just as he was lamenting, in what sounded like genuinely despairing tones, the sexual attractions of the women students passing in the street. He had a beatific smile as he was hauled off.

Right on, they were beautiful. ★

2003

Marion Winik

Born in New Jersey, Marion Winik came to Texas, to Austin, in the 1970s. She began her writing career as a poet (*Nonstop*, 1981) and later wrote several collections of essays and memoirs, including *First Comes Love* (1996) and *Above Us Only Sky: Essays* (2005). Winik now lives in Glen Rock, Pennsylvania. Anybody who has spent a summer in Austin (defined as May to October) will recognize the symptoms of suffering in the poem below.

The Texas Heat Wave

The Texas Heat Wave broke over my body
as if I was a beach, and could take it.
The heat wave shortened our lives,
it shortened our hairdos, it shortened
our sentences, great novels were struck down
when no more than tiny phrases,
by August, nothing was left of the lawn.

The summer reeled by
like an insane home movie
one pointless scene after another
People walking abruptly in and out of the room
smiling like idiots, never in focus
Decisions were hasty, judgments were snap
It was too hot to argue I never said no
The heat made me easy
The heat was white it swallowed all colors
the days were bleached there was no night

to speak of We had to get up at five
to drink coffee before sunrise
The heat was the excuse for everything that happened
Nothing happened anyway
A few car accidents, a long distance phone call,
a lady in high heels died in the desert,
made the front page every day for a week
Everything senseless was violent
Everything violent was senseless
Air conditioning was thorazine
Those who did not have broke beer bottles
over each other's heads
The Texas Heat Wave turned the entire state
into an Intensive Care Unit
Anyone who could afford it was at the airport
leaving for Boston
The rest were driving nowhere with the windows down
having car accidents
It was desperation
I tell you, even I was half-crazy
with thirst, with exhaustion,
with lethargy, with lust: I dreamed
I wore long pants
in the daytime

Insects ruled the earth.
They commandeered the food supply
and would not let us sleep.
Willing slaves, we did nothing without orders.
Only showers came from the heart. ★

1981

CHUCK TAYLOR

Chuck Taylor grew up in the Midwest and graduated from Northwestern University. Eventually he made his way to Austin, where he founded Slough Press in 1973 and worked in a variety of venues, including the Paperback Plus bookstore in downtown Austin from 1980–1988. His experiences brought him into contact with Austin's diverse community. Today Taylor is a lecturer in the Department of English at Texas A&M University-College Station. He has published several chapbooks of poetry and a collection of essays and poems that speak to the countercultural scene in Austin in the 1970s and '80s: Only a Poet: Selected Stories and Essays, Practical, Literary, and Personal (1977–1984), 1984. His poem "Texas," from that volume, offers a wry and very true take on Texans' self-absorption with their state.

TEXAS

texas, I'm told I'm supposed
to love my country
but does the monarch migrating south
passing over this region
say to his buddies
hey we are now passing over texas
do the birds stop at the rio grande
to have their luggage checked
Texas, I'm told you're supposed to exist
I look out my window
I see sidewalks
I see sky
I see a boy carrying

an eight track silver and black
stereo tape deck radio player
blasting funk—
but I don't see—
wait a minute,
there went a license plate
it says texas
so the cars belong to texas
the cars are texas
a yellow car is the yellow rose of texas
or if the cars aren't texas
it is our taxes that are texas
that's what it says
over at the comptroller's office
your taxes your texas
I mean where is this texas
I'd like to meet him
so many people
turn cow eyed at the word
the guy must be something special
the way the hearts flutter
when I say texas
you'd think it was the virgin mary or god
I picked up a rock the other day
and looked for some letters
that said texas
I scooped water out of the Colorado
and held it to my ear
but it did not whisper texas
I asked the pine trees in the east
I asked the ocotillo in the west
I asked the fabled cow and a rusty derrick

who went just moo and clank
nobody was talking
who I respected
all I could get was the static
of lawyers and literary men
buzzing texas, texas, texas ★

1984

Betty Sue Flowers

Betty Sue Flowers, born in Waco, took her B.A. from the University of Texas and a Ph.D. from the University of London. Eventually she returned to Texas to teach poetry and literature in the Department of English. A poet, editor, and business consultant, she has published several chapbooks of poetry and four television tie-in books in collaboration with Bill Moyers, among them, Joseph Campbell and the Power of Myth. In 2002 Flowers became Director of the Lyndon B. Johnson Presidential Library and Museum at the University of Texas. The place imagined in the poem included here, though unnamed, is Austin.

BEING IMAGINED

At five thousand feet over Texas,
I am being imagined. A man
builds a picture of me in his mind.
Clearest to him are my eyes, hands, hair.
My lips are there, but shaded. He forms
me, feature by feature, and my eyes
widen, my nose straightens, and a wind
lifts my hair.
He imagines me below, watching
deer under Spanish oaks, or chasing
armadillos through the cedar. I
stand, he thinks, by the broken windmill—
so still the circling turkey buzzards
lower their black ring to look. His high
canvas is covered with bluebonnets

in all weathers.
His imagination has silvered
the glass I see through, mirrored me back
to myself as a plane in the sky
flashes light. My chin lifts to the sun,
and a strong wind blows through the tall grass
and my hair. Knowing he could never hear
the mockingbird at five thousand feet,
I listen well for both of us. ★

1976

JOSEPH JONES

Joseph Jones (1908–1999) was born in Nebraska and received his Ph.D. from Stanford University in 1934. He joined the Department of English at the University of Texas in 1936. Jones traveled widely throughout the British Commmonwealth and, with his wife Joanna, published books on Canadian, Australian, and New Zealand fiction. Upon retirement in 1975, Jones devoted himself to studying and preserving Waller Creek, a stream that flows through the eastern side of the campus of the University of Texas. His book, *Life On Waller Creek* (1982), is, among other things, a natural history of Austin. Jones appeared in the famous Richard Linklater film, *Slacker*. In the following excerpt Jones explains his fascination with the creek and its ancient history in a manner that Thoreau would have appreciated.

from LIFE ON WALLER CREEK

FORTY YEARS AND MORE I HAVE PACKED MY LUNCH TO Waller Creek. Only since retirement, though, have I felt I had time to spend undertaking small improvements along its rugged banks: ephemeral gestures to be sure, but good for body and spirit alike—an hour or so, three or four days a week, before lunch. Instead of going up the wall I go down to the creek. If it doesn't really "keep me young" as we sometimes sentimentally allege of our elderly pursuits, it may keep me from aging as rapidly as otherwise I might; and I have been perennially grateful for my brief yet almost daily contact with earth and rock and flowing water along this beautiful stream.

Early after reaching Austin in 1935 I must have fallen in love with Waller Creek, I feel sure, because of its clear water and limestone bed, and the shade trees kept green by its moisture. In southeastern Nebraska, where I grew up, we had plenty of creeks but they were nearly always muddy from the too-easy erosion of the bountiful loess topsoil. We swam and waded and fished in them anyway, of course, but what wouldn't we have given for a stream like this one!

For one of my self-appointed tasks my shovel stirs the gravel in the creek-bed, producing a nearly imperceptible change. Plenty of gravel: The few cubic feet spread along the rock border of the nature trail can easily be spared; and anyway the next rain will reclaim part of it, nature habitually, quite unconcernedly making practical mincemeat out of my "pure" speculative projects. I don't wear a ten-gallon hat, but I do lug along in a five-gallon green plastic paint bucket the rest of my tools: machete, (or corn knife, as I knew it in corn country), light sledgehammer, pruning shears, homemade hand pick (patterned after the Polynesian digging stick, which was made from forking tree-branches), and—occasionally—pruning saw and bobbed-off broom-rake. Fitting all this into my modest-sized locker in Bellmont Hall is something of a ritual: First this, then that, must go in or I end up with too much gear, not enough locker. I sweat—pints, quarts, liters: For a couple of hours of a morning I too am a "wet-back," and more, since I slither across the algae-festooned rocks and get my feet wet as well. My clothes, such as they are, are daubed with particolored creek-bed sediment. In short I must appear to be a curious sort of pick-and-shovel troll, possibly not quite rational. All of this I like very much, and in my come-lately capacity as a limited day-laborer I fancy that now, after several years of the pursuit, I have some hazy conception of how the man with the hoe views, or may view, his job. That's useful. Henry Thoreau found that "incessant labor with the hands, which engrosses the attention also, [was] the best method to remove palaver out of one's style," but for me—to judge from my title page—hand labor may have conspired to put the palaver in.

Farther south thirty paces or so, I—trading no longer over the classroom counter—meet up with one of my current customers, a young walker who asks how long the trail has been under construction. A few weeks, I tell him, cautioning about the poison ivy. He assures me he's not allergic to it and I congratulate him on his good fortune. A student, I surmise (we don't introduce ourselves and the exchange is so brief, so casual, that we don't reveal ourselves either), taking half an hour's break to explore his campus home. He says he likes the trail and hopes it will be kept open. I thank him and we walk on, he north, I south. There are thousands upon thousands of him/her on the Forty Acres, within a few minutes' walk, but as yet only a few along the shady, limestone-littered reach of Waller Creek just east of Freshman Field, the site of the Waller Creek Riot of October 1969. Others will show up, as energy supplies in the immediate and long-range future grow increasingly precarious and our machine-pampered minority of the human race rediscover our feet. (Coincidentally, for some months in 1980–81, during the construction of a cluster of new courts, Freshman Field was blocked off and as a result this virtually unknown nature-trail served as an unofficial detour, the only pedestrian thoroughfare available to Waller Creek visitors in that area. The 1981 floods washed parts of it out, but it soon became walkable again.)

Waller Creek began as no more than a trickle along a stretch of Cretaceous limestone, known more precisely as Austin Chalk—but when? Forty-five to fifty thousand years ago? Possibly no more than fifteen thousand? Geological estimates of its age may fall anywhere between these extremes, creeks being less easily pinpointed than substances datable by Carbon-14. It is much like hundreds of other streams draining the Central Texas limestone region whose processes of erosion have left us, through many a rarely visited mile, smooth white beds and chalky banks that for intensity at least, gleaming in the summer sun, would easily outdo even the White Cliffs of Dover. Underground, these same limestone deposits contain some remarkable caverns. Anything green growing in or along such creek banks and beds looks greener for having chosen that spot for its home, which likewise enhances the wildflowers—verbenas, gaillardias, bluebonnets, bull nettles, primroses, poppies, thistles, winecups, Indian paintbrush, along with dozens of others—and the occasional flowering tree whose blooms are showy enough to be readily seen.

The limestone abounds in small fossils and fragments of large ones— weathered remains of ancient oysters and other bivalves together with much else. There are more than 120 species of the microscopic organisms called *Foraminifera* ("perforation-bearers"), and in the upper part of the West Branch (immediately behind old Kirby Hall) the Eagleford formation—just below the

Austin Chalk, exposed along a fracture system—has yielded large quantities of fish-remains in its chalky shale. All this tells us that these beds of rock were deposited as sediment on the floor of a marine embayment that once extended at least this far into Texas, or probably even farther west, but there the rocks have all been removed by erosion and are no longer available for study. In such terrain a sizable creek, threading its way through parts of a city, adds a contrasting natural element of continual aesthetic interest besides affording other civic advantages. Town creeks are important for all sorts of reasons.

Austin, like every other city, has an anatomy and physiology all its own. Except to a very few citizens, this wholeness of function will never be wholly grasped, and perhaps only within restricted limits of growth can it be grasped: What individual Japanese, for instance, really knows all of Tokyo; what New Yorker can comprehend the totality even of Manhattan, or Brooklyn? Nevertheless, there are unique or unusual physical features that give a city its special character, if it has one—and who can say that any place is altogether faceless, however much it may seem to have wanted to remain so? In London it is quite evidently the Thames, or in Sydney or Hong Kong the harbor, that the parts of the city all finally relate to, and bodies of water seem to have the same kind of organizing, unifying, particularizing function the world over. That is not to suggest that cities were founded with an eye to the picturesque: Water, for any number of reasons, must be seen as practically useful before its "pure" aesthetic qualities are fully realized; but once a city is founded and generates its momentum, a civic consciousness begins to relate to its natural features.

For Austin these genetic organizers are first of all the Colorado River with its original three principal local tributaries, Waller Creek, Shoal Creek, and Barton Creek—now extended to many other creeks; second, the fascinatingly varied landscape which through long ages these streams have shaped and prepared for its mantle of vegetation. As urban growth continues, other parts of the area watershed are being added, but the three creeks and the river remain the original nucleus which determined Austin's shape and her strong individual appeal. For these reasons, along with others, a special Creek Ordinance, said to be unique in American urban legislation, has come to be enacted; and thoughtful citizens are more than casually aware of the need for protecting the river and its chain of lakes against ever-present threats of abuse. They wish, if they can, to keep us from submitting indiscriminately to "progressive" mutilations which finally add up to municipal suicide. The task is not easy, particularly when abnormal growth-rates over a span of three decades have created a climate of activity in which, it sometimes seems, "The best lack all conviction, and the worst Are full of passionate intensity." ★

1982

Tom Zigal

Tom Zigal was born in Galveston, grew up in Texas City, and arrived in Austin in the late 1960s as an undergraduate at the University of Texas. After sojourns in Northern California, Aspen, New Orleans, and Atlanta, he always returned to Austin, where he lives today. He is the author of the Kurt Muller mystery series, set in Aspen, and he has published short stories in literary magazines and fiction anthologies for the past thirty years. A collection of stories, *Western Edge,* appeared in 1982. His latest novel is *The White League* (2005). In "Recent Developments" Zigal explores changing times in downtown urban Austin—a familiar theme in writing about the city.

Recent Developments

WHEN THE TELEPHONE RANG, MELISSA SIMS WAS IN HER dark room, processing a batch of color photographs she had taken the previous week, the new series of abstract architectural patterns in the downtown development area.

"I feel like such a fool," said Rhona Kirchner, her gallery representative in New York.

Last evening, after locking up and leaving the gallery, she was knocked to the pavement by a young thug who ran off with her handbag. Among the items in the bag were several sheets of Melissa's latest slides.

"Rhona, I'm so sorry," Melissa said. "Are you okay?"

"My pride's a little wounded," Rhona laughed dryly. "Fifty years in this city and I get mugged like a tourist."

Melissa assured her that there were copies and that she would send them in tomorrow's mail.

"I like what I've seen so far, Lissa," said Rhona Kirchner. "Formalism is back, you know. This new series may be just the ticket to pull you out of the doldrums, my dear."

Melissa thought nothing more of the mugging incident, sent off a duplicate set of transparencies the following day, and continued with her study of the runaway construction projects downtown, the shadows and dark tonalities created by cold steel girders, the shimmering reflections of glass in the new highrises. Then, a week later, she received in the mail a large stained envelope postmarked New York, the name and address of the original recipient scratched out and Melissa's residence supplied in pencil. Inside were her missing slides.

"Dear Miss Sims," the letter began, large simple handwriting that reminded Melissa of her mother's. "I found these pictures in a dumpster near where I stay. I couldn't figure out why you would throw away such nice pictures and then it dawned on me they might have been heisted from you. Thank goodness you are a smart lady and put your address on the plastic. I have read that we should always mark our valuables in some way so as to identify them to the police."

The letter was written on mismatched scraps of paper, the backs of someone's discarded receipts.

"I myself was born and reared in Texas so I felt it the neighborly thing to return your pictures to you. I'm sure you would have done the same for me," the letter continued. "I cleaned them off. Hope you can still use them."

The plastic sheet smelled of rotted garbage, but the slides themselves appeared in satisfactory condition.

"I am no expert on the subject but I wonder why there are no people in your pictures. I like the colors and the great old buildings but you must get up awful early in the morning to take them because I didn't see a single person on the street or even in a window. Maybe you are working for a construction outfit, I don't know."

Melissa smiled. She hadn't shot people in over a year, she realized, the shift in esthetics vaguely matching the changes in her troubled life. Perhaps she should look up this fellow the next time she was in New York and arrange a critique of her most recent work.

The correspondent went on in rambling sentences, revealing bits and pieces of a transient life. He was born in Gladewater, Texas, he said, the son of a roughneck drawn there by the oil boom. His mother died when he was in high school, "some kind of cancer," and his father not long after. He had a brother who once drove a truck for Gulf Oil, but he wasn't sure if he was still alive.

"Do you know a Bill Duncan of Longview, Texas?" he asked. "Married a woman named Gladys, I believe."

His sweet young sister, he said, "had a heck of a time poor thing got mixed up with some navy romeo she met during the war and he left her PG and then went off and got himself killed."

Melissa turned the soiled pages, fascinated by the man's account.

"The last time I saw my brother and sister was the end of 1946," he wrote, "just before I re-upped in the army. I have asked myself many times over the years why I have not written to let them know where I am or called maybe on Xmas at least or spent a little money to go and visit them. I don't know the answer Miss Sims. I always intended to get in touch and then the months and years rolled by and it just got easier to stay away and not write or talk to people you hadn't seen for so long. I guess I was a little ashamed of myself and thought maybe they would not forgive me or understand or approve of the life I have come to live. You see Miss Sims I have enjoyed a drink from time to time. They use to look up to me, my brother and sister. I guess I never wanted them to see me down on my luck."

Melissa placed the pages on the kitchen table and poured herself a glass of iced tea, her fingers strangely weak and trembling.

"If you got people you care for," the letter concluded, "don't ever let them go. Take it from one that knows." It was signed, "Missing in action, Sammy Duncan."

After reading the letter, Melissa lay on the couch and cried a little, remembering her father in those last months, when he could no longer keep his balance and so often wet his pants without noticing. He began to fall asleep at the supper table, in the doctor's office, behind the wheel of his pickup. One afternoon mother found him passed out in the garden, red ants crawling in and out of his slack mouth.

"I'm getting too old to watch him every minute of the day," her mother had said. "We're going to have to put the poor thing in a home."

After he'd survived several near-tragic accidents involving the riding mower, Melissa had no choice but to break the promise she'd made to herself as a young woman. She put one of her parents in a retirement home.

The burst of emotion fatigued her and she fell into a shallow sleep. When she woke, she put on her bathing suit and walked to the neighborhood pool, where she tried to exhaust herself doing laps. To her disappointment, none of the tanned young men lounging at poolside took notice of her.

At home she phoned Rhona to tell her about the returned slides.

"Life gets weirder and weirder," Rhona said, laughing her raspy laugh.

She told Melissa that everyone at the gallery was impressed by the fresh group of photographs they'd received from her. "We're working on a title for the show," Rhona said. "Something about the Dynamics of Structure, the Graphics of Light. We're all getting excited here, darling. When can you get us more? To fill the main gallery we'll need twice what we've got so far."

At sunrise the next morning, in those peaceful hours before traffic and the patter of heels on concrete, Melissa set out into the deserted center city, a place of stark abstractions and monumental silence. They intrigued her, these formal qualities of stone and steel and glass, they somehow suited the empty dimensions of her heart. Sammy Duncan was right, she thought. I find no use for people anymore. Only lines and planes and the cool hollow moulds of structure, the negative spaces, which trick the eye with the most facile formulations.

Camera strapped to her shoulder, Melissa wandered the abandoned streets, searching methodically for something to capture her imagination—a honeycomb of windows, a pattern of brick, a sensuous curve of highrise glass. She soon realized she'd mined this area already and there was little left to fascinate her. A sudden feeling of melancholy swept through her, a faintly recalled moment from yesterday, a glimmer of loss, and for the first time since this project began, she had doubts about its value.

After a few lazy snaps at a building paneled with black glass, purely an exercise in mechanics, she returned home and made breakfast. In the morning clutter of mail was a secondhand envelope, the pencil script one she recognized immediately.

"Dear Miss Sims," the letter began, "I hope you don't mind me writing again but I got to thinking about your pictures of those tall buildings which I took to be maybe Austin because of your address and then I started wondering how on earth they got up here and in that dumpster, but then it dawned on me that is how it always goes, you start out one place and end up another so far away and nobody knows how or why it happened that way. And then you wake up one day and the years have come and gone and you don't know how to find your way back."

He tried to explain himself, to sort out the when and where of a life that had slipped away from him, but the chronology was confusing and Melissa found herself rereading the passages more than once. From what she could decipher, when Sammy Duncan had returned home from the war, a young man of twenty-five, there was no work in East Texas, so he drifted down to Houston and hired on as a dock hand. But after a year of backbreaking labor, friendless and confused, he reenlisted in the army, the only life he knew.

"Uncle Sam has always been good to me," he said. A purple heart in World War II, a bronze star in Korea. And when he contracted tuberculosis while stationed in the Philippines in the 1950s, they sent him to recuperate in Valley Forge Hospital.

"Good grub, pretty nurses. After they removed part of my lung I spent a long time in rehab and they built me back up like a football player. I tell you Miss Sims it was the best damn treatment I ever had."

Now that he was an old man he had only one regret, he said. "My sister use to write me when I was in the service and I even got a few letters forwarded to the hospital in Valley Forge. I don't know why I never answered her. I always loved that little stinker. I guess I felt sorry for her with the kid and all and I didn't know what to do for them and just kind of give up thinking about it."

Melissa wondered if the woman was still alive. How old would her daughter be? A few grades ahead of Melissa in school? Had they found happiness, mother and daughter, in those hard years following the war? Had the woman married again to someone who had raised the girl as his own? That was how life was supposed to work out, wasn't it?

"It's still rainy and cold up here my friend and a little hard to find a dry spot at night. I bet the spring has already come to Texas. I always liked the wildflowers on the side of the highway.

"Sometimes I miss the old place and wonder what it would be like to go back," Sammy Duncan said as he concluded his letter. "I have not lit foot there in forty years."

For the next three weeks Melissa received a letter nearly every day. Sammy Duncan was in a reminiscent mood, almost as if he were composing his memoirs. He described a mundane post-war career working in the motor pool in the army. Although he'd never achieved a rank above corporal, not in nineteen years of service, it suited him just fine, he said, to have a steady job, three squares a day, a roof over his head. He had no grand ambitions beyond his comfortable life on the base.

"I wish to the lord Uncle Sam had never let me go. But I don't blame them or harbor ill will. I guess they had to. Once my lungs give out again, I wasn't fit for service anymore."

He told her that in 1959 he was discharged because of medical complications stemming from his lung surgery for TB. The government provided a small retirement pension and an extra fifty-four dollars a month in disability payments. He was thirty-nine years old, a decorated veteran of two wars, something of an invalid. Fifty-four dollars a month.

Then came an endless string of temporary jobs and rooming houses in snow country and handouts from churches.

"I'm not saying I'm some kind of Einstein but they didn't give me much of a chance, those garages I applied to for mechanic work. I can fix a car, anybody can tell you that. But something about the people up here, Yankees, they don't take to the slow way I talk and I heard one fellow tell another he thought I was retarded. Can you beat that? I have always been a book reader Miss Sims. Do you think those men that turned me down have ever read a book in their life?"

Melissa wondered how she could help. She wanted to send him money, but there was never a return address on the greasy envelopes.

"I am a veteran Miss Sims and as such have tried to work for a living and did my best to avoid the kind of riff raff that bum around in cities," he wrote. "I have had to jungle up maybe only three or four times in my whole life much to my regret. I once went to an AA meeting but didn't have the clothes to go back."

Melissa didn't know what to do. She phoned a friend who worked in Social Services and he suggested that she send a contribution to one of the shelters in New York.

"I wish I could save every case assigned to me," her friend said. "In the beginning, when I first started this work, I brought people home, let them use our shower, fed them, gave them a bed, a few bucks to spend. It nearly drove Eileen crazy. It's a revolving door, believe me. They go out and come back. Sad to say, but you get immune to it. You build up a tougher skin," he said. "Take my advice and send some money to New York, Lissa. You'll feel better about it. There's not much else you can do."

Melissa began to worry about her own aging mother, alone in a dusty West Texas hamlet, forty-odd years a beautician working out of a small shop next to the house, her business now drying up with the passing of the elderly ladies who had been her steady clientele. I need to visit her more often, she thought. I ought to be sending her a monthly check.

Her sleep became erratic. Early mornings she spent roaming the downtown area, but she'd lost interest in form and contour and the physical qualities of light. Those things no longer appealed to her.

She knew where the street people gathered, in the crumbling decay of the warehouse district and in church doorways and under the trees next to the river. There was one camp underneath a bridge only a few blocks from the heart of her project.

"Don't come around here with no camera," she was told by a bearded man missing half his front teeth. Seven o'clock in the morning and he was already drinking from a brown bag.

Still she strayed into their midst. Bony, shirtless young men rose from the cardboard packing they'd slept in. Children emerged sleepy from a broken-down car. A woman with fresh bruises on her face clutched her knees, rocking back and forth in the dirt, mumbling to herself. The stench of urine was overwhelming.

Melissa felt no urge to take their pictures. She felt instead the coldness in her hands that always signaled fear. Two ragged young men with tattoos, their hair pulled back in ponytails, approached her with rude suggestions. Someone asked for money. The bearded man with the brown bag wanted to see her camera.

"Don't run off," he said as she turned to leave. "We're just getting acquainted."

Back home, Melissa stripped and took a long hot shower. As she was drying her hair she received a phone call from Rhona.

"Is everything okay?" Rhona asked. "It's been a month, dear, and we haven't seen any more of your work. I just wanted to touch base. We're booking you for early January. Does that sound good to you? I've shown your images to some friends at *Aperture* and *American Photographer*, and you've caused quite a stir. People are talking about you again. Frankly, Lissa, I'm seeing this as a real mid-career turnaround. Very few artists ever make this kind of leap and get away with it. Not at your age, doll."

Melissa confessed that she had been distracted lately and that the work had not come as easily as she'd hoped. But she would get back to it, she promised. She just needed a little time.

"Fine," Rhona said. "As long as you know what you're doing, darling, I'm happy."

A new letter from Sammy Duncan related that the rooming house he'd lived in for several months had been torn down recently—"to put up some fancy shops, I suppose"—and he'd been forced to rely on the Salvation Army, and then a men's shelter.

"I don't know what I'm going to do," he wrote. "I wish I had the jack to leave this town. I've got an old army buddy down in Tampa and he tells me you can live there pretty cheap. At least the weather treats a man better."

It was a warm sultry evening and Melissa sat on her porch swing, remembering those early backpacking years with Brian in Europe, when they'd slept in ratty youth hostels and under the stars on the beaches of Spain. Tonight the crickets sang like jingling bells and she drank a little too much Lillet, reading and rereading the collection of letters in the yellow, moth-swirling light of the porch. When it was very late she went inside and found the musty bedroll she'd carried on that trip many years ago and unraveled it in the tall grass. Lying on her back, she peered up through the thick verdant branches of the oak trees and remembered a story her father had once told her about a vacation trip to a Mexican border town. He and mother had crossed the bridge and come upon a poor ragged beggar with a tin cup, a naked child clinging to her side. They gave the woman a handful of change and then went off to enjoy themselves in the cantinas. But the next evening, when they returned for another outing, they discovered the woman begging again in the same place. *She was still there!* her father had said, shaking his head incredulously. *I gave her money and she was still there!* A simple man who'd run a hardware store for most of his life, he couldn't understand why his two dollars in change hadn't eradicated the poor woman's misery.

The rain was light at first, almost a dew. Melissa closed her eyes and let the drops wash her face. But soon the grass began to hiss and her T-shirt clung to her skin. Sammy Duncan has slept in the rain, she thought. He has slept in worse. She turned on her side, water now spattering from the tree limbs high above. Lightning split the sky and thunder rumbled. It was silly, she thought, to continue lying out here. I will catch a cold. This won't save anyone.

Melissa dried off in her bedroom and crawled between fresh sheets. She thought again about Brian, their twenty years together and how he'd walked out on her a month after her father's funeral for a woman young enough to be their daughter. She thought about her mother, no doubt still awake at this hour, smoking in bed, reading a dog-eared paperback romance novel, the kind she devoured like Halloween candy. In the morning the dear woman would pour herself a stiff bourbon and then go to work cutting hair. At least she had a house to live in, a shop that was paid for.

At daybreak Melissa drove to her favorite bakery and bought three bags full of croissants and a dozen cups of coffee. She took them to the grassy slopes of parkland near the downtown bridge and left them near a huddle of waking bodies. The strong fresh coffee steamed in the early morning air.

"Hey, camera lady," someone mumbled. "Where's your camera today? Ain't you gonna take my picture?"

She walked to her car and sat there at some distance, watching early risers tear at the bags. She felt a little like a curious girl who had set out birdseed. A familiar bearded man looked toward the car, smiled through gaps in his teeth, and raised a croissant to her in salute.

"Mare-see buckets," he said. "Viva la France."

She smiled and waved back.

Their hair matted from sleep, a little boy and his sister ran giggling toward the food, a threadbare blanket covering their shoulders. A stray dog snooped near the camp, searching for scraps. Melissa watched the scene for a long time, struggling to convince herself to get busy and go take photographs in the business district a few blocks away. After a few moments she laughed at the idea, cranked her car, and drove home.

Rhona phoned at the end of the day. "Have I got news for you," she said. "I've managed to sneak around the conference this week and dangle your new goodies in front of the right eyes."

She was referring to photography curators at their annual meeting.

"They're starting to bite, darling. Can you believe it? I'm throwing a party for you tomorrow night. There's a ticket with your name on it at the Austin airport," she said. "Your work is getting legs, Lissa. People at the ICP and Eastman House are sitting up and taking notice. Houston and Minneapolis are on-line. I think I've even caught the attention of the Californians, poor dips. Get here as soon as you can, sweetheart. We're going for the jugular."

Melissa's mind raced to invent an appropriate excuse for not attending, but nothing suggested itself. In the end she could only respond with a halfhearted acquiescence.

"Is it my paranoia, dear, or do you sound less than ecstatic?" Rhona questioned her. "Don't you understand what's at stake here? This kind of opportunity comes around only once in a lifetime."

❧

Guests at the party knew one another. Old grad school chums, fellow interns once upon a time at one prestigious museum or another, business contacts over the years, rivals. Although Melissa was acquainted with their names, had lunched with several of them and dropped off her slides at their galleries in the twenty-plus years she'd been promoting herself in this world, she still felt like an intruder at a private club.

Rhona paraded her around like a new bride, and people greeted her with genial curiosity. One curator had forgotten they'd been dancing together at a New York disco only a year ago. Another confused her work with someone else's. There was a tendency, Melissa noticed, to speak to her only until the cocktail glass was drained.

"Have you heard what our boy is doing now?" Melissa eavesdropped on several conversations at once. "He's hopping freight trains, if you can imagine, and taking portraits of bums. Thinks he's Mapplethorpe, I suppose. His career has bottomed out, poor dear. His own fault, of course. Just goes to show how quickly the curtain comes down in this crazy business."

There was a lot of talk about the latest advances in color processing in France, and who was showing where. Melissa found herself fading from the chatter, her attention marginal, and on several occasions she had to ask the speaker to repeat a question. Out of desperation she let the roving waiters fill her wine glass much too often, and she soon realized she'd passed her limit.

"I know this sounds like heresy," said an older woman wearing a silk scarf tied around her forehead, "but I've always appreciated the painterly possibilities of the medium." A morsel of pâté stuck to her lower lip. "I think I can persuade the magazine to do a little something on you. Rhona says you give a marvelous interview. I always admire that in an artist. So many spoil their work by talking about it."

As people were being seated for dinner, Melissa took Rhona aside. "I can't do this," she told her old friend. "I have to get out of here."

Rhona looked horrified. "What's the matter, darling?"

"I'll call you tomorrow," Melissa said, grabbing up her jacket and bag.

"This is unforgivable, Lissa!" Rhona said. "What am I going to tell everyone?"

"Tell them I'm sick to death," Melissa said, searching for the door.

She hailed a cab to take her down to her midtown hotel, but when they

287

approached the final block she leaned forward and spoke through the opening in the Plexiglas shield. "Do you know where any of the shelters are?" she asked the driver.

"'Scuse, please?" The driver peered at her in his mirror. He was a Middle Eastern man who needed a good shave.

"Shelters for the homeless," she said. "Do you know where they keep them?"

The driver shrugged. "On Third," he said, "I have seen. The East Village. You know where is that?"

"Yes," she said. "Take me there."

He turned his head to gaze at her. "It is not a place for ladies," he said with courtly concern.

"Take me there."

They arrived in time to see a bus unloading a long file of the city's poor and wretched. The cab driver explained that each night these buses rounded up the needy off the streets and delivered them to places with food and toilets and sleeping mats.

"Lady, if you please," the driver said. "What do you want with such a place? Let me take you to your hotel."

The man in charge of the shelter was a bespectacled, middle-aged monk wearing a long brown robe with a cowl, his beard neatly trimmed around a puzzled smile. He seemed surprised by the sudden appearance of a woman in evening dress.

"I'm looking for a man named Sammy Duncan," Melissa began.

The monk offered her a seat in a typing chair, the best in the room, and brought her a paper cup filled with coffee from a pot warming on a hot plate burner.

"The people here go by all sorts of names," he said, pouring himself a cup. "Can you tell me more about him? Is he a relative?"

Melissa claimed that Sammy Duncan was her uncle. "My mother is worried about him," she said. Then she told the monk an amazing amount of detail about a man she had never met.

"There are so many," he sighed, rubbing a hand through his sparse hair. "Hundreds a night, and that's only a small fraction. I wish I could be more helpful," he said, "but I'm drawing blanks tonight. Do you think you'd recognize him? I'd be happy to show you around the facility."

He led Melissa through the large open dormitory where thin mats were arranged on a tile floor. It was shortly before lights out and some men were already asleep; others milled about, bumming cigarettes, talking quietly among themselves. The stench of unwashed bodies was suffocating.

"Would you like me to call out his name?" the monk asked.

Melissa searched the ravaged faces. She remembered her father at the retirement home and the smell of disinfectant that did little to neutralize the overpowering decay of flesh. The walk down that long mildewed corridor to his room was a passage through the lowest circle of hell, moans escaping the closed doors, forgotten souls babbling to the blank walls. It was the darkest, saddest place she'd ever seen. Until this.

"Miss Sims," the monk spoke again. "I can call his name, if you like."

"No," Melissa said, growing lightheaded from too much drink and the hallucinatory decomposition of spirit all around. She felt the eyes of a dozen desperate old men reaching out to her. "No, thank you, father. That won't be necessary. I think I've made a mistake."

Back in her hotel room she showered briskly, took the phone off the hook, and sprayed the room with tea rose cologne, hoping to eliminate the lingering odors of a claustrophobic city.

In the morning she did not call Rhona, as she'd promised. She changed her plane reservations to Dallas, rented a car, and drove to the little town near Abilene where she grew up and where her mother still lived. She found her sitting in the beauty chair in the one-room shop next to the house, smoking and reading a ladies magazine, waiting for a late-afternoon customer to arrive.

"Goodness gracious," her mother laughed, rising slowly to embrace her daughter. "Why didn't you tell me you were coming, you dickens? I woulda made some banana pudding."

"Mama," Melissa said, "I want you to think about moving to Austin, where I can keep an eye on you."

"Come on to the house," her mother said, patting her hand. "Let's get you something to drink, sweetheart. You must be dry."

The house Melissa had grown up in was showing signs of neglect. Her mother had let things go, and for the next two weeks Melissa tried to make improvements. She cleaned yellowed linoleum, scrubbed the stains from porcelain, shampooed carpet that stank of cat urine. Kitchen wallpaper was coming loose in scrolls, so she bought new floral patterns and re-stripped the room. The outside trim needed a coat of paint, the garden was overgrown, the old pickup wouldn't start.

"It's funny," her mother said, "how almost nothing bothers me anymore. When your daddy was alive, we were quite a pair. A drop of food on the floor, I'd run get a mop. A few weeds near the fence, daddy'd race right over and pull 'em up. I wonder what he'd think of the place now?"

Every evening they would watch television until eleven o'clock and then take up the paperbacks her mother purchased with her prescriptions at the drug store. After an hour of quiet reading, mother would always say, "How 'bout something a little sweet?" with a girlish twinkle in her eye, and they would retire to the kitchen for cake or cookies or ice cream, something new and inventive each time. And then Melissa would try to convince her mother to move to Austin.

"I've got to where I won't even go into Abilene anymore," her mother said one night. "Too much meanness in this world. So what on earth would I do in Austin? All my friends are here."

"There aren't a whole lot of them left."

"Enough to play Uno," her mother said with an elfish grin. "That's all that counts."

They were eating banana pudding with vanilla wafers on top, Melissa's favorite treat since she was a toddler.

"What's the matter, anyway, sweetheart?" Her mother looked across the table at her. "You don't seem like your old self. Is it Brian?"

Melissa shook her head. "I'm pretty much over that," she said.

"Well, then, what?"

Melissa dawdled with her spoon. "I'm not who I wanted to be at this point in my life," she said.

Her mother placed both hands on the tabletop, two wrinkled white appendages, the wedding band still in place. "You are a wonderful lady," she said. "And you've taken some of the best pictures that have ever been taken in this whole blamed state. Doris says she is sure we will see you on the Tonight Show some night."

Melissa ducked her head. "Tell Doris not to wait up."

"What do you mean you aren't the person you thought you'd be?" her mother asked, that wonderful strength of voice resonating from her chest, the voice that always seemed so wise and sure and knowing. Over the years, just when you were ready to shunt her aside as a country woman with small town ways, another woman inside her would surface to face you down with the simplest, most astonishing profundity.

"Look where you started out." Her mother gazed around the modest kitchen. "And look where you've gone. Would you like to see the awards and citations my daughter has won? I've got a drawer full in yonder."

Melissa licked the spoon. "I think I've lost the calling," she said. "It doesn't interest me anymore. There are more important things."

"You are forty-five years old, Melissa," her mother said, those strong venous hands still flat on the table. "You have given up having a family in order to chase after a wonderful dream. Don't stop now, darling. See it through. When you were up on that stage getting your diploma, your daddy turned to me and said, 'She is the first Sims to earn a college degree, and she will be the first Sims to shake hands with the President.' Look how far you've come, child."

Melissa pressed the heels of her palms against her wet eyes. "This is as far as I can go," she said, "and there are so many years left to me. Don't you understand how disappointing that is?

"What am I going to do with the rest of my life?"

Her mother brushed wafer crumbs into a tiny pile. "You'll do what we've all done," she said with force and determination. "You'll stop feeling sorry for yourself and plant another garden."

After nearly three weeks away, the mail was jammed through the door slot and scattered onto the living room floor. Dozens of calls filled the answering machine, including several messages from Rhona that ranged in tone from anger and frustration to panic and finally to an abiding motherly concern. "I want what's best for all of us," she said in her final message. "No, I take that back, Lissa. I just want what's best for you."

Melissa searched through the litter of mail and found only a single letter from Sammy Duncan.

"Dear Sis," the letter began, and Melissa sat down on the floor to read the lines that followed his strange salutation. "I am so sorry for not getting in touch sooner but I was waiting for the right time and an improvement of circumstances to send you a little money for the child and to let you know my latest address."

Four worn one-dollar bills were enclosed between the pages. But in spite of his declaration, there was no return address listed anywhere.

"I have not been feeling too good of late," he continued. "A little congestion in my chest and some fever. The accommodations here leave much to be desired in the way of conveniences so maybe its just a summer cold."

He went on to say that he was going to retire from military service next year with a full pension in accordance with his officer's rank. He asked if her daughter had received the birthday present he'd sent, a Filipino doll he'd picked out for her in Manila.

"I'm going to try and get down there in the spring," the letter concluded, "before mama and daddy forget what I look like, ha ha." It was signed, "With love, Sammy."

Melissa was paralyzed with sadness, unable to put the pages down, unable to read them anymore. She finally lay back on the hardwood floor and closed her eyes. She lost track of time. Twilight entered the room like a gray wintry fog, and then darkness. Before long she could hear wind rustling the oak trees and crickets rubbing their wings in the eerie ritualistic rhythm of nighttime.

When the phone rang, Melissa was slow to rise. She listened to the voice on the machine, and when she determined it wasn't Rhona, she lifted the receiver and said hello to the man calling long distance. He was an intern at a hospital in New York.

"He listed you as next of kin," the young man said. "Directory Assistance matched your name and address with this number. I'm very sorry to have to inform you of this."

"How did it happen?" Melissa asked. She knew it was only a matter of time.

"Complications in the respiratory system. He didn't have full capacity of his lungs, and apparently he lacked proper treatment and medication." There was a pause. "Were you aware, ma'am, of his condition?"

"I'm not sure what you mean."

"Mrs. Sims, your brother was living on the street here in the city. We might've saved him if we'd gotten to him sooner. A squad car found him unconscious on the sidewalk and EMS brought him in."

"I appreciate everything you did for him," Melissa said.

A moment passed, the line hissing with static. "Would you like us to send you his belongings?" the young man asked.

"Belongings?"

"Yes, ma'am. He had a duffle bag with a few odds and ends. We'll be happy to box them up and send them to you."

Melissa considered this. "Yes, thank you," she said. "I'll take them, if it's no trouble."

The package arrived by UPS, a cardboard box containing reading glasses, a hand-sized transistor radio that had to be one of the earliest models ever made, a heavy silver cigarette lighter engraved with the initials SD and the insignia of the United States Army, a used paperback novel by Louis L'Amour, and a small velvet-covered box that held his military medals and pins. The last item in the box was his wallet, a flat, dark brown ancient piece of leather stained by sweat. There were no bills, but the change purse hoarded several nickels and a quarter. The plastic picture holders were stuck together by moisture, but Melissa carefully pried them apart and found an NYC library card, a blood-donor card, a VA hospital identification card, and one photograph, circa the 1940s, of a pretty young blond-haired woman and her infant baby. His driver's license was issued by the state of Virginia, the picture of a middle-aged man of no remarkable aspect, no distinguishing features. This was Sammy Duncan ten years ago; the license had now expired. Short hair combed neatly, brown eyes, 5'10," 158 pounds. The average American male of her father's generation. Melissa studied the small rectangular photograph, trying to fit what she knew of him, his personal chronicle, the accretion of setbacks and misfortune, with that blank visage fixed straight ahead at the camera. He could have been anybody.

She placed these items in the bureau drawer with her father's mementos, the collection of watches, cuff links, tie clasps, and his own assortment of decorations from the war. Then she set about cleaning out all her closets, piling up things she hadn't touched in years—blankets, sheets, pillows and cushions, shoes by the dozens, winter jackets and sweaters. She went through the kitchen and extracted silverware, glasses, cups, cooking utensils, all but the bare essentials for her own use. Finally she gathered together the cameras and photographic equipment that seemed superfluous now, packed these in the back seat of her car, and loaded the trunk with everything else.

She donated the cameras to the St. Vincent de Paul Society store, then drove to the bridge and began to lug the rest of the giveaways down the long sloping riverbank to the homeless camp.

"Looky here," said the bearded man, approaching with the usual brown bag in his hand. "The camera lady is having a garage sale."

Children rushed from the doorless Buick perched on cinder blocks. Others started rummaging through the boxes she'd set on the grass.

"I hope these things are useful," Melissa said.

The bearded man grinned at her and offered his bottle. "You want a receipt?" he asked.

That afternoon Melissa gathered her courage and called Rhona.

"Lissa, you're making a terrible mistake," Rhona said with clear disappointment. "The worst thing you can do to a curator or a critic is to show them great promise, tease them a little, and then blow off their entire world as if it's trivial. These people never forget. Next time around they'll eat you alive."

"I can't finish the project," Melissa said. "It is trivial. I don't know if I'll ever take another photograph."

"Oh, Lissa, darling, I wish I could save you from whatever it is that's troubling you. Are you going through some kind of midlife crisis? I had mine ten years ago and bought a Fiat."

Melissa laughed weakly. "I need some time away from it all," she said. "Maybe a permanent vacation. This thing called art—it makes you a tourist most of the time. You forget where the real people live."

At daybreak the next morning she drove through the empty streets of the business district, seeing the tall glass structures for what they were, places where money was exchanged and mortgages were recorded, where savings collected interest and trust funds were set aside for the future, where those who wore the right fashions and spoke properly could make a comfortable life for themselves and their families. She was not cynical about these things, as she had been in her youth. Prosperity and leisure were admirable enough, and the rewards of a certain cultivation. There was no reason why, at forty-five years of age, anyone would turn their back on these easy consolations. Wasn't it time to get serious about those final frail decades to come?

She parked in the warehouse district next to a railroad track no longer in use. Across the street was the entrance to the Least Brethren Hospice, a dingy brick building that had once been a tortilla factory. She rang the bell and waited.

"May I help you?" said the man who appeared at the door. He was a monk in full habit, his hair tousled from sleep.

"Actually," Melissa said, "I've come to help you."

The monk rubbed his eyes and smiled. "We're just getting breakfast on," he said. "We could use a pot scrubber."

Along the quiet street, from every direction, old men in tattered clothing were making their way toward the shelter. One of them was holding a small radio to his ear. Melissa wondered if he was living on fifty-four dollars a month. ★

1989

PART SEVEN

Our Scruffy Eden: 1990s-2006

LARS GUFSTAFSSON,
      from *The Tale of a Dog* 300

ELIZABETH HARRIS,
      Give 305

THOMAS CABLE,
      Trail Markers 310

MOLLY IVINS,
      How Ann Richards Got Elected
            Governor of Texas 312

BILL MINUTAGLIO,
      from *First Son: George W. Bush and the
            Bush Family Dynasty* 322

LYNN FREED,
      from *Reading Writing and Leaving Home:
            Life on the Page* 330

DAVID WEVILL,
      Home Improvement 334

LAWRENCE WRIGHT,
      Heroes 336

KEVIN BROWN,
      Literary Playscape 338

JAMES MAGNUSON,
      The Week James Michener Died 343

BERT ALMON,
      Austin Odyssey 348

ROBERT DRAPER,
      Adios to Austin 351

LYMAN GRANT,
      Co-Op 360

KURT HEINZELMAN,
      Way Out West at 51st and Berkman 363

STEVEN MOORE,
      Salon of the West 365

JOHN SPONG,
      King's Ransom 373

GARY CARTWRIGHT,
      Statues of Limitation 378

LAURA FURMAN,
      The Woods 384

DON WEBB,
      from *Essential Saltes* 401

SCOTT BLACKWOOD,
      Nostalgia 410

Don Graham,
 Ghosts and Empty Sockets 416

Karen Olsson,
 from *Waterloo* 425

Betsy Berry,
 Human Sexuality 427

William J. Scheick,
 Gridlock 443

LARS GUSTAFSSON

Lars Gustafsson was born in Vasteras, Sweden, and received his Ph.D. in theoretical philosophy from Uppsala University in 1978. He is the author of numerous novels, including some with Austin settings, most notably *The Tennis Players* (1983) and *The Tale of a Dog: From the Diaries and Letters of a Texas Bankruptcy Judge* (1993). For a number of years Gustafsson has lived in Austin and taught at the University of Texas. His fiction set in Texas, like the chapter "Whole Foods" from *The Tale of a Dog*, always has an interesting off-beat slant and nuance. He is a close, whimsical observer of the Austin scene.

from THE TALE OF A DOG

I USED TO DO MOST OF MY SHOPPING OUT WHERE I LIVE, on the other side of the river: in an old shop which is called Tom Thumb at the moment, but which has had many other names. I live in a house right by Town Lake, or Colorado River if you prefer.

I knew just about every assistant there. For a couple of years, until last summer, they had a very pretty student who used to work at the checkout on Sunday evenings, a small dark girl with a somewhat dejected, hunched, and deliberate air. Jennifer. I liked her. We often used to have a chat. I always paid at her till. She said she was studying advertising at the University and always helped me out to the car with my bags herself. There was obviously some kind of unexpressed fellow-feeling between us. She disappeared at the end of the spring term. Yes, it must have been last spring. I presume she finished at the University.

All that summer she was my main reason for shopping there on Sunday evenings, a task that otherwise Claire would usually do. Now that the girl's gone I've changed shops. *Mutatio delectat*, as the Romans say. I go shopping in Clarksville instead. It's more or less on my route home in the afternoons or evenings from Court. I always take Seventh Street and Exposition Road anyway as far as the dam that I have to cross, so it's not much of a detour. It gives me an interval of welcome relaxation between work and home. So I've started calling in at Whole Foods some afternoons on the way back from Court. That's the name of the health-food shop on Lamar Boulevard. It's just below Clarksville, a part of the city up on a hill, where the little white wooden houses were once home to a fine middle-class black population (with washing machines out on the verandah and some still living there; and the tiny grocery shop up on the hill still selling paraffin—can there really be houses there without electricity even now?). Clarksville started changing in the early Eighties, in the Seventies in fact. It began when the younger professors at the University noticed that house prices were fairly low there. A few professors appeared among the old black families. Younger ones. Associates.

A little hash, a few co-operatives, piano-teachers and herbalists, lesbian women jogging in pairs in long silk stockings, the characteristic mix of healthy and unhealthy activities of the period. A lawyer, whom I had met occasionally at Court, in my own Court, was found murdered, lying in the boot of his own Jaguar in the garage of one of those elegant condominiums that gradually began to rise up out of the old overgrown gardens like exotic mushrooms. I presume it had something to do with cocaine that hadn't been paid for. But that's just my entirely personal assumption. The cocaine business has no bankruptcy procedures for people who don't want to pay. I sometimes say as a joke that all commercial life would be like the cocaine business if we didn't have regulated arrangements for the suspension of payments and rescheduling of debts. After the hippies came the yuppies, which was when the expensive condominiums shot up like mushrooms out of the soil. Lawyers, artists, and foppish homosexuals of various professions in velvet trousers and cowboy boots. A few young professionals with a bit more money, lawyers, and doctors, slipped in at the beginning of the Eighties when some of the builders started erecting the huge, smart condominiums up in Clarksville. Spanish palaces and functionalist tower blocks. And Whole Foods, of course, did well out of it all along. I've seen at least three different extensions built. In the Seventies it was a scruffy little co-operative with organic tomatoes and guaranteed toxin-free potatoes on the shelves, and pale red-haired ladies (the kind that always have big dogs waiting in the car), goat's milk and ginseng and very serious young assistants at the checkouts, students and earnest little girls with soft silk ballet shoes in net bags beside their handbags. (I have, I must admit, an interest in supermarket checkout girls that's virtually a hobby, and always have had. Most of them of course are as stupid as cows: spotty, fat and boring lower-class young women. But you constantly come across intriguing exceptions. The very transitoriness of the encounter has a charm in itself. Yes, I keep remembering what Claire often says about my never-fading interest in supermarket cashiers and the women in men's hairdressers, those *gentle priestesses of the fleeting moment*, as I privately call them.)

In recent years Whole Foods has grown in size and become a more cheerful place, as well as noticeably more expensive. But their principles are still intact of course. The pale and, in statistical terms, abnormally thin ladies who stand for ages picking and choosing at the long shelves of vitamins and among the glass bottles of unusual sorts of tea have been joined by the boys in velvet who've been creeping in. But they mostly buy French wines and fuss around the choice grain-fed beef and smoked salmon up at the charcuterie counter—served by the charcuterie assistant's gloved hands, thank goodness—and chat about God knows what in the lengthy queues. Then there are the really delightful young girls in leggings; nowhere else in town can you see so many beautiful figures as in Whole Foods.

What do they do? Modern ballet, perhaps? I've never actually understood what aerobics is though I've always been quite good at Greek. I would guess that the Veuve Cliquot and the well-marbled beef have been biodynamically produced in some mystical way too. Since they're sold here, along with the goat's milk. There was some kind of argument with the authorities about the goat's milk, but I didn't follow it, because I don't drink goat's milk—nor, as far as I'm aware, does anybody else I know.

Over the years the shop has become damnably expensive, but that doesn't seem to have frightened off the health fanatics, and it's probably even been an inducement to the boys in velvet. What is striking is how it has become a meeting place for two different types of people.

The anxious, who worry about vitamins and biodynamic and cholesterol, and the snobs. The anxious, who are easiest to recognise, come because they're afraid that our whole era is poisoning them. They probably also read all the weird magazines, vegetarian and occult, that you see by the checkouts. The snobs, who are a little harder to detect, come because they enjoy food and cooking. And fine wines, of which there are plenty. And to a certain extent they come because the shop has developed into something of a club. They call the cashiers by their first names, and expressions of affection like kisses on the cheek and hugs between customer and cashier are not infrequent. I actually wonder whether the contacts here are more significant than they may appear at first sight. But that's just my own, extremely subjective guess.

Then of course there are ordinary people such as myself. We come because the fruit and vegetables are so good. The tomatoes have a flavour. The apples are wonderful. The wine selection, as I've said, isn't at all bad. Professor Dehlen, my German-born former neighbour who moved to Cherry Lane from the river a couple of years ago because he got rheumatism from living so close to the water, a grand old white-haired university teacher whom I sometimes see there on Fridays, assures me that whoever puts the price labels on the wines makes some rather interesting mistakes from time to time. A *Trockenspätlese* that would cost sixty marks in Berlin will occasionally be going for eight dollars .

So it's quite an entertaining kind of shop. (But it's no compensation for the relationship I had with that little brunette in my old one.)

What has always fascinated me most is the noticeboard. It's right by the exit and is always filled with slips of paper announcing runaway cats, oriental massage (I wonder a lot about what oriental massage consists of), a lesbian lady seeking a female friend with an interest in canoeing. These little pieces of paper, all in different colours, often provided with tear-off strips with a telephone number that you can take away with you, give a glimpse into other worlds than the one I normally inhabit.

I came across something new the other day, a very tiny note, right at the bottom of the board, fixed with a drawing pin that must have caused its owner's small fingers a lot of problems. It was insecurely pressed in, at an angle:

HAS ANYONE SEEN MY DOG? The person who took my dog! a wire-haired fox-terrier called Willie, from the street outside Garner & Smiths Bookshop on Guadalupe Street while I was working there last Saturday, is kindly requested to contact me by telephone. The dog needs his medicine, and I really need the dog.
Theresa Biancino. Phone 512–477 68 59
or (work) 512–477 97 25.

On the way out with my two big bags—one of which was pretty awkward, because it really had too many bottles of wine in it—I took a careful look around. Then I tore off one of the strips from the poorly-fastened paper that had Theresa Biancino's phone number and stuffed it into the breast pocket of my suit. I was in a hurry to get home. ★

1993

Elizabeth Harris

A native Texan, Elizabeth Harris attended Carnegie-Mellon and Stanford Universities. She joined the Department of English of the University of Texas in the late 1970s, where she teaches creative writing. Her stories have appeared in several anthologies, and in 1991 *The Ant Generator,* a collection of stories, was published. "Give" examines a kind of redneck/hippie culture that has existed in Austin just about forever. The motif of searching for gold is an old one in Texas writing. O. Henry searched for gold in Pease Park, and J. Frank Dobie wrote two books about lost gold mines and such.

Give

He's a finder, the Pope. We call him the Pope 'cause his name is John Paul, and 'cause he's a biker—biker's got to have a nickname. 'Course the Pope don't have a bike right now. What the Pope's got is a wife and nine kids and a job driving a gravel truck. Still, scooter trash. And the Pope is a finder. He's always looking around him, so he sees, like not just whether there's any good looking babes or anybody coming at him, but really sees, what's there.

One time he's climbing a rise in the road with his old lady in this '81 Ford of his, and he thinks he's got tire trouble, so he pulls over, gets out. Fat guy, belly slung out over his jeans, and he's got one of them Fu Manchu mustaches, hanging down. So he's walking around the car, where you and me'd've seen a long distance view of that capitol building that's supposed to belong to us, and settled for a level place to crank a jack. And the Pope is looking, looking like he always does, and he sees something shiny, laying in the dirt alongside one of them motorcycle boots. Bends down, picks it up, and it's a three-quarter carat diamond. Just loose, like that, where it fell out of somebody's ring.

He knew, right away, what it was. His old lady was sitting up there in the front seat like she's gonna make him jack her up with the car. She's something else, wears them big dresses you could crawl under there with her. I wouldn't mind. She's got a mouth on her, too.

The Pope shows her this diamond and she says, "That's a piece of glass, John Paul, rhinestone. Or one of them cubic zirconias you get at the discount house, thirty-nine ninety-five."

But the Pope don't say nothing, just reaches out with that diamond and scratches a big X right across the windshield on her side of the car. 'Cause he knew.

He sold that diamond, too. Probably bought meat for the freezer. The Pope is always cooking meat. His old lady—they live in one of them quadriplexes out near me, with the master bedroom down the end of the hall?—she's always laying down back in the bedroom, having a baby. So the Pope does the cooking. You ought to see their place, rug rats and yard-highs everywhere, and the Pope trying to keep them in line. Can't do it, but when he serves out what he's cooked, the piece of meat he gives you is just how he's feeling about you that day.

What the Pope can find ain't only gold and jewels, it's all kind of valuable things. You'll be driving along the interstate with him, not seeing nothing but shopping centers and housing developments, and the Pope'll look over at some sudden little valley with a few trees at the bottom and say, "Creek down there, got fish in it." I never tried him on any of those, but Ernie—him and me shoot pool and I get us into bar fights down at Spellman's: I was born to bust heads—he says the Pope can pick the spots.

Course most people don't pay the Pope no mind, 'cause he don't seem real smart. Sometimes he can't hardly talk, he sorta jitters, or he can't understand you good 'cause he can't remember what words mean. Might be something wrong with him in the head, one of them road accidents or getting beat up too much. But maybe he never learned. Ernie says the Pope's just a hill country cedar-chopper.

Whatever the Pope is, people disbelieve him to their loss. Another thing he found, one time we went to one of these pioneer swap meets out at Oak Hill.

Like a flea market, only people trading flintlock rifles and them enormous-mother Bowie knives. All kinds of stuff, wagon wheels and axes and churns. A whole log cabin you could take apart and haul someplace else and put back together. This one old man had a bunch of arrowheads and clay jars and things spread out on an Indian blanket, and the Pope is real interested in Indian stuff. He looks at the things one by one, and when he gets to this pipe, long clay pipe with a kind of decorated stem laying there, he gets real excited, like he does.

"That's old!" the Pope says. "That's real old!"

Grandpappy, skin so thin you can see the blood of his face through it. Smiles, kinda humoring the Pope.

He picks this pipe up and looks at it real close through them little round John Lennon glasses, he never seen anything like it before. Puts it back down on the blanket like it was a new baby. Then he asks the guy if he means to swap it. 'Course this gives the old guy another curl—'cause it's a swap meet, see.

"Wait." The Pope holds up his finger, "Wait. Don't go away. Just wait," and we go back to the car for this pair of Indian tomahawks the Pope had, that he always thought a lot of. All the way there and back the Pope gabbles on about how old that pipe is.

"Man," he says, "that's the oldest thing I ever seen."

"How old, you figure?" I ask him. "Older than America? Older than Jesus Christ, or the Bible?" The Pope don't know about any of that, he just knows that pipe is the oldest thing he ever seen.

That old red-faced man, he liked them two tomahawks. He traded that pipe for them two tomahawks like he believed he got the best of that deal. Said he got that pipe maybe eight, ten years ago, from a man robbed it with a bunch of other stuff out of an Indian mound in Louisiana. But the Pope, I'm telling you, he handled that pipe with respect.

And—this is the kicker—later him and Ernie took it to a professor Ernie found out could tell how old a thing was, and this professor kept it for a while and did something to it that didn't hurt it none, and you know what he told the Pope? Told him that pipe was five thousand years old. Wanted him to donate it to the natural history museum. Had to explain to the Pope that means give.

Pope says, uh-uh. Man like me can't afford to donate nothing except to his wife and children. He's still got that pipe, wrapped up in paper towels on the top shelf of his closet.

That ain't the biggest thing the Pope ever found, neither. They thought there was a vein of gold in this county—them big geologists and mining engineers been looking for it for years—went out of sight over in the next county, they figured it cropped up somewhere over here. Guys on the job were talking about it. I'm the one told the Pope.

He was interested, but he didn't set out to look for it. Ernie says the Pope don't have to think about looking, he's just bred to it, from hundreds of years of hunters and fishermen and moon-shiners watching out for the Feds. Which ought to be good for *him*, I guess, only he ain't any richer than the rest of us. I mean, what if some men were bred to things that there ain't enough call—for them, anyway—to do anymore?

Like, one day the Pope drove his truck up on the construction site where they were building that extension to the highway, and he seen that vein of gold, just seen it, striping across a fresh bulldozer cut. He got real excited—I wasn't there, but Ernie was—and the Pope got down and went over and tried to tell the site engineer and the surveyors.

"That's that," he says. "See? That's gold! That's that vein of gold!"

They wouldn't pay him no mind, though. Just laughed at him, the way guys like that are going to do at a guy like the Pope. "That's pyrites," they told him. "Fool's gold, son." And I reckon they had another laugh about it over lunch: one of them crazy truckers, fat guy with the evil-looking mustache.

But the Pope knew it was gold. He went back with a pick and shovel the next day—being a state job they weren't working Saturday—and he shovels him up a bucket of that gold dirt. He showed me, and we went out there at night and loaded up half my pickup full, brought it home. I thought, way he's talking about it, least I might get me a nugget, have it made into an earring, like Willie Nelson. Only there wasn't no nuggets, just rocks and dirt with gold dust sprinkled through them. It was gold, all right. The Pope took some of that dirt to a place to have it what they call assayed, and sure enough, he got a letter to prove it. They told him it was good as that ore they mine in South Africa. 'Course it takes tons, and you have to do a bunch to it before you actually get any gold. They leaned on him to tell them where it came from; he thought they had a suspicion it was from around here, but he wouldn't. Told them he bought it back from Colorado a while ago.

He pretty much lost interest in it after that—soon's he found out he wasn't gonna buy his old lady an El Camino with it. So far as he's concerned, it's just a pile of shiny dirt laying out back of his carport.

But every now and then, maybe something expensive broke down on one of us, or the boss or some engineering guy's been on our asses, and the Pope and me'll be driving home together and come up towards the spot on the new highway where that vein of gold is—you can't see it anymore: The state done covered it over with about a million yards of concrete. But the Pope'll sort of hunch over with his head cocked around and look up at me from under those little glasses. And he'll be paying attention, and then he'll say, "That's it! There it's at," he can feel when we go over it, he says, like a little thump. Like driving over one of them expansion joints in the highway. ★

1991

THOMAS CABLE

Born in Conroe, Texas, Thomas Cable graduated from Yale University and the University of Texas, from which he received a Ph.D. in 1969. Cable joined the Department of English at UT in 1972. His books include *The English Alliterative Tradition* (1991) and, with Albert C. Baugh, *A History of the English Language* (5th ed., 2001). He regularly teaches a graduate course in prosody and poetics, and his poem "Trail Markers" indicates both that interest in prosody and another, notably Austin one as well: running. The site is somewhere on the hike and bike trail on Town Lake, a favorite venue for walkers and runners.

TRAIL MARKERS

To say their minds that afternoon were one
    doesn't suffice. There was identity,
molecule for molecule: the sun,
    the bench, the bridge, the leaning cypress tree,
these registered the same in their two brains,
    as did their plain desires. This happens rarely.
        Runners passed the bench, wildflowers bloomed,
            inspired by late March rains.
        They knew that much was changed by what was barely
            said, and much unsaid would be assumed.

One afternoon of talk can change a year,
    or change two lives, or be a reference mark,
a milestone, like the chiseled marker near
    their bench, half a mile inside the park.

From point-five miles they would return to zero,
    but for now, stillness held. In the vacuumed air
        it was as though a film projector failed,
            and in the silver glow
    of silence there was meaning everywhere,
        more than the words and all the words entailed.

To leave the park and go their separate ways,
    for a while at least, was their unsure intent,
the world all before them. In later days
    each would trace a sharp impoverishment
to this lush setting: two red-winged blackbirds hopped
    across the trail and paused; a slope of grass
        and Indian paintbrush rippled; beneath an arch
            two women rowed and stopped;
    all stopped—all to start again, to pass
        on through this unremarkable day in March.★

                                                    1997

MOLLY IVINS

Born in Monterey, California, Margaret Mary Tyler (Molly) Ivins grew up in the River Oaks section of Houston, Texas. Educated at Smith College and Columbia University, she has worked as a reporter and nationally syndicated columnist for several newspapers and magazines, including the *Texas Observer*. She is known both for her staunch commitment to progressive politics and her humor. Her books include *Molly Ivins Can't Say That, Can She?* (1991), *Nothin' But Good Times Ahead* (1995), and *You Got to Dance With Them What Brung You: Politics in the Clinton Years* (1998). In the essay reprinted here, Ivins recalls one of the brightest political highlights of her life, the election of her good friend Ann Richards to the governorship of Texas.

How Ann Richards Got To Be Governor of Texas

The way Ann Richards got to be governor of Texas started back when Bill Hobby decided not to run. Hobby had been lieutenant governor since the memory of man runneth not to the contrary. Lite-Guv-for-Life, we used to call him, and during eighteen years in office, the quiet, studious Houston millionaire had earned the esteem of almost everyone in Texas.

But he'd just come off some killer special sessions in 1989, about workers' comp, for pity's sake, and the man was tarred. Plumb tuckered. His advisers told him he couldn't even take a vacation—no fox-hunting in Ireland, which is what Hobby actually does for fun. Who the hell ever heard of a governor of Texas who fox-hunts? No vacation, they said, you've got to face Jim Mattox right now. If he was going to make the race, he'd have to poop or get off the pot right then.

No wonder Hobby got off the pot.

Mattox, then the attorney general, is the pit bull of Texas politics. Mattox is so mean he wouldn't spit in your ear if your brains were on fire. He is such a fearsomely vile campaigner that he got elected as a liberal out of Dallas for twenty years. Aside from that, he's a pretty decent public servant.

So that left no one but Richards to run against the Dick Nixon of Texas Democrats. "Lite Guv," all her friends said. "Go for Lite Guv." Trouble with Lite Guv is, it pays squat: $7,200 a year, just like the members of the Legislature. You have to be as rich as Hobby to hold that job. Richards got some money out of her divorce, but she used it to buy a house and then she had to earn a living. Fifty-four years old, single, recovering alcoholic—hell, what the woman needed was a pension. Governor of Texas makes $94,000 a year. Don't ever let anyone tell you giving politicians a raise won't attract better candidates.

It all seemed fairly simple at the start: Richards had been state treasurer for eight years; she had a genuinely terrific record in that office; she had national name recognition from her funny keynote address to the Democratic Convention of 1988; and she had a negative rating of 4 percent. Six months later, she won the Democratic nomination for governor with her negatives at 50 percent and half the people in the state under the impression that she was a lesbian drug addict. That's politics in our time.

Yo, well, it was a doozy, start to finish. In addition to the formidable attorney general, Richards faced former Governor Mark White (1982–86), who, as these things go, had been quite a decent governor. (In Texas, we do not hold high expectations from the office; it's mostly been occupied by crooks, dorks, and the comatose.) White would have been counted one of our more successful chief executives, had not the price of oil—indeed, the entire economy of the state—not crashed to ruin on his watch. It wasn't his fault that the price of oil slid from $30 to $9 a barrel; on the other hand, who else could we blame?

So here are these three Democratic candidates—Richards, Mattox, and White—putting on a primary so ugly it became a national joke. Incidentally, the state was in crisis. State governments have four basic areas of responsibility: roads, schools, prisons, and what Governor Allan Shivers used to call "your eleemosynary institutions." In Texas, three of the four were so bad they'd been declared unconstitutional. The schools, the prisons, and the state homes for the mentally retarded and mentally ill were all under court order. On top of that, the state faced a huge deficit and clearly needed to restructure its entire tax system, an utterly regressive, jerry-built, patched-up fiscal disaster area designed to encourage "a healthy bidness climate." So what was the big issue in the primary? The death penalty.

They held a Fry-Off. Mattox got on television and announced he couldn't wait to pull that old death-penalty lever; when he was A.G. he used to go up to the state pen and watch guys get fried for the fun of it. Mark White got on television and actually strolled through a gallery of baddies who'd been fried when he was governor while he talked about how keen he is on frying people. Richards kept saying, "Me too." Mattox found some prison newsletter that had endorsed Richards and put up an ad that said, "Vote for Jim Mattox: He hasn't been endorsed by anyone on death row." You'd have thought they were all running for State Executioner. "Saturday Night Live" did a satirical skit on the primary in which the candidates wore black hoods and carried axes.

Mark White was the first casualty, knocked off by a third-place finish in the March primary that left Richards and Mattox in a run-off. Everyone thought the primary race was pitiful—the run-off was just flat ugly. White stomped off in a huge huff, swearing he'd never vote for Richards, who had run an attack-ad on him he thought was below the belt. Below hell, there was no belt in that race. Then Mattox showed the world how to be really crass. Richards had discussed her alcoholism openly; at the end of a televised debate, she was asked if she had ever used illegal drugs and she refused to answer the question. All hell broke loose. It was widely known that in the crowd of writers, country singers, liberal politicos, and freelance fun and funny people Ann Richards went around with in Austin in the late sixties and early seventies, almost everyone tried marijuana.

Richards's position was that if she answered the drug question, everyone around the state who was still out there drinking and doping would be discouraged from coming in for help, because if they could still beat you over the head with it after ten years of sobriety, there was no point in sobering up. The Texas political world went bonkers. Why doesn't she answer the question? Why won't she answer the question? Half her supporters thought she should just 'fess up;

the other half warned that it would finish her candidacy. Some thought she should say, "I was too drunk to remember." Everybody had a scenario, everybody thought they knew what she should do. None of it had anything to do with roads, schools, prisons, or taxes, but it was the only issue in the run-off. She was asked "the question" again at the second televised debate and again refused to answer. After that debate she was surrounded by a mob of screaming reporters, all demanding that she answer the question. By the time her staff waded into the scum and dragged her out, Richards was white and shaking. I never saw her enjoy a single day of the campaign from then on. She became tight and guarded with reporters, answering every question as though it were booby-trapped.

Mattox put up an ad posing the new question: "Did Ann Richards use cocaine?" More flap. The issue just would not go away. Everybody started running ads saying the other guy's ads were unfair. It got wonkier and wonkier. Some guy showed up claiming he had seen Mattox, who is a teetotal Baptist, smoke dope. This citizen was put on television making this claim in both Houston and Dallas before anyone could even check out whether he'd just been released from the state nuthouse. Someone else popped up to say he'd seen Richards use cocaine ten years before, at a Jim Mattox fund-raiser. The press did not cover itself with glory. The citizenry was disgusted. Richards limped through the run-off in April with 54 percent. And there stood Clayton Williams.

He had a thirty-point lead. He had $10 million ($8 million of it his own money). He had the best television ads anyone had ever seen. And he was a likeable guy. He wasn't a politician, he had no record to attack. His big issue was drugs. He, Clayton Williams, proposed to stop drug use in the state of Texas. (This also has nothing to do with roads, schools, prisons, or taxes, but whatthehey?) His announced plan was to take young drug-users and "teach 'em the joys of busting rocks."

Claytie Williams is in truth a perfect representative of a vanishing Texas. He's white, he's macho, he's rich (oil, cattle, banking, and communications). He really does wear cowboy boots and a cowboy hat all the time. He worships John

Wayne, has a statue of Wayne in the lobby of his bank in Midland. Williams is open-hearted, sentimental, and gregarious. He's not only an Aggie (a graduate of Texas A & M University), he still gets tears in his eyes whenever he hears the Aggie fight song. He's got a trophy-wife named Modesta. He hunts. He drinks. He occasionally gets into fistfights. And he believes the world simple.

One of his most brilliant ad series would give some simpleminded, tough-talk answer to a complex problem and then close with, "And if they tell you it can't be done, you tell them they haven't met Clayton Williams yet." If they'd just shut him up in a box for the duration of the campaign, he'd be governor today.

In late March, he invited the press corps out to his ranch for roundup. They got bad weather. Sitting around the campfire with three male reporters, Williams opined, "Bad weather's like rape: As long as it's inevitable, you might as well lie back and enjoy it." Bubba, the shorthand we use to denote the average, stereotypical Texan, has been using that line for years. But it was Williams's fate in the campaign to keep unerringly finding that fault line between the way things have always been in Texas and the way things are getting to be. Richards shrewdly picked up on the difference with her endlessly reiterated slogan about "the New Texas." Claytie Williams is Old Texas to the bone.

Later, a bizarre rumor about "honey hunts" out at Williams's ranch began circulating. I don't know who started it, but I do know it was ably spread by George Shipley, a campaign consultant known to the press corps as "Dr. Dirt," who was then working for Richards. According to this rumor, to reward his top employees, Williams would hire a bunch of whores and then take everyone out to the ranch and let the boys hunt down the whore ladies. Apparently in an effort to address this rumor, Williams publicly allowed as how the only truck he'd ever had with prostitutes was when he was a student at A & M and would go to Mexico because it was the only way you could "get serviced" in those days. (Technically speaking, it is the bull that services the cow, not vice versa.) Texas Hispanics naturally do not enjoy being reminded that Anglo Texans have been using Mexico as a whorehouse for generations. And Texas women don't like being reminded that Bubba thinks of them as a service station.

This touched off a new round of bad Claytie Williams jokes: "How many Republicans does it take to screw in a lightbulb?" "Republicans don't screw in lightbulbs: They screw in Mexico."

Polls showed the gender gap in support for Richards or Williams getting wider all summer. Williams had enough money to keep his ads on during the hot season, Richards didn't. Unfortunately for Williams, three of his ads were so full of egregious errors and misstatements they had to be pulled down. This lent incentive to the press's "ad police" efforts: Most of the state's major newspapers took to dissecting new political ads to see how their content measured up to the truth. This was done most effectively by television stations, notably WFAA in Dallas and KVUE in Austin, which were better able to show how the pictures used in ads can be misleading.

Interestingly enough, one of Williams's ads showed Ann Richards at the political highlight of her career, making the keynote address to the Democratic Convention in 1988, specifically, the famous line on President Bush: "Poor George. He can't help it. He was born with a silver foot in his mouth." The ad ran in August, at the start of the Persian Gulf crisis, when patriotism was at flood tide and criticizing the president was tantamount to treason. But I was astonished at how many people objected to that line and held it against Richards throughout the campaign. The line itself is already classic and will be used in every anthology of political humor published hereafter. Yet a surprising number of men are alarmed by the thought of a witty woman. They think of women's wit as sarcastic, cutting, "ball-busting": It was one of the unstated themes of the campaign and one reason why Ann Richards didn't say a single funny thing during the whole show. Margaret Atwood, the Canadian novelist, once asked a group of women at a university why they felt threatened by men. The women said they were afraid of being beaten, raped, or killed by men. She then asked a group of men why they felt threatened by women. They said they were afraid women would laugh at them. Williams blooped again on October 11, not a slip of the tongue, but a carefully planned confrontation that just didn't work. The press had been gnawing on a story about Williams's bank, Claydesta National (that's a combination of Clayton and Modesta, you see; very Texan) illegally selling credit insurance, particularly to poor black people applying for auto loans. Richards's campaign planted that story (Dr. Dirt again), but since it was a legitimate story, the press ran with it. All Richards herself ever said about it was that she only knew what she read in the papers. Richards was to appear before Williams at a forum in Dallas. Television cameras caught Williams just before he went up on the dais, saying to a friend, "Watch what I'm going to do to her now, watch this." As Williams moved behind the seated line of dignitaries on the dais, Richards, who had already spoken and was fixing to leave, got out of her chair, put out her hand, and said, "Hello, Claytie." Williams feigned surprise, then indignation. "I'm not going to shake hands with you," he says, "I won't shake hands with a liar." And he moved past leaving Richards to say after him with commendable self-possession, "Well, I'm sorry you feel that way about it, Clayton."

Bubba didn't mind the rape joke or Claytie's shooting an endangered species of mountain sheep or ripping off black folks, but Bubba did not like that scene. It played over and over on television and Bubba thought it was tacky. Bubba may screw Mexican whores, but Bubba is not rude to a lady. Williams then managed to observe within hearing of the press that he planned to "head her, hoof her, and drag her through the dirt." When Richards predicted she would win the race, Williams giggled on camera and said, "I hope she hasn't started drinking again," a line so tacky Richards used it in one of her own ads. A spoof of the Williams' tagline became popular: "If you think Texas doesn't have a village idiot, you haven't met Clayton Williams yet."

But the polls still showed Williams ten points ahead, then seven points ahead. The Richards campaign was praying for Williams to screw up again, and he cheerfully obliged. Williams's people had sagely dodged all requests for a debate, since Williams knew almost zip about state government, but two Dallas television stations, KERA and WFAA, managed to rope him into "in-depth" interviews. He gave a shaky performance, his ignorance more visible than usual. Then one interviewer asked, almost as a throwaway, "What's your stand on Proposition One?"

"Which one is that?" Williams inquired. "The only one on the ballot." He was still lost, so the interviewer told him what the proposition was about—concerning the governor's power to make late-term "midnight" appointments. Williams still didn't know if he was for it or against it.

"But haven't you already voted?" inquired the interviewer.

"You told us you voted absentee. Don't you remember how you voted?"

"I just voted on that the way my wife told me to; she knew what it was," Williams explained.

He was so clearly a candidate in a world of trouble, the clip made the national news. The polls now showed her within three points. All Richards had to do was stay out there plugging away, not make any mistakes, and keep drawing that line about the difference between the Old Texas and the New Texas. There were Richards yard signs all over upper-class Republican neighborhoods in Dallas and Houston, thanks to the women. Texas politics features an astonishingly dedicated corps of Republican women who woman the famous Republican phone banks—notoriously more effective than anything Texas Democrats have ever been able to pull together. Republican women not only weren't working the phone banks, they were lying about who they were going to vote for. It wasn't just the abortion issue: Many upper-class Republican women are pro-choice, but they were also wincing over how it would look to the rest of the world to have Claytie as governor of Texas. He's such a throwback, like a character out of *Giant*. The old Texas stereotypes, which these women have been struggling to bury for years by their good works for art museums and symphony orchestras and ballet companies, would be so reinforced by Governor Clayton Williams they could hardly bear to think about it. And let's face it, Modesta is a tacky name.

The candidates went into the last weekend dead even, but Williams got President Bush down to work for him nonstop. Bush pretended he was running hard against Saddam Hussein and might have pulled it off, had not Williams blooped again. The Richards campaign, which had been trying hard to get Williams to reveal his tax returns (Richards had already made hers public), kept faxing tax questions to reporters wherever Williams went. On the Friday before election, asked again about taxes during a small-town television interview, Williams replied as he always did, "I have paid millions of dollars in taxes." Then he added, "Except in 1986, when I didn't pay anything." The press almost missed it. The throwaway line made it into one wire story, but was buried. Richards's campaign people saw it and went ballistic. Bill Crier, Richards's press secretary, had a hard time getting her to pick it up and use it. She was in Houston that night, but it hadn't made the Houston newscasts, it wasn't on the wires, she was tired, she couldn't see it. But Crier insisted she bring it up in front of a union audience. The audience went nuts. Clayton Williams, a multimillionaire, paid no taxes in 1986. Perfectly legal, of course. Like everyone else in oil, he lost a lot of money that year. But it reminded everyone one more time what they don't like about rich Republicans—the guy is sitting on a bank account with at least $10 million in it, he had enough money that year to make thousands of dollars in political contributions to Republican candidates, but he didn't pay any taxes. Everyone else in Texas had a bad year in 1986, too. Unemployment was almost 13 percent. But the rest of us had to pay taxes. It's not fair. The rich get all the breaks.

A subsidiary theme was, "Can you believe he was dumb enough to say that?" The half of the press corps traveling with Williams missed the whole thing. First of all, they got into a fight with the pilot of the press plane, who wouldn't let them drink. When they got to Laredo, they were told their rooms at La Posada were not available. Actually, the Williams's campaign had cancelled the reservations and then shipped the reporters across the border to a Mexican hotel with no telephones. Editors trying to find their reporters that night to check out the story were S.O.L. The ploy backfired: Several papers did miss the story Saturday, but that meant it hit the Sunday papers, with a much larger readership. Richards's campaign people stayed up all night making a radio commercial about Williams's failure to pay taxes. Monte Williams did the voiceover and volunteers drove hundreds of miles all over the state to get it to radio stations, where it aired Sunday and Monday. It was the last impression voters got of Clayton Williams before the election. His campaign was in free fall.

Richards won with 52 percent of the vote. We knew it was over at 7 P.M. election night, before any official returns, when Clayton Williams's press secretary, Bill Kenyon, started berating the press. Williams was exceptionally gracious in defeat, reminding everyone of why they'd ever liked him in the first place.

The scene at Richards's headquarters hotel on election night, the Hyatt in Austin, was like nothing ever seen before in Texas politics. It's true Ann Richards had some heavy-hitters give money to her campaign—some wealthy trial lawyers, the Jewish socialist insurance millionaire from Waco (a class of one) Bernard Rapoport, and a few Texas women with their own money. But by and large Richards had done something unprecedented in state politics. She raised almost $8 million in $25 contributions—it was the great bulk of her money. When Texas lobbyists back the wrong candidate, they say among themselves that they have to catch "the late train" over to the winner. With Richards, it was a Midnight Special. The lobbyists started pouring into her hotel around 9 P.M. and it looked like a conga line—oil, insurance, timber, chemicals. Upstairs, there was no one "insider" party for the big givers, as there usually is. Instead there were at least ten different parties for people, most of them women, who had raised big money in small chunks. There was an intensity of celebration normally felt only by the family and staff of a victorious politician. Perhaps because women show emotion more easily than men, the intensity factor was formidable. People were packed into the main ballroom like sardines. They sang and laughed and greeted one another with that peculiar female Texan greeting call that sounds like calling pigs, "OOOOOOOOOOOO, honeee, how good to see yew again!" Finally Ann spoke and everyone laughed and wept some more, and then she reminded them to drive home safely. ★

1991

321

BILL MINUTAGLIO

A native of New York City, Bill Minutaglio is the author of *First Son: George W. Bush and the Bush Family Dynasty* (1999) and *City on Fire: The Forgotten Disaster that Devastated a Town and Ignited a Landmark Legal Battle* (2003). Minutaglio's career spans twenty-eight years as a prize-winning journalist for major newspapers in the U.S. He lives in Austin. His most recent book, *The President's Councilor: The Rise to Power of Alberto Gonzales,* was published in 2006.

from FIRST SON: GEORGE W. BUSH AND THE BUSH FAMILY DYNASTY

November 3, 1998

FROM INSIDE THE LINCOLN TOWN CAR, ALL BLUE-SILVER like the river snaking through Willie Nelson's smoky rancho deluxe, it's impossible to miss the cloud cover beginning to burn off over the Texas Hill Country. It's a little after 9 A.M. on a slightly chilly day, and as the clouds are erased there are the soft bumps and shoulders, the same loping country that LBJ retreated to, bouncing along in his own Lincoln on the banks of the capricious Pedernales River... in the same bit of Texas that Willie Nelson and his aging coterie of snaggletoothed mad-dog musicians like to claim as their outpost.

Sometimes the Midland good old boys remind him: Back in '75, back then his West Texas friends would yodel and snort when they saw him. Here comes the Bombastic Bushkin, George W., that SOB...George Dubya! Back then one night, he and Charlie had had some beer and had finally decided, hell, that it would all right, important really, to walk onstage at the Ector County Coliseum with Willie and his band. And all the while Willie was vaguely aware of something happening behind him, all the while Willie kept staring in his usual goggle-eyed way into the cosmic otherworld and the band was going to be playing "*Whiskey River, take my mind.*"

His Lincoln is in downtown Austin now, and it's slamming hard off Lavaca Street and straight onto a sloping driveway. Wheels flashing, it's surging just inches from the still-opening automatic wrought-iron gate. It's rolling right to the rear entrance of the faded white governor's mansion. The building, Greek Revival-meets-southern-plantation stately, is crawling with splattered, callused remodelers, many of them Hispanic, dressed in soiled jumpsuits and hanging from a cobweb of scaffolding. They're smiling. And they're nudging each other: *"Señor Suerte..."* "Mr. Lucky," whispers one of the admiring workers, nodding toward the Lincoln. He's riding shotgun, his right arm is hanging out the window as if he's in the lead car in the homecoming parade in Amarillo, as if he's cruising downtown Fort Worth in a T-Bird, as if there's somebody out on the Drag by the University of Texas whose attention he desperately wants to get, as if it's Midland in the 1950s or Houston in the 1960s and the smiling mothers on the baking sidewalk are halfheartedly shielding their curious daughters' eyes. George W. Bush's brow is doing a Lone Star two-step up and down. It's election day. He's leading by an extraordinary margin and projected to be the first Texas governor ever elected to consecutive four-year terms. The numbers are huge, and in the shadowy piney woods creeping toward the Louisiana border, a woman comes up to him at an old fashioned political rally and presses a jar of fresh Henderson cane syrup into his hand. Outside the weathered Camino Real Hotel in El Paso, an elderly Mexican immigrant grips his shoulders and won't let go as he stares into his eyes. In the soul of the new high-tech Texas, in Austin, computer billionaire Michael Dell invites him to his yawning hillside manor one Saturday in January; on Monday, the first thing George W. does is write a note, just like his father trained him to do, carefully scribbling notes by the thousands, shorthand—scrawled missives suggesting an intimacy, a lingering friendship: *Dear Susan & Michael: Laura, the girls, and I had a fine time Saturday at your party. We especially appreciate the tour of your home. It is great. I look forward to future visits. Sincerely, G.W.* Looking out the car window, he can see the little army waiting for him outside the mansion. It makes him laugh, he can't help it, and it makes him want to scream something out the Lincoln: "Hey . . . welcome to Reality Day!"

The driver brakes the car hard just short of the porte-cochere. The governor of Texas bolts from the car and takes a few strides to the back door of the mansion. Up close, the 142-year-old refurbished building looks like any one of a thousand fraternity houses, one of those older homes that the family of an iron-willed nineteenth-century industrialist donated to the local university—all Ionic capitals and ribbed columns, all stately and ghostly, a witness to twinkling soirées, toga party chants, and pregame rallies. Bush shoots the cuffs of the white dress shirt under his gray suit. The rolling amoeba of coffee-clutching reporters that has been waiting all morning for him begins to tumble in his direction. CNN, *The Washington Post*, Associated Press. He's winking at his boys, the fraternity of security detail men and the armed, white-hat-wearing Texas Rangers, who can't help but grin too as they line up outside the mansion's back entrance. The energy level out here is set at the usual, nice, rollicking pitch. He suddenly shrugs his shoulders.

"I'm glad Reality Day is here!" he yelps into the air. "Yesterday was Speculation Day. Today is Reality Day!"

He starts to bob in a bantam rooster strut across the hand-laid bricks in the circular driveway. His head is tilted back, all chinny defiance. He's done twenty-three press conferences in the last seven days: Dallas, Austin, Waco, San Antonio. His caffeine-sucking press handlers, saggy faces, bad skin, and droopy shoulders, are all dragging, but he's still up at 6 A.M., still crackling to jump on the King Air campaign plane: San Angelo, Wichita Falls, Sherman. There have been dozens of reality days, speculation days, one after another.

&

"Oh, it's been a long campaign!" he shouts, still beaming, still antsy.

For weeks, the first son had been on the phone, taking meetings in his cavernous second-floor office and debating the merits of the new slogan. It was, he and his advisers had decided, compact. Al Gore will deride it and the knuckle-draggers will complain, but it will really put some velvety distance between himself and Newt Gingrich, between himself and all those other soon-to-be defrocked bastards. And it was, though hopefully no one will notice it, the exact same slogan his father's closest aides had once devised to describe the elder Bush to Christian voters back when he was finally sure his 1988 presidential campaign was rolling forward: *Compassionate Conservative.*

This morning, the first thing was to call his father. They had been making these calls for decades, these election-morning calls. They talked about the same things they had talked about face-to-face several weeks before, during the annual, almost giddy August retreat at the ninety-six-year-old seaside family compound in Maine. In Kennebunkport, it was obvious. It was celebrative. The numbers were impressive. The crafty backdoor Democrats in Texas were still falling all over themselves for the first son. Jeb was going to win in Florida. His father had said he'd decided he would take Jeb's and George W.'s mother and go to Florida. He wouldn't be coming to Texas, where he had done all that grinding backroom muscle work to force the modern Republican Party onto its feet and out of that pockmarked landscape in oil-stained West Texas, out of that sickening humidity in Houston, every day his starched white shirt sticking to his chest like a moist blanket. He wouldn't be coming to Texas, where he had done all those things that had made it possible for his first son to become governor. More important, he said, that I go to Florida. The first son had agreed.

Exactly twenty-five years ago, he'd had a different conversation with his father. That night, he'd been drunk, and he was out driving with his fifteen-year-old brother, Marvin. After he had rammed through the garbage cans with his car and walked in the front door of the house...he was ready, if it was going to be that way, to fight his father. He was from Houston, Texas, he was beery, he had no real career, it was late, and for most of his life he, more than anyone in the family, had been measured against his father, his grandfather, the Bush legacy. That night he'd stood in front of his father, in the den, and asked his father if he was ready to fight:

"I hear you're looking for me. You want to go mano a mano right here?"

Now, this morning, he was happy his father was traveling to Florida and would be with his younger brother. Through five decades, there has always been a Bush as governor, senator, congressman, or president. Since the early 1950s, there have been only rare, random interludes when a Bush hasn't been in a prominent political office. This one, for the first time, is one the first son is going to claim on his own without all those losers, all those *psychobabblers*, who pretend to know him, who want to analyze him, who waste their time looking for some deep-rooted angst, some inner, complicated undulations...all those soothsayers from the Northeast...all the weak-willed products of the 1960s, the people who fell for all that claustrophobic, indulgent William Sloane Coffin guilt at Yale and Harvard...the ones who whisper that they can always see his father's shadow hanging, nagging, pacing off to the side.

&

All year, the extraordinary poll numbers have been delivered to that second-floor office at the State Capitol, the one with the collection of 250 autographed baseballs neatly arranged in a dark-wood display case, the Western painting with the lone rider that his Midland oil buddy Joe O'Neill...*Spider!*... had loaned him, the rows of framed photographs on the counter behind his chair, the photos, staring at his back, of his stern grandfather and his misty-eyed father. All year he has led by pneumatic numbers in every poll, including the national prepresidential ones that say he's more popular than Colin Powell, Steve Forbes, and Al Gore. All year in Texas it's speculation squared: He had already made the calls to set Newt Gingrich's resignation in motion, hadn't he? Larry Flynt was investigating him, wasn't he? Hasn't a Texas reporter called up his press office and asked if the governor ever killed anyone? Six years ago the *Houston Chronicle* ran the wrong picture of him. It was on a Sunday, the final day leading up to his carefully scheduled official announcement that, without ever holding any other elected office, he was going to run for governor of Texas. Of course, by mistake, the newspaper had run a picture of his father:

"In some copies of Sunday's State section, the wrong picture was used in a story about George W. Bush's address to the Texas Federation of Republican Women."

He said it didn't bother him. But whenever the extended BushWalker clan assembled for their annual meetings at Kennebunkport, they watched him, as they always did, because they wanted to see what he would do or say next. He was the oldest, most incendiary, of the five kids, but he was always more than that: *Primus inter pares,* as his erudite, wordy Uncle Bucky liked to harrumph. First among equals, maintained Bucky.

His uncle, especially, loved to watch his nephew, wondering how he would turn out. He could see the patterns emerging, even when he had taken him to his first ball game at the old Polo Grounds, watching the New York Giants play the Cincinnati Reds, and even later, sitting in box seats at Shea Stadium, keeping tabs on the New York Mets, one of the baseball teams the Bush family would own a piece of over the years. Bucky saw the way Jeb, Neil, Marvin, and Dorothy deferred to Little George...no one ever called him Junior, unless he allowed them, unless it was someone he knew very well. Bucky saw the way the three younger brothers stepped out of his way, just the way they stepped aside for their mother. Little George, Bucky liked to tell people, was "as close to being the boss as you could be. I mean...they looked up to him and respected him and were...maybe...a little afraid of him from time to time."

Now the glum Texas Democrats, truth be told, knew what people had said inside the walls of the Democratic National Committee offices in Washington after he first got elected: "The guy is a fucking giant killer," said one normally soft-spoken, level-headed DNC researcher. The Bush clan had assumed that Jeb was going to be elected to high office first. Jeb was the ideologue, Jeb's face wasn't going to wash over with anger, with rage, as his older brother's was prone to do. There might be a time for George W. Bush, but not in 1994, not in Texas, not against Ann Richards. He would raise his profile, establish his own identity, but he wasn't going to beat the high-haired populist incumbent with the splendid approval ratings...the way she pounded the Bushes, sounding like rusty nails at the bottom of a coffee can when she went on the national talk shows. What about the cover of *Texas Monthly*, the photo of her sitting on a motorcycle? Don Henley from Eagles loved her. So did Steven Spielberg. They gave her $50,000 each. She got money from Robin Williams, Annie Leibovitz, Linda Ellerbee, Gloria Steinem, Willie Nelson, Marlo Thomas, Rosie O'Donnell, Donald Trump...*Donald Trump!* She'd ladled Texas acid on George W.'s father at the Democratic National Convention; the one-liner, about George Bush being born with a silver foot in his mouth, was one for the ages. In 1994, she'd done it again, unblinking and over and over again, serving it up as pointed as an ocotillo, talking about an anemic link at the tail end of a gilded Bush dynasty. Her family had grown up desperately poor, on hardscrabble Texas farms in hamlets called Bugtussle and Hogjaw. She had been raised as an only child in a microscopic town outside of Waco, the small city sometimes called the "Heart of Texas," and her relatives survived from paycheck to paycheck provided by her grandfather's job driving trucks with Humble Oil. And Richards called the New Haven-born Bush the Little Shrub.

As the campaign between the most popular governor in America and the most powerful political family in America ground forward, Bush was confiding to a friend in Dallas that he was worried that Texans would never see him as a "real person"; that he was in his forties and that when they heard his name, they still simply thought of his father.

Early on, his chief political adviser ordered him to avoid the media, to avoid all the people wanting to talk to him about his father, about a modern American dynasty. The strategy, instead, was to carry around four ideas, four issues, only four campaign issues—education, crime, welfare, and tort reform—to one more town hall meeting in Waco, one more 4-H show in Abilene, one more rusted-out cotton gin in faraway, forgotten Lubbock. The strategy was to make him more Texan than Ann Richards and also to extinguish any anger. He was always moving, wrapping his lean arms around the Luby's cafeteria lady, her cheeks slathered with dollops of hopeful rouge, and posing for a picture in some population 600 Texas town, or he'd go to the high school in Sherman, not far from the Red River, insisting to the fidgeting juniors and seniors, *I have no ill will or feel negatively toward Ann Richards . . . I find her to be an interesting soul.*

That was exactly when the family thought that maybe, maybe, something had happened to him. His favorite cousin, Elsie Walker, couldn't believe it: Little George, the turbulent cosmos inside every family gathering in Maine, the combustible brother who doled out what he liked to call "behavior modification" to the wandering, disenchanted members of his father's White House staff? Now, somehow, he was holding it all back, holding on to it "like a dog with a bone," said a vaguely worried Elsie. She immediately sent off a telegram to Barbara after she saw the way Richards was working him over in their debate, trying to get him to snap and he wouldn't...not this time. Elsie's telegram to his mother began this way: "WHAT HAS . . . WHAT DID HE DO?"

He was supposed to buckle and erupt. His sister, Dorothy, knew he was still wrestling with it. They all watched him, his brothers and the cousins—Elsie Walker, John Ellis, and others—who swirled around him every summer at Kennebunkport.

"Then he just kicked the living shit out of Ann Richards!" yelled John Ellis. ★

1999

LYNN FREED

Lynn Freed, who was born in South Africa, is the author of seven books—a memoir, a collection of essays, and five novels, including *The Mirror* (1997) and *House of Women* (2002). Her short fiction and essays have appeared in leading journals, magazines, and newspapers. She now lives in Northern California. In the early 1990s she was a visiting writer at the University of Texas, and in this section of her memoir, *Reading, Writing and Leaving Home: Life on the Page* (2005), she recalls those days of living in Austin and teaching creative writing.

---

from READING, WRITING AND LEAVING HOME: LIFE ON THE PAGE

SIXTEEN YEARS LATER—WITH MARRIAGE, TWO NOVELS, a world of travel and a career as a part-time travel agent behind me—I was back in the classroom. The invitation had come from a large university in the Southwest, offering a decent sum to spend two semesters teaching creative writing. This time, there hadn't even been a question of what I really wanted: I needed money. The modest advance on my last book was long since gone, the next book was hardly on the page, and working full-time as a travel agent would have paid little more than the cost of my travel, leaving me no time at all to write.

So I packed up my car and drove across the country to a city lost in the fold of the Rand McNally map. And then suddenly, after fifteen years, it was back to dips and chips on a Saturday night and Marvin Gaye with the rug rolled up. Not to mention "lay" for "lie," split infinitives, falafel stands, office hours, memos from the Chair—the whole baggage, in short, of my new and unnervingly familiar patron, the Academy.

Had marriage been this bad? I tried to remember.

"Ma'am," said a C student, "I just want you to know I'm shootin' for an A." He was a young man who seemed to suffer incurably, like so many of the others, from television ear ("Son, I'm leaving." "But, Dad, just think of Mom, think of what this will do to her." "I am thinking of your mother, son. Trust me. One day you will be old enough to understand all this.") He was taking my Undergraduate Creative Writing Fiction class "to better sharpen his verbal skills," he claimed. The fact was, he said, he was headed for law school. He needed the hours and he needed the grades.

I stared at him, wondering what my writing life would have been like had I become a lawyer. Lawyers could work part-time. As it was, my writing itself had come to a standstill. Every time I switched on the computer, I remembered the student stories I had to grade. And then, once they were read, it was as if all the vigour had dropped out of my own desire to write. Writing felt like homework I was setting for myself in a subject of which I had long since grown tired.

Every day, letters arrived from my mother. "What are you writing?" she wanted to know. "Don't put your all into teaching, darling, or you'll regret it." She understood quite well what she was saying. Given greater talent than she had, she would have stayed on the English stage. As it was, she put much of her own all into her acting school, kicking off her shoes and hiking up her skirt to demonstrate, yet again, to a hopeless student how to fall down a flight of stairs without killing herself.

In the office next to mine was a famous Indian writer, also visiting for the year. Recently he had become a bestseller in India when one of his novels was turned into a television series. His office was filled with women in saris all talking at once—this one was a daughter, that one a daughter-in-law. They lived in a furnished apartment nearby and all came to the university together, carrying marvelous-smelling food.

"What are you doing about grading?" I shouted at him. He was very old and quite deaf, and hardly seemed to understand why he was there at all. But I was in transports of exasperation myself, subject to the assaults and imprecations of students every time I handed back a set of graded stories. With every week that passed, I felt stupider, less sure of my right to be teaching at all, let alone grading. Perhaps, after all, the student writing of his father's "uncircumsided" penis was not to be faulted for his English if, as the story seemed to imply, he had suffered the repeated assaults of such a weapon as a boy himself. But then again, so what? Why did such a thing have to land up in my Undergraduate Creative Writing: Fiction class when it belonged more properly with social services?

"How do you teach them writing? I shouted at the Indian writer. "How do you teach them to write?"

"Oh! Teaching!" he laughed. "Either they are reading my books, or they are not!"

I made my way back to the Versailles townhouse complex in the spirit of an outcast. It was ninety-eight degrees. My car had no air-conditioning, and my townhouse itself was infested with crickets. So was the one across the pool. My friend the handyman had told me that the redhead who lived there was a medical student and had two diaphragms under her bed, one on each side, both of which he had sprayed for crickets.

Gazing across the pool, with its dozens of crickets skittering on the surface, I wondered if things would have been easier had I become a doctor. Doctors could work part-time. The redhead herself was home a lot, and men came and went there constantly. One wore an army uniform and carried a ghetto blaster. Another wore Bermuda shorts and a baseball cap turned around backwards. When I had instructed the students in my class to remove their baseball caps, they had complained to the chairman. He called me in and asked whether I would please relent. Things are different in this country, he explained to me. Students tend to wear hats the way they wear shoes. In addition, they have concerns about "hat hair." Perhaps I should consider the teaching evaluations they would be turning in at the end of the semester. Such things counted for future employment, he said.

It was at about this point that it began to dawn on me that I had landed myself in a situation in which the inmates were running the institution. I might have known. I had arrived at graduate school in New York in the late sixties, right at the onset of the Age of Relevance—a time when, as Isaiah Berlin lamented, a whole generation of youth confused crudity with sincerity.

What I was encountering now was simply the logical result of that revolution—the supreme relevance of the self in an institution that had come to depend for its continuance on the pleasing of that self. It was a self that took its reference not from history, philosophy, and literature, but from psychology, a variety conveniently adjusted to the pursuit of personal happiness. And so the Age of Relevance had become the Age of the Self.

It is one thing to understand the points of the compass, quite another to use them in order to find one's way in a life circumscribed by one's own refusals—the refusal, in my case, to consider permanent full-time employment and the refusal to abandon the freedom to travel.

Once the year in the Southwest was over and I was back in California, I found myself again facing the problem of how I was going to earn a living. Freelance writing was all very well, but it was haphazard, unsuited to a temperament prone to anxiety. And so, when other offers of temporary teaching positions started coming in, I would accept them. ★

2005

David Wevill

Wevill, a Canadian American, was born in Japan, grew up in Canada, and went to Cambridge University in England. He has lived also in Burma and Spain. He has published nine books of poems and some translations, including such recent titles as *Figures of Eight: New Poems, Selected Translations* (1987), *Child Eating Snow* (1994), and *Departures: Selected Poems* (2003). He has lived in Austin for many years, where he teaches poetry in the Department of English at the University of Texas. The poem "Home Improvement" derives from the poet's bemused observations of a local worker hired to do some repairs at Wevill's dwelling in the Bee Caves area west of Austin.

Home Improvement

Dogs and cats, he said, they ain't that different.
Both front loaders and both dump from the rear.
Good machines you ask me, cats and dogs.
Course you can train a dog but no damn cat.

As to trainin I got to France with the boys on D-Day.
Survived on Omaha because I knew
just when to cut and run and head for cover.
How deep you want me to cut this driveway now.

Had a dog once could eat cats. Nothin left
of the cat but an old helmet with a hole in it.
That was some cat too. Cats never give up.
Not like some boys you got to train to fight.

I'll get my nephew to saw down them cedar trees.
The worst fightin we did was in the Ardennes
couldn't see nothin. Went at it cats and dogs
and Lord knows what other crap thrown in besides.

Still I'm alive ain't I. Should take about a week
to get that drive graded proper. That old dozer there
ain't exactly a Sherman. That your dog I see
staring out at me from that jasmine bush

or is it a big old cat? I reckon it could take
another week before we get to Berlin.
That is if it don't rain and the ground ain't hard.
We'll talk about the cost when we get there, friend. ★

1994

LAWRENCE WRIGHT

Lawrence Wright was born in Oklahoma City, grew up in Dallas, and was educated at Tulane University and the American University of Cairo. He is the author of, among other works, a memoir, *In the New World: Growing Up With America, 1960–1984* (1987); a novel, *God's Favorite* (2000); and the screenplay for the film *The Siege*. His most recent book, *The Looming Tower: Al-Qaeda and the Road to 9/11*, appeared in 2006. Wright, a staff writer for the *New Yorker*, lives in Austin. In "Heroes" he writes of the statue of Dobie/Bedichek/Webb located near the entrance to the swimming pool at Barton Springs. Public statuary seems to be a minor obsession of many of the Austin literati.

HEROES

EVERY AGE HAS ITS HEROES. WANDER THROUGH THE world of bronze and stone and you will see the striding pharaohs of the First Kingdom and the muscular gods of Olympus, Roman lawgivers and French thinkers, fifty-foot dictators and monsters of the proletariat, cross-legged Buddhas and politicians on horseback, martyred presidents, pioneer women, doughboys, and even creatures out of fairy tales. Statues say as much about an age and a culture that chooses to honor such figures as they do about the people whose lives are enshrined. Moreover, the very act of encoding cultural values in art often signifies a loss: We mourn the passing not only of the great person but also of our own moment in the sun.

Thus the case can be made that the statue of J. Frank Dobie, Walter Prescott Webb, and Roy Bedichek sitting on the rock in Barton Springs that they made famous by their frequent attendance is a valedictory farewell for the very qualities these men embodied. We think of them as the fathers of Texas letters, but despite their talents they were worth more as men than as writers.

Their greatest gift to themselves and their community was their friendship. Wit and humor, biting and intelligent conversation, an open and accessible humanity, a love of teaching and an endless quest for learning—these were attributes that made these men heroes to our particular place and time.

Barton Springs is a part of their legend. It was Bedichek who loved it most. He became such a fixture at the Springs that his perch is still called Bedi's rock. Most afternoons Dobie would join him, and the two would hold court. Webb, who didn't swim, would come by for picnics. This is how they are so fondly remembered in Austin. Barton Springs is more than the setting where they worshiped nature. It is the community bath where they joined their neighbors. It is the matrix that held them together in its pure, and purifying, artesian embrace.

The statue of these three men commemorates not only their friendship but also their love of this place. In honoring them this way, we pay homage to our own love of Barton Springs and its spiritual power to bring us together in mutual shivering appreciation. ★

1993

KEVIN BROWN

Kevin Brown grew up in El Paso and moved to Austin to attend the University of Texas but dropped out in the late 1970s to take a short break from higher education. During this period he wrote a bit, drove a school bus for a living, and helped landscape the governor's mansion. Sixteen years later he finished his degree and is now pursuing an MFA in the Bilingual Creative Writing Program at the University of Texas at El Paso. The first draft of Brown's "Literary Playscape" was written when he was enrolled in my course in Life and Literature of the Southwest.

LITERARY PLAYSCAPE

WITH TYPICAL IRREVERENCE, SOUTH AUSTIN PUBLIC sculpture honors not famous statesmen, Confederate soldiers, or metaphorical figures representing the ideals of Greek philosophers. Tastes below the Colorado River lean more toward blues guitar-slingers and geezers playing in the water. One such statue of the latter, called *Philosopher's Rock*, is located in Zilker Park and features likenesses of the three compadres J. Frank Dobie, Roy Bedichek, and Walter Prescott Webb. This trio of UT-Austin professors, each in his own right a homespun Texas legend, is depicted cavorting on Bedichek's favorite rock in Barton Springs Pool. Dobie and Bedichek are swimsuit-clad and looking a little rowdy, like schoolboys playing hooky. Webb is included symbolically standing to the side, ankle-deep with his pant legs rolled up; apparently he enjoyed the water about as much as a hydrophobic cat. All three gesticulate philosophically, bronzed in the moment as if they had been plucked up and dipped in burnt butterscotch. Philosopher's Rock fits into its surroundings near the entrance to the pool as naturally as the huge pecan trees which shade it.

One time on my way to the park where *Philosopher's Rock* resides, I stopped at a used record store and saw an old vinyl recording for sale called *The Ghost Bull of the Mavericks and Other Tales*. It was Dobie reciting some of his stories. On the cover was a pencil drawing of Dobie in a classically crusty pose, squinting through his wrinkles with his pipe in hand—locked down and loaded. Scattered around the yellow background were the typical images which populate his stories: Indians, broncos, longhorns, wranglers, and a canine animal of some sort. Dobie's record, with its $35 price tag, was hard to miss, displayed as it was directly behind the cash register, next to *The Birds, the Bees and the Monkees* and some other high-priced collectibles.

Considering my destination, running into this relic was prophetic. Actually, only slightly prophetic; less like predicting that Michael Jackson would marry Lisa Marie Presley and more like finding a Capital Metro token on the way to the bus stop. Dobie might well be proud that his record had such an impressive price tag—it couldn't have cost more than $1.99 brand new. The owner of the store told me he sells as many copies of the album as he can get, three or four a year. One pristine copy sold for $45. Dobie won't be awarded a gold record anytime soon, but $45 for a 40-year-old spoken-word record ain't a boot in the butt. I felt proud for the old cuss. Apparently someone besides me knew who he was.

A scant half hour after I left the store, I was at the sculpture with Dobie still on my mind. I discovered that virtually none of the other visitors seemed to know exactly what *Philosopher's Rock* represented. Personally, I couldn't pin down where I learned what I know. The bulk of my knowledge about Dobie and his two buddies is folkloric in its source. Their myth overwhelms reality, even though much of their work is still in print. On my bookshelf I have Dobie's *I'll Tell You a Tale* and Webb's *The Texas Rangers*. The writings of Dobie, the storyteller, I believe provided a lot of material upon which Larry McMurtry based *Lonesome Dove*. The historian Webb, in his account of the famous Rangers, manages quite a feat of overstatement by portraying the Texans as a breed of superhuman while maintaining historic accuracy. I have never read Bedichek's most famous book, *The Adventures of a Texas Naturalist*, but for the longest time

I entertained the impression that it concerns nature about as much as *Zen and the Art of Motorcycle Maintenance* concerns motorcycle repair.

As for the myth, it goes like this: Bedichek loved Barton Springs Pool and went there to pass the time and beat the high humidity of the hot Austin summers. Dobie often joined him on the rock. I've heard that Bedichek would abruptly roll off his perch into the water to cool off, sometimes right in the middle of a sentence. I get an image not dissimilar to a California sea lion falling off a seal-rock. Dobie and Bedi got into rollicking discussions that involved a lot of cussing and tried not to drop their books in the water. No doubt their visits also involved a fair amount of babe-watching. A plaque near the sculpture claims that Webb joined his friends in debate while not actually getting in the water, but according to legend he hated the pool and never went near it. There's an old joke about a fan of the trio who was curious about the original location of the famous boulder. He inquired at the lifeguard station.

Fan: "Where's Bedichek's rock?"

Lifeguard: "What do I look like? A geologist?"

Philosopher's Rock (the sculpture) is set into footings of natural limestone, and I always wondered if it is true to the actual site, which is down the hill a couple of hundred feet away. The three cast figures are approximately life-sized—not much larger than life, anyway. The bronze rock is roughly six feet across, about waist high, and lightly splattered with bird droppings like some kind of pox in the clearing-up stage. Dobie, Bedichek, and Webb are, curiously, always unsoiled.

Activity around the metal men is consistent from day to day. Children endlessly climb about the sculpture while their parents fidget and glance nervously at a sign that reads "Climbing on the statue is forbidden." Indeed, the design was made to be scaled; I have been up there myself. On one of my visits a ten year old told me it was more fun than the monkey bars. Why? "Because it's metal," he answered loudly, giving the hollow boulder a hearty slap. The satisfying reward for his effort was a thunderous echo.

Smaller children can stand upright atop the rock and be eye-level with the literary icons. They sit in Dobie's lap, trade handshakes with Bedichek's gesturing free hand and, like the king of the hill, slouch casually on the book Bedichek holds in his other. They lean over to gaze into the forged eyes, searching for a return glance. I once saw a little girl, probably three or four years old, rub Dobie's head as if she were trying to muss his hair, then slap Webb's bald pate noisily and repeatedly with squeals of delight. That same time, another child on the ground kicked Webb in the shin, waited for a response, glanced around to see if he'd be scolded, then kicked him again. Though they don't know who the three old guys are, the youngsters enjoy them the most. Will they ever know that their odd playscape represents part of Texas literary heritage . . . the roots of Texas intellectualism...the free-flowing exchange of ideas . . . and all that other hifalutin' folderol? I doubt it. If the rowdy kids ever learn the names of these men, they're not going to rush over to Barnes & Noble and buy the Dobie/Bedichek/Webb catalogue, but maybe they'll remember summer days when they played on *Philosopher's Rock*.

The newest generation surely won't be hearing those names from their parents. The older passersby show only a fleeting interest. They think it's a nice statue but don't know much more about the men than what's on the descriptive plaque. The lady who runs the nearby Austin Nature Center gift shop is an exception. She loves *Philosopher's Rock* and is able to enjoy its presence daily. One can see it from the long, curving window at the front of the store. She once informed me that there's a good bit of information about the men and the sculpture on the informational computer terminal that sits glowing amidst the rubber salamanders, gaudy sun-visors, and environmentally approved T-shirts, but I never did interface. Legend is always more fun than fact, and I hate to get bogged down in details. Still, when I talk to people around the sculpture, I send them to the store if they show any interest in learning more about it.

In their time, Dobie, Bedichek and Webb brought a legitimacy to Texas' literary arts, and they deserve the honor of being immortalized. That doesn't alter the fact that they are relics, dead and gone. The work of Dobie and Webb, while vital, projected a latent racism that is mildly disturbing. Maybe "latent racism" isn't even the proper phrase. It's more of a condescension that, despite the lofty ideals and friendly tones, inevitably leaves the white Texans firmly planted on a superior moral plateau when compared to the lowly Mexican peasants. This is a glitch in the myth that must be acknowledged, though it's not likely to happen very soon in a state as heritage-proud as Texas.

As for Bedichek, I plan to read *The Adventures of a Texas Naturalist* someday; I can't say when. Turns out, the book is about nature, and the chapter about chickens is supposed to be a real gut-buster. His rock was long ago washed away in a flood, but local lore placed it at the upper end of Barton Springs, just west of the diving board. Until recent modifications on the pool, that area was roped off to swimmers for the protection of the endangered Barton Springs blind salamander. What Bedichek would think about that, we can only speculate. ★

2000

James Magnuson

James Magnuson was born in Madison, Wisconsin, and received his B.A. from the University of Wisconsin in 1964. For a number of years after college, he lived in New York as a playwright. In 1985 he joined the Department of English at the University of Texas. He is the author of eight novels, including *Ghost Dancing* (1989), *Windfall* (1999), and *The Hounds of Winter* (2005). Magnuson has also written for television, including *Knots Landing, Class of '96*, and *Sweet Justice*. He is currently Director of the Michener Center for Writers. The center is located in J. Frank Dobie's house, at 702 E. Dean Keeton Drive. In the piece reprinted here, Magnuson recalls the death of the benefactor of the Michener center—the man who earned millions from novels such as *Hawaii*, *Space*, and *Texas*.

The Week James Michener Died

The day after the first newspaper articles appeared announcing James Michener's decision to go off kidney dialysis, the students began to call me. Was there anything they could do? Could they bring him a cup of tea? Could they make him a dessert (they all knew that he loved sweets)? One former Michener Fellow, now a successful screenwriter in Los Angeles, phoned, nearly in tears. She was flying into Austin on the weekend. Was there any way she could see him or speak to him, even for a minute? There wasn't. He died on a Thursday night, twelve hours before she arrived.

Back in the early eighties, when James Michener came to work on the novel *Texas*, he was given the red-carpet treatment. He was wined and dined by Governor Clemens, flown to private airstrips in Marfa, taken on jeep tours of the biggest ranches. He was also given a ten by ten office at the University. It was a particularly astute move, because one thing you quickly learned about Michener was that he was a lover of universities. Soon thereafter he bought a

343

house in Austin and every so often a rumor would waft through the halls of the English Department that he was considering endowing a creative writing program.

I had just come to teach at the University myself, so when I was approached by an administrator who wanted to know if Michener could sit in on my graduate fiction workshop, it didn't seem wise to say no.

The students were in awe of him and he took their work very seriously. He was like a stern Dutch uncle—encouraging, but concerned that no one got too big for their britches. "I'm just your T.A.," he told me and he was a remarkable T.A. He attended every class and gave detailed notes on their stories. He passed out lists of the most common grammatical errors—the differences between lie and lay, between there, their, and they're.

If he could be intimidating, it also quickly became apparent what an old-fashioned idealist and an enthusiast he was and that he had a lot more nerve than the students. One afternoon a group of young writers were talking about their plans after graduation. One woman said she was thinking about going to Bosnia to work with the rape victims of the war. Michener jumped right on it.

"Go," he said. "Do it now. Drop out of school if you have to." Her eyes went wide. She stammered something about needing to finish her thesis, but Michener didn't seem to really understand that. There was an opportunity. It needed to be seized. He did not believe in half-measures.

In 1988 it was announced that James Michener was giving two million dollars to create an interdisciplinary MFA at the University of Texas. It would not only train students as screenwriters, poets, playwrights, and fiction writers, it would ask them to work in more than one genre—"to give them another arrow in their quiver," Michener said.

I remember how dubious I was. Having fellowships for our students would utterly revive our program, but wasn't it hard enough to teach students in one writing discipline, how could we possibly do it in two? Wouldn't our students be spreading themselves too thin? It sounded very grand and Michenerean in its ambition, but it also sounded as if we'd just bitten off a lot more than we could chew.

In 1991 I went on leave, taking off for Los Angeles to write television. While I was there I began to receive faxes from Joe Kruppa in the English Department, proposals for how this new MFA would work. Then in the summer of 1992, just before I came back to Austin, the announcement was made that Michener had endowed an additional sixteen million dollars to fully fund the program. I was stunned; it was far and away the largest gift ever made to support creative writing anywhere.

The year after I returned I became director of the Texas Center for Writers, succeeding Rolando Hinojosa-Smith. I soon discovered that James Michener was not a man who was going to give you eighteen million dollars and then forget about it. Each fall he would invite every member of the entering class to his home. He would offer to read their work, give them advice about their work, tell them stories.

When we held our annual barbecue at the Salt Lick he would always be there in his bolo tie, his Hobo Times baseball cap and his tennis shoes with the velcro straps, sitting at the center table, greeting everyone. He was well into his eighties and not in good health. He was not a meddler, but he was a man used to seeing results and there was not much time.

The students had a genuine admiration for him as well as an understandable gratitude. Yet they were often shy around him. There was something in him that didn't invite intimacy, and he could be gruff. "Young lady," he once told an aspiring fiction writer in front of the class, "your teachers have told me that you have talent, but I didn't see it until this story." At another gathering, when he was feeling particularly glum, he said, "All my life I've wanted to support a talented young writer, but I've never found one."

But his darker moods would always be answered by bursts of enthusiasm. I remember when he decided to throw a party for the students at Louie's Mexican Restaurant in Dripping Springs, a spot that had become a favorite of his. He spent two days on the invitations, typing out the menu on his typewriter ("crispy taco, rice and beans, guacamole...") and gluing various pieces of it to a big piece of construction paper.

He was deluged with requests. One person wrote declaring that with a little financial backing from Mr. Michener, they were prepared to write an

American novel in the style of Nikolai Gogol. Someone else was more direct; he wrote saying he knew he couldn't get into the program, but he needed the money; he had included a deposit slip. A third wrote requesting money for a sweet-potato farm that would help save the starving populations of Africa. Every one of these got a polite, considered reply.

It seemed as if he had known everyone, from the Pope to Arthur Miller to every president since Truman. When I asked him once what he thought about Marilyn Monroe, he said, "We all thought we could save her." He had sailed with Walter Cronkite and corresponded with bullfighters.

But for all his fame, if there was one key to his character it was the fact that he had been an orphan. In the last couple years of his life, it seemed to come up a lot. He could be quick to feel rejection and would write letters to his friends saying that he was thinking of moving again. One of his last books was entitled *The World Is My Home*, yet I had the sense that he never felt utterly at home anywhere.

The first full class of ten was admitted to the Texas Center for Writers in the fall of 1993. Within two years there would be forty students supported by 12,000-dollar fellowships. Michener's endowment would make it possible to bring in some of the finest writers in the world to teach and give seminars: J. M. Coetzee, David Hare, W.S. Merwin, and Michael Ondaatje.

Our program was certainly not the only one to benefit from Michener's generosity. Over the last decades of his life he gave an estimated one hundred and sixty-five million dollars to universities and museums, as well as individuals. No writer had ever amassed such a fortune and now it seemed as if he had set about, in his characteristically methodical way, to be sure that every penny would be used.

The question I was never able to bring myself to ask Michener was why. What would motivate a person to give in such an unprecedented way? My guess is that a lot of it had to do with his Quaker background and that he grew up in a time and place where you could utter words like service and duty with a straight face. Constitutionally he was a man incapable of squandering anything. He had lived through the Depression and known hard times. He loved to eat at the Marimont Cafeteria and if there were left-overs he would have the waitress wrap them for his lunch the next day. If he saw an Arby's two-for-one coupon fluttering across the sidewalk he would pin it to the concrete with his rubber-tipped cane and announce, "Skipper, this is where we're going to eat lunch."

Part of it too was that he had been, throughout his life, in love with the grand enterprise. He was a man who enjoyed being feted. Even as he grew more feeble, he had an incredible ability to rally for an interview on *Good Morning America* or an appearance at Barnes and Noble where two thousand people stood patiently for up to four hours to have their books stamped.

In the winter of 1997 the university gave him a gala birthday party. It began with the inevitable and interminable receiving line. Governors, publishers, and college presidents spoke and Stan "The Man" Musial played "It's A Small World" on his harmonica. Michener read from a book of one hundred sonnets he'd published the month before. After it was over I walked out into the lobby of the Alumni Center and there he was, inexplicably sitting alone.

"Happy Birthday," I said.

He looked up at me. He seemed incredibly tired. He gave me the thinnest of smiles and, as always, his chin was up.

By autumn, he was too ill to meet the incoming students. There were so many things to tell him—two years after the first class had graduated, three had published books, one had a full-page rave review in *The New York Times,* another had a film at Sundance, another had her play produced Off-Broadway—but the last couple of times I called his house, he was sleeping. He had taken himself off dialysis and the end was near.

At the funeral one of the students told me, "He was such a chronicler. Wherever he went, he would always come back and tell us everything he learned, everything he found. This is the first time he's gone someplace where he can't tell us what it was like."

Once again this fall, forty young writers will meet at the Salt Lick. A lot of it you can count on being the same: The vegetarians will complain about having to eat all that meat, the professor of poetry will get lost on her way out, someone will break up with their boyfriend in the parking lot. The only difference is that the center table will be empty. ★

1997

BERT ALMON

Bert Almon was born in Port Arthur and grew up in El Paso. He teaches creative writing at the University of Alberta and loves to visit Austin and the Harry Ransom Humanities Research Center to gather material for his books on Texas authors: *William Humphrey, Destroyer of Myths* (1998) and *This Stubborn Self: Texas Autobiographies* (2002). His poetry collections include *Calling Texas* (1990) and *Mind the Gap* (1994). In the poem below Almon casts a sharp eye at the passing scene in and around the Harry Ransom Humanities Research Center, located on the campus of the University of Texas.

AUSTIN ODYSSEY

If I sit in the dark on the patio
of the bedandbreakfast
feasting with three empty chairs
drinking Pecan St. Beer against the heat
and eating a barbecue sandwich
that passes for roasted ox
—if I sit alone in the dark
with Whiskers the cat
as my apathetic only companion
Then I find my mind singing
with dislocated motifs from the *Odyssey*—

Because three times tonight
a muttering emeritus has walked by
a nonagenarian version of Nestor

Because this afternoon I sailed
along Guadalupe Street
at the University campus
past the slackers caught in lotus dreams
wearing their dirty army fatigues
flashing their homemade tattoos
their pierced tongues and nostrils

Because early this morning
I passed a beautiful woman
in a short night gown
who was walking her mastiff
(and when I told my Penelope
on the Internet, she typed back
"Odysseus you'd better steer clear
of that young Circe"
The original Penelope didn't have email)

I have no sign from Athena
though I spent all day
in the Humanities Research Center
I think she has abandoned the emeritus
who just walked by again
escorted by his faithful wife

On the way back tonight I passed
frat houses where partygoers caroused
like drunken suitors
There's a movie called *Sirens*
showing in the Union Theatre
It's full of breasts
jiggling in the Australian Outback

but I don't think it's a musical
If I feel like a lost mariner
in the middle of this parched city
it's because I can imagine
the presence of the limestone layer
under the thin topsoil
—the gardener's curse
laid down 350 million years ago
when the sea covered Texas—
It's because I feel I've been away
almost that long

An ash tree as high as the roof
brushes our bedroom window at home
when I finish my beer and sandwich
I can go inside and place a call to that room
a thought that turns the sultry night intimate
so that I take a deep breath on this patio
suddenly tasting the winedark air ★

2000

ROBERT DRAPER

Born in Houston, Robert Draper graduated from the University of Texas in 1979. In the late 1980s he became a staff writer for *Texas Monthly*. He is the author of three books: *Rolling Stone Magazine: The Uncensored History* (1990), the novel *Hadrian's Walls* (1999), and *Four Trials* (2004). He currently lives in Washington, DC, and writes for *GQ Magazine*. In "Adios to Austin" Draper charts the changes that he saw in modern Austin over about a ten-year period. Nobody has made the case better than Draper does here.

ADIOS TO AUSTIN

I FELL INTO THE URINE BUSINESS IN 1987 THE WAY YOU landed any job in Austin back then. My prospective employer and I knew the same writers and musicians, and one of them had told Nightbyrd I was something of a weird guy. When Nightbyrd, a former Abbie Hoffman sidekick and underground-newspaper publisher, shared this tidbit during the job interview, over Dos Equis and chips at a downtown bar, I remember feeling stung, because even in 1987 pretty much everyone in Austin was weird, so when someone actually called you weird, it in fact meant you were not content to be weird. It meant you were ambitious. Strictly speaking, I was. But I was also like everyone else in town, long graduated and destined, at least in the short run, for underemployment. And so after Nightbyrd picked up the check, I followed him across the street to Byrd Labs, to begin my six-month career of packing vials full of synthetic drug-free urine to sell desperate military men and bureaucrats preparing to submit to drug tests. Nightbyrd offered me $6 an hour—which, if your girlfriend had a job, as mine did, and you were paid in cash, as Nightbyrd offered to do, amounted to a plum Austin gig.

Byrd Labs operated out of a warehouse on the popular cruising axis of East 6th Street. In times of high urine demand, I performed my gnome like labors into the evening while the windows rattled from the melee of human heat-seeking missiles soaring in from quiet little towns all over central Texas. Occasionally, I'd wipe the grubby yellow powder off my fingers and approach the windowsill of the darkened lot, where I'd linger for several minutes like Quasimodo in the belfry, dumbly surveying the mischief below. In those days, the spectacle didn't yet make me feel ancient—though I did feel weird, being ambitious by Austin standards. Even Nightbyrd, the urine king, faced ridicule for his strivings, despite his lefty portfolio, his nocturnality, and the mentholated ease with which he lied about his age. New tartlets materialized in the laboratory foyer without warning, unfailingly dressed for midday sex, at which point my boss would clock out, though never without first reminding me, in a somewhat anxious voice, "Deposit all the checks before the bank closes."

Just before noon one morning, Nightbyrd sauntered into work and promptly instructed me to sweep his floor. When I refused, his predatory eyes narrowed. "What's the matter?" he sneered. "Are you too proud?" It was a cruel question to put to his urine lackey. But he was correct. I had no intention of submitting to something so common, especially since my citizenship in this strange, somnolent backcountry of charming malingerers and inspired if fainthearted balladeers was tenuous enough already. The term *loser* had not yet entered the popular lexicon; in Austin, if nowhere else, being a character was vocation enough. Preoccupied as I was with reconciling eccentricity with ambition, I deemed myself better off leaving the floor unswept. A couple of months after I quit Byrd Labs, I received a sizable book advance. After the book was published, *Texas Monthly* hired me as a staff writer. In the summer of 1997, fully ten years after Nightbyrd had taken me in, I began to work for *GQ*.

No one asked me to relocate from Austin, so I didn't. In the meantime, Nightbyrd went to Havana to start an English-language newspaper. I don't know what kind of reception he got. But one fall evening in '97, a prominent local restaurateur clinked his wineglass against mine and unctuously declared, "Austin needs people like you."

How sweet, I thought at the time. The illogic, the portent, went right past me. At last. Austin needs people like me. Well, it got 'em. *Hordes* of them. So this one's out the door.

I want to tell you about a place that never was. The blissed-out cartographers would mark it in the very midsection of Texas, on a dais of limestone among undulating emerald hills, bisected by the Colorado River. The state endowed it with its capital and a sprawling public university, which together conferred upon the town a sensibility of frisky enlightenment. As such, it became a haven for musicians, writers, seasonal Marxists, free sex, and dirt-cheap Tex-Mex. So idyllic was the city that its few violent criminals were assigned monikers—the Hyde Park Rapist, the Tower Murderer, the Choker Rapist—and thus banished to mythology. So vigilant were its stewards that when some spiteful bugger saw fit to poison a more-than-500-year oak tree, they hauled him into the brig and flayed him in the local press as if he'd been caught boiling babies on the lawn of the governor's mansion. So learned were its inhabitants that they were commonly (and unprovably) said to buy more books per capita than any other citizenry in America. This was Athens, Atlantis, Utopia. This was Austin, one big unswept patio of groovy daydreamers.

It was groovy, that is, if you didn't care much for spring or autumn, enjoyed a good drought and were impervious to cedar fever and 95 percent humidity. In truth, if you were one of the city's dark-skinned inhabitants east of Interstate 35, you saw quite a bit of crime, though that kind of riffraff got little play in the *Austin American-Statesman*, whose editors never bought into the above-cited boast of Austin's brainy readership. Yes, there were hills, off in the distance, where the rich kept their boats and their deer rifles. We had our bards, none so hallowed as Billy Lee Brammer, an enormously gifted fuckup who published all of one book and then slowly drugged himself into an early grave. Even as the city boosters yodeled on about "the Live Music Capital of the World!" it was axiomatic among habitués of the music scene that if you ever nurtured dreams of reaching a national audience, your best bet was to get the hell out of Austin. Otherwise you'd stay small—because in Austin, that was the whole point. Dulcet and drowsily antic though it could be, and beyond the five months every two years when legislators gathered there to affirm their contempt for Big Gub'ment, Austin possessed a singular raison d'etre: to be unlike Dallas and Houston. It was the place that never was, nor ever could be, Dystopia.

Until recently, Austin's chief claim to fame was its relative docility. Visitors to the twin demon cities would crumple with gratitude to discover that from that searing infinity of empty boasts, big hair and proud ignorance composing the Great Nation-State of Texas, there shimmered a mirage of dope-smoking cowboys and women with little makeup. Even though this was Texas, one could go months, even years, in Austin without witnessing an ass stomping or hearing racial insults. Casual druggies didn't get hard time in Austin. The churchgoers didn't litter your lawn. (Hell, Madalyn Murray O'Hair lived there.) Janis Joplin was only the most famous among the thousands of culturally dispossessed Texas youths who fled their native hellholes for the liberal oasis that was Austin. The result was positively, and negatively, Woodstockian. Like Joni Mitchell's rhapsodies about Max Yasgur's "garden," Brammer's dewy description of "a pleasant city, clean and quiet, with wide rambling walks and elaborate public gardens and elegant old homes faintly ruined in the shadow of arching poplars" would prompt guffaws from even the local chamber of commerce. Better to regard Austin as a blank slate for the tribes who gathered there—and that was more than enough, until rent was due.

The inability to find a decent-paying job anywhere in Austin became evidence of virtue. In a state where the only thing more oppressive than the month of August was its braying ostentation, Austin developed a knack for elevating unpretentiousness to an art form. The oft tossed-off refrain "Hey, it's Austin" means you could eat at the city's fanciest restaurant without running a comb through your hair or changing out of your well-pocked cut-offs. It meant it was OK to crash parties and make off with as many links of barbecued sausage as you could jam into your denim jacket. It meant you didn't have to own a necktie—and this became its ideology. Austin the Un-City, never-never land, beloved for what it was not. Let them eat nachos. Everyone was broke and everything was beautiful.

The imminent defilement of our scruffy Eden—which would mean we'd all have to move back to the megalopolis and learn how to shave regularly— insinuated itself into everyday chatter the way weather forecasts do in rural communities. Each of us could calculate to the day when Austin went to hell. It was when some ethos-drenched five-year-old local institution (the Nothing Strikes Back ice cream parlor, the Mad Dog & Beans hamburger stand, the punk club Raul's, the slacker coffee joint Quackenbush's on Guadalupe) fell prey to the evil spirit of capitalism and expired amid bitter eulogies. It was when Don Johnson began flying to town to strafe the local titty bars. It was either the day a former hippie flower salesman named Max Nofziger was elected to the city council or the day Nofziger left public service to do TV commercials for a car dealership. More likely, it was when your carpetbagging ass moved there, one month after mine did.

Fortunately our nymph knew how to pick herself up from the barroom floor. The first bewailings of innocence lost came in 1966, when Charles Whitman climbed the University of Texas tower and introduced America to the peculiar phenomenon of mass murder. Then Wilie Nelson drove in from Abbott by way of Nashville and all was made right. Epitaphs were penned when the Armadillo World Headquarters shut down in the early '80s and an IBM office took its place. But a few years later, local girl Ann Richards won the Texas governorship and ratified Austin liberalism as the law of the land. In 1991 four teenage girls were raped and murdered in a local yogurt shop, horrifying proof that Austin had at last been led to the urban slaughterhouse. The years that followed saw the rescue of the storied swimming hole Barton Springs from contamination and the emergence of nationally recognized music and film festivals. Now the tourists flew in from Helsinki and Berlin, and their ill-disguised wonderment renewed our own. Jaded little bastards that we were, we remained, at bottom, Texans—*Super-Americans*, as John Bainbridge termed us in his obscure 1961 classic: simultaneously self-enthralled and self-conscious, weavers of our own mythology, which we swallowed as absolute gospel, as long as outsiders did the same. Austin needed only believers. And so there we sat together, on the shadeless patio, licking our sundry wounds, peeling the labels off the beer bottles with our thumbnails, pronouncing doom to and from the urinal and then splitting the tab—which was never high, unless some asshole ordered the imported swill.

That asshole was me. Even in the best of times, my relationship to Austin approximated a lovers' quarrel: She was ever the languid, vintage-attired pixie, hoarse from laughter and reefer smoke, and I the uptight aspirant. In the early '80s, I managed a profoundly untalented new-wave band, the Shades, and the bombast with which I promoted them did not play well among the hipster elite. My early scramblings as a freelance journalist won me further scorn. After winning my first feature assignment from *Esquire,* I bought a new blazer and made the mistake of wearing it to the office of the *Austin Chronicle,* the arts-and-entertainment weekly and nexus of reverse snobbery, where any regalia tonier than a New Order T-shirt meant you were either a Bible sales-man or a narc. "So," said Sylvia, the sultry young woman at the front desk, as her olive eyes took in my ensemble, "is this what an *Esquire* writer's supposed to look like?" The editors killed the piece, and I completed the humiliation by becoming a scribe for the prestigious journal *Meetings & Conventions,* which paid decently but late, as the New York accountant insisted upon sending my checks to Ostin, Texas—no doubt my kind of place, if I could only find it on the map.

A very unexpected thing happened to Austin a few years back. It became a place where one could earn a fortune. By 1997 you began to see them all over town: the fabled Dellionaires, loping from golf course to wine shop to sailboat in the middle of everyone else's workday, garbed in pastels, like plump Easter eggs. Many of them were humble geeks who'd caught the high-tech wave just right. We'd known them back when, and though it was conceiv-able that the leader, the young schemer Michael Dell, was the Antichrist, he made a fine laptop and kept his sprawl far from Barton Springs, who could complain? The long-repudiated notion of getting rich in Austin was an idea that now seemed divinely compatible with the Church of the Holy Slacker. Yesterday's philosophy grad student became today's Webmaster. All writers great and small began to craft screenplays. The preeminent local ad agency, GSD&M, flush with success from its Clinton connections, relocated to a cavernous office adorned with the strikingly unironic sublogo IDEA CITY. That idea was, of course: Let's act like Republicans!

So accustomed were Austinites to forecasting the apocalypse that the depths of the transformation eluded them at first. The handsomely weathered face of Ann Richards was no longer in evidence: She'd moved to Washington to become, among other things, a tobacco lobbyist. Now the grande dame of Austin was Barbie look-alike Susan Dell. The city's freeway traffic jams were at first blamed on NAFTA, then on bad drivers transplanted from Silicon Valley. The guru behind the inane bumper sticker WHAT'S THE HURRY YOU'RE ALREADY IN AUSTIN began marketing a somewhat more plaintive battle cry: KEEP AUSTIN WEIRD. But why the fretting? Dogs with bandannas still snagged Frisbees in Zilker Park. The great blues club Antone's still hosted timeless riffs even as its overlord, Clifford Antone, was cooling his heels in the federal prison near Bastrop on a dope-smuggling charge. Las Manitas still served up quintessential *huevos a la mexicana*, if you could find a parking place. And when, very late on the evening of November 7, 2000, the main boulevard of Texas's most liberal city teemed with revelers cheering the apparent election of a conservative Republican to the presidency, you could still say, employing the same casual condescension with which we dismissed the touristic banalities of East 6th Street, "Let 'em have the place."

So let me tell you how the place that never was Dystopia is today. The city of Austin, a manageable burg of 300,000 when I arrived in 1976, now contains 1,225,000 inhabitants in its metropolitan area. Its newest arrivals are primarily from the West Coast, seekers of a more perfect geekdom. Austin, pledged the corporate handouts, was a Quality of Life city. Affordable housing in Round Rock, just minutes from work! No state income tax! No racial tension that we know of! An "entertainment district" for you night crawlers! Live Music Capital of the World! And so on. Today Austin's Old Guard mutter among themselves in the margins of coffee shops and Tex-Mex dives. The rest of the city has been subsumed into the generic colossus of Greater Silicon Valley, a wasteland so smug and culturally vapid that Dallas circa 1963 seems flamboyant by comparison.

Here is what the new economy and its cocky little offspring have done for Austin. According to a recent study, it ranks among the top seven American cities in traffic delays—right there with Dallas and Houston. The region's chief private-sector employer, Dell, laid off approximately 5,000 workers in the first five months of 2001. Owing to its past denunciation of high commerce and its more recent high-tech sputterings, downtown Austin is a butt-ugly morass of Stalinist bureaus and half-finished concrete shells. There may be an unsightlier cityscape among the nation's prosperous burgs, but I have yet to be pleasured by it. Dozens of new restaurants chased the yuppie dollar into Austin in the past three years—and nearly all of them, if there is any culinary justice, will be chased out before the next boomlet. It is still possible to two-step at the Broken Spoke and strike a sullen pose at the Continental Club, possible as well to be turned away from velvet-rope discos and saunter into shadowy swingers clubs; possible, above all, to live within the bland sinews of the sprawl and never once visit the center of town. Of course, weird-ness endures, here and there, as it always has in Houston, Dallas, Atlanta, Charlotte, San Jose, Kansas City, and Phoenix. Austin is better than these cities in many ways, worse in many others. But those who maintain there's nothing in the world like Austin either don't live there today, or do and don't go out much.

As recently as a year ago, the disclosure that I was considering a move after twenty-five years was met with looks of astonishment and pity. Leaving Austin now? When it had everything figured out, at long last? When everyone had begun to dress smartly but still screwed with hippie abandon? When you could repair to the parking lot of the Back Yard while Lyle Lovett crooned inside and smoke a joint crouched between two SUVs, yours and your boss's? When the student flophouse you bought a few years ago was now worth a half mil and counting? When you could claim Sandra Bullock as your neighbor, could throw back shots of Don Julio with Jenna Bush and, if you knew one of Laura Bush's longtime pals, would stand a decent chance of having a White House sleepover, which would in no way disqualify you from denouncing her husband a few days later over wine and reefers? Had you lost your mind—or worse, your Dell stock options? A friend of mine, a realtor who'd swum many an ocean of margaritas and now found herself gyrating atop the high-tech boom, proclaimed without irony, "If Austin's so bad, why is everybody moving here?" Meanwhile, Houston and Dallas sat back and watched with knowing smiles.

Any lamentation from this corner would ring false. I spent more than half my tenure in Austin scheming to move to a place where personal initiative was not held in similar esteem as venereal warts. Often what made me reconsider was my strange but abiding love for Texas, and if I was going to stay in Texas, where else but Austin? At other junctures, love, work, or inertia held me back. Meanwhile, grudges mellow with the years. There came a point when I looked around and realized I'd become a town fixture, a surprisingly sweet accomplishment. Austin was, at bottom, a civilized place. When it did not let fear of achievement darken its heart, it could be the most inviting refuge imaginable. Alas, Austin invited me in, when it had every reason to fear hustlers like me. I knew it then, when I berated the town for its proud puniness, and above all, I know it now, when the city's chortling motto, "Onward through the fog," has long been discarded in favor of that most compelling of exhortations, "Smart growth."

This past Memorial Day, my wife and I left Austin for good, and absolutely no one asked how we could do such a thing. The downturn will cease in time, but Peter Pan's leotards lie puddled in the dust. Among longtime dwellers at Billy Lee Brammer's gay place, the ever fashionable wry pessimism has been replaced by a somberness born out of genuine loss. Well, we've all aged. Still, I must confess this singular regret: I wish to hell I had swept Nightbyrd's floor when he'd asked me to. I wish I'd shown a little character instead of trying to be one. You know what I mean? There was real work to be done in the city, and when the place that was really Austin called my name, I was somewhere out on the patio, statuesque as a cactus, saying something really goddamned clever that I can't remember anymore. ★

2001

Lyman Grant

Lyman Grant moved to Austin in 1971 and graduated from the University of Texas in 1975. He has taught at Austin Community College since 1978 and currently serves as Dean of the Arts and Humanities Division. He has published one volume of poems, *Text and Commentary,* two textbooks, and two works concerning regional literature. "Co-Op," making its first appearance in print, is set at one of the co-op grocery stores in the city, probably the Wheatsville Co-Op on Guadalupe north of the campus of the University of Texas. The poem reflects, among other things, the tendency among long-time Austin dwellers to recall the constant ebb and flow of favored venues.

Co-Op

Inger checks me out, soy milk, chocolate Tofutti bars,
El Gallindo corn chips, green chili salsa, Shiner Bock,
organic carrots for juicing, beets, Good Flow orange juice.
Where you been? Her spiked hair is pink tonight. She turns
so she can scan the items with the universal price codes,
and I can see the leopard's paw rising over her left shoulder
under her wife beater's t-shirt, the purple bra showing through.
I wonder how close the golden claws come to her nipple.
No where much. *Hey Jacob.* Jacob, in his cowboy hat and boots,
red shorts, and greenish-yellow tie-dye, is pulling on my arm
and swinging into the counter. *We've missed you at park day.*
For some reason, Jacob turns shy and pulls my arm even harder
behind me and tries to hide. We catch each other up on the families.
I tell her Colleen's on her way home with the baby, that they
had been in town and we met for dinner at El Patio.
Inger's girls are good, staying with their dad for a few days.

I tell her our kids played together last month at Kerrville
Folk Festival. Jacob warms up and says that Jade read
Where the Wild Things Are to him at the kid's tent and they sang
Woody Guthrie's children's songs that we know from the Smithsonian
collection. I introduce her to Will, who's started bagging.
She says *I've seen you in here before.* He tells her he knows Anson,
back in the deli section. She says *that's right. That's where I
usually work. I'm just up here cause we're short tonight.*
Will's been in town a few weeks on break from college.
So you know Anson? Will nods and sets the bag of corn chips
inside the paper bag with the beer. I tell Will that Inger
is the person who burned the Christmas CD with our new
favorite Xmas song that goes "Mamacita, donde esta Santa Claus."
He nods and says cool tune, and she whoops *Little Augie Rios!*
I'm already finding new stuff for next year's disk.
I think I see Will's eyes reach out toward the Leopard's paw.
No one's in line behind me, so I mention we read the article
in the *Statesman* with her in it about alternatives in home schooling.
Someone has to say that it's not just radical conservative Christians
who distrust the schools with our children. You did a good job.
Thanks. She winks *They cut some of my best lines though.*
Too much for them I think. I bet you're right about that.
She tells me we need to come back to home school park day
at Little Stacy Park. *All the construction is finished, thank god.*
Where's Colleen been? We miss her. It's just hard for her
to get into town. I remind her that we had to move out of town,
that the taxes were getting too high. We're in the country now.
Well you guys still should come some time. You could meet Jen.
She's my new girlfriend. She smiles and I smile. Will smiles.
I'd like that. Looks like it's agreeing with you. I bet she's younger.
No comment. Then she asks me for my member number and I
tell her, and she says *That's an old one. How long you been a member?*
I don't know, twenty, twenty-five years. *Shit, I was just a kid,* then

she looks at my work clothes, khakis, button down, Rockports.
That's a long time. *Will, how old is your dad?* Pretty old, I think.
And I think about the old Good Food Store down the block,
where my freshman year I would buy heavy loafs of whole wheat bread,
local honey, and raw milk. The pizza place down another block,
where I first heard Alvin Crow play fiddle, "Give me a bottle of Ny-Quil
for the restful sleep my body needs," that became Antone's
and now is a laundry. Emmajoe's where Townes was too drunk
to sing and got booed off the stage and where Will's mom
and I listened to Mose Allison. "Your mind is on vacation."
Emmajoe's closed and now maybe is Supercuts. I don't remember.
The old Quaker Meeting House was just a few blocks to the west.
There one morning Otto Hoffman, the organ builder, remarked
on the beauty of "The Ode to Joy" that KMFA was playing
as he drove to church and he was noticing the blossoming
pear trees and the bright March sun and he just had to tell us.
Another morning, Bill Owens sat there quietly, while two blocks
away in my little house on King Street after being up all night
I completed some work editing *The Letters of Roy Bedichek*.
When he returned, he read what I had done, and shook my hand.
All that information accessed faster than all those digital cables
laid throughout the city in past five years. Inger asks
Will that be all? Yeah, for now. I swipe my debit card
and punch in the code. It was nice seeing you, Inger.
Is the tattoo new? *Naw, I've had it a long time. Park day.*
Don't be such a stranger, she says. Jacob holds my hand
as we cross the parking lot. Will puts the groceries in the cooler
for the drive home, grabs a Tofutti bar for each of us.
As we pull on to Guadalupe, I ask Will, Who's this Anson guy?
O, he's a jerk. He owes me money and he stole my girlfriend.
Jacob giggles. I laugh and swerve and almost drop my ice cream.
Then I take a look at Will in the rear view and I see he's laughing, too. ★
2005

KURT HEINZELMAN

Kurt Heinzelman, born in Wisconsin, received his Ph.D. from the University of Massachusetts. In the late 1970s he moved to Austin to teach at the University of Texas. *The Economics of the Imagination* (1980), a critical study of British Romanticism, appeared in 1980. In 2003 he edited *Make It New: The Rise of Modernism.* He has also published two volumes of poetry, *The Halfway Tree* (2000), and *Black Butterflies* (2004). In this poem Heinzelman illumines the present as juxtaposed with the past—a recurring pattern in writing about the city from earliest times to now.

WAY OUT WEST AT 51ST AND BERKMAN

Bicycling west toward the freeway
less than a mile from your house
you come upon some letters weathering
in polished granite facing the ghost
of an airport from the corner of a park
and all within sight of the Capitol
where a settler stopping here for water
(a dry creek-bed still depresses the bull-
dozed landscape away from the monument)
was "stabbed & scalped by the Indians"
(it was 1832) while "surveying lands
for the colonists." He lived a dozen
years more, dying in Bastrop, "a true
patriot." That's what the sign says, etched
in stone, as truth is, and just as few stop to
read it as any poem. You don't. You turn
here—what?—maybe three times a day, but

who's ever on foot (or looking even now)?
As wind strums the high-tension feeds
to the PROMISELAND of the nearby World
of Pentecost, a faded pennon crying 6 PAX
* BLOCK ICE circles its U-Totem: flycatchers,
scissor-tailed ones (remember, you are still
looking up), bulk up here before moving on. ★

2000

STEVEN MOORE

Steven Moore was born in Bloomington, Illinois, and graduated from the University of Chicago in 1993. In 1994 he moved to Austin and founded Austin's Physical Plant Theater. In 2005 he received an MFA in playwriting from the Michener Center for Writers at the University of Texas. His play about Dobie, Bedichek, and Webb, *Nightswim*, was produced in Austin in 2004. In this essay from the *Austin Chronicle*, the local alternative newspaper, Moore seeks to recapture the lost times and places of the three figures whose lives are so woven into the texture of the city's culture and memory.

SALON OF THE WEST

ON ANY GIVEN EVENING IN THE 1940S OR 1950S, AN OLD MAN named J. Frank Dobie might walk over to the house of another old man named Roy Bedichek for a conversation and a little beer. To get there, he turns left from his front door at 702 Park Place (now East Dean Keeton), heads two long blocks east, and crests the hill at Red River. He can see the last of the after-work traffic sliding up East Avenue (already an artery, soon to be I-35). The sun falls behind him, and the evening light pulsing on the chrome is the signal of an unfamiliar code. He turns right and bears south for three blocks to 23rd Street, then takes a left and heads east two blocks to Oldham Road. Bedichek's house sits on the southeast corner of 23rd and Oldham; Dobie jaywalks the intersection, climbs the porch steps, and knocks. If it takes him more than eight minutes door-to-door, the night has been hot enough to move through slowly or he found a cat or a friend along the way.

I made the same walk last night, but Oldham Road was gone, and 23rd was gone, and Bedichek's house was the parking lot of the LBJ Library. The night was hot, but encountering no friends and no cats, I made it in seven-and-a-half minutes—including the pretend knocking on the pretend front door.

And then I was done—and alone in a wide space. With my remaining seconds, I imagined the moment was part of a movie: The camera cranes up to show the parking lot, then the neighborhood and the new city, like a map, but with everything that's gone now shaded in with blue.

Dobie and Bedichek knew each other for forty years. Together with Walter Prescott Webb, they comprised an intellectual triumvirate at the center of what their contemporaries sometimes called the Salon of the West. Webb, a historian, wrote the epic tale of the Great Plains. Dobie, a prolific folklorist and professional iconoclast, charmed and cussed and typed his way to the center of Texas popular writing—such as it was at the time. Bedichek, the great and gentle naturalist, spent a life watching birds, telling stories, writing letters, and holding together a community of thoughtful men by the power of his personality.

Those are the standard designations for these once-famous Austinites—one historian, one folklorist, one naturalist—but it is truer to say that each of them had strains of historian, folklorist, iconoclast, naturalist, storyteller, and conversationalist, not to mention philosopher, crusader, and cowboy. Despite differences in personality and variations in discipline, their similar childhoods spun all three into the same kind of man. They were each raised in tiny Texas towns around the turn of the century, after the Indians had all been run off or killed. Each lived among hardscrabble farms, one-room schoolhouses, and contentious battles over the proliferation of barbed wire, an invention that all three loathed. They grew up outside, working hard and learning about trees and water, about snakes and horses, and about the people who'd lived on the land before them—settlers, Indians, Spaniards, other Indians. And still young, they left their small towns for jobs as teachers and journalists, settling finally in the world of Austin academia at UT: Dobie and Webb as teachers, Bedichek as head of the University Interscholastic League, and all three as curious, enthusiastic, well-read, hard-working intellectuals.

And so they were friends. Like the best of friends, they became better at being themselves by mutual influence and encouragement and saved one another from boredom and despair. They were the acknowledged giants of Austin at a time when Austin was not so different from the rest of Texas: boring and desperate. Liberal-minded men with ability and learning rarely rolled suddenly out of the country—a country notorious for its distrust of brainpower. Still, they all three loved that country and longed for it, for that frontier, which was disappearing even as they grew into men. (If the imagined map were large enough and old enough, of course all of Texas would be shaded blue.)

Despite their connection to that land, they could never belong there, and so they took refuge in Austin and in one another.

Under their influence, Austin made a major shift from typical Texas town into an oasis of open-mindedness. To the wider world they were writers acknowledged for their stories and their ideas, but here in Austin they were far more than that. They were real men. Here, they represented a spirit of deep and well-aged friendship and friendliness. They spent long, lazy days in conversation around the swimming hole, with one another or anyone else who might approach them. They offered and asked for camaraderie and got it and gave it to each other and everyone around them. They did their best to take care of the world.

But every friendship is particular, and the better it is, the more particular it gets. Just so, these three each offered something peculiar to one another. Dobie acknowledges his debt to Bedichek in the dedication to his book *I'll Tell You a Tale:*

> To the memory of my cherished friend Roy Bedichek, a whole man of just proportions, a rare liver, in solitude as well as with genial companions; ample natured and rich in the stores of his ample mind; always understanding, whether agreeing or not; always enlarging both his own views and those of others. In talk he called forth all my powers, made me laugh, live more abundantly, love life with more reason.

Their conversations were more than friendly banter. They were often a crucible to refine and distill ideas that Dobie funneled into his weekly newspaper column. By contrast with his books, which are nostalgic and apolitical, his newspaper column eloquently condemns fascism, blacklisting, censorship, when those things desperately needed condemning. The arguments Dobie made bear Bedichek's stamp of rigor, humor, and sympathy.

What Bedichek offered Webb was different. Webb was well on his way as a thinker and writer before meeting Bedichek, and so the influence seems to be more purely Bedichek's force of heart than his force of mind. Webb had a reputation as a quiet man, almost morose, even among most of his friends, but Bedichek could always open him up with his playfulness and curiosity. Webb liked best to have Bedichek to himself, camping out in the wilderness, exchanging thoughts and feelings that Webb had no other way to express. Bedichek endorsed and encouraged and understood Webb as no one else seemed able to do. It is a great testament to Bedichek that he had so many friends and took such particular care of them individually. And yet he had a reputation of being always the same, not bending himself to suit the people he encountered, but simply welcoming them freely into his roomy good humor and compassion.

From Dobie and Webb, Bedichek received—besides their loyalty and admiration—constant encouragement to record in some permanent form his innumerable stories and reflections about nature, which he finally did. He wrote his first book, *Adventures With a Texas Naturalist,* after Webb and Dobie all but locked him in a room to do it, taking a year for the task and finishing at the age of sixty-eight. He died suddenly twelve years later, having written three more books, though *Adventures* stands out as the best of the lot. Sixty-eight might seem like a late start, but Bedichek had actually been writing for years—not books, but letters. He corresponded with friends and family almost maniacally for all of his adult life. His days began early at four A.M. with a few pages of Plato, followed by hours of reading and writing his letters. Though Bedichek's books are full of a hearty earnestness and reams of fascinating facts, the writing is ornate and rambling; in contrast, his letters are simple and clear, and at times they contain arresting confessions of doubt and of outrage, but most often they tell of his satisfactions and little surprises of discovery.

The letters tell us that Bedichek liked tomatoes (particularly his own), fresh milk, sleeping in sheets that sat in the sun all day on a lavender shrub, urinating and defecating out of doors, and cooking vegetables in the ash of a fire. He liked great empty spaces—as documented in a wonderful PBS special, "Roy Bedichek's Vanishing Frontier," which aired in April on KLRU—and he liked to do things that took all day. The letters paint a picture of a whole and particular man. (If you're curious to read them, Bedichek's letters have been collected into two volumes—*Letters of Roy Bedichek*, edited by William Owens and Lyman Grant, which deliberately omits any family letters, and *The Roy Bedichek Family Letters*, edited by his daughter-in-law Jane Gracy Bedichek).

You could suppose that living in the same town and seeing them almost daily would mean that Bedichek didn't write letters to Dobie or Webb—or they to him. But in fact, Bedichek, Dobie, and Webb traded scads of letters. Usually they exchanged anecdotes, elaborated a point from some earlier conversation, or just told the day's news, but often they wrote letters from deep inside the mind, set to one side of daily life, as if to conduct a second friendship parallel to the first, but on secret terms. The letters carve out a wide space for poetic speculation about nature, injustice, old age, and death. Although a few fascinating audiotapes remain of the three in conversation, and although their other friends told many tales of them in writing, the letters stand as the best record of the men and their friendships.

They weren't perfect by any means. Readers of Webb's book *The Texas Rangers* often accuse him of playing apologist for racism and butchery—and they're right. Dobie chased the spotlight, and in the end he became a cowboy cartoon of himself. And even Bedichek had strains of self-satisfaction and preachiness. In spite of these faults, their energy, intelligence, and integrity drew others into this so-called Salon of the West—fellow professors, storytellers, journalists, and other New Dealers and civil libertarians like themselves.

Among the youngsters in their clan were John Henry Faulk and Ronnie Dugger. Faulk was Dobie's protégé, for whom Austin's downtown library branch is named. A writer and humorist famous for his nationally syndicated *John Henry Faulk Show*, on the radio from 1951 to 1957, Faulk's greater notoriety comes from his tenacious battle against the blacklisting of the fifties. He tells the story of his ultimately victorious five-year court battle in *Fear on Trial*, dedicated "[t]o the three persons, Texans all, who influenced me the most in respecting the liberated mind and the joys and responsibilities of citizenship: My mother and father and J. Frank Dobie."

The other youngster, Ronnie Dugger, founded *The Texas Observer* in 1954 when he was twenty-four years old, and the magazine has served as an engine for intelligent and progressive analysis ever since. Throughout the *Observer's* first ten years, articles by and about Dobie, Bedichek, and Webb appeared frequently, and at last Dugger collected the articles into a book called *Three Men in Texas,* an extended flattery by friends and admirers—including the men themselves admiring one another.

The admiration has everything to do with the men and almost nothing to do with their writing. In truth, Dobie, Bedichek, and Webb earned their local fame more by who they were than by what they wrote. Dobie's books, like Bedichek's, are less compelling than one might hope, often consisting of related anecdotes loosely tied together. In his 1968 essay "Southwestern Literature?," Larry McMurtry convincingly demotes Dobie from literary giant to respectable scribe. Dobie's audience, he predicts, "will probably not outlive him much more than a generation." When McMurtry published the essay—only four years after Dobie's death—disciples leapt to Dobie's defense, but now, forty years later, the disciples are mostly dead as well, and Dobie's books are fading from the shelves.

Bedichek fares better. McMurtry credits him as a "stylist" and says he "used language better than either of them." I disagree. Of the three, I think Webb's writing is the keenest and most readable. Even with subchapter titles like "Conservation of Soil Moisture" or "The Evolution of the Range and Ranch Cattle Industry, 1866 to 1928," his writing is confident, enticing, and propulsive.

It helped me get through the books to imagine Bedichek, Dobie, and Webb in person together, reading the books aloud to one another. I wanted to imagine their voices. They were famous above all for their conversations, which lit up back yards and campgrounds, car rides and restaurants—in particular the Night Hawk at 20th and Guadalupe, now shaded in with blue on the imagined map (a Schlotzsky's). They talked about the things that were important to them: birds, grass, books, the weather, freedom of thought, and citizenship. In 1994, a group of Austin philanthropists commissioned a statue to celebrate those conversations, specifically those that took place on one particular rock at the Barton Springs Pool. In the statue, which sits outside the main entrance of the pool, Bedichek, Dobie, and Webb all in bronze gather around a bronze version

of their old rock. The sculptor, Glenna Goodacre, called the statue *Philosophers'*
Rock, though the men themselves and the pool regulars in those days referred
to that particular rock as Conversation Rock, or more commonly, Bedi's Rock.
Bedichek's friend, Wilson Hudson, even wrote a little poem about it:

Bedichek sat on Bedichek's Rock,
The water was cold but Bedi was hot.

For forty years, from July to October, Bedichek drove to the pool every
afternoon at 3:30 to sit for two hours with his friends on that rock. It was
part of a limestone outcropping just west of the diving board and just above
Parthenia, the largest of the pool's springs. A small sycamore cast shade along
the back of the rock for those who liked to stay cool. Bedichek didn't. He
preferred the direct sun, and, when he got hot enough, he'd stand up and fall
backward into the cold water as it rushed from the spring and let it drift him
a little downstream.

The rock is gone now. After all three men had died, an epic flood washed
it toward the Colorado. The Texas writer Don Graham says that flood came
in the late sixties, but he can't remember how he knows that, and no one else
seems to know at all.

Bedichek was the first to go. He died suddenly in his home on May 21,
1959. Webb outlived him by four years, Dobie by five and a half. Earlier I
tried speculating about what each man owed to the others, but never mentioned what Dobie owed to Webb or Webb to Dobie. In fact, they were never
considered terribly close friends, though they spent much time in shared
conversation with Bedichek. The topics ranged far and wide, but death was
a common one, especially as they saw it coming for them. I try to imagine
the conversations that Dobie and Webb might have had after the passing of
their dear friend. Perhaps they met at Barton Springs to reminisce, struggling
together through the gaping loss, and hoping to forge a new connection
across his absence. (I imagine a dot that haunts the map, from house to house
and down to Barton Springs and back, shaded with a deeper blue than what
he moves among.)

We all know and remember some few things and forget the rest, and we remember best what is still present and alive. The books, though worth remembering, won't ever be widely read again; McMurtry was mostly right about them. But thanks to the statue, we can remember the vision that these men shared of the good life, a life spent with each other in a quiet and beautiful place—thankfully still present and alive. What's difficult to remember, or even to believe, is that dead people whom we never knew were once actually there as well and that they splashed in the water and had voices and missed each other when they died.

Even with their flaws, they were good and worthy, continually fighting to understand the world, and brave enough to try to make it better. Maybe they were old men whose wives took care of them. Maybe they never escaped their childhood fascinations with the dying frontier—and had to die with it. Maybe they weren't imaginative enough or smart enough, or maybe in 2003, we're just smart about other things, darker things, about irony, change, worry, and loneliness. They were smart about birds and the weather and what a person owes to another person, and what he owes to the general good.

Well, to each his own.

If you have time, read one of the books or read the letters. Remember the individual lives and their friendships with one another. Remember their fondness for Austin and Barton Springs, and their love of conversation and nature and liberty. Forget the walk from house to house. Forget the house. Forget the porch steps. Forget the porch. But remember that blue sound of someone in the evening, knocking on his friend's front door. ★

2003

John Spong

John Spong holds a bachelor's degree in history and a J.D. from the University of Texas at Austin. In 1997, after a brief yet dramatically unfulfilling stint as a civil litigator in Austin, he joined *Texas Monthly* as a fact-checker and became a staff writer in 2002. Spong has lived in Austin since 1970. "King's Ransom" offers testimony to the amazing collection of intellectual, literary, and artistic wonders to be found at the Harry Ransom Humanities Research Center, located on the University of Texas campus.

King's Ransom

When I was a student at the University of Texas at Austin in the early nineties, a story got around about the Harry Ransom Humanities Research Center. It didn't qualify as campus legend; too few people had heard it. It was more like a rumor, and it went like this: If you rode up to the fifth floor of the HRC—that is, if you could find the HRC, which was a chore before $14.5 million in renovations were completed this spring—you could fill out a request form and then be allowed to look at the journal Jack Kerouac kept while he was writing *On the Road*. That's right: the very journal, written in Kerouac's own hand in a small, spiral-bound notebook that was no doubt kept in the back pocket of his dirty blue jeans while he was, literally, on the road.

But there was one thing you had to keep in mind. To see the journal, you had to have a valid reason. And if you weren't writing a biography of Kerouac or making a documentary on the Beats and you didn't feel comfortable lying, you could still get in if you remembered the magic word. Write "inspiration" in the space marked "purpose of research," and the keys to the kingdom were yours.

I didn't give the story much thought at the time. But a few years later, when I was between careers and in possession of plenty of free time, I went by the HRC to suss things out. It happened that the rumor was true. A particularly helpful librarian pointed me not just to Kerouac's journal but to other items in the Kerouac collection. In papers obtained from the widow of Neal Cassady, Kerouac's friend and role model, were dozens of letters Kerouac wrote while he was struggling to find his voice. The stream-of-consciousness flow was there in his prose but none of the confidence. That changed, though, with the letters he wrote after *On the Road* was published. Suddenly his signature was taking up half a page. An afternoon at the HRC turned into a week. I'd arrive in the morning, think of an artist, and ask for the moon. Half an hour later, I'd be holding a handwritten draft of Dylan Thomas' *Do Not Go Gentle Into That Good Night* or a letter from jazz saxophonist Charlie Parker written during his court-ordered dry-out at a California mental hospital. (Parker's handwriting was immaculate; each g looked like it had taken five minutes to write. But the message was less deliberate: "Man—please come right down here and get me out of this joint. I'm about to blow my top!") I've since learned just how much HRC there is. It owns one of the surviving copies of the Gutenberg Bible, the first book printed with movable type. It owns the first photograph ever taken. As an American cultural archive, it is ranked not far behind the Library of Congress and the New York Public Library; the only university libraries consistently mentioned in the same breath are the Beinecke at Yale and the Houghton at Harvard. The HRC has the personal papers—manuscripts, journals, letters, and the like—of a long list of true literary lions, including Joyce, Twain, Faulkner, Beckett, Hemingway, Ginsberg, Singer, Wilde, Waugh, and Pynchon. Its photography collection is one of the finest in the world, with thousands of images from the Farm Security Administration's famous photo project and more than a million taken by San Antonio panoramic photographer E. O. Goldbeck. Then there are the oddities that show the artist behind the art. Gertrude Stein's pens. Carson McCullers' cigarette lighter. Edgar Allan Poe's desk. Marlon Brando's address book. If you took the time to find the HRC, the allure was simple, and it wasn't a desire to be nearer to celebrity. It was something more. The HRC humanizes the superhuman. When you pick up a page of Joyce's final revisions to *Ulysses*, you're not looking at the most important novel of the twentieth century. Rather, you're glimpsing a moment in time, an instant when Joyce was just a man and *Ulysses* just an idea.

"Ransom believed that the book represented the end of the process," HRC director Tom Staley told me in his office one morning in August. "You get the story down, you print it, and then other people read it. But where did that story come from? What you really ought to study is this trajectory, as I call it, of the imagination. What are the false notes? What was thrown out; what was kept? So in the end, what the student studies is the creative process."

That was Harry Ransom's vision when, as vice president and provost of UT, he founded the Humanities Research Center in 1957, and it still guides Staley as he presides over almost everything that happens at the HRC: fund-raising, acquisitions, conservation, exhibits. Staley has the refined charm of a Pennsylvania-born Fulbright scholar turned university administrator. Yet he's a passionate storyteller, particularly when the conversation gets around to the right topic, like James Joyce—nearly every inch of shelf and wall in Staley's office is occupied by books about or pictures of Joyce—or the HRC.

"When Ransom decided in the fifties to make a special collection and create the center," Staley said, "he believed Harvard and Yale had the great collections of eighteenth- and nineteenth-century literature, Cambridge and Oxford had the great early collections, and Texas was just a young university. So he decided to collect what wasn't already gathered up, as it were, and he went after the late-nineteenth and twentieth. He bought a great deal from a man named Hanley, who was very wealthy and who lived in Bradford, Pennsylvania, which is, as you know, where the oil industry really started—they still have that famous Pennsylvania crude, which they use in motor oil. Hanley married a belly dancer named Tallulah, and her twin sister lived in the house with them. But anyhow, Hanley had this great big house that he filled full of books. His accountant would say, 'Look, you don't have the money for this, and it is so dangerous to keep these in this wooden house. You could burn them all.' So Ransom would send a truck up there and buy them. And Hanley would always tell him, 'That's it! I'm getting out of this collecting business forever!' And two years later Ransom would have the truck at his door again."

Part of Ransom's success owed to a small market for twentieth-century writers and a nearly nonexistent one for manuscripts. But it was due also to his ability as an administrator; four years after founding the HRC, he became the

UT system chancellor. "There was always this myth," said Staley, "that Ransom had made a pact with the devil, meaning [Board of Regents chair Frank C.] Erwin. 'Let me have money for the libraries, and the football teams can do this or do that.' Now, I don't know if that's true. But there is one extremely important thing in all this that people lose sight of: Ransom was able to convince the regents that the part of the Permanent University Fund that went to capital expenditures, meaning the money from the university's oil leases that was originally used only for buildings and roads and not academic programs, could be used on books. That's the crucial point."

Although Ransom served as director of the HRC only from 1958 to 1961, he was a presence there throughout his chancellorship, from 1961 to 1971, and until he died, in 1976. Two years later the HRC purchased the Gutenberg Bible in his honor for $2.4 million. The next ten years saw continued growth and, more significantly, the development of a world-class conservation department, beginning in the early eighties.

Staley became the human face of the HRC in 1988. Until recently, his biggest gets were works by Pynchon, Burgess, and Singer and by contemporary British playwrights like Tom Stoppard. Although he has opted not to pursue Texas writers—they have, for the most part, deposited their papers in the Southwestern Writers Collection at Texas State University, in San Marcos—he has pushed the HRC to take a chance on first editions of contemporary authors like Jonathan Franzen and the *McSweeney's* magazine crowd. "Maybe we'll make a mistake on a writer and lose eighty bucks," he said. "It will be historically interesting, and it's cheaper than the alternative."

This spring, however, Staley raised eyebrows when the HRC acquired Bob Woodward and Carl Bernstein's Watergate archive for $5 million. Announced at a time when higher-education funding was being slashed, the purchase caused a small ruckus even though it was made entirely with private funds. Staley said the controversy should have been over how little he had to pay. "The trick was finding the funds outside the university," said Staley. Containing more than 250 reporter's notepads, memos, photographs, drafts of stories, and *All the President's Men,* both the book and the screenplay, the collection realizes Ransom's vision in all ways but one: It is not complete. Documents relating to confidential sources, including Deep Throat, have been kept in Washington. Only after the sources die will their names be revealed and the documents sent to the HRC.

Staley's ultimate legacy, though, will be the HRC's heightened public profile. Its anonymity has been partly the fault of its location, or lack thereof; when Ransom started the collection, it had no home. Then, when the HRC's current building was built, during the student uprisings of the early seventies, it looked like a bunker. "Oh, they wanted to keep people out," said Staley. "We didn't want any riots in here." But six years ago Staley and the university embarked on a drive that raised $26 million to bolster the HRC's endowment and give the facility a makeover. The resulting renovation, executed by San Antonio's Lake/Flato architecture firm, is striking. The front facade is now windows, with images from the collections—photographs, drawings, signatures—and pieces of text etched into the glass. Inside, for the first time ever, the HRC has space to exhibit its own materials. Staley has also beefed up the HRC's Web presence, putting its catalog online, along with a virtual tour of the Gutenberg Bible. "There's a possibility here for a mecca of culture," said Staley. "And this used to be a quiet place."

It remains quiet in the new reading room, which is where the real magic happens anyway, even for someone who walks through the stacks every day. "Oh, those *Ulysses* page proofs are a special place for me," Staley said. "And Graham Greene's collection. He did a series of postcards in which he wrote a story on the back of each one for his grandchildren. And there's a letter Faulkner wrote to his parents from Connecticut, with a passage describing a ship that he's watching, afloat on Long Island Sound. And he's talking to his folks about it, and all of a sudden, my God, there, for the first time, is his writer's voice."

And there also, in a moment, is what makes the HRC a special place. One writer, one idea. You might call it inspiration. ★

2003

GARY CARTWRIGHT

Gary Cartwright was born in Dallas and grew up in Arlington, Texas. He graduated from Texas Christian University in 1957 and worked as a newspaper reporter and sports writer for newspapers in Fort Worth and Dallas. His books include the novel, *The Hundred Yard War* (1968); a nonfiction crime book, *Blood Will Tell* (1979); and a collection of journalistic pieces, *Confessions of a Washed-up Sportswriter* (1982). Cartwright collaborated with Edwin (Bud) Shrake on the screenplays for *J.W. Coop* (1972) and *Another Pair of Aces* (1990). Cartwright has lived in Austin since 1973. His work appears regularly in *Texas Monthly*. In "Statues of Limitation" he takes on the ever-popular Austin subject of public statuary.

STATUES OF LIMITATION

SOME TIME THIS SUMMER, STROLLERS AT 6TH AND Congress will come upon a huge bronze of a berserk woman firing a cannon. No, she's not trying to blow away the statue of the goddess of liberty perched on the capitol dome, though that's not all together a bad idea. The bronze commemorates an Austin innkeeper named Angelina Eberly who from this very spot in 1842 fired the town cannon to warn citizens that a band of Texas Rangers was stealing the government archives. The Rangers were sent by that rascal Sam Houston, who believed the capital of the young republic should be in his namesake city rather than the isolated village on the western frontier that had recently changed its name from Waterloo to Austin. She missed the Rangers but blew a hole in the General Land Office Building, rousing the populace who chased down the thieves and recovered the archives. Angelina's bold, reckless, historically whimsical action is the reason that Austin is the state capital rather than a wide spot on the banks of the Colorado. Whimsy is a value that we in Austin cherish, one of the things that sets us apart from the rest of Texas.

Angelina won't be everyone's idea of a proper public monument. When a photograph of the model created by Pat Oliphant, the Pulizer Prize winning cartoonist, appeared in the *American Statesman* some readers called or wrote complaining of the generous proportions of Angelina's bosoms. One irate caller said, "Angelina is no hoochie-mama!" Statues are powerful statements of the values and trusts that a culture holds dear, as evidenced by the fact that every revolution concludes with an attack on the statues of the previous regime. Saddam is only the most recent example of how people who have been betrayed take out their rage on symbols of the betrayer. When a culture can no longer agree on its values, truths, or even its history, it implodes. Fortunately our democracy and tradition for tolerance seem to have anticipated the diversity, short attention span, and limited sense of humor that might otherwise be our ruin. Some folks in San Marcos are in a snit because a statue of the legendary Texas Ranger Jack Hays has him wielding a pistol. This was no doubt the sculptor's point: The old Indian fighter is celebrated for proving that the six-shooter was the ideal weapon for gunning down Comanche. Nevertheless, some believe that the statue sends the wrong message. But messages are what statues are about, the synergy that makes them more than hunks of rock.

I've read that the original gift of forty acres from Col. Littlefield that established the University of Texas was predicated on the condition that all statues on campus should face south, in commemoration of his beloved Confederacy. Though statues have been installed over the years facing directions the colonel wouldn't have approved of, mobs have yet to storm the Tower. At the south edge of the campus there's a fountain named for Littlefield, a monument much reviled by the grand old man of letters, J. Frank Dobie, who also suggested that UT turn the Tower on its side and use it as a farm house. I'll bet that not one student in ten on the UT campus can identify either Dobie or Littlefield. On the other hand, almost everyone knows that when one views the statue of George Washington on the South Mall at just the right angle, the father of our country appears to be holding an erect penis rather than a sword. Supposedly, this was the sculptor's revenge for some slight by his UT benefactors. Legend has it that before sculptor David Addickes' sixty-five-foot high statue of Sam Houston was installed beside a busy freeway near Huntsville, the artist was asked to reduce the size of Houston's crotch, which apparently was *too much* larger than life.

Curiously, the small towns of Texas appear more aware of who they are and where they came from than do our major cities, Austin being an exception. Maybe it's because the frontier hasn't entirely vanished in places like Odessa, Fort Stockton or Glen Rose, where giant concrete jackrabbits, roadrunners, dinosaurs, watermelons, mules, and pecans honor the past and proclaim the present. Lubbock has a statute of native son Buddy Holly, Austin has Stevie Ray Vaughn, and outside the library in Mason is Fred Gipson's statue of the fictional Travis Coates and his dog Old Yeller. Crystal City, proud producer of spinach, has Popeye, and Iraan has a huge dino in its public park, honoring V.T. Hamlin, creator of the Alley Opp comic stripe, whose inspiration for things prehistoric came while working in Iraan's oil fields. Public statues in cities tend to be abstracts by famous sculptors, probably because the people who pay for them—developers and corporate presidents—want monuments that offend no one.

When Phyllis and I visited Moscow in 1999, we joked about the number of statues of Lenin that had vanished since our guidebook was published. The only remaining statue that we saw was a seventy-foot bronze Lenin that towered above what was formerly called October Square. We speculated that it had been spared so that the Old Bolshevik might be tormented a while longer by the sight of the neon-roofed Starlite Diner across the street. The motif of the diner was straight out of 1950s America, bobby-socked waitresses serving frosted Cokes while Buddy Holly jammed on the jukebox. We were surprised at the number of statues in Russia honoring poets and writers, long the conscience of that tragic country. A popular hangout for young people was a fountain just across from the Kremlin where bronze sculptures illustrated characters from Pushkin's *Fairy Tales*.

Texas has yet to produce a Pushkin, or even a Joel Chandler Harris, but we have produced some first-rate writers—among them Larry Wright, Steve Harrigan, and Bill Wittliff, three of the founders of Capital Area Statues, Inc., or CAST. The statue of Angelina Eberly is CAST's second and most recent project, but one future project is "Critters' Park," where some day you may see Br'er Armadillo frolicking with Br'er Raccoon. Ten years ago CAST gave us our first monument to writers, Philosopher's Rock, a larger-than-life statue of Dobie, Roy Bedichek, and Walter Prescott Webb, that sits near the entrance to Barton Springs pool.

The epiphany for an organization such as CAST struck Larry Wright in 1991 when he happened to spot a cheesy concrete statue of Stephen F. Austin that had sat virtually unnoticed in a small park on South Congress for nearly half a century. Having traveled in Europe and the Middle East and observed how ancient cultures cherish their heroes, Larry reflected how few public statues existed in his hometown. Cities express their identity and demonstrate their sense of dignity, or humor, or humanity by the monuments they chose. The seated figure of Hans Christian Anderson, reading his *Fairy Tales* in New York's Central Park (usually with a child or two nestled in his lap) somehow marries the genius and the spirit of that great city. Larry remembered the statue of "The Pioneer Woman," in his boyhood home of Ponca City, OK, a bonneted mother holding the hand of her child and striding into the future. It wasn't great art but it was the one thing that distinguished Ponca City from its neighboring towns.

As fate had it, someone took a sledgehammer and demolished the statue of Stephen F. Austin before CAST could hold its first meeting. Bowing to whimsy, they declared that the attack on the Father of Texas was a "brutal but aesthetically defensible" act and went ahead with business. At the second meeting Wright decided that CAST needed a sacred object with which to convene its meetings. He cited one Jeremy Bentham, who died a hundred years ago, had himself stuffed, and willed his body to the Oxford Historical Society where it is wheeled out at the beginning of each meeting. Harrigan suggested they recover Austin's head from its resting-place at the park department and carry it from meeting to meeting in a bowling bag.

Philosopher's Rock should have been a no-brainer, yet it attracted some sharp criticism and random bewilderment. "Even though it was a gift, we still had to sell it, make people believe in it and buy the idea," Harrigan told me. "We weren't naïve. We knew there were all sorts of opinions and current of thought, but we were surprised by the vehement reaction." Some people thought the monument desecrated one of Austin's most beloved locations—it sits in an open space, about halfway between the men's locker room and a hot-dog stand. Others complained that sculptor, Glenna Goodacre, belittled Dobie and Bedichek by putting them in bathing suits; Webb, who didn't swim, has his trousers rolled up. One sculptor approached by CAST rejected the project as "distasteful and degrading" to the three icons. Way-serious *ar-tists* objected that the statue was *figurative,* a post-modern pejorative: If Goodacre had made the trio look like a plate of spaghetti instead of three guys, the work would presumably be acceptable. Goodacre captures perfectly three old men locked in conversation, their friendship, the pleasure they share in enlightened company, and this magic place unspoken and obvious. A decade later you'd swear the statue has been here forever. Like any enduring work of art, it has gradually dominated its surroundings. Small children swarm over its bronze surface, or cuddle in Bedi's lap, pretending he's reading to them. When Phyllis and I were there in December, posing with our dogs for our Christmas picture, we decided that permitting kids to crawl over public statues should be encoded in law.

This summer CAST must weather the new controversy of Angelina Eberly. There are people who think it frivolous, or incomprehensible. "Angelina was an idea we'd been kicking around for years," Harrigan told me. "The problem was none of us had a vision of what it should look like." Wittliff had commissioned Pat Oliphant to do a sculpture of the storied Texas writer John Graves and suggested that the artist might have some vision for the Eberly project. "He sat down and did this sketch and it was magic right from the beginning," Harrigan remembers.

As was case with *Philosopher's Rock,* the fund-raising centers on selling bronze miniatures of the statue—in Angelina's case, for $10,000 a donor gets both a maquette and an acknowledgement on the statue itself. Most of the people who have seen the sketch or model have rallied behind the project, but to no one's surprise there have been critics. Some thought the idea was frivolous and some found it bewildering. Then of course there was the matter of Angelina's prominent balcony. When the complaints filtered back to Oliphant, the artist sketched his reply in a cartoon, titled "A Fine Fine Arts Committee." One black committee member says "Hey, didn' that bitch keep slaves?" to which a fat white guy with his finger in his nose replies, "So what? She's got great tits."

So how will CAST top itself? Nobody's sure. Critter's Park seems safe, but other suggestions are fraught with peril. Oat Willie, the endearing but goofy cartoon symbol of Austin in the '60s, carries the baggage of drugs and hippies. Cabeza de Vaca is seen by some as a white European conqueror. In my opinion, both criticisms are lame: Austin is what it is and what it was. Let the forces of political correctness deal with it. ★

2003

LAURA FURMAN

Laura Furman, a native New Yorker who has lived in Austin since the 1980s, is a professor in creative writing at the University of Texas in Austin. She is the author of two novels (*The Shadowline*, 1982, and *Tuxedo Park*, 1986), a memoir (*Ordinary Paradise*, 1998), and three collections of short stories, the most recent of which is *Drinking with the Cook*, 2001). She is currently serving as series editor of the O. Henry Prize Stories. Several of her stories are set in Austin or Lockhart (where she also lived for a time). "The Woods" takes place in the rolling, cedar-covered acres of Westlake Hills, a favorite residential suburb for many of UT's faculty.

THE WOODS

ONE WINTER SUNDAY WHILE BEN WAS OUT WEST, CARLOTTA took Josh for pizza. It was a melancholy night, and raining so that it was hard to see. They crossed the Colorado River, drove toward downtown, and they were lucky. The juggler was performing at their favorite pizza parlor. While Josh ate stuffed-crust pepperoni pizza and she had a big salad and the crusts Josh didn't want, the juggler worked with three balls and then four and balanced a bar stool on his chin.

They had seen him before, one night in late spring. He was a small boy who lived in their neighborhood and went to the high school Josh would someday. The juggler worked for tips and to force himself to practice. He could do everything but he had no showmanship, which Carlotta liked. After he finished one bit, he'd pause and think what to do next. When the pizza eaters applauded or called out asking him if he could balance this or juggle that, he looked a little startled, then nodded and responded to the challenge.

While they ate and watched, Carlotta wondered if the juggler drove himself to the pizza parlor or if his parents brought him. He was twice Josh's age.

He could drive legally in Texas and that put him out alone at night. Was he in danger less than five miles from the woods in which they lived? Of course he was in danger. They were in a city that was growing every day. People were moving in from everywhere around the world, strangers who knew nothing about the state much less the city, and some of these people were criminals for sure. Even if they were a band of angels, they'd be driving cars and cars were dangerous. It was dangerous altogether being a boy, a young man. As the juggler threw a fork, a shaker of grated parmesan, one bottle of chili sauce, and an empty coffee mug around his head, she thought of drugs, sex, cars, and the normal accidents of living, the diseases that struck the young, Hodgkin's Lymphoma.

When they were finished eating, she gave Josh a five dollar bill to put into the paper coffee cup labeled *Juggler's Tips*.

On the way home, Carlotta told Josh that before he went to bed he would have to read his chapter in *A Paradise Called Texas*, his social studies textbook that weighed about twenty pounds and had on its cover a head shot of a monstrous bronze mustang. He told her he would read it in the morning; he'd read most of it at school and he knew it already. She differed. As they argued back and forth in a tired way, Josh stared out the car window at the married student housing. The streetlights diffused on his watery window. The car turned down the hill. Josh looked up into the trees high above the river. He saw a man who stood as tall as a tree and as still as a tree. Then the car moved onto the bridge and they were crossing the river.

&

For a long time after the Comanches had been driven out, not many people lived in the woods or the limestone hills. There was no easy way to get there from the rest of the city until, forty years ago, a man who owned some of the hills persuaded the city to build a bridge across the river. The chosen site was at a dam, and the cliffs on both banks were blasted through to make a place for the new road. When the bridge was completed, a new road wound upward to the hills and valleys, and people moved out, building houses for themselves. New trees grew and maidenhair ferns covered the scars on the cliffs.

&

Just below the dam was a turbulent pool where kayakers practiced for bigger whitewater. Down river, at the opposite bank, fly fishermen cast where smoother water flowed. Between the banks was an isle covered with scrub trees and rocks. Often people fished or drank beer there, throwing sticks into the river for their dogs to retrieve. When the floodgates were opened, the isle disappeared, all but the tops of the trees.

The neighborhood in the woods was zoned so that the woods would be preserved, though the zoning and preservation were compromised by shifting times—trees did come down, houses did go up above the treeline, small and large infringements—still the woods were protected. Overprotected, some said, for what was the use of protecting the cedar trees that took the water and light from the oaks and sycamores? Beyond the city, on the ranches, the cedars were cut on a regular basis but here they were allowed to take over and become a hazard. If the neighborhood ever caught on fire, the cedars would fuel the flames beyond control.

In addition to the plague of cedars there were the deer.

Trapped between the river and the new highway to the west, herds of deer wandered through the woods, browsing, standing still and blink-eyed, close to the people who soon got used to them. Between the cedars and the deer, the neighborhood in the woods had grown barren. Get ambitious, grab a shovel, ram it into the ground with all your might, and you hit bone crushing, spine rattling limestone. There was no soil, just a deceptive layer of rotted leaves. Even native plants that deer were supposed to despise disappeared. The serious gardeners fenced their lots, acres to a half-acre, brought in truckloads of topsoil, threw in their old vegetables and fruit composted to richness, and made a garden and a lawn so that, driving along, you saw the brown of the deer territory, the green claimed by the people.

Most people lived with the devastation or tried to establish shrubs and plants the deer would ignore. Deer families crossed the roads in their perambulations, and the people who lived in the woods soon learned that when a fawn crossed, the doe wouldn't be far behind. The does were cautious and the fawns were not, so you had to wait and wait to be sure you could drive on. Somewhere, watching over the enterprise, might be the buck, who crossed even more slowly, bearing the weight of his antlers. Strangers to the roads or impatient residents hit deer; sometimes the careful drivers did as well. The deer flung themselves suddenly out of the woods onto the path of the car or stood waiting to be killed. The worst was when one limped off, for the deer would die if lame and unable to browse.

&

When they first moved to the neighborhood, Josh liked to play in the woods with his friends. Carlotta would sit on the deck, reading and listening for their voices. Once, the boys came running back to the house, excited. They'd found an arrow! It was a deer arrow, a rigid steel shaft with razor blades embedded at the tip. Carlotta reached for it but Josh wouldn't let go and for a terrible second it seemed that his hand was grasping the razor blades. He finally relinquished it and she promised to keep it in a safe place. She talked to other mothers, and they too worried about letting the children loose, for other children had found cruel arrows. It was illegal to hunt there but that didn't seem to stop anyone. A few women also confirmed what Carlotta thought she'd mistaken: the report of guns.

Josh had spotted the arrow first, so it was his, and he wanted to keep it in his room, which his mother wouldn't allow. He thought of taking the arrow to school for sharing time, but Carlotta wouldn't let him carry it on the bus. She drove him to school herself and insisted on carrying the arrow to the classroom. She stood at the door and watched as Josh held the arrow above his head so everyone could see and told the class where he'd found it. All the kids wanted to touch it.

When she moved to the woods, Carlotta left fruit for the deer but a neighbor convinced her that she would only attract opossums and raccoons who would invade her house, so she stopped. She grew used to the sight of fawns staring at her as she got the mail in the afternoon, the mothers looking protective and fearful. The same neighbor told her that once in the spring a rutting buck had attacked a woman, but Carlotta and Ben decided that was ridiculous. They heard that a buck had gored a dog, a yellow Lab, and they couldn't decide if that was true or not.

Their house was anchored to the side of a valley, and their steep half-circle of a driveway led down to their carport and climbed back up to the road. One night when Carlotta, Ben, and Josh first moved there, before she was used to the sharp incline, she left her car parked up by the mailbox. In the morning, when she went up to get the newspaper, she saw that her left passenger window was shattered. The police came, took pictures for the insurance company, and told her the window had been shot out. The back seat and floor were riddled with glass. There were tiny pieces everywhere, even up front on the driver's seat and in the sun roof. The estimator at the body shop didn't ask Carlotta what had happened, but when he gave her the bill a week later he said that all the guys in back wanted to know what she looked like.

Carlotta figured that the person who shot her car was after the deer but then there was a rash of mailbox tippings. During a morning walk when Josh was safely in school, she saw a rugged stone column with a regulation U.S. Postal box embedded, lying on the ground like a one-eyed giant with rigor mortis. High school kids, her neighbors said. It was a fad. Carlotta didn't believe it. Who had the strength to pull over something so heavy? It was possible with a pick-up truck, she was told, and she wondered again who had shot her car.

&

"I saw him," Josh said.

"Who?"

"Turn around, Mom. Look."

"I'm driving across the bridge, I can't turn around. Who did you see?"

"I don't know who he is," he said as if he were talking to the stupidest person in the world. "He's standing there."

"It's raining so hard, sweetie. Who would stand there? Maybe you thought you saw a man but it was really a tree."

The boy had quick eyes and often saw things the parents couldn't: a clown in the middle of an oilfield, tiny birds against the sky.

Josh wished she would turn the car around so he could look again but he knew she wouldn't.

"Do you want to read the book aloud to me?" she offered. And when he didn't answer, she asked, not in a friendly voice, "Well, do you?" Her voice startled her. When they quarreled Josh told her she was mean and now she recognized that he was right.

When Carlotta was a child, younger than Josh, she lived in the country, ten miles from the nearest town, in a state where lawns grew easily and the deer stayed away from people. One summer day, family friends threw a party, and just below the house, tables were set up with five-gallon tubs of ice cream, and drinks. There were hot dogs and hamburgers, and a bar for the grown-ups. The gathering was larger than most of the parties her parents went to and there were people, grown-ups and children, whom she didn't recognize. Maybe it was the Fourth of July.

At some point, she walked down the sloping green lawn. When she got to the pond, she saw her father standing by the wooden shack where people changed for swimming, a dark place with its own musty smell. At the entrance was another man, the father of the girls she played with most often, the host of the party. He was drying himself with a towel. Her father didn't notice her but the other man did.

"Get out of here," he yelled. "Go away!"

Her father turned and saw her for the first time.

"Go on, sweetie," he said. "Go find your mother."

She ran back up the hill as fast as she could. Her heart was pounding. She had done something wrong but she didn't know what.

The man had been naked, drying himself, and he thought she'd seen him. But if he didn't want to be seen, why was he standing out in the daylight? It reminded her of something in the Bible.

Why had she gone down the hill? Had her mother asked her to find her father? She couldn't remember and her mother was dead, so was her father, for that matter. The only one left was the man and he was too mean to ask, even if she thought he would remember the moment.

Why hadn't her father defended her? He could have said, *Don't yell at Carlotta*, or *No need to shout*, but he hadn't. *Go find your mother. Go on, sweetie.* The endearment didn't matter because he used it all the time and she barely heard it. She recalled the other man's voice, harsh and unfriendly all the way back up the sloping lawn. Carlotta tried to stand again among the party-

389

goers, near the tables with the abundance of the sweet ice cream she loved. Everyone was taller than she. All she could see were their legs. Why had she gone down the hill? Why was she looking for her father?

"It wasn't a tree, Mom, it was a man."

"I can't turn around now, Josh. We're almost home, it's dark, it's raining. Your father's away." Then, "Tomorrow, we'll go back and look."

She promised him things all the time to put him off, to quiet him, to try to forestall his disappointment or disagreement. She didn't like the idea that he was seeing a man in the woods. It might be real, it might not. Homeless people lived in the woods on that side of the river (on their side, too, she suspected), or so she'd heard. The police patrolled all the time, and strangers, homeless or not, certainly strangers on foot, would be questioned and, probably, escorted back to the other side of the river.

Josh didn't argue with Carlotta, though he knew that, even if she remembered her promise, it would be useless to return the next day. Tomorrow the man wouldn't be standing there. Who would stand in the woods all day and all night?

&.

At home, in bed, Josh read what he had to in his book about Texas. They were studying Quanah Parker's mother and the Comanches who'd kidnapped her and kept her for twenty-four years. When Josh finished his homework, Carlotta read him *Chicken Little,* a picture book with wild, extravagant drawings. Lately, Josh asked for books he'd liked years before. Ben tried to persuade him to read to himself, but Josh refused. He liked being read to before sleep, and Carlotta indulged him because she also clung to the comfort.

Carlotta sang to Josh, then fell asleep by his side. She awoke with a start and went to her own bed in the adjoining room. When Ben was away, Josh sometimes asked to sleep in her bed but he hadn't that night.

Carlotta tried to read her mystery but soon turned out the light. Sleep was slow in coming, so she listened to the rain on the metal roof and wondered why her son was so fanciful. He was an only child, and he might imagine seeing things because he needed companionship. She had brothers and sisters and so did Ben, and they'd always wanted to be only children. She thought again of the party, the crowded lawn, going down the hill to find her father. She turned the light back on and tiptoed past Josh's door to the little room where they shelved their dictionaries and atlases, and returned with the Bible, but when she settled back into bed, she realized that there was no index to look up seeing someone naked. She read the Twenty-third Psalm. *My cup runneth over.* She turned out the light, and, still listening to the rain, fell into a dreamless sleep.

By the time Ben came home, the weather had cleared and a series of high blue days replaced the gray rainy ones. He and Josh went off quarreling for a walk every evening. The boy never wanted to leave the house but liked it once he got going. They visited a cat up the road whose name they knew from the tag around its neck. Carlotta was allergic to cats but she liked looking at them. She would have liked an outdoor cat. Ben was sure the cat would be run over or would disappear in the woods. Josh was content for the moment with his pet mouse. He didn't want a cat unless it could be everywhere in the house, curled up on every soft piece of furniture, and that would never happen.

While Ben and Josh walked, Carlotta finished cooking their dinner, chicken for them, chick pea soup for her. She didn't eat meat but Ben and Josh did. Josh wouldn't eat any green vegetables but he'd tolerate a carrot every day. Ben would eat green vegetables and meat, or no meat. He was glad someone else was cooking dinner.

On the way home, Ben and Josh met a neighbor who'd retired from the state insurance board and was now the Republican precinct chairman. He told them that mountain lion droppings had been spotted in the woods near their house. Yes, it was true. He said that mountain lions were strong enough to haul off small children and then he looked at Josh who was big for his age and said, "This is what the neighbors are saying. There's probably no danger."

"It would be natural if there was a mountain lion," Ben said. Out West there were mountain lions that came down to the town when they were hungry enough. "There's all this food walking around. Not you, Josh."

When they got home, they told Carlotta about the mountain lion and she told Josh not to play outside for a few days.

"Yes," said Ben, "until the rumors die down."

Carlotta had trouble sleeping again and, in the nature of things, she began wondering if they were giving Josh the childhood he deserved. He might be happier in a flat place where he could ride his bike and visit neighbor kids and develop autonomy. The kids who lived in the woods depended on their parents for rides and couldn't wait until they could drive. This made the roads even more dangerous than the natural curves and inclines did, because you never knew when a sixteen-year-old in an SUV was going to come hurtling at you.

But the school district was so good. They might move to a house in a flatter part of the neighborhood but that would entail doing everything to their house that needed to be done before it could be sold and then doing the same to the next house, and who was to say that they would like it? The noise of the highway could be heard over there. Where they were now, you heard cars from the road below but mostly birdsong and kids calling from across their little valley.

She found her robe at the foot of the bed and pulled it on, draped the comforter over Ben who had kicked it off and she felt around and found the Bible on the floor where she'd left it. She hesitated at the door of Josh's room which glowed like an aquarium with the green of his favorite nightlights, small wafers he plugged into the wall, three of them so far. He too had kicked off his covers but he held them pinned beneath him so she unfolded a nap blanket and covered him with that.

Downstairs in the kitchen, she emptied the dishwasher and heated up a cup of milk in the microwave, then stirred in a spoonful of honey. She liked dark crude honey and this was refined and pale amber, and reminded her of the round jars of orange blossom honey her grandparents had sent from Florida every December in a crate of grapefruit. Every year she had tried it, hoping it would taste like oranges.

She looked up Genesis 9:22 as Ben, who had won a prize at Bible camp when he was Josh's age, had suggested. She read the whole chapter because the one verse didn't make sense. The first part was complicated and fearsome: The Lord told Noah to be fruitful and multiply and gave Noah and his descendants the Earth, pronouncing (truthfully) that the dread of man would be upon every beast of the earth, every fowl of the air, every fish in the sea. Everything moving on the earth would be food for man, and every green thing too. Man was made in God's image and human life was sacred except if killers were being killed, and that left a world of latitude. No more deadly flood but a covenant between God and man. Noah took up farming, planted a vineyard, got drunk on his wine, and lay naked in his tent. Ham entered the tent, looking for him innocently, Carlotta thought, some domestic errand, a question for his father, and saw Noah naked and asleep. Ham left the tent and told his brothers what he'd seen. They, savvy, put a cloak over their shoulders, entered the tent backwards, covered their father without seeing his nakedness, and left the tent, but when Noah woke up he somehow knew that Ham had seen him and cursed him and his descendants.

She wondered why she had remembered that verse: seeing his father's nakedness. Reading the Bible always gave her more than she'd sought and not exactly what she wanted. How had Noah known that Ham had seen him naked?

It seemed accurate that Noah was furious, waking up befuddled from the stupor of a drunken afternoon nap. It wasn't his nakedness, perhaps, but being seen unconscious and vulnerable, that made him so furious. The naked man had frightened her, and her father said, *Go find your mother*.

What had Ham wanted? What had she?

Carlotta took the sweet hot milk and went outside on the deck that hung over the valley. She saw the three radio towers on the farthest ridge, their red lights blinking, and the lights of the sports court across the way. The neighbors with the sports court always forgot to turn out their lights, and once a year Carlotta called the city inspector and he went over and explained about the light ordinance. For a few nights they remembered and then they forgot again.

When she finished the milk she climbed back upstairs and waited again for sleep.

ঌ

The next Saturday night, Ben and Carlotta went to dinner across the river while Josh played with the boy next door.

Their dinner hosts had moved to Texas from the Midwest, knowing only Carlotta and Ben, but they'd been here so long that they no longer asked for advice. They were invited everywhere. Carlotta wasn't sure if she was envious or not, which probably meant that she was. There was another couple at dinner, a droll woman who had once cut off the tip of her finger and since then kept only dull knives in her house. Her husband was a lobbyist. Toward the end of dinner he told a funny story about the governor, and then Ben and Carlotta went home. They drove through the quiet streets near the river, silent after the talk of the little party.

Carlotta asked Ben if he thought Josh was all right.

"Yes, he's all right," Ben said. "He's certainly sure of what he wants to do and doesn't. What do you mean, is he all right?"

"He sees things," she said.

"He's always seeing things," Ben said. "Remember—"

"I was wondering if he sees things because he's lonely. If he saw someone in the woods because he wants someone else there." She wanted to ask Ben if she'd been right to insist that they have a child so late. Not every life had everything it yearned for, she could have survived.

"There's no reason, Carlotta. Or no reason we'll ever know. He's a boy with great eyesight and an imagination. Just leave it alone. He's fine. He's a kid. That was pleasant tonight. I miss them when we don't see them. Why don't we see them more often?"

"We won't see them at all if we move all the way out west."

"We'll see them more. They'll visit. Everyone visits out there. We'll have to take numbers."

"They'll visit once," Carlotta said.

"The drive's not bad."

"Once you give yourself over to it, the drive's not bad. There are hours when you wonder, but eventually you relax. But most people, even Texans, consider driving eight hours each way for a weekend a bad drive."

"I haven't been offered the job, Carlotta. They only approached me about it. I don't have to take it if they offer it. There's a long way to go."

Mercury vapor lights cast an orange glow over the water. As Ben made the turn down to the bridge, Carlotta glanced up and saw a tree with something odd about it, a double trunk but the second trunk was a strange shape for a trunk, almost like a man but too still to be a man. Standing funny.

But then a car behind them passed illegally, in a big hurry to be over the bridge first, and she forgot what she'd seen.

 è

Carlotta worked two days a week at a private school, teaching art to the oldest children who were beyond the age when they concentrated easily. They were more interested in each other, which Carlotta found restful. The school wanted her there every day but she wouldn't do that, and they wanted her to talk to the children about the creative process and she wouldn't do that either. She believed that the important thing she did for the children was to provide them with a large clean airy room, paper in interesting colors and patterns, scissors and glue, pencils and paint, and then set them a task that would engage their minds enough for them to start working. She loved the moment when one by one the children fell silent, looked at the paper, and recognized that it was a vast desert. The moment didn't last long.

After work, she rushed to her yoga class, which met in a karate dojo at the edge of downtown. Sometimes during class they heard the rhythmic pounding and screams of practice sessions from the next room.

Her teacher started with the tree pose, which Carlotta was sorry about because she wasn't any good at balancing poses. The tree required simultaneous groundedness, relaxation, and uprightness. The more effort she made, the worse she got. She had to have an awareness of her right foot on the ground, her right thigh working and flexed, not hyper-extending her knee as she wanted to. Her left foot was planted in her right groin, though it slipped and she had to lower her hands to correct it. She'd once asked her teacher why her foot slipped and he told her it was because she didn't have enough strength in her thigh to hold her foot up, which hurt her feelings. Now, years later, she saw that he was right because she could hold her leg up a little better. She backed up and used the wall so that her legs would get work even if she couldn't balance. From here she could see the class, each student standing upright on one leg, arms in front of the sternum, palms resting against one another, like dancers frozen in place. But were they like trees, she wondered, and tried to see them as a sparse forest. The tree part of the pose came from the foot rooted to the ground. Now her teacher was bending forward, his left foot still firm in the opposite groin. His nose was touching his standing calf. His hands were flat on the ground. He instructed them to stick their sit bones up in the air. She tried not to fall over. Once she succeeded in bending forward, then straightening her leg, she wondered how she would ever get up, which was fatal in yoga. To look ahead was to jinx yourself. Coming up, her hands still pressing together, she bent her knee and was able to rise with only a little help from the wall.

Repeating the pose on the left leg, the class looked more like trees, an esplanade of one-legged trees. This leg was easier. The whole enterprise felt easier to Carlotta. She lifted her body out of her hips. She balanced.

At the end of the class they lay on their mats and the teacher took them through a relaxation and as Carlotta sank into the floor, she remembered a trip with her parents to a large party somewhere by a lake in Pennsylvania. It had seemed like a terribly long way but it was probably only a few hours. Compared to the drive to West Texas, it was nothing.

The house was full of people and behind it a lawn sloped sharply down to a string of picnic tables by the lakeshore. She stuck with her mother who gravitated to the kitchen to offer help, but her mother struck up a conversation with another woman and Carlotta was handed a tray of glass dishes of red Jell-O. Alone among strangers she carried the tray across the flat part of the lawn, and then she started down, the Jell-O wobbling and glinting in the sun. The tray was heavy and when she reached the downward slope—always in this part of her memory she told herself that her foot had slipped on the slick green grass, but this wasn't so. Her knees had trembled and the tray grew too heavy. She put one foot before the other carefully, carefully, until she came down too heavily on one foot and the rest was a disaster of glass bowls and glistening mounds of Jell-O.

On the way home there was a storm that was the beginning of a hurricane. A giant maple, as tall as the house, right outside her bedroom window, had been uprooted. When she lay on her bed, reading in the summer afternoons, she'd missed the particular green the tree cast into her room.

"That's it," her teacher said. "Clean up your mess. Go home."

Carlotta had to go to a dentist appointment, and after school Ben took Josh with him to the office where Josh drew pictures and Xeroxed them, colored them in, Xeroxed them again, and then played Math Blaster on a spare computer. On the way home, they picked up pizza for dinner. It was Wednesday evening so the juggler wasn't there.

Josh looked up again at the scruffy trees high above the river. The man was standing without moving, as tall as a tree.

"He's still there," Josh said.

"Who?"

"The man I saw. He's still standing there."

"What are you talking about?"

Ben didn't like the bridge. There were no guardrails on his right, only a barrier about a foot high. He wondered why no one drove off into the water. Ben had heard of boys diving from the bridge into the water thinking it was deep.

"I saw him standing there when Mommy and I got pizza. She wouldn't stop. She never stops."

Ben waited for Josh to say that Mommy was mean, ringing the triangle of their family, Carlotta was like a horse nearing the stable when she was heading home.

"Well," said Ben, meaning to say that he wouldn't stop either because the pizza would get cold, and then, no cars behind him, he pulled over between the bridges and parked.

They had often seen people walking across the bridge and spectators who came to watch when the floodgates were open, but they'd never walked on the narrow pathway that led over the bridge, inches from the passing cars. The cars weren't speeding, Ben thought, but they were so big and powerful that it would take only an instant of forgetfulness for one of them to hit Josh or him. He made Josh walk in front of him and they both tried not to look down into the churning water.

On the other side of the river, Josh pointed up. From below, the man was easy to see. He wasn't standing. He was hanging by his neck from the tree.

The man was in the woods, the way a deer was when pretending not to be there, still as the air, blending in, wishing itself away. If thoughts could cause invisibility, then he was invisible.

He hung quietly, hidden at first by the leaves, dressed in cloth the color of the winter trees, gray and brown, his skin long ago losing its living redness and turning the same parchment color as the trunks when the sun hit them toward sunset. Even the rope, plain rope from the hardware store, soon blended in, and if the boy had not seen him, then the rope would eventually have grown moss and rotted and become part of the woods. The animals had been at him, of course.

"You stay here," Ben said. "Don't cross the road. I'm going up to look. Don't move, do you understand?"

"Yes, sir," Josh said.

When there was a break in the traffic, Ben ran across and stood for a moment, figuring how to get up the sharp bank. Then a path seemed to appear, rocks for him to step on, roots that he could grasp, and he made his way up, hand over hand.

There was a lot of noise, water and cars like two great herds crossing paths, but it was peaceful on this high lookout. Ben saw the water, the woods across the river, and the darkening sky.

The tree from which the man hung was near a chain link fence and the parking lot of a building housing the river commission. People used to design low buildings along the river.

Ben fought down nausea and listened to the ringing in his ears. When he could, he made his way back down to Josh.

❧

The water had just come to a boil and Carlotta was looking in the refrigerator for the chunk of parmesan she'd bought last week and for the tomato sauce she'd made on Sunday but she couldn't find either. She was wishing she'd asked Ben to pick up some spinach pizza for her when the phone rang.

❧

The police didn't want Ben and Josh to leave even though Ben pointed out that they knew nothing. Traffic was stopped on both sides of the bridge, backed up into the city.

Carlotta was allowed to walk across the bridge when she insisted, "That's my son, I need to get over to him," pointing to Josh who looked very small behind the police barricade. Josh flung himself at her and hugged her as he hadn't in a long time, but then he stood away from her and said, "I told you."

"You were right, honey," she said. "But it was raining so hard."

"It's getting dark," Josh said.

"They'll let us go soon," Carlotta said. "Won't they?"

"Don't look," Ben said.

Standing here, below the cliff, she could see the hanged man clearly now, surrounded by the policemen in their bright rubber jackets and the EMS men. She had ignored him the first time she saw him, she had decided she hadn't seen him, but he had been there all along.

"Don't look, Josh," she said.

"There's nothing to look at," he said. "I saw him first, remember?" but he held her hand until a policeman came to them and said, "You folks still here?"

&

She watched over Josh night after night, as she hadn't since he was an infant, waiting for a sign that the whole adventure was bothering him. And why shouldn't it—a hanged man by the river? She was proud of him of course and that was what she and Ben emphasized, that Josh had been sharp-eyed to see him in the first place and correct to tell about what he'd seen. If Josh hadn't told, then the poor man would still be there.

The man's obituary appeared a few days later in the paper and they searched it for a clue. He had been missing since autumn. He had a child of his own and a wife. His parents lived in a neighborhood at the northern edge of the city. The obituary didn't mention where he'd worked. Obituaries in the local paper were written and paid for by the families of the dead and contained few revelations. There was no news story, Ben said that he must have been crazy, although they'd never know. He'd been missing for ten weeks. Carlotta and Ben figured that he'd been there about six weeks when Josh first saw him.

Ben was furious with the man for showing himself to Josh and doing God only knew what to the kid and to him, to Ben, who would never forget the sight.

"Why did I have to see that?" Ben asked. "Why did Josh? Someone was going to find him sooner or later, and I guess he just didn't care who it was."

The next morning, while they waited for the school bus up by the mailbox, Carlotta asked Josh if he was going to tell his friends about finding the man. He said that he didn't know, he hadn't thought about it, and she wondered if that was true. Usually he liked to tell his news but maybe this was too big or gruesome. Maybe Josh just wanted to forget it. The bus came and she told Josh, as she always did, "I'll be here when you come home." She waved to the driver and the big yellow school bus lumbered off down the road.

She was sorry for Josh and Ben and for herself, that, as Ben said, they'd seen what they had, and she felt the horror of the man's family that they had slept all the nights he was missing, that they had gone on living when he hadn't. All along he had been waiting for them to come and cut him down, and they hadn't been the ones to find him.

Still, these sensations were the privilege of the living and no longer his to feel. Thinking of him alone, as a man who'd lived and now was dead, Carlotta felt glad for the man, and she considered that he'd chosen well for himself, the high bank over the river, the beautiful view of the woods. ★

2000

DON WEBB

Born in Amarillo, Texas, Don Webb holds a B.A. degree in English from the University of Texas. He has published widely in sci-fi and fantasy magazines. His books include *Uncle Ovid's Exercise Book* (1988), The *Double: An Investigation* (1998), and *Endless Honeymoon* (2001). Webb lives in Austin and teaches in Hayes County. The chapter "Chronicles," from *Essential Saltes* (1999), is a play on the title of Austin's free alternative weekly newspaper, *The Austin Chronicle*, which is always running a "Best" something feature.

---

from ESSENTIAL SALTES

"YOU LOOK LOUSY," SAID SELMA SACKS. SHE HAD COME to thank him for the party and to show off her boobs.

"I didn't sleep well last night," said Matthew.

"Well, you know, if you're not sleeping you can always give me a call, and I'll talk to you. You could even come over and maybe we could work on some kind of stress reduction."

"I, eh, thanks. I'll keep that in mind."

"Did you get a lot of feedback from the party?"

"Oh, yes. I found out many things because I had the party. I can't thank you and Yunus enough. It was eye-opening, I mean, to know how many friends I had."

"Well, I want you to know you always have me."

"You're on the top of my list." *After all, you suggested the damn party, which is the first time I let you in my house in over two years. What did you want?*

"While I'm here, where are the Hull books?"

"You liked what you won?"

"I'm hooked. I just finished *Little Gardens of Happiness.*"

"Mysteries are over there." He gestured with his left hand, suddenly inspiration-struck. "You know, I'm writing a mystery short story."

"Really?"

"I thought it would be good therapy to spend some time putting my words down. I know you can't get rich off of short stories, but I figured it would give me a nice little hobby, force me to learn to use Haidee's computer, and maybe give the store a little publicity."

"You're going to write about the New Atlantis?"

"Well, I figured I'd mention it in the stories, and then people would want to come by if they're in Austin. But I'm not very good at it."

"Trouble plotting?"

"I can't come up with a MacGuffin I need. See, I've got this guy that's being stalked and I want him to communicate with the stalker—you know, have them meet. The stalker's a nut, so I think he's apt to walk into a trap, but I don't know how to contact him."

"And this is set in Austin, right?"

"Yeah."

"Well, in *Little Gardens of Happiness* there's the same situation where the lady who works at the Wildflower Research Center is being stalked by someone from her past. So she puts a personal ad in the local free paper. The stalker calls up the discreet phone service and then she calls the police."

"Did it work out OK?"

"Well, not really, but you don't want me to go into that because if you knew too much about that other plot, wouldn't that be plagiarism?"

"Well, I wouldn't want my hero to have any problems I hadn't thought through."

"In the book, it happens that the stalker has her phone bugged and knows what's going on."

"That sounds a little farfetched."

"No, the stalker's this ex-phone company guy, which lets Hull go off on these riffs about the Network."

"Well, then, presuming the stalker doesn't have access to superior forms of information, this would be a safe idea."

"Coming up with the ad would be half the fun."

Selma wandered off to the mystery alcove. Matthew restrained himself from picking up the *Chronicle*. His store was one of their free distribution places. Matthew had a secret relationship with the *Chronicle*. Years ago, after he had his falling out with John, Haidee and he had wanted to keep on playing Dungeons & Dragons. They had tried putting little ads in gaming stores for active groups, but they kept being called up by teenagers, so they did an ad for the *Chronicle*— "Looking for Adults for Fantasy Role-Playing Games"—and gave their phone number. They started getting calls from a man named Frank, who would leave boozy messages on their answering machine, "When it gets too kinky for most people I am just ready to go."

Eventually Frank called when Haidee was home, she tried to explain that they were interested in an entirely different type of fantasy role-playing and suggested that Frank place his own ad in the *Chronicle*. He did, and then others did, and eventually the ads became a mainstay of the little weekly paper. Matthew had meant to mention this to the editor many times to see if he could get a free ad for his store, but the whole thing seemed farfetched.

Selma came back with *Dad's Last Pitch*. And he had a *Chronicle* in his hands before her butt was out the door. It was one of their "Best of Austin" issues. His eyes fell on the "Best Street Name" entry. The *Chron* had picked Kumquat Court (over Ferret Path, Gnu Gap, Possum Trot, Whiskey River Drive, Hangman's Court, Bunny Run, Cooing Court, Dati Lane, Cockelburr Cove, Festus Drive, Sugar Shack, the High Road, Cotton Picking Lane, Alimony Cove, Capsicum Cove, and Easy Street). Ah, here's the section on personal ads. He would have to mull this over for a while. It didn't fit in any of the existing categories, and other niceties—like whether or not to use the optional 9-point-type headline—would need to be thought out. He should probably call the police for their advice, but he felt he was going to do it anyway. As his mother had once said (although not while talking to her kids), it is easier to ask forgiveness than to ask permission.

There were some other customers; one said "angiosomething" to his equally elderly blue-haired companion, and Matthew's mind raced back to his fluorescent angiogram, which he had had two months after his diagnosis of diabetes. The procedure is simple—your eyes are dilated, an orange dye is pumped into a vein in your arm, and a series of pictures are made of your retinas to see how much dye leaks out in a few minutes' time. Haidee had taken him, really because he was scared of how much of his eyesight might already be lost to retinopathy, but nominally because he couldn't drive after the test.

As the strobe light lit his eyes, and nausea filled his being, he grew very guilty at having killed the dream of Haidee becoming a doctor. For some reason it was all he could think about.

By the end of his senior year Haidee Bomars and Matthew Reynman had progressed so far in love that the world was not big enough for anything else and they made love anytime, anyplace, trying to reinvent it each time they did. They had the naive belief that the power of their love, which to them was as constant and obvious as gravity, was a true force in the objective universe, so that whatever objections their families might raise (and who could truly object to an interracial couple in the eighties, for God's sake?) would pass like a cloud in the light of their love's sun. Their news was met by a distant reception from Elaine and Hennan Reynman, who explained that with Hennan's growing health problem they would not be able to send Matthew to graduate school. But Haidee's family was not overburdened with politeness. She was abandoning her dream. She still intended to be a doctor, but they pointed out marriage was the last thing that aids one's academic career. *Of course* if she were marrying a man of color, she would at least be furthering their dream—the collective dream they all had. Besides, her grades at UT had been terrible; only after she had fallen into the pit of romance had her academics suffered. Where was the valedictorian who had given the racial pride speech? Where was the "I am going to come back to my community and give?" Their daughter was dead. (That she had had white ancestors was not to the point, nor that her brothers were lighter skinned than she.)

But it was true. Matthew knew it was true as the lights flashed into his eyes. He had killed her dream. He had killed their dream, and now years after the fluorescent angiogram he realized that he had killed her as well. She wouldn't have been in the store if she hadn't fallen in love with him. With that special knowledge that guilt brings of one's total responsibility for the fates of others and even the mechanical properties of the objective universe, Matthew was ready for William's bullet. It wasn't as if these feelings hadn't occurred before, but no matter how well banished, they needed only to have a certain name spoken to return to see him.

Speak of the devil.

Matthew had long ago decided that his announcement of his intent to marry Haidee had killed his father as well. At least helped along that disease he had caught years ago in Brazil.

The announcement was that he would marry Haidee when she had finished her bachelor's degree. Since this plan didn't get the support they had wanted, they moved to plan B, which was to get married immediately.

Matthew had his B.A in English after all, and they had the enchantment of love—what could indeed stop them? Perhaps they would have to live in a garret downtown while Haidee finished her degree. Perhaps they would have to get scholarships of the most promising sort, but it could happen.

It didn't happen.

Matthew went to work for the largest chain of used-book stores in Texas as a buyer and spent long hours telling people just how damn little their accumulated books, records, and magazines were worth. The garret proved to be a third-floor apartment on Lamar Street next to a bus stop, which had roaches the size of small dogs. Lots of meals with John and Cassy, just like the barbecues with William, Matthew suddenly realized. He hadn't realized that he had equated William with John on some emotional level.

His father died.

His mom went into isolation and mourning for a few years. John got his divorce.

Paul and Saul had their own troubles as the New York legal scene knew boom and bust as the Reagan years cycled through the American economy bringing ruin and relief and setting up certain long-scale tides that would chaotically create the U.S. in the next century.

And William shot Haidee.

It was his fault.

Just as the diabetes had been his fault for eating too much. He started to fill out the ad form.

Apparently you filled out the form, and they billed your credit card, unless you were getting one of the free ads from e-mailing on a certain day or using a fax on a certain day or having a name beginning with a certain letter. The cost went to the person calling in to answer the ad. Now that was a weak point: William did not have a phone just yet. But he had a car somehow. He seemed a pretty resourceful guy. (It would be a shame to be stalked and terrorized by someone who wasn't resourceful; you mustn't be easy prey.) Then after they billed you, you called in a voice message to go along with the ad, and then people could call you up and leave a message. This was the ad:

"Dear William, I read the message you left. I too want to
talk. Let's get together. Matthew Reynman."

He mailed off the form at lunch. He closed the shop for half an hour and walked over to the central post office.

Two days later the confirmation came in the mail, and he called and left the following message: "William, I know you're out there and I've given a lot of thought to many things and think you may be right. Why don't you call me up and we can meet and talk. Then if you still have business to do, you can take care of it."

He didn't know what he was going to do when William called him. He could work out a scheme with the police to catch him, or he could go and end William's life, or he could let William kill him for the very real crimes Matthew had committed. Each had a certain goodness to it, but he tended toward a mixture of the last two. He could go armed to the meeting and try to have a shoot-out. Shoot-outs were, after all, in his blood. He was the nephew of Lullaby and Pegleg Reynman.

He had been amazed that Haidee hadn't heard of Lullaby. It was one morning after he had gotten in the habit of sleeping in her dorm room. They were watching her roommate's black and-white TV, some Tom Mix—no, Gene Autry—movie about him fighting the evil forces of some underground kingdom and she had made fun of the whole idea of a singing cowboy. He pointed out that his uncle, who had died before his birth, had gone out west to make a career in Hollywood as a western band leader and had got really and truly involved with Japanese and Nazi spies and killed some of them in a shoot-out in rural California. At first she hadn't believed him, but as it came to be more and more clear that it was so, she at least conceded that it must be family legend. He promised to some time tell her the whole legend of Lullaby Reynman. He realized that he hadn't done this, and this was a bad thing. He had always had certain hopes for his marriage that he hadn't gotten to do. One of the first courting gifts he had given Haidee had been Sir Francis Burton's translation of the *Arabian Nights,* which he very pedantically always called by its real title of *The Thousand Nights and a Night.* It had been for sale in a publisher's discount catalog, only about $150, and money was easy to come by before they were wed. He had got the long box full of the black volumes with gold and silver titles and carried it to her dorm room on a cool December day. (It seldom got truly cold in Austin.) She found it after chemistry and he promised that they would read a story to each other every night. They got to night twenty or so, when reality cut the head off of that project, but the vow was made again and again. One night he had thought of reading aloud to her ashes, but that had struck even him as too morbid and pathetic. If he lived out his encounter with William Delaplace, he would find her ashes and do so. There had been too many unfulfilled vows in his life. Looking back, he decided that all of the happiness he had had—which he would be the first to admit was more than most men—had come from the vows he had fulfilled, and even if he did not have another really happy day, he would fulfill his vows anyway. His honor would be known by his faithfulness.

The sheet that explained how to call in for the ad he put by his work phone. It would remind him to call once a day. More than that would be obsessive.

Thursday came and he saw to his horror and amusement that the ad was placed under "Variations" as opposed to "Men Seek Women," "Women Seek Women," and so forth. He tried to visualize William picking up the free paper somewhere. If he could think about it strongly enough, maybe William would do it. That was no doubt the origin of magic, people being unable to do something about a situation so they thought strongly about it. It was either that or worry. It had to do with excess psychic energy, which is what separates us from the beasts. The brainpower of a cat or a goldfish is sufficient for the job, so when the job is done the brain is done. People have an excess of the energy, so when the tasks at hand are done the brain comes back to whatever occupies it. This gift of energy is what makes or breaks people. They can use the energy to worry about things, to obsess, to tear themselves apart which is the natural way of the world and why our lives are filled with cigarette smoke, gin, heroin, and romance novels.

Or someone can use that gift to create him- or herself in art or music or just plain good thinking. People need to be reminded of that often, which is why they read books or watch TV. They like to see others using the gift, they like to think that they would be clever or creative with the contents of their minds. However, some folk—and Matthew realized that this was a very good thing (otherwise the New Atlantis wouldn't pay for his blood-test strips)—become confused in the difference between the quest for inspiration and the actual process of inspiration.

He felt better for having launched the plan to meet with William. He was hoping that the police wouldn't read the ad. He doubted that the police department had a person that read the ads in the paper, but you never knew. There were all those spy movies and novels where someone takes out an ad like "The wolves are placed diagonally on the game board" and this alerts some secret operative in the world. Christ, a real secret message would be "The Sunday morning book club will meet an hour later next Sunday."

Matthew wondered idly if you did put a message in the personals like "The game board is a box which is a building" how many people it would set off. How many seemingly normal folk lose their rules at an unexpected stimulus? What if some secret understanding of brain chemistry existed so that a book with messages aimed entirely at the amygdalae of the world could be created?

Heck, such a book might already exist. He might even have copies of it on his shelves. The real world-changing book might not be Plato's *Symposium*. It might be James M. Cassutto's *Guide to Austin* for that matter. That was a great idea for a story. Maybe his words to Selma were prophetic. Like he would have the time to write stories, if he was going to inventory his life for unfulfilled vows.

He would tell the next writer that came into the shop.

He looked up and saw Rex Hull walking in.

What were the chances? ★

1999

Scott Blackwood

Scott Blackwood grew up mostly in Arlington, Texas, and graduated from the University of Texas in 1988. Blackwood traces his ancestry back to William Blackwood, the founder of *Blackwood's Edinburgh Magazine*, which first published Joseph Conrad's *Heart of Darkness*, in 1899. Blackwood's collection of stories, *In the Shadow of Our House*, was published in 2001. He directs the Undergraduate Writing Center at the University of Texas in Austin. His story "Nostalgia" draws upon one of the most famous literary sites in the city, the O. Henry House Museum located at 409 East Fifth Street in downtown Austin.

Nostalgia

"Your new eye looks good," my wife Nona tells me, sitting beside me on the front steps of the house we once shared. She puts her hand under my chin, turns my head towards her and stares into my prosthetic eye.

"Can you tell?" I ask.

She squeezes my arm gently, a distant familiarity reserved for soon-to-be ex-husbands. "Well, I knew you before," she says.

For half a minute, I say nothing, watch the sprinkler stream move over the yellow FOR SALE sign, onto flower beds, and then back again. "Sometimes things I should've done differently stand out in relief," I say, surprising myself. I grin stupidly to cover my inexplicable seriousness, wondering how this comment will mesh with asking for my old lathe and table saw back.

"Please don't start," Nona says. "I'm happy with the way things are. I wish you were." Nona used to say, because I couldn't see the whole picture, I made up the other half. But back then, beneath the joke, she had sympathy, even grudging love, for my attachment to the untapped possibilities of the past.

When we stood on these same steps eleven years ago, Nona's hands clutched her round belly, longing for this clapboard house with its Dutch gables, wraparound porch, the front yard, its oak branches lacing the blue sky. The realtor had given us a key to look around, telling us he'd be late. Inside, Nona opened all the bedroom windows, and we lay on our backs on the musty carpet, mentally furnishing sunflecked rooms. Nona rolled her round melon weight over onto me, her face flushed, her hands unbuttoning my jeans. I kissed her hard, hiked up her dress to the Apex of her tight belly with its navel stem. The heavy, lurching rhythm of her moving against me, half-closed eyes.

Now, here on the porch, I'm overcome and want to kiss the nape of Nona's neck where a few wispy gray strands stand out against tanned skin. But this is out of the question. She looks hard at me and, for a moment, I wonder if she notices my eye's limited motion.

I look over at the large U-Haul backed into the driveway. "Adventure In Moving," its black lettering says. Wes, Nona's intended, lopes down the ramp with an armload of orange blankets. Wes winks at us, his craggy face full of encouragement. He's been through these heart-to-hearts before, the wink says. But by late afternoon, he'll gleefully move Nona and my daughter Melissa down to San Antonio.

"I'm worried about you," Nona says, giving me a look that's sympathetic but not exclusively so. She's wondering if I'll cause more trouble. That's a reasonable worry, I decide, watching boxes of albums, some of which are mine, leave in Wes's thick hands.

Last summer, I was arrested and put in jail for breaking into O. Henry's house. This was after Wes remodeled our kitchen and I found the Bill Monroe cassette he'd made for Nona. On the cassette, Wes's careful hand-lettering: "For Nona—High Lonesome Sounds." Nona even suggested having Wes over for dinner back then, a thank you for our expanded kitchen, she said. Besides, he and I had things in common. For instance: woodworking, bluegrass music, and, though she never said it, her. A part of me knew then where things were headed. I lost my appetite, dropped eight pounds. When something's missing, your body knows it before your head does.

Absent but not forgotten. That's what the embroidered plaque said hanging above O. Henry's wife's china cabinet. In the plaque's center, a washed-out photo of his wife, Athol, her hair pulled into a hard bun. I'd thrown a brick through the front window of the museum, crawled inside and later fell asleep on their quilted bed. "What were you thinking, Stan?" Nona said the next morning on the jail phone. I explained I'd gone drinking at Deep Eddy with a friend (which was true), and then blacked out (which wasn't). Sometimes what you're thinking can't be dovetailed with what you do, though Nona doesn't believe this. What was I thinking outside O. Henry's house? When I was a kid I read an O. Henry story about a dying woman who's saved by a fake leaf painted on the wall outside her window. Silly, sure, but this is what my reeling mind clung to, standing in O. Henry's front yard, brick in hand.

"Stan," Nona says to me now on the porch, narrowing her eyes, pale ovals of skin crinkling around them, "do you think you'll get married again?" After a few seconds I realize this question is a kind of referendum, and what she's really asking is not so much my opinion on future marriage as it is: Can we slough off one skin and enter another? Because she doesn't wholly believe she can.

"I'm seeing somebody," I say, surprising myself, the stupid grin returning. "A woman named Charlotte. She lives in Bastrop."

"Charlotte of Bastrop," Nona says in a dramatic voice. She smiles, genuinely happy for me.

"She has two teenage kids, Ben and Jennifer, so we try to be discreet." I watch Nona sweep her gray-brown hair from her face, tuck it behind her ear, then fiddle with an earring loop. She's interested, maybe even a little jealous. Charlotte's my ocularist. She took the putty mold of my eye socket and made me the eye, its painted hazel iris and red-dyed hairs for veins.

Charlotte and I have restoration in common. I run a furniture refinishing shop where I mostly restore antiques. Armoires, dining room tables, credenzas. Ornate, early-twentieth-century pieces. One afternoon, Charlotte brought in a glass-top oak display case she wanted refinished—"to display her eyes," she said.

She'd stared at my own eye, which, at the time, looked like a pale grape. When I was ten, my grandfather's table saw kicked back a wedge of pine into it.

Kids used to stare. At the rec swimming pool, I'd say, "Wouldn't open my eyes underwater if I were you," point to my eye. "Too much chlorine." My grandfather and I were in the tool shed when it happened. He yelled to me for his tape measure over the table saw's whining. I grabbed it from the shelf, pulling the tape out long, and cut the air with it, a sword. The wedge of pine made a thwacking sound against my skull. Later, my grandfather joked to hide his awkwardness, saying, "Stan thrust when he should've parried." How different would things be if I had?

I looked the display case over. After I explained the sanding and staining process, she said, "Ruptured cornea?"

"What?" I said, like I hadn't heard.

"Your eye," Charlotte said.

"Something's wrong with it?" I said.

She smiled. "I could make you a new one—but it's just for looks," She paused. "Some people misunderstand."

"I'm on the transplant list," I said. I wanted to hop in my truck, head home, my ruptured eye still containing the possibility of sight, however slight. Staying meant closing off options.

She stood with one bare leg crossing the other, looking at me, an appraisal, while I gave a refinishing estimate. I was staring at the pad, but I could see a silver anklet circling the hard ball of her ankle.

"I make beautiful eyes," she said. I looked up quickly, my heart thudding.

On the porch with Nona, I crunch ice between my teeth and look down at the Pattersons' adjoining lawn, where a kiddie pool sits and two bikes sprawl on their sides. Across the street a mower starts up. My shirtless, tanned former neighbor Earl Gunter appears along the side of his house, an allergen mask strapped over his nose and mouth, dust and dry grass swirling around him. He sees us and waves cautiously, as if saying, I've done all I can for you both, so keep your future plans to yourselves. Earl's in his sixties. A retired justice of the peace. He has good reason to think I'm a nut: He went with Nona to bail me out of jail—though he never lets on that he does. It says something about me that I avoid him now. I give him a hearty wave from behind the windshield of my truck every time I pick up Melissa for a visit.

It's getting hot on the porch, concrete warming the backs of my thighs. Wes ambles up, still grinning, asks if I could help him with a few boxes. "Sure thing," I say, and for a second I feel the urge to shove him down the steps. Then it passes. I walk inside my former house and a hollowness settles in my stomach. My shoes squeak on the living room's parquet flooring. Wood I cut, laid and stained.

People used to grow old and breathe their last raspy breaths under their own roof. I remember my grandfather's house, the skin-tightening warmth of space heaters, the smell of Mentholatum. His bed faced the window, where, outside, bloated tomatoes hung on a trellis. His cataract eyes couldn't see the vines, though we pretended they could. Sons and daughters hovering. Help me roll him over, someone said. Rust-colored bedsores. The outline of his body in the mattress, a mold, where he'd been. Later, though I wasn't in the room, his teeth ground, his white-crusted lips parted. He's gone, someone said. A county nurse's slender hand gripped the oak bedpost. In the window light, dust motes (his sloughed-off skin and ours) carrying souls (my grandma said this) from our earthly house to the other, beyond.

This is what I want to know: How much dust has already floated away and how much is me now?

Through the front window, I can see Nona looking over her plants, deciding which ones to take. Across the street, my ex-neighbor Earl is sitting on his porch, wiping his face with a towel. Bags of grass nearly line the road in front of his house. Look at that poor son of a bitch, he's probably thinking, as I pack my wife and kid off to another man's house.

"You okay there, Stan?" Wes says in front of me as he heads down the steps with a cardboard box.

I'm sweating now, a belated hangover from last night. What will happen if I pass out, go crashing down with Nona's china? "I'm fine," I say, and remember how last December, a few months after the separation, I got high late one night and decided to come over and put up Christmas lights for Nona when she was on her shift at the hospital. A favor, I thought in my daze. I still had a key. So I pulled the boxes of Christmas decorations from the attic, grabbed a ladder from the tool shed, and climbed onto the roof. It was cold and I blew on my hands while pulling strings of lights across the roof. I stepped on a loose shingle and slid. Down went the lights pow pow pow onto the driveway, like firecrackers. I tried to get back up but I'd twisted my ankle. I thought about yelling for help, then I thought about the state I was in. Half-gone. Semi-departed. From where I sat, I could see Earl and his wife Clara standing in their kitchen window, watching. In my addled, never-still mind, I imagined Earl dialing Nona at work, saying I was crazy. I crawled back up against the chimney and held my ballooning ankle and watched my breath billow, then disappear.

2001

DON GRAHAM

Don Graham was born on a farm in Lucas, Texas, and graduated from North Texas State University with a B.A. and M.A. In 1971 he acquired a Ph.D. in English from the University of Texas. After a five-year stint at the University of Pennsylvania, Graham returned to Austin in 1976, where he has taught Dobie's Life and Literature of the Southwest ever since. Along the way he has written and edited several books, among them *Cowboys And Cadillacs: How Hollywood Looks At Texas* (1983), *No Name On The Bullet: A Biography Of Audie Murphy* (1989), *Kings Of Texas: The 150-Year Saga Of An American Ranching Empire* (2003), and *Lone Star Literature: From The Red River To The Rio Grande* (2003). The title of the short story below is taken from a Paul Simon song.

GHOSTS AND EMPTY SOCKETS

IT WAS AN OLD-FASHIONED COCKTAIL PARTY HELD IN AN old-fashioned house in one of the older districts of the city, and Harry and Jamie were excited about the prospect. They rarely got invited to anything anymore, as they never repaid invitations. They lived hugger-mugger in the high style, paycheck to paycheck, and traveled widely and spent lavishly and dreamed of third-world countries where they could hide out against the day their fragile credit-card empire came crashing down. They lived in what was called a townhome but was really just an apartment, with lots of computer hardware, and a cat they adored. The tone of the complex was being lowered year by year. The siding had begun to fade and fray, more neighbors seemed to have more dogs than ever, and the trash pickup was unstable. Still they dressed well and by all appearances were as plugged in as anybody. They were learning to use e-mail and had a passing acquaintance with the Internet. They both had day jobs and wrote and drank in the off hours. Jamie had taken to shooting a pretty good stick of pool, and Harry, who liked the game less, but consented to play on occasion, would go with her to the expensive cigar bars in the city and play rather well until he got drunk and crossed over into belligerent incompetence.

Jamie liked to go in the afternoons by herself to an old-fashioned pool emporium as big as a warehouse and shoot nine-ball with the air conditioning repair guys whose names were stenciled on their shirts and the ex-cons who frequented that establishment. Pool was perfect for those with time on their hands. The pool hall mob were entranced with both Jamie's looks and education. "How does a girl like you get to be a girl like you?" one of them named Art always asked. And Jamie always said, "Salon 505...and several degrees." She told Harry the story later, and he enjoyed it.

The house into which they were ushered had a warm, Christmasy-year-round feel to it. There was a staircase and coat-and-hat racks and a fireplace and bookshelves and, best of all, a man who came round asking what they'd like to drink.

"I'll have a Cuba libre," Harry said.

"And I'll have a fast Eddie," Jamie said.

"Uh, I'm not exactly sure what that is, m'am."

"That's ok, nobody knows what it is, but I'm gonna tell you. It's like a Cuba libre only with less coke. It's rum & soda, with a splash of coke, and a lime twist."

"Oh yeah," said Harry, "I'll take a lime twist too." And the man, who was black, was off in a whisper and back in seconds with the drinks on a tray. It had been a long, long time since Harry and Jamie had been to a cocktail party served by a black waiter. "Who are these people?" Jamie asked.

"A lot of one-time movers and shakers," Harry said. "Looks like somebody stashed away some money to have a house like this."

"Whose house is it?"

"I'm not sure."

"Hi, I'm glad you could come," said a woman in her late sixties/early seventies, Harry couldn't say exactly. He'd found that lately he could tell almost no one's age except the people in Hollywood who wouldn't talk to him about his script. They were all twenty-four and had not seen anything prior to *Forrest Gump*.

Introductions were exchanged. The woman *d' un certain age* turned out to be the owner of the house.

"Wonderful house," said Harry, diving into his rum & coke.

"Oh, thank you. You must mingle; there are a lot of interesting people here tonight."

"We will," said Jamie, "and thanks so much for having us."

The woman was just as much in the dark about who they were as Harry and Jamie were about her. But it was a party, and there was the commandment to mingle.

Harry and Jamie decided to split off. Divide and conquer, one of the rules of cocktail parties. Later they'd share stories, except often Harry couldn't remember whose stories were whose. He and Jamie would sometimes spend hours trying to reconstruct the very interesting person he'd been talking to but whose name he couldn't recall. At times it was disheartening. Harry was afraid that in the age of networking he was pretty much of a flop. Usually, too, he forgot his cards, so he hadn't anything to hand out, to lift his profile as his friend the Australian writer Marvell always put it, and so Harry was always riffling through his pockets later, finding slips on which someone whom he'd forgotten ever meeting had scribbled a meaningless name and address. As a consequence, he never followed up any of these very promising leads, or so they seemed at the time. In the stark light of morning, the day beginning, the writing there before him, the hours stretching ahead till his and Jamie's own private cocktail hour began, the tags of paper seemed futile, meaningless; he always began such days by discarding them.

In front of the fireplace stood a promising circle of local celebrities. Harry knew one of them slightly, the daughter of a locally famous deceased writer who had been the confidant and later author of a *roman à clef* about a president of the United States. It was she who had invited Harry and Jamie to the party in the first place. She, as a child, appeared in the novel. So did her sister and a brother, and both were introduced to Harry. Their mother, who appeared as a wife and mother in the novel, was somewhere in the house; Harry could meet her later. Another woman in the small circle interjected herself into the conversation, announcing that she had been a lover of the dead novelist's, though their affair had come later, after the novel, and as there had been no second novel, she had not been memorialized.

Was there anybody here who wasn't in the book, a ghost out of a novel? As a matter of fact, there was. The oldest daughter of the deceased local novelist was attached to a member of a once and still famous singing trio. Even Harry, who didn't follow music, recognized his name when she introduced him. Harry thought the group had long ago disbanded. It was surprising how such things kept going through the decades. The trio had been big in the sixties and retained, apparently, a following out there somewhere in America, playing upwards of forty concert dates a year. The female of the group had grown quite stout; Harry recalled a glimpse of her on TV recently. The male singer's great talent, the one standing before him, apart from his singing, was that he'd kept his money instead of stuffing it up his nose. Harry wondered what he himself would have done with real money. Dunno. Wd. like to find out, he memoed himself in his shorthand style.

When the little circle broke up, Harry drifted along to another room, in the back, a sort of add-on, a covered-porch it felt like. Here the table with the drinks was set up, and that made it nice. The bathroom was just down the hall. Everything you needed, right there. People were talking, and Harry leaned against the wall, listening, observing, sipping his drink. On the edge of the group hovered a man who had to be in his seventies. He wore an elegant black suit with a wonderful, flowing yellow bow tie, old school. He had great beetling brows and looked like one of the oldtimers who gather around Rosemary's baby at the end of that movie. Harry could almost call his name, he had been a member of Congress at one time, and he had been married to two or three of the women who were present tonight. Harry could never keep all that straight, who had been married to whom, and when, but they all knew, and they all got along. Amazing. The former congressman had at one time been married to the ex of the locally famous deceased writer, then to the ex of another locally famous writer who had been a close friend of the locally famous deceased writer, and who, of late, still writing, had entered into a depressing phase, recycling his very Southern past. His last book had been about a dog, and Disney was said to be interested. It wouldn't be long before he entered permanently into the purlieus of self-parody, if he wasn't there already. He of course had been a character in the novel, back when he lived in Texas and the novelist had been alive and they had been close friends. The old congressman, who had been friends of both and who—it must be restated—had married, in sequence, not at the same time, the ex's of the two writers, he was in the novel, too.

The locally famous writer's first ex was awfully nice, and Harry was happy to be in her company and to listen to her because by that time, two Cuba libres later, Harry had moved into that zone of the party when his job, his self-appointed task, was to wax interested. He'd himself no more stories to tell, that night. It was all consumption and listening. The subject turned to the former American ambassador to France, who had lately died, suddenly. Someone in the group had met her once. That was the thing about the gathering; everybody had met somebody once; and this party would be added to that string of meetings and later embellishments that form the loamy subtext of the next party, the intertextuality of association, the romance of third-hand reports, the glamour of near brushes with near greatness. Odd it was, but this was the second person in two weeks whom Harry had met who had known, or met, the dead ambassador. One of his former students, in Paris on an internship, had dined with the not-then-yet-dead ambassador several times. Once in the company of another man who was here tonight, a prominent local whiz-bang who had money the way most people have a dog; it was his; money loved him, slobbered over him, it seemed, exactly like a faithful mutt. Money clung to him, accrued to him like the filings to a magnet.

The local whiz-bang was on all the boards and all the councils, and he had a very simple philosophy of life which he would share with you unbidden or not, but usually after hours, over a last brandy. It was that life is a succession of pledge-ships. And had been so for him since the rather second-rate fraternity he had joined at a second-rate university in Virginia where people with wealth were wont to send their sons in order for them to acquire a certain tone, a feeling of entitled fellowship that made them excellent stewards of the old money they would inherit upon achieving their majority.

Meantime the group was talking about the former ambassador's upward succession of men. Harry pointed out that he'd heard a network anchor call her one of the great courtesans of the twentieth century. What was that you said? Did you say one of the great cortisones of the century? put in an older bloke whom Harry hadn't met. In any case it was a very good line, and Harry meant to use it some time if he got the chance. The locally famous writer's ex said you could write it on the ambassador's tombstone: "She never strupped down."

These were the old-line Democrats of the genteel left, Harry thought to himself. They traced their bloodlines back to the New Deal. They loved the dead President to whom most of them owed their current status and livelihood. They all basked still in that glow. They knew there had been mistakes, failures (Vietnam came to mind, but they didn't talk about that much); still they tendered to him the most allegiance of anybody they knew who was dead, including Jesus. Alive or dead, the former president had kept them propped up through the years.

The buxomy wife of a locally famous singer who was not at the party began to enjoy some success with her stories. Her husband's having to be somewhere else that night was by implication a sign of ongoing importance because the rest of them, presumably, had nowhere better to be. Harry knew he didn't, he was very happy to be where he was, this night, with Jamie, who was somewhere, oh, there she was, right there, listening to the buxomy wife (who really did have extraordinary breasts). Later, a few years ahead, they would form a shelf, but for now, they were in their last blooming glory. The wife was mentioning, in passing, their house in Belize (causing tremors of envy to course through Harry), before telling a joke. As a rule, Harry didn't like jokes. He couldn't remember them, for one thing, and he could almost never tell one correctly. He was a poor joke teller and rememberer. But the buxomy wife was good, very good.

It was a joke about an African-American, a Jew, and a Texan. (The African-American waiter was not present during the recitation. Which was a

good thing, Harry thought. Were any of the listeners Jewish? Harry wondered.)
When the narration began, Harry felt a slight apprehension, the way he always
did at the launching of a joke. He wanted the joke to be funny so he wouldn't
have to fake-laugh. He hated fake-laughing. He didn't want to experience that
uncomfortable embarrassment that follows a badly told or badly calibrated joke,
one that was inappropriate to its audience. One that crossed some invisible line
and left everybody feeling bad. He hoped this one would not be a source of
embarrassment.

The joke turned out to be quite funny, and everybody had a good laugh.
Harry detached himself and slipped away to the bathroom, hoping the circle
didn't start telling one joke after another but knowing they would. Eventually
somebody'd tell a clunker. Jokes were like TV; they stopped conversation. What
Harry wanted from a gathering like this was the exchange of gossip, innuendo,
and slander.

After the bathroom Harry hung around in another room where he fell into
conversation with a woman of whom, it turned out, he had some faint knowledge, though they'd never met. She was a local actress who had appeared in a
few grainy, black & white, neo-realist, low-budget, independent art-house films
shot in decidedly down-market neighborhoods, the kind of films that when
people talked about responsible, non-Hollywood cinema, they always singled
out if they could remember them, the kind of films that in any group only one
person had ever seen, though several thought they had heard something about
it, the title sounded familiar.

When Harry heard her name, he recognized it because he had analyzed
one of those obscure films, and the delicate tracery of the characterization she
had brought to her role, in a book he'd once written about film-making in Texas.
The book was out of print, of course, as were all of Harry's books, a point he
liked to dwell upon when given an opening, but tonight he decided to forego
the pleasure he always got from talking about how all his books were out of
print. He had recently garnered new pleasure from tracing the o.p. titles on the
Internet, where they were invariably listed as "Hard to Find." But Harry wasn't
hard to find; it's just that nobody was trying to find him.

He trained his attention on the woman. What had happened to her since? he wanted to know. A great deal, it appeared. She had had some kids and then she had had to get away from them, they were driving her crazy, they were bad for her aura, and so she had made the first of several trips to India. Harry's heart raced. India was one of his favorite places. He was in love with a certain British imperialist version of India, the Raj, all that. But he liked hearing stories about modern India, too. Though he'd never been. It was on his dream itinerary.

The actress's India was very spiritual. She went there to do the guru thing. India made her crazy, though. All the people touching you all the time, the constant now-ness of the experience, everything being lived crazily in the present, without a sense of Western becoming, everything instead a matter of being, Eastern style. Of the moment.

Harry liked her sort of deranged account of India. Once, she told him, she was on a bus and simply started screaming, everybody was so close and it was so frightfully hot. It was a very Indian thing to do, she said, to scream like that. And, too, she added somewhat breathlessly, she had seen a man beat a dog to death in the street. Harry gasped, but she said, oh no, it was all right; the man expelled all of his rage in the act; and the dog, well, the dog would have another shot at being. Still, it must have been horrible, Harry suggested. Oh, no, not in the least, not if you are truly Indian and of that moment. Yes, well.

On that note, Harry decided to have a martini. Just one. A sort of night-cap and homage to the lost good old days of the former dead president. By now Harry had sorted out nearly everybody at the party. They were all ghosts and empty sockets, living off the still powerful beam cast by the former dead president's energy. Many of those party-goers worked in jobs created by his dead body, in the Library or in adjuncts of the Library, or for politicians whose careers dated back to the former dead president's majesty and largesse. The former dead president even accounted for the literature that explained a number of the connections, Harry's own included.

For Harry had written an introduction to a new edition of the novel by the locally famous novelist, long since dead himself. He, the locally famous novelist, had drawn his own inspiration from the source itself, working as an aide to the man of inexhaustible energy. Who had still died, Harry reminded himself. But lived on, his body metamorphosed into foundations and libraries and ancillary oscillations that took on a life of their own. And drove the fuse that flared, however flickeringly, through the now paling life of this party.

Goodbyes were tendered, commitments to keep in touch with promising new-found alliances, the hopeful exchange of cards (Harry had forgotten his), the party dissolving onto the lawn into the moist night.

On the way home, Jamie asked, "Did you ever find out who the woman was who was giving the party?"

"Oh, yes, I did. That was Ellen Streeter."

"Ellen Streeter? That name sounds familiar."

"Yes, she's one of the characters in the novel written by the locally famous novelist."

"Of course. She was the pretty one, wasn't she? Who hung out at the locally famous watering hole."

"Exactly."

"Was everybody at the party locally famous?"

"Yes, almost everybody, I think. Or else they knew somebody."

"Yes. Still, it's better than the departmental parties, isn't it?"

"So's the maggots in a dead mule's ear."

"What a disgusting image. Where did you get that?"

"I adapted it from something Hemingway said about James Jones. Perfectly scurrilous."

"Well, don't tell me."

"I won't."

"Harry, is everything in literature derivative?"

"Yes it is, Jamie. If it's any good it is. ★"

2000

KAREN OLSSON

Karen Olsson was born in Washington, D.C., and graduated from Harvard University in 1995, where she majored in math. In 2005 she received an MFA in Creative Writing from Warren Wilson College. Her writing has appeared in *The Washington Post,* The Nation, and numerous other publications. She worked for a time as editor of *The Texas Observer.* In 2005 she published her first novel, *Waterloo.* In Spring 2006 she was a visiting creative writer in the Department of English at the University of Texas. In a brief preface to her novel, Olsson revives the original settlement's name, *Waterloo,* and provides an impressionistic sketch of the city's history while paying homage to Billy Lee Brammer's *The Gay Place.*

from WATERLOO

WATERLOO (POP. 600,000). THIS PROVINCIAL CAPITAL, known for its friendly, laid-back atmosphere and vibrant local music scene, is nestled between blackland prairie to the southeast and limestone plateau to the north and west. The Alameda River dips below the center of town like a fat man's belt. The city is home to the state's flagship university and its governing assembly.

Surrounded by attractive hills and spring-fed streams, Waterloo is regarded as a pleasant city by locals and visitors alike. Its climate, however, is often unpleasant. In most years a thick, hot haze descends upon the region in mid-April and suffocates the populace until late October. A north-south interstate highway, built fifty years ago and annually responsible for dozens of traffic deaths, divides the city: poor sections to the east, downtown to the west. Farther west are violet hills that used to afford genial vistas of the town, before the smog and subdivisions arrived. "From the hills it is possible to view the city overall, and draw therefrom an impression of sweet curving streets and graceful sweeping lawns and the unequivocally happy sound of children always at play," a writer once observed. "Closer on," he continued, "the feeling is only partly confirmed, though it should seem enough to have even a part." That writer died in 1978.

The majority of Waterloo's residents don't bother themselves with the city's history, such as it is. During the early years of the Republic there was much debate over where to locate the capital, until a commission of the region's gouty elder statesmen chose Waterloo, a frontier encampment, over a more civilized but fever-prone rival on the coast. The encampment became a town, and pioneers arrived, full of grand ideas, but they soon discovered that the thin soils were inhospitable to their more ambitious schemes. They settled. They suppressed their fantasies and consoled themselves with books, music, and ale. Waterloo grew to be a center of learning, a good town for live entertainment, and an incubator of laziness. Rather than visionaries, the city would eventually harbor state legislators and musicians, two populations who, despite their very different styles of dress, were united in their desires not to have to work too hard, to be locally renowned, and to drink beer paid for by somebody else. In this they were generally content, though when the weather shifted, one could occasionally catch a whiff of old buried ambitions.

Only then, only after Waterloo had spent more than a hundred years wallowing in the sun, was it hit by boom times, much as this ran counter to its indigenous spirit. At the turn of the twenty-first century, the city sprung an economy like a leak, like a tear in the cloud cover, and money poured down, into new enterprises created with the toss of a wrist, a couple of keystrokes. High technology sent its conquistadors; builders rushed into action. The air grew thick with sawdust and receipts.

And the poor old musicians, the state employees, the bookstore clerks—they stumbled through the malls and office parks, bewildered, uneasy, cursing under their breath, hoping that some portion of the windfall might find its way into their own ragged pockets, yet forever wishing it had all turned out differently. They couldn't help themselves. ★

2005

BETSY BERRY

Betsy Berry was born in Aguadilla, Puerto Rico, and attended high school in San Antonio, Texas. After graduating from SMU with a BFA in Film, she worked for the Dallas Cowboys Football Club as staff writer for Tex Schramm. In 1994 Berry received a Ph.D. from the University of Texas-Austin, writing on the British Modernist Jean Rhys. Berry has published critical essays, short stories, and poetry. She is a Lecturer in the Department of English at the University of Texas. In her story "Human Sexuality" Berry tackles the parallel universe of college footballers and finds that learning is a two-way street.

HUMAN SEXUALITY

JP DID THE DIRTY WORK. HE WAS JONATHAN PAULSON Phitzmer, and he had the most unenviable job on campus. "Worst job in the world," he called it. "My life is not my own," he would say often, sometimes out of frustration but mostly out of pride. He was the Academic Advisor for University Football. He had a master's degree in Sports Education from a respectable southern university, and the idea that college players might actually learn something while they were fighting for a shot at the NFL had captured JP's fancy.

Everybody called JP JP except for the head coach, who more formally addressed him as Phitz. "Watch that kid like a hawk, Phitz," Coach would growl about one of his prize players. "Get the grade. B to win. C okay. D acceptable. No F. F stands for failure, and we are not about failure."

Getting those "kids" a C was going to help put me through school, taking into account that I hadn't gotten a dime from that damn doctor I'd been married to.

The rhetoric of sports is clichés, and JP would trot 'em out and string them together if you didn't watch him. In our interview he told me I had the "right stuff," that I seemed "tough for a girl."

JP had a little orientation session in his office for each new tutor.

"So the idea here is that while you are not actually writing the essay for them you are explaining the process in detail as you go along," he would begin.

"You mean, like telling them what an essay *is*?"

He arched his eyebrows, thought I was trying to be cute. I was not trying to be cute. Students need to know what an essay is.

"Grasp the point here," he said. "These guys do not need to know what an essay is." He folded his hands on his desk. "They need to *have* one when one's due."

"Tests I'm not as worried about," he said. "Multiple choice especially." He needn't be. Even I knew they had a system for tests. It was the "designated player" system. One player each time from the group of test-takers was adequately prepared to answer questions from the unique basis of having actually studied. Next came an ingenious little signaling pattern, which pleased the other players enormously. Naturally faculty could never spot the signal but knew something was up, especially when a player in the same class taking an alternate test with questions in a different order got all the answers wrong but those answers would be in *precisely the same order* as in the test taken by the designated. The players were very subtle about it. It fit their character. They were masters at misdirection, faking one way and going another. And that playbook was constantly evolving. Championship level, very successful, they spent a lot of time on strategy. They were a team. When a prof pulled a last-minute switcheroo to an essay exam format they were pretty bummed.

JP clung to his ideal of the "student-athlete," but his loyalty to the athletic department called for him to be in continual contradiction with the term.

"Something gets dicey, academically speaking, with any of these guys you come to me."

I nodded, waited.

"Do not pass go," he added for emphasis.

I could tell he was ready for the meeting to end. "Look, I appreciate the job, JP. I really do." I pushed off from my chair and slung my book bag over a shoulder. "I appreciate all the advice. I'm glad I can talk to you when I need to."

He had a phone in one hand and a report in the other as I walked out. "I'll do the best I can," I said.

"You mean 'we'll,'" he said. "*We'll* do our best. There's no 'I' in team."

ਡ

All the players had nicknames; it was a longstanding tradition. There was Bouncer, Ray Gun, T-Rex, Tiny, not to be confused with Teeny, and Toad. Mini-Me, Ranch Dressing, Stein and his best bud Franken. Alley Oop, Playmaker, Stare-Royd, Rat Man, Dodger, Go-To, Go-Long, Flyboy, Big Toke, In-Out. Diddy Dawg, Draft One, Lift-Off, Love-Joy, Lover Boy, Snooze-Lose, S&M. There was Wide Load, Shit-fer-Brains (affectionately shortened to "Brains"), Top Mock, Big Ball, Last Chance, Mac-Run, Final Stand, Highs-Man, Ho Poke, Pod-Jock, and Sneaky. Tex-Ray, Gonzo Guy, Goo-Roo, Get-Some, Dooney. Cheese Whiz, Wiz-Kid, Mars Bar, Fast Eddie, Fast Flex, GoFast, Spec Sheet, Slider, and Brokeback. A guy who came in with the name Bones Baxter became Bax-trax, because they already had a Bone Yard and a Bonedaddy.

I became Toot. I asked why. "It isn't, um, drug-related, is it?" In my new position in life this was the kind of thing you were supposed to half-ass police, particularly so with the football team. The question met with the usual eye sliding and guffaws.

"Because I'm a tutor," I said.

"Lots of tutors round here," said Teeny, a 367 lb. nose tackle who prided himself in answering tutors' questions as long as they were of no academic rigor. "Only one Toot. You Toot."

JP assigned me as mentor to Michael Rawlings, known as Big Mike. A mentor was kind of like a promotion. A few more dollars per hour, a few more hours. A tutor could tutor many but a mentor had just one mentee. I had some questions for JP, and I'd learned my shorthand well. With JP it wasn't so much a short little attention span as it was a minus degree when it came to patience.

You were welcome in his office, but just like the coaches wanted the guys on the field, JP wanted tutors back on the floor, in tutoring position.

"JP?" I said. "Mike. Position. Year in school. Major. Behavior pattern. Run down his case."

"Interior lineman. Indeterminate. Kinesiology. HD, ADD." A pause. "Smart ass besides."

After another pause he had a change of heart. "Could take us to a national championship," he added, with a little boy quiver of excitement I came to recognize well when any of them uttered either word: "national" or "championship." I learned later that Big Mike's ability to take us to the championship was not necessarily a distinctive characteristic. JP said that about all the players. JP and the coaches wanted a national championship, they just wanted it so damn bad, it was a relentless theme, and their job was to remind you about it, like, *every day of a tutor's life.* It was like therapy for them.

"Also important," said JP, "it's *Big* Mike. He goes by 'Big Mike.' Dudn't go by nothing else."

"367 lbs.," he added, automatically, even though I hadn't asked his weight.

"Learning capacity?" I asked.

JP sat back in his chair. "Uhm, I'd say, let's see, uh, low to middling to coach-gonna-kick-him-in-the-ass if he doesn't get on the bandwagon. And fast. 'Cause then I'm gonna kick your ass," he said. "And I'm just the man to do it."

"Isn't that a specialty of the house around here?" I said. Still, I was pretty pumped about the challenge.

I wanted to bond with Mike quick, get him interested, inspire his confidence in me, that kind of introductory occupational stuff. Behind that tree-trunk neck and hands as big as a briefcase, the guy had eyes that could melt you. There was a kind of *je ne sais quois* about him, there really was. A real charmer underneath a body of steel and what appeared to be maximum laissez faire.

"Mike, where you from?" I said, propping my feet up on a converted card table in the study room. I was casual. It was our first meeting. Let the chips fall where they may.

"What course would you want to start on first?"

He was listening intently to his iPod.

"Mike, you with me?"

"Mike, do you read me?" I swung my feet down and stood up.

TURN OFF THE BLOODY HEADPHONES, I said.

He pulled out an earpiece. "It ain't playing nothing," he said, and gave me a level look. "And I'm *Big* Mike."

"Well, can we begin, Big Mike?" I said. He disattached himself not so easily from the desk chair he was sitting in. "Gee, I'd like to, Coach," he said. "Just ten minutes to get to Sex."

"I'm Toot," I said, but he was out the door.

Ten minutes to sex, he said. Almost every player at one time or another took Human Sexuality, offered in Ed Psych. They took it because they figured that going in they had a jump on things, already having uncovered a lot of source material right in line for the subject of the course. Once they were in sex they suffered a blow when they found out about the heavy biological component, as well as a constant focus on STDs: cause, symptoms, and appearance in various forms. There were Petri dishes loaded with nasty microbes, and plenty of photos of ugly pustules and worrisome, off-kilter claudifications. As for the chapter on Erectile Dysfunction, well, nobody wanted to go there. Sex turned out to be no gut course, but they continued to take it because it had a pleasing name. And these guys had a surprising linguistic interest in names.

&

I tried my best with Mike, Big Mike from Beaumont, Texas, graduated high school one Michael C. Rawlings and headed for greatness in grace and brawn.

But Big Mike wasn't coming along as JP had hoped. Two out of three times he didn't show for sessions. I only got to charge an hour of my time when he did that, so it bothered me in a financial sense as well as personally. I had things to *impart* to Big Mike. I was going to show him something outside of football. I was gonna make something of the kid.

"What matters is that we need Big Mike. *This team needs Big Mike,*" JP had reminded me a thousand times.

And, boy, didn't I know they needed Mike. Didn't I know. I could hardly walk down the hall beside Mike without some coach or trainer or some such angling up and clapping him on the back, saying to me, "You take care of Big Mike, eh, Toot? Big game comin' up. We need Big Mike bad out there. Do what you can to keep Big Mike on the field. We need him out there. We need him bad." Sometimes it would be the sports shorthand. "Toot," somebody would say, "Big Mike." Toot and Big Mike. Toots, get Big Mike on the field. Need him bad. Bad, Toot. I'd heard it so much it was getting to be a mantra. A mentor mantra. I wanted to get a T-shirt that said on the front, "TOOT KNOWS YOU NEED BIG MIKE BAD," and on the back, "TOOT TRYING TO KEEP BIG MIKE ON THE FIELD."

The lines between tutor, coach, and cheerleader blurred together. And always Big Mike, Big Mike, Big Mike. Big Mike, who continued to be a thorn in my side, sharper by the week.

I busied myself tutoring students. I held study sessions in Rhet/Comp for Bonedaddy and T-Rex and Go Long.

With three weeks to go in the semester, still no Big Mike. The wind-down. Crunch-time. This was the time when instructors were sometimes seeing students they'd never seen before, then seeing them every class until the end. This was the time when even dim bulbs flickered into some academic life. But no Big Mike.

We had gone a ways towards a friendship, I thought. Towards trust, I thought. Mike was a quiet philosopher, no dummy. Mike had come from hard times; his father had left his young wife in a tenement in the Fourth Ward before Mike had his first birthday. From then on she'd had turbulent, troubled romances with a string of men, some addicts, some cons, some gamblers, sometimes all three—all losers trying to play the spread. When Mike was fifteen she moved him and his two sisters to Beaumont, give Mike a chance at a high school where he didn't have to always watch his back. Mike muscled up, tough and street smart, and in football he saw where he could put it to some purpose. He'd studied life off the field and preferred it on. He saw his future in playbooks, not in lesson plans. One of his assignments was an essay on life goals. What did he think was his ultimate goal now, and what did he think it might become? It was supposed to be two pages. Mike did it in two words. GO PRO. Mike seemed not to care so much about that hallowed national championship.

I'd tried to talk to him about his situation, using the old "Supermodel" argument: You're finished at thirty, thirty-five if you're lucky. Mightn't a degree be good to have then, I asked him? I mean, when he thought it all through, that future at the end of the line?

But the ring Mike was reaching for wasn't made of brass. It was made of gold—and diamonds. Even if it's true, how you going tell a guy who can become a multimillionaire just by signing on the line which is dotted that he'd be a better man if he'd read Toni Morrison?

ða

In a wrap-up study session, nobody knew his whereabouts either. "Where's Mike, you think?" I asked. The group just looked at me for a while, but I guess I sounded kind of plaintive. So T-Rex piped up. "Oh, Big Mike?" said T-Rex. "Yeah, he's gone. Mike's gone away."

"*Gone away?*" I said. It sounded like the Mafia.

"He had to leave. Taking some time off from things, like," T-Rex said. "He, uh, said to tell you 'bye and stuff.

"He told me, uh, to say he'd see you later and stuff, but I been studying so hard I forgot." The group got a laugh out of this one, T-Rex always being the class clown of class clowns. Even a little laugh made Rex talky.

"Big be back sometime," he said. "Now Go Long, he ain't here 'cause he's in some trouble," he said. "Whacked some guy downtown last week."

"*Whacked?*" I said.

"Decked him pretty good," Bonedaddy said.

"Stitches," said Rapster, a player of few words.

"Guys your size *could* kill somebody when they hit 'em, you know."

They knew this of course, and still they looked surprised. Their *job* was to hit people all the time. But they liked the way the conversation was tracking. They wanted me to think it was their way of taking my mind off Mike the MIA, when what they were doing was buying time, time they could avoid talking about American lit. Here they saw the opportunity for a favorite subject.

"Good hitters," Rapster said.

"Bring 'em down," Bonedaddy chimed in.

"Bring 'em on down." Rapster said. "Down to the turf, severe grass stains. Win that national."

They looked down at their hitting hands, solemn—and stirred up at the same time. Raw pulsating masses of muscle fibers and springboard reflexes and overtime hormones.

"Back to Crane, oh gladiators," I said. It was like pouring a bucket of cold water over their heads.

They looked startled, then blank.

"Stephen Crane. The author at hand, gentlemen. Where should we start?"

T-Rex's eyes lit up with a thought. "Mr. Davidson said that we should all be like looking at what we're looking at."

Silence. So our first act of business today would be to examine T-Rex's statement for possible meaning.

"Like, you know, starting with what the thing's named and all," he added.

And because distractions were catching among this thick-necked testosteronic group, I temporarily steered off course myself. "*Mister* Davidson?" I asked. "That's how you guys address him? Not *Dr.* Davidson?" No harm in adding a little academic etiquette to the lesson plan.

They exchanged a smile. "Coach give him two fifties first game," somebody piped up as if that settled the matter, let the guys call him anything they wanted. 'Cause they weren't talking about money, they were talking fifty-yard line seats, treasured far above money and worth substantially more than a hundred dollars.

I gave up and deftly tacked our sailing craft back to the discussion.

"Okay, good, Rex, let's go with Davidson's advice. What it is we're looking at. The title. First off, we know it's a story, right? It's called a short story."

"Don't seem short to me," Rapster said. It was the longest line I'd heard him utter. Rapster was fondest of monosyllables, and frequently he just grunted.

"Okay, Rap, " I said. "That's just what you call it. That's its *form*. Now let's move to that title."

"There's four men at sea, right?" I said, going with the title. "Why are they there?"

"They were going somewhere, and they, uh, crashed. And now they're, you know, like floating around."

"They're rowing," I said.

"Rowin' to beat the band," said T-Rex.

"They rowin' for sure," Bonedaddy agreed.

Sweet victory. A literary round table discussion had been launched!

"Good," I said. Remedial Review time. "The *big* boat crashed, I mean *sank,* and now four survivors are in a *little* boat.

"They're open to the elements," I said. "They're in this little boat open to the elements. Are you with me?"

"It's an open boat!" said Bonedaddy triumphantly.

"Better write that down, smart boy," T-Rex told him, though none of them had a pen or paper.

"The men are being beset upon by nature," said Last Chance, a walk-on kicker. "They're where they are at the behest of fate, who's like a woman. And they're not doing well with her."

The rest of the group looked at Last Chance like he was some kind of a god. "Mr. Davidson said," he explained. "I wrote it down here in my book."

"You don't get as much back for the book if it's got words in it, smart boy," T-Rex told him.

"Everybody in their own boat," said Rapster.

"Nah, Rap, man, we a team," said T-Rex. "Coach say so."

❧

Next week Big Mike came to our last scheduled session, like an apparition. But I knew it was in the flesh. He had two fresh tattoos and a set of CZ ear studs. The tattoos looked like hell, swollen, sore, Vaselined. But that Mike had returned, that was what mattered. Then there was a second miracle. He'd made a B on his next to last English test.

"You know that guy Billie in that boat?" he said. Mike said this. He said *You know that guy Billie in the boat?* "I feel for that dude, man. I feel for him."

"How so?" I said, as casually as I could.

"He seems like a nice guy. Strong. He's the big guy in the boat—like me. He could make something happen, 'cept he don't talk much, which is good for him, 'cause of that other guy always jabbering.

"The Correspondent?" I ask.

"Something like. Man, that dude won't give it up."

I took a deep breath and dug in. "You know how in class Dr. Davidson talked about a way of looking at things called 'naturalism?'"

"You mean that we're all ants and animals and shit and life is one screwed deal and God doesn't give a shit, and nature's one raw bitch and then we die stuff?"

"Something like," I said. "Not bad. Now, these kinds of ideas, they seem like they're coming from the Correspondent, right? That's why he's called what he is. But the things he feels are shared by all the men in the boat."

"They're brothers in a boat," he said.

"Theirs is a 'subtle brotherhood.'"

"Now, Billie, he's scared," he said. "That dude's scared."

He stood up to go and looked me in the eyes. "Guess I'll hang on a bit yet," he said. "I ain't scared.

"Know what. Maybe we could make a team, you and I," he said.

"You and *me*," I said. There's no I in TEAM.

❧

Later that day Mike and I left the athletic center and took a walk in a spring sun ready to heat to a sizzle. "Two-a-days coming up," Mike said, looking up at the sky. Two work outs a day, he meant, getting ready for the season. "August's brutal."

"Cruel month," I said. "But leading to your goal."

We walked to where Mike was obviously steering us, away from study hall and to the football field, the turf *he* owned. Out onto the middle of the field we walked and stood, looking up at the tens and tens of thousands of seats that were all packed with fans at game time, screaming like maniacs. Big Mike stood tall, but I was a tiny speck in the center of that field. I took it all in, my smallness and how he carried himself proud and upright, with the kind of dignity that could never be taught. I could see, taking it all in, how things that happened here could really go to your head. Kids wanted autographs and girls wanted a little something more.

"*My* boat," he said, gesturing with his arm the expanse of green. "That's what all this is here. I ain't so interested in other stuff.

"This is my boat," he said.

"Pretty open," I said. "Remember what we talked about, after all this goes?"

"Yeah, I surely do," he said. "Still trying to figure it out." We sat down in the grass. I picked a blade of grass and started folding it into shapes.

"Who's Georgiana?" I asked. He didn't answer.

"She your girl back home?" I pointed to an old tattoo.

"Not the kind of girl you're thinkin'. And I don't ever get to see her."

I kept looking down. "She's my baby," he said. "Almost three now." He pulled a picture out of his wallet. A little girl with apple cheeks and a red and white checked pinafore. She had a big grin, was bent forward with her little hands grasping the toes of her shoes. She looked like she might have big feet. She looked like Big Mike. She was beautiful.

"Her father's daughter," I said.

He put the picture back without looking at it.

"Georgie don't know Big Mike, really," he said. "Hardly ever did see her much. She came around my last year in high school. I'm not with her mother now. Everybody back home see to that."

We got up to start walking back. "Tell you what, though. I'd sure like to get to know her someday."

"Bet so," I said.

"Yeah," he said. "I'd like that.

"Not gonna end up with her mother. I wasn't ready for a family. I've still got stuff to do.

"It's not so easy," he said. "Girls always wanting something, and me, you know, always wantin' something else, I guess."

I remembered one of Mike's Personal Statements, a writing requirement for Human Sexuality. *Personally I worry that my actions are part of a negative stereotype of men, of men like me, because I'm getting to chase my own dreams where*

I'm at right now. And my mother's daughter, my daughter too—well they can't really do that where they're at right now.

"Maybe you should have taken Human Sex earlier, Big Mike," I said.

"*May-be*," he said. He looked down at the picture he still had in his hand. "That's some little girl there, though, huh?

"I never did tell ya, Toot, I learned something from you. Think I probably did. I always thought it was weird you didn't have no guy, a girl like you. You oughta take you a vacation."

"Tend to your own knittin'," I said, turning my face away so he couldn't see I was kind of teary. Not by the thought of a guy, or a vacation, but of saying goodbye to Big Mike. But goodbye it was. Our time was up.

❧

In two other courses Mike ended up with Ds, and in a course he hadn't bothered to drop he got an F. Everything added up he wouldn't be able to play in the fall.

I only saw him once more. He called my cell phone and left a message he wanted to see me. Wanted to give me one of the only two pictures, he told me, he had of his little girl.

"Keep it for me," he said. "I'll be back to get it."

All the players could tell me is that Mike had taken off for somewhere.

I ran into JP one day in the players' cafeteria and I couldn't avoid sitting with him.

"You see," he said, buttering a piece of his bologna sandwich bread before adding potato chips, and happy to share his woes, "Big Mike got a boot on his car. Admin. Assistant to the Dean of Students calls. Tells me Big Mike can never park on the campus again, ever, in his life. He's gonna be out on his keister, and so on. Mike happens to be in my office when the call comes in. I ask him where his car is. He tells me. It's right outside the Dean's building, for chrissake. It's booted, he tells me. Had it there for two weeks. Two weeks. So I say how can it have been there two weeks? How can your car be there for two weeks? Well, it's booted he says. Can't move it. Haven't had to in a coupla weeks.

"Now. What ya supposed to do with this guy?"

"Have you tried reading Mike the riot act?" I asked. "Have you actually yelled at him?"

"Have I read him the act?" he said. "Have I *yelled* AT BIG MIKE?" His voice mounted in volume.

"I've yelled at him. I've kicked his ass with the sole of my shoe. I've gotten on my knees. I've praised his mother. I've insulted his mother. I've cajoled and wheedled. I've negotiated. Hell, I've hugged Big Mike.

"I've hugged Mike," he said again quietly.

"I was just asking," I said.

"I have used all the tools in my box," he said, adding some more chips to his sandwich.

And I must say, I felt kind of bad for JP, the man with the worst job in the world. Then he told me what motivated Mike in a single metaphor. "Let me tell you one more story, Toot," JP said. "You're good with stories."

"Say you got a pie. You show the pie to Mike. Custard, freshly baked. It's warm, it's wafting. You wave it under his nose, tell him it's a good pie, and he can have it, and he doesn't have to pay for it or anything. He can have the whole pie right now.

"*OR*—if he waits a week, holds off on the pie for seven days, he can have the pie *factory*. He can own the whole pie-making factory. He can have a pie a day, for life. He can make money on the pies. Okay, so, pie now, or factory next week?"

"He's gonna take the pie," I said.

"Big Mike's gonna take the pie," he said. "He's gonna take the pie, 'cause he's gonna be looking at the person offering the pie. He'll listen to their offer. Then he's gonna turn and eyeball that pie. Smell it. He's gonna say 'Hey, don't try puttin' one over on *me*. You mean I can have *this* pie, *right now?'*

"He takes the pie. Instant gratification," he said. "Why wait? See, you gotta always keep in mind what is consistently, inarguably, inevitably in their hearts.

"You know where Big Mike's from in his heart?"

"Beaumont by way of Houston?" I said.

"No, in his heart he's from Silsbee, Texas. That's where his grandmother lives. She raised him almost single handedly. Look around this room, this one we're in. This *room's* bigger than Silsbee, Texas. Then another hicksville town, just bigger. *Then* the big city, the big university. I bet Mike hasn't spent a single night alone in his little dorm bed since he got here. See my point?"

"You make it well," I said. "But you have it both ways. You say you care about these guys—and I think you do, and then you'll defend them. All the while thinking they're a bunch of losers off the field. You're always waiting for the next shoe to drop."

"Ah, but I always know *when* it's going to drop—and whose foot it belongs to.

"It's my job," he said, pushing his chair back from the table and turning to leave. "Only the following matters to these guys. Food. Football. Foreplay and follow-through. Sometimes the order changes up is all.

"See, it's not *personal* with these guys. It's *physical.* It's all physical."

"Sure you're not selling some of them a little short? And maybe yourself in the bargain?" It was a risky play, but I took the chance and said it. Even when all the time I was feeling a little bit sorry for the guy, for poor ol' JP. He did have the hardest job around, no doubt about it. I think I let out a kind of nervous little giggle.

But he took it okay. JP wasn't a king of spin for nothing. You could see that trademark smirk start up at the corners.

"You think I'm funny?" he said. "You think I'm making fun of these guys? I am *not* making fun of these guys. My business is to know them, to know *their* business. These are their basic needs I'm talking about here. Together they complete them—okay, not all of them, but many of them—as living entities. Who am I, or you, to say this should not be the case? Who are we to apply logic to what are essentially free agents on this planet?

"These are the men," he said, worked up to a pitch—"and I mean men, not boys. These are men that are going to take this university to the National Championship of College Football."

He was quiet for a moment, reverential really. Calling on the gods.

"Oh, but nice job with Big Mike though, Toot," he said.

"He got a B in English, JP."

"A B in English," he said. "Well, that's great. Maybe he can write a book."

"In the meantime, you get him out there on the field in the fall, let me know. 'Til then I'm holding you alone responsible."

꙳

A year passed, and a few things happened. The football season came and went. Last Chance turned out to be a pretty good kicker, graduated, and got drafted by the NFL. T-Rex left school and got signed; he'll have a shot at the big time in the fall. A quarterback named Langston Supra, Supra-Man, graduated and fulfilled his dream "to open up a *La Madeleine*" in Midland. He'd never be known as Supra-Man again, of course. Plenty of guys would return to their Midlands, but no self-respecting football player would have ever wanted to open a *La Madeleine* anywhere.

Bonedaddy, the 367-lb. defensive tackle from Tyler, Texas, had the best season of his career. Every scout in the country was said to be wildly attracted to him.

That damn team won their damn national championship. First time in thirty years. After a frenzy of excitement a kind of pall descended upon the place. They'd done it, and it was over. All the fans, all the local businesses, the mayor and the city council, all the colonial outpost neighborhoods skirting the city—all had given the team their life's blood in spirit and thanks, and now it was done. It was over. NCAA rules dictated that the commemorative rings be not a bursting star of real diamonds but one of cubic zirconium stones, stones that as it turned out got permanently cloudy when they came in contact with any liquid. The upcoming stars, just graduating from high school and joining the team, would be sad, knowing they had just missed out on being national champions. The players who had graduated from or left college before the big win would be sad, knowing they had just missed out on being national champions. For a number of the players who had won, this national championship would be the apex of their lives, and they knew it. Soon enough, they would be sad. And then the massive march towards greatness would begin all over again.

JP called me to his office, told me he oughta have my ass but made me a mentor again instead. But I might take a breather. For a semester, say.

At present I'm dating again, just one guy, who of all people if you can believe it, is JP's brother. I met him in JP's office. He's a half brother, so his last name isn't Phitzmer. Thank god. And he doesn't like sports much, very artsy. Very sexy. JP had about two heart attacks and then decided the two of us belong together. Maybe it is more than a passing thing. Who knows? It's all a darkness.

A couple of weeks ago I got a postcard. On one side was a picture of Big Mike with a big grin, his arms around two women. The postmark was New Orleans. The card read:

> TOOT, HOW GOES. GOT YOUR DEGREE? (THIS IS FROM BIG MIKE.) REMEMBER ME. GOT THAT PICTURE I LOANED YOU? THINK I MIGHT NEED IT BACK PRETTY SOON.
>
> YOU WOULD LIKE THAT I'M USING SOME BRAINS OVER HERE (WHICH MAY NOT SHOW THROUGH IN THE PICTURE). THINKING IT ALL OUT.
>
> ABOUT DONE, I'M THINKING. WON'T BE LONG. STRONG TIES IN BEAUMONT. WHATCHA KNOW— MAYBE YOU AND ME'LL WORK AGAIN.
>
> LOVE, MIKE

You and I'll, Mike, I said out loud as I read the card again. You and I. Maybe there is an I in team after all. ★

2006

WILLIAM J. SCHEICK

Born in New Jersey, William J. Scheick received his Ph.D. from the University of Illinois at Champaign-Urbana in 1969. That same year he joined the Department of English at the University of Texas. A nationally recognized authority on colonial American literature, with numerous books on such figures as Edward Taylor, Jonathan Edwards, and Cotton Mather, he has also published books on English fiction, modern American women authors, and other literary subjects—twenty-two books in all. He is also a widely published creative writer who continues to publish stories and photo-journalism dealing with plants, another one of his interests. His story "Gridlock," published here for the first time, captures a very real aspect of modern Austin. Many Austinites pretend there is no traffic problem because they live in sequestered old suburbs and do not experience the other life of Austin, the one lived on Mo-Pac and various other clogged arteries.

GRIDLOCK

ANOTHER RED LIGHT. A TRIP THAT SHOULD TAKE FIFTEEN minutes now requires at least thirty-five, on a good day with no accidents. The new Austin—Gridlock City.

He presses the brake pedal and grips hard on the steering wheel. There are seven cars, he counts, doubting he'll make it through the intersection before he loses the next green light.

It isn't just the increasing proliferation of cars, he is convinced. Certain city overseers seem intent on worsening traffic by beginning numerous road projects at the same time—most notably, as far as he is concerned, on the two major intersecting arteries of Enfield and Lamar. He was not at all surprised, though he was still irked, to learn that federal or state road-money only flowed into the city when construction sites were actually underway. So it paid for the city to tear up far more roadway than it would or could complete in a reasonable amount of time. Projects were started, then left for another day while the money appeared promptly in some bureaucracy bank account.

He doesn't make it through the green light. So he's waiting again, reading a sign: Your taxes at work. He feels the scorching sunlight through the windshield despite the air conditioner blowing a sharp cold eddy into his face. His eyes burn even more from the insistent cloudless glare. Out of the blue, a line of verse some English professor explained years ago races into his mind: "Things fall apart; the center cannot hold."

Actually he had found a way—not efficient, but manageable—around the Enfield-Lamar debacle. He took Guadalupe to Sixth, then turned west. But there was a tricky left turn, before entering Mopac Expressway, where cars backed up in a single lane for several blocks as the traffic signal went through successive changes.

Within a week—he rubs his aching left temple remembering it—Sixth Street was also torn up. No workers present, only cautionary-orange barricades, a few chunks of concrete, and signage alerting speeders about fines doubling in work areas. A long line of cars, nearly bumper to bumper, inched forward for 1.3 miles toward the tricky turn at Mopac.

He's moving again, but a fire-engine red SUV suddenly speeds past him in the turn-lane to his right and then abruptly cuts in front of him. He slams on the brake pedal, the steering wheel cutting into his ribs. It's not a teenager in that miniature tank, he reports to himself. It's a silver-haired woman. Another new phenomenon—grandmothers driving like teenagers or bats ascending fiercely at dusk from the Stygian darkness beneath the Congress Avenue bridge.

Bats, an Austin treasure he'd heard on the nightly news, are a valuable tourist attraction. In still another effort to find a way home about a month ago, he was crossing the Congress Avenue bridge when a bat crashed into his windshield. Hardly left a mark other than a slightly bent driver's-side wiper. The wiper no longer quite clears the window any more, but still he hopes it will pass the state vehicle inspection in a few months.

Resorting to the road shoulder, the silver-haired bat has leap-frogged and intimidated five more drivers, he notices when he is forced to bring his car to a sharp halt once again. Getting to the Wal-Mart today is clearly going to take more than thirty-five minutes. At least he is far from the roads closed for the 5.3K Keep Austin Weird run. He squeezes his mouth with his hand.

With Sixth Street no longer viable as a way home from his job, he had opted for Twelfth Street, far from ideal because it crosses Lamar very close to a construction site. Twelfth leads to West Lynn southward, somewhat beyond the construction point on Sixth, where heading west would then take him to the tricky turn.

Twelfth Street worked for three days before it, too, defaulted into "the road not taken." Not the Lamar intersection, where he had expected trouble eventually, but an old house under renovation near West Lynn forced a road closure. As he sat behind the wheel watching one vehicle after another slowly flagged away from the blockage, his car radio weirdly picked up the crackly voice of an unintelligible construction worker. It hadn't been in the least consoling to think of the mere $8-per-diem penalty the renovating company would be fined by the city. Remembering, he tugs a little too hard on an ear-lobe.

Later that particular day in his study, with a frayed city map spread on the floor, he settled on Guadalupe all the way across the Colorado River. It would be congested, he knew—its traffic signals are timed only in theory and in press releases. But within a week there was a water-main break—nobody's fault, just old buried lines taxed by droughty conditions—and so he was forced to turn west on Riverside that day and, this course proving hopeless, west on Barton Springs the following day. He had crept along Barton Springs toward a seventh change of the Lamar traffic signal.

Living alone, he thinks, has never been an issue for him, but he is feeling something peculiar, something like loneliness. Sleep often eludes him, too, as his mind maneuvers through alternate routes, real and imaginary. Whenever he does sleep, he dreams of Whitmanesque open roads, empty except for him traveling uninterrupted at a comfortable clip to nowhere in particular. This recurrent dream, he reminds himself again today, is a simple fantasy like the final scene of the first version of *Blade Runner*.

Fantasies notwithstanding, mornings always come early. He notices that the darkness under his eyes has only deepened. He feels clammy. The air conditioner can do only so much with Austin's pervasive humidity.

Attached to his door-knob, last Saturday, was a city notice announcing that his driveway would be obstructed when road-work commenced in two weeks for an indefinite period. He crunched the flyer into a ball, its resistant card-stock hurting his hand. He could park his car around a corner, but what's the use? They'll find it, dig around it, and force him to park farther and farther and still farther until he might as well move out of his home. Every road he'd choose would eventually be shut down. Everywhere he'd go, a city work-crew would follow.

Is this, he playfully wonders, a Capital Metro conspiracy to make him ride the bus? The bus was hardly an option. None passed near his home. The closest pick-up station for the route he needed was a few miles away. Even then, the ride on musty, bone-crunching seats took an hour, on a good day. Then from the drop-off point there was a hefty, sweaty walk to the office. He had already tried the bus for several months some time ago. It was far from suitable, and his memory could recite a bitter litany.

At least he knows they are coming now. The road by his mailbox is likely the least of their plan. He turns that over in his mind as he pulls into the crowded Wal-Mart parking lot and anticipates the hot hike across the tarmac to the store. They'll want his driveway next. Then, claiming some other underground problem needed fixing, they'll want the walkway to his door, maybe even the portico of his home. A funny thought (he admits) that does not feel funny, as he calculates how much the road tax will be on that discounted shotgun inside the Wal-Mart. ★

2006

446

SELECTED BIBLIOGRAPHY OF
ADDITIONAL NOVELS SET IN AUSTIN

Abbott, Greg. *Panic.* 2005. Young documentary filmmaker returns to Austin to visit his mother, only to discover that she has been murdered. This novel is full of what reviewers like to call "jolting plot twists."

Adams, Hazard. *The Horses of Instruction.* 1964. With a title courtesy of William Blake, this academic *roman à clef* dramatizes the machinations of the Department of English at UT in the early 1960s.

Anderson, Rex. *Cover Her With Roses.* 1969. Murder mystery set at UT-Austin, 1960s.

Ball, Margaret. *Mathemagics: A Chicks in Chainmail Novel.* 1996. Fantasy/SF novel set in Austin. From back cover: "Just because mild-mannered suburban mom Riva Konneva was a warrior woman from an alternate reality. . . ." You get the drift.

Banks, Carolyn. Author of a series of novels involving the equestrian world and a woman detective whose husband is Food Critic for the *Austin Daily Progress.*
Patchwork. 1986.
Death by Dressage. 1993.
Groomed for Death. 1995.

Bird, Sarah. *The Alamo House,* 1986. Satire set in UT area and based on the premise that women are smart and men are not.
The Boyfriend School. 1989. Comedy set in Austin made into a lame film.

Blankenship, William D. *The Time of the Wolf.* 1998. Private auction in Austin for Jim Bowie's knife brings murder.

Brady, L. E. *Lone Star Fire & Ice.* 2004. Austin music scene.

Charyn, Jerome. *Pinocchio's Nose.* 1983. Quirky, off-beat novel set partially in Austin. Author, held in high regard in France, taught creative writing for a semester in the English Department at UT in the 1970s.

Crider, Bill. *The Texas Capitol Murders.* 1992. Murder mystery set in and around the capitol in Austin, 1980s, by a prolific author of crime novels who attended graduate school with the editor in the palmy days of the late 1960s.

Cross, Ruth. *The Golden Cocoon.* 1924. A poor farm girl from Lamar County (northeast Texas) attends the University of Texas and along the way has an affair with the governor of Texas. Cross herself graduated with an M.A. from the University of Texas in 1911.

Davis, Claire Ogden. *The Woman of It.* 1929. A novel by a newspaper writer about the first woman governor of Texas, Miriam "Ma" Ferguson. In the novel the Governor battles against the KKK. The real governor liked the novel.

Dewlin, Al. *The Session.* 1981. Political novel set in Austin about a young representative who discovers, surprise, surprise, that the legislature is a corrupt bunch of lawmakers and law-breakers. Some excellent descriptions of a skid-road-like 6th Street before it got upgraded into a tourist attraction.

Dodge, Kirsten. *Let Me See.* 2004. Lively first novel set in Austin and Mexico during late 1990s, narrated by a bright, sassy female immunologist. Author shared an office with the editor in the late 1960s.

Grape, Jan. *Austin City Blue.* 2001. Police corruption and murder in Austin.

Gustafsson, Lars. *The Tennis Players.* 1983. Austin, UT, 1980s. Some good local color from a foreign perspective, including a memorable description of the UT Tower,

Harrigan, Stephen. *Jacob's Well.* 1984. Austin, 1980s. Young Austin marrieds live the good life until one of them, a scuba diver, suffers a fatal diving episode at Jacob's Well, a deep, dangerous, mysterious watery cave in Wimberley, Texas, southwest of Austin.

Hearon, Shelby. Author lived in Austin during the 1960s-80s and set several of her novels here.
>   *Armadillo in the Grass.* 1968. An upper-middleclass wife who is bored with her affluent life turns to art and nature in an effort to affirm her creative and independent spirit.
>   *Hannah's House.* 1975. Relationship novel about a liberal, divorced mother and her uptight, conservative, sorority-style daughter; several scenes set at UT where the mother is having an affair with a University professor.
>   *Now and Another Time.* 1976. Set in Houston and Austin, this is a family saga about successive generations of upwardly mobile Anglo Texans.
>   *Group Therapy.* 1984. Set in Austin among Junior League types who strive to make a difference.

Hynes, James. *Kings of Infinite Space.* 2004. More comic misadventures taking place in Lamar, the author's fictional version of Austin. This time out, the narrator's job is at a state office building where bureaucratic boredom battles with satanic supernaturalism.

Jolly, Andrew. *A Time of Soldiers.* 1976. An ambitious novel about three generations of a military family from WWI era through Vietnam. The middle section is set in Austin and contains interesting local-color ambience of the 1940s as well as vivid portraits of characters based on Walter P. Webb and J. Frank Dobie.

Kahn, Sharon. Author of a series of novels based in Austin and featuring Ruby the Rabbi's wife.
>   *Fax Me a Bagel.* 1998.
>   *Never Nosh a Matzo Ball.* 1999. Contains recipes for matzo balls at novel's end.

Leavenworth, Geoffrey. *Isle of Misfortune*. 2003. The novel's first half deals with an attempted murder in Galveston, and the second half with its aftermath in Austin, in the Bee Caves area.

Lindsey, David. Long-time Austin dweller set most of his earlier crime novels in Houston or more exotic locations in Mexico or abroad, but of late has turned to Austin for the scene of high crimes and terrorist plots.
The Rules of Silence. 2004. Thriller based on terrorist kidnapping of a computer tech bigwig, set in the affluent hills west of HW 360 (Capital of Texas Highway).
The Face of the Assassin. 2004. This one deals with a forensic artist who lives in Austin, and exhibits the author's trademark command of arcane technical knowledge.

Magnuson, James. *Windfall*, 1999. Austin, UT, 1990s. Caper novel about an underpaid professor in the Department of English at UT who finds a stash of money, after which things go awry. Some brief cameo appearances by recognizable colleagues of the author.

Markovits, Benjamin. *The Syme Papers*. 2004. Complicated literary fiction set partly in contemporary Austin and in Europe in the early 19th century, as an academic seeks to prove the genius of an obscure and largely forgotten pioneer in the search for the theory of continental drift. The author grew up in Austin and now lives in London.

Meyer, Charles. Murders in Austin solved by an Episcopalian priest.
The Saints of God Murders, 1995.
Blessed Are the Merciless. 1996.
Beside the Still Waters. 1997.

Pollock, D. J. *The Austin Affair*. 1994. Murder mystery revolves around an Austin night-club singer-college student.

Redd, Louise. *Hangover Soup*. 1999. The heroine of this novel set in Austin and the University of Texas is a young woman who tutors UT athletes.

Reid, Sally Helen. *Close Call*. 1994. A free-lance journalist in Austin gets entangled in a murder.

Riordan, Rick. *The Devil Went Down to Austin*. 2001. Tres Navarre, the San Antonio detective featured in several of the author's novels, comes to Austin to solve a high tech murder case.

Ripley, J. R. *Lost in Austin: A Tony Kozol Mystery*. 2001. A mystery involving country music set in Austin.

Roberson, Chris. *Voices of Thunder*. 2001. A supernatural murder mystery set in Austin, involving a journalist working on the case.

Saylor, Steven. *A Twist at the End*. 2000. Interesting fictional account of the servant girls' murders which occurred in Austin in 1884–85. This was during William Sydney Porter's time in Austin, and the author does an excellent job of capturing the savory (and at times unsavory) world of pre-modern Austin.

Shrake, Edwin. *Peter Arbiter*. 1973. Satirical novel set in Austin, with some scenes at the University of Texas.

Sublett, Jesse. The author, who lives in Austin, has written three novels arising from the Austin music scene, featuring a musician/debt collector named Martin Fender.
The Rock Critic Murders. 1989
Tough Baby. 1990.
Boiled in Concrete. 1992.

Ventura, Michael. *Night Time Losing Time*. 1989. Story of a blues pianist with a penchant for wild women and wild ideas, set mostly in Austin in the music world of 1980. Also contains a long sequence concerning the making of a low-budget film.

Walker, Mary Willis. Four crime novels set in Austin, featuring journalist qua detective Molly Cates, who writes for *Lone Star Monthly*. A governor modeled on Ann Richards appears in *The Red Scream*.
Zero at the Bone. 1991.
The Red Scream. 1994.
Under the Beetle's Cellar. 1995.
All the Dead Lie Down. 1998.

Webb, Don. *The Double: An Investigation*. 1998. Murder investigated by an Austin computer game designer.

PERMISSIONS

Adams, Michael. "Crossroads at the Broken Spoke." *West Texas Historical Association Yearbook.* Spring, 1991. ©1991 Michael Adams. Reprinted with permission of Michael Adams.

Almon, Bert. "Austin Odyssey." *New Texas 2000.* Belton: Center for Texas Studies, 2000. © 2000 Bert Almon. Reprinted with permission of Bert Almon.

Bedichek, Roy. *Letters of Roy Bedichek.* Edited by William A. Owens and Lyman Grant. Austin: University of Texas Press, 1985. ©1985. Reprinted by permission of Roy Bedichek's Literary Executor, Alan Pipkin.

Berry, Betsy. "Human Sexuality." ©2006 Betsy Berry. Published with permission of Betsy Berry.

Blackwood, Scott. "Nostalgia." *In the Shadow of Our House.* Dallas: Southern Methodist University Press, 2001. ©2001 Scott Blackwood. Reprinted by permission of Scott Blackwood.

Bracker, Jonathan. "Garten of the Gods." Austin: *Texas Observer,* October 15, 1964. ©1964 Jonathan Bracker. Reprinted with permission of Jonathan Bracker.

Brammer, Billy Lee. *The Gay Place.* 1961. ©1989 Shelby Brammer, Sidney Brammer, William Brammer Eckhardt. Reprinted with permission of Shelby Brammer, Sidney Brammer, and William Brammer Eckhardt.

Brown, Kevin. "Literary Playscape." *Analecta,* 26 (Fall 2000). ©2000 Kevin Brown. Reprinted by permission of Kevin Brown.

Cable, Thomas. "Trail Markers." © Thomas Cable. Published with permission of the author.

Carpenter, Liz. *Getting Better All The Time.* New York: Simon and Schuster, 1987. © 1987 Liz Carpenter. Reprinted by permission of Liz Carpenter.

Cartwright, Gary. "Statues of Limitation." *Texas Monthly,* May, 2004. Reprinted with permission of Gary Cartwright.

Clausen, Andy. "Conversation With A Lady I Took To The Airport Who Loved Austin Texas." *Austin, Texas Austin, Texas.* Austin: Place of Herons, 1981.

Cousins, Margaret. "The Beatific Memories of an English Major." *Texas, Our Texas: Remembrances of The University.* Ed. Bryan A. Garner. Austin: Eakin Press, 1984. ©1984 The Friar Society.

Curtis, Greg. "Austin, May 15, 1973." *Lucille,* No. 2 (Fall 1973). Reprinted with permission of Greg Curtis.

Dobie, J. Frank. "For Three Years We Three Sat Together." *Texas Observer,* July 26, 1963. Reprinted with permission of J. Frank Dobie Library Trust, JP Morgan Chase Bank, N.A. Trustee.

Draper, Robert. "Adios to Austin." *GQ Magazine.* November 2001. ©2001 Robert Draper. Reprinted with permission of Robert Draper.

Dugger, Ronnie. "So There It Is." *Our Invaded Universities: Form, Reform and New Starts.* New York: W.W. Norton & Company, 1974. ©1973 Ronnie Dugger. Reprinted with permission of Ronnie Dugger.

Dwight, Olivia (Mary Hazzard). *Close His Eyes,* Revised Edition. Lincoln, Nebraska: iUniverse.com., Inc., 2000. ©1961, 2000 Olivia Dwight (Mary Hazzard). Reprinted with permission of Olivia Dwight (Mary Hazzard).

Faulk, John Henry. *Fear on Trial.* ©1963, 1964, 1976 John Henry Faulk. ©1983 University of Texas Press. Reprinted with permission of the University of Texas Press.

Flowers, Betty S. "Being Imagined." *Extending the Shade.* Austin: Plain View Press, 1990. ©1990 Betty Sue Flowers. Reprinted with permission of Betty Sue Flowers.

Frantz, Joe B. "Triptych: Bedichek, Dobie, and Webb." *The Forty Acre Follies.* Austin: Texas Monthly Press, 1983. ©1983 Joe B. Frantz. Reprinted with permission of Betsy Chadderdon Frantz.

Freed, Lynn. "Doing Time." *Reading, Writing, and Leaving Home: Life on the Page.* New York, Harcourt, Inc., 2005. ©2005 Lynn Freed. Reprinted with permission of Lynn Freed.

Friedman, Kinky. "The Left Bank of Texas." *Texas Monthly,* May, 1989. Reprinted with permission of Kinky Friedman.

Furman, Laura. *Drinking with the Cook.* Houston: Winedale Publishing, 2000. ©Laura Furman. Reprinted with permission of Laura Furman.

Ghose, Zulfikar. "It's Your Land, Boss." *The Violent West.* London: Macmillan, 1972. ©1972 Zulfikar Ghose. Reprinted with permission of Zulfikar Ghose.

Giles, James R. "One August Day in Texas." *Quartet,* VII, Nos. 51–53 (Summer-Fall-Winter, 1975–76). ©1976 James R. Giles. Reprinted by permission of James R. Giles.

Gonzalez-Gerth, Miguel. "Borges and Texas: Farewell To An Old Friend." *Vortex,* 1, No. 2, Fall 1987. ©1987 Miguel Gonzalez-Gerth. Reprinted by permission of Miguel Gonzalez-Gerth.

Graham, Don. "Ghosts and Empty Sockets." *Southwestern American Liteature,* Vol. 25, No. 2 (Spring 2000). ©2000 Don Graham. Reprinted with permission of Don Graham.

Grant, Lyman. "Co-Op." © 2006 Lyman Grant. Reprinted with permission of Lyman Grant.

Greene, A.C. "The Founding of Austin." *Texas Sketches.* Dallas: Taylor Publishing Company, 1985. ©1985 A.C. Greene. Reprinted with permission of Meredith Greene.

Gustafsson, Lars. *The Tale of a Dog: From the Diaries and Letters of a Texan Bankruptcy Judge.* Translation by Tom Geddes. London: The Harvill Press, 1993. ©1993 Lars Gustafsson. Reprinted with permission of Lars Gustafsson.

Harrigan, Stephen. "Foreword." *Cuentos de Austin/Tales from Austin.* Edited and translated by Luis A. Ramos-Garcia. Austin & Lima: Studia Hispanica Editors, Texas, 1980. ©1980 Stephen Harrigan. Reprinted with permission of Stephen Harrigan.

Harris, Elizabeth. "Give." *The Ant Generator.* Iowa City: University of Iowa Press, 1991. ©1991 Elizabeth Harris. Reprinted by permission of Elizabeth Harris.

Heinzelman, Kurt. "Way Out West at 51st and Berkman." *The Halfway Tree.* Austin: Verser, 2000. ©2000 Kurt Heinzelman. Reprinted by permission of Kurt Heinzelman.

Helmer, William J. "The Madman on the Tower." *Texas Monthly.* August, 1986. Reprinted with permission from the August 1986 issue of *Texas Monthly.*

Hinojosa-Smith, Rolando. '50s Austin: A Variform Education." ©2006. Rolando Hinojosa-Smith. Published with permission of the author.

Hudson, Wilson M. "Bedichek's Rock." *Three Men in Texas: Bedichek, Webb, and Dobie.* Ed. Ronnie Dugger. Austin: University of Texas Press, 1976. ©1967 *The Texas Observer.*

Huffstickler, Albert. "The Ghosts of College City." *The Remembered Light.* Austin: Slough Press, 1980.

Hynes, James. "Casting the Runes." *Publish and Perish: Three Tales of Tenure and Terror.* New York: Picador USA, 1997. ©1997 James Hynes. Reprinted with permission of James Hynes.

Ivins, Molly. "How Ann Richards Got To Be Governor of Texas." *Molly Ivins Can't Say That, Can She?* New York: Random House, 1991. Reprinted with permission of Random House.

Johnson, Lyndon B. "Tarnish on the Violet Crown." Radio Address, *Congressional Record.* January 23, 1938. Not copyrighted.

Jones, Joseph J. *Life on Waller Creek: A Palaver about History as Pure and Applied Education.* Austin: AAR/Tantalus, Inc., 1982. © 1982 Joseph Jones.

LaSalle, Peter. *Strange Sunlight.* Austin: Texas Monthly Press, 1984. © Peter LaSalle. 1984. Reprinted with permission of Peter LaSalle.

Lasswell, Mary and Pool, Joe. "The Big Middle." *I'll Take Texas.* Boston: Houghton Mifflin, 1958. ©1958 Mary Lasswell and Joe Pool.

Lavergne, Gary. *A Sniper in the Tower: The Charles Whitman Murders.* Denton: University of North Texas Press, 1997. ©1997 Gary Lavergne. Reprinted with permission of the University of North Texas Press.

Lomax, John A. *Adventures of a Ballad Hunter.* Macmillan Reference USA. ©1947 Macmillan Reference USA. Reprinted by permission of The Gale Group.

Mackintosh, Prudence. *Just As We Were: A Narrow Slice of Texas Womanhood.* Austin: University of Texas Press, 1996. ©1976 Prudence Mackintosh. Reprinted with permission of Prudence Mackintosh.

Magnuson, James. "The Week James Michener Died." *Texas Monthly,* December, 1997. ©1997 James Magnuson. Reprinted by permission of *Texas Monthly.*

Mewshaw, Michael. *Earthly Bread.* New York: Random House, 1976. © Michael Mewshaw. Reprinted with permission of Michael Mewshaw.

Middleton, Christopher. "The Armadillos." *111 Poems.* Manchester: Carcanet New Press, 1983. ©1983 Christopher Middleton. Reprinted with permission of Christopher Middleton.

Minutaglio, Bill. "Reality Day." *First Son: George W. Bush and the Bush Family Dynasty.* Times Books, 1999. © 1999 Bill Minutaglio. Reprinted by permission of Bill Minutaglio.

Moore, Steven. "Salon of the West." *Austin Chronicle,* July 4, 2003. ©2003 Steven Moore. Reprinted with permission of *Austin Chronicle.*

Morris, Celia. *Finding Celia's Place.* College Station: Texas A&M University Press, 2000. ©2000 Celia Morris. Reprinted with permission of Celia Morris.

Morris, Willie. *North Toward Home.* New York: Houghton Miffliln, 1967. © 1982 Willie Morris. Reprinted with permission of JoAnne Pritchard Morris.

Oliphant, Dave. *Austin.* Fort Worth: Prickly Pear Press, 1985. ©2000 Host Publications, Inc., 2000. Reprinted with permission of Dave Oliphant.

Osborn, Carolyn. "The Vulture Descending Each Day." *A Horse of Another Color.* Urbana: University of Illinois Press, 1977. ©1968 Carolyn Osborn. Reprinted by permission of Carolyn Osborn.

Owens, William A. *Three Friends: Roy Bedichek; J. Frank Dobie; Walter Prescott Webb.* Doubleday & Company, Inc., 1969. ©1969 William A. Owens. Reprinted with permission of Jessie Ann Owens and David Owens.

Porter, William Sidney. "Austin. A Brief Glance At Her History And Advantages." *The Rolling Stone,* June 9, 1894, p.1.

Prokosch, Frederick. *Voices: A Memoir.* New York: Farrar Straus Giroux, 1983. © 1983 Jack H. Bady. Reprinted with permission of Jack H. Bady.

Ransom, Harry Huntt. "Frontier Museum." *The Song of Things Begun.* University of Texas at Austin. ©1998 Hazel H. Ransom. Reprinted with permission of Miguel González-Gerth.

Ransom, Hazel Harrod. "Quorum Pars Parva Fui." *A Vacation in the Sun and Other Stories.* Austin: The University of Texas, 1996. ©1996 Miguel González-Gerth. Reprinted with permission of Miguel González-Gerth.

Richards, Ann with Knobler, Peter. *Straight from the Heart: My Life in Politics and Other Places.* New York: Simon and Schuster,1989. ©1989 Ann Richards. Reprinted with permission of Ann Richards.

Richards, David. *Once Upon a Time in Texas: A Liberal in the Lone Star State.* Austin: University of Texas Press, 2002. ©2002 David Richards. Reprinted by permission of David Richards.

Rota, Bertram. "The Night of the Armadillos." Bodley House, 1960. ©1960 Anthony Rota. Reprinted with permission of Anthony Rota, literary executor for Bertram Rota.

Scheick, William J. "Gridlock." ©2006 William J. Scheick. Published with permission of William J. Scheick.

Shrake, Edwin. *The Borderland: A Novel of Texas.* New York: Hyperion, 1999. ©1999 Edwin Shrake. Reprinted with permission of the author.

Spong, John. "King's Ransom." *Texas Monthly,* October 2003. ©2003 Texas Monthly, Inc. Reprinted with permission from the October 2003 issue of *Texas Monthly.*

Sprague, Kurth. *Frighten the Horses: A Rusty Coulter Mystery.* New York: Writers Club Press, 2003. ©2003 Kurth Sprague. Reprinted with permission of Kurth Sprague.

Taylor, Chuck. "Texas." *Only a Poet: Selected Stories and Essays, Practical, Literary and Personal (1977–1984).* New Braunfels: Cedar Rock Press, 1984. Reprinted with permission of Chuck Taylor.

Taylor, Pat Ellis. "Spring Water Celebration." *The God-Chaser and Other Stories.* 1986. ©1986 Pat Ellis Taylor. Reprinted with permission of Pat Littledog.

Webb, Don. *Essential Saltes*. New York: St. Martin's Press, 1999. ©1999 Don Webb. Reprinted with permission of Don Webb.

Webb, Walter P. (J. Frank Dobie Roast). *The Texas Observer*. July 24, 1964.

Westbrook, Max. "Bartons Creek." *Confrontation: Poems*. Austin: Thorp Springs Press, 1982. ©1982 Max Westbrook. Reprinted with permission of Frankie Westbrook.

Wevill, David. "Home Improvement." *Child Eating Snow*. Toronto: Exile Editions Ltd., 1994. ©1994 David Wevill. Reprinted with permission of David Wevill.

Whitbread, Thomas. "Argumentative Poem Against Certain Articles." *Triad*, No. 3, 1964. © 1964 Thomas Whitbread. Reprinted with permission of Thomas Whitbread.

Whittier, Julius. "The Last Bastion." *Texas, Our Texas: Remembrances of The University*. Ed. Bryan A. Garner. Austin: Eakin Press. ©1984 The Friar Society. Reprinted by permission of Julius Whittier.

Winik, Marian. "The Texas Heat Wave." *Nonstop*. New Braunfels: Cedar Rock Press, 1981. ©1981 Marian Winik. Reprinted with permission of Marian Winik.

Wright, Lawerence. "Heroes." *Barton Springs Eternal: The Soul of a City*. Eds. Turk Pipkin and Marshall Freck. Austin: Softshoe Publishing, 1993. ©1993 Hill Country Foundation. Reprinted with permission of the author.

Yarborough, Ralph. "The Music of Running Waters." *Barton Springs Eternal: The Soul of a City*. Edited by Turk Pipkin and Marshall Frech. Soft Shoe Publishing: The Hill Country Foundation. ©1993 Hill Country Foundation.

Zigal, Tom. "Recent Developments." *New Growth: Contemprary Short Stories by Texas Writers*. San Antonio: Corona, 1989. ©1989 Tom Zigal. Reprinted with permission of Tom Zigal.

ACKNOWLEDGMENTS

MOST ANTHOLOGISTS, I SUSPECT, RELY ON ADVICE AND help from others, and that was certainly the case with me in the preparation of this book.

My thanks, therefore, to the following:

Susan Taylor McDaniel Regents Professorship in Creative Writing—support from which provided some invaluable release time in Summer, 2006.

Dave Oliphant and Tom Zigal, who were especially helpful in identifying poets from the past.

Cathy Henderson of the HRHRC, who offered useful information about authors who had written about Austin, including several from Great Britain.

Dick Holland and David Dettmer for help with addresses of authors and heirs.

The staff at the Center for American History at the University of Texas, especially Patrick Cox, John Wheat, Paulette Delahoussaye, Linda Peterson, Jane Boyd, and all who helped out in various ways.

Benjamin Grillot of the Austin History Center for his help with the O. Henry photograph on the cover.

Steve Davis and Rollo K. Newsom of Texas State University for "Scene of the Crime: An Annotated Bibliography," available on-line at www.library. txstate.edu/swcc/exhibits/mystbib.html.

Wanalee Romero, a work-study English major at the University of Texas, for her skills in scanning gnarly copies of texts.

Amy Stewart of the Department of English staff, who provided some timely Xeroxing aid.

John Broders and Cathy Casey of *Texas Monthly* for their help in running down various authors and addresses.

James Garrison, Chair of the Department of English, for his scholarly and contextualized translation of a quotation from Vergil.

Susan Petty of TCU Press, without whose generous aid in scanning, editing, and performing related tasks, this project would probably still be meandering on.

Judy Alter, Director of TCU Press, for her patience and support in what turned out to be a longer undertaking than either of us imagined.

The students in my course, Life and Literature of the Southwest, Fall, 2004, who read a number of Austin-based novels and offered advice on what to include and what not to.

All the authors and heirs who granted me permission to reprint the pieces included herein.

INDEX

Adams, Michael. Crossroads at the Broken Spoke. 229

Almon, Bert. Austin Odyssey. 348

Bedichek, Roy. [Letters on Sculptures] 40

Berry, Betsy. Human Sexuality 427

Blackwood, Scott. Nostalgia. 410

Bracker, Jonathan. Garten of the Gods. 132

Brammer, Billy Lee. From *The Gay Place*. 119

Brown, Kevin. Literary Playscape. 338

Cable, Thomas. Trail Markers. 310

Carpenter, Liz. From *Getting Better All The Time*. 44

Cartwright, Gary. Statues of Limitation. 378

Clausen, Andy. Conversation With A Lady I Took To The
    Airport Who Loved Austin Texas. 243

Cousins, Margaret. From The Beatific Memories of an English Major. 30

Curtis, Greg. Austin, May 15, 1973. 208

Dobie, J. Frank. For Three Years We Three Sat Together. 97

Draper, Robert. Adios to Austin. 351

Dugger, Ronnie. From *Our Invaded Universities*. 237

Dwight, Olivia (Mary Hazzard). From *Close His Eyes*. 134

Faulk, John Henry. From *Fear on Trial*. 59

Flowers, Betty Sue. Being Imagined. 270

Frantz, Joe B. From *The Forty Acre Follies*. 116

Freed, Lynn. From *Reading, Writing, and Leaving Home: Life on the Page*. 330

Friedman, Kinky. The Left Bank of Texas. 177

Furman, Laura. The Woods. 384

Ghose, Zulfikar. It's Your Land, Boss. 220

Gilb, Dagoberto. From a Letter to Pat Ellis Taylor. 259

Giles, James R. One August Day in Texas. 197

Gonzalez-Gerth, Miguel. From Borges and Texas: Farewell To An Old Friend. 156

Graham, Don. Ghosts and Empty Sockets. 416

Grant, Lyman. Co-Op. 360

Greene, A.C. The Founding of Austin. 6

Gustafsson, Lars. From *The Tale of a Dog*. 300

Harrigan, Stephen. [A "School" of Austin Writers?]. 257

Harris, Elizabeth. Give. 305

Hazzard, Mary. (*See Olivia Dwight*) 134

Heinzelman, Kurt. Way Out West at 51st and Berkman. 363

Helmer, William J. The Madman on the Tower. 184

Henry, O. (*See William Sidney Porter*) 2

Hinojosa-Smith, Rolando. '50s Austin: A Variform Education. 64

Hudson, Wilson M. From Bedichek's Rock. 71

Huffstickler, Albert. The Ghosts of College City. 209

Hynes, James. From *Publish and Perish: Three Tales of Tenure and Terror* 251

Ivins, Molly. How Ann Richards Got Elected Governor of Texas. 312

Johnson, Lyndon B. From Tarnish on the Violet Crown. 50

Jones, Joseph J. *Life on Waller Creek.* 272

Knobler, Peter. (*See Ann Richards*) 80

LaSalle, Peter. From *Strange Sunlight.* 247

Lasswell, Mary and Pool, Joe. From *I'll Take Texas.* 54

Lavergne, Gary. From *A Sniper in the Tower: The Charles Whitman Murders*........ 179

Littledog, Pat. (See Pat Ellis Taylor) 215

Lomax, John A. From *Adventures of a Ballad Hunter.* 19

Mackintosh, Prudence. From *Just As We Were.* 165

Magnuson, James. The Week James Michener Died. 343

McMurtry, Larry. From *In a Narrow Grave.* 124

Mewshaw, Michael. From *Earthly Bread.* 212

Middleton, Christopher. The Armadillos. 153

Minutaglio, Bill. From *First Son: George W. Bush and the Bush Family Dynasty.* .. 322

Moore, Steven. Salon of the West. 265

Morris, Celia. From *Finding Celia's Place.* 91

Morris, Willie. From *North Toward Home.* 87

Oliphant, Dave. From *Austin.* 11

Osborn, Carolyn. The Vulture Descending Each Day.. 137

Olsson, Karen. From *Waterloo*.. 425

Owens, William A. From *Three Friends*.. 34

Pool, Joe. (*See Mary Lasswell*). 54

Porter, William Sidney. Austin: A Brief Glance at Her History and Advantages. 2

Prokosch, Frederick. From *Voices: A Memoir*............................. 23

Ransom, Harry Huntt. Frontier Museum. 155

Ransom, Hazel Harrod. *Quorum Pars Parva Fui.* 161

Reid, Jan. From *The Improbable Rise of Redneck Rock.* 223

Richards, Ann with Knobler, Peter. From *Straight from the Heart.* 80

Richards, David. From *Once Upon a Time in Texas.* 76

Rota, Bertram. The Night of the Armadillos. 110

Prokosch, Frederick. From *Voices: A Memoir.* 23

Scheick, William J. Gridlock. 443

Shrake, Edwin. From *The Borderland.* 8

Spong, John. King's Ransom. 373

Sprague, Kurth. From *Frighten the Horses.* 262

Taylor, Chuck. Texas. 267

Taylor, Pat Ellis. Spring Water Celebration. 215

Webb, Don. From *Essential Saltes.* 401

Webb, Walter P. J. Frank Dobie. 73

Westbrook, Max. Bartons Creek. 255

Wevill, David. Home Improvement. 334

Whitbread, Thomas. Argumentative Poem Against Certain Articles. 129

Whittier, Julius. From The Last Bastion. 172

Winik, Marian. The Texas Heat Wave. 265

Wright, Lawerence. Heroes. 336

Yarborough, Ralph. The Music of Running Waters. 27

Zigal, Tom. Recent Developments. 277